TEACHING SPEECH
IN THE HIGH SCHOOL

Principles and Practices

TEACHING SPEECH IN THE HIGH SCHOOL

Principles and Practices

Mardel Ogilvie
QUEENS COLLEGE

New York

APPLETON-CENTURY-CROFTS, INC.

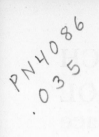

Preface

THIS BOOK IS ADDRESSED to the prospective or the new teacher of speech in the high school. It is intended to (*a*) help the teacher develop for himself a workable philosophy of speech education, (*b*) give him a sense of his role in the school and community, (*c*) help him find materials and methods for teaching, (*d*) guide him in preparing courses of study, units, and lesson plans adapted to the needs and abilities of his students, (*e*) suggest to him ways of organizing and administering a program in speech therapy, (*f*) aid him in evaluating his own work and that of his students, (*g*) give him direction in planning and conducting extracurricular activities, and (*h*) counsel him in his professional development.

If the young teacher of speech could observe a number of superior teachers in his field, he would borrow and adapt some of their ideas and discard others. I, therefore, have tried to describe principles and practices used by many such teachers of speech. The beginning teacher will find some of these principles and practices appropriate for him, his students, and his situation; others he will find inappropriate. The paramount purpose of this book is to guide prospective or new teachers rather than to tell them exactly how to teach.

I am indebted to Dr. Wilbur Gilman, Chairman of the Department of Speech at Queens College, for his sympathetic encouragement and for his many helpful suggestions and to Dr. Andrew Weaver of the Department of Speech at the University of Wisconsin, for his kindly and constructive criticism and for his wise counsel for making the book useful to high school teachers.

Appreciation is also due the many superior high school teachers of speech whose classes I have visited and who have given me their materials freely. These mentors of those of us who teach speech education are Dorothea Hubschmitt, Chairman of the Department of Speech of Bryant High School, and Ann Brignoli, Bennett Parstek, Lillian Tacomi, and Constance Bernardi of her staff; Rose Kirchman, Chairman of the Department of Speech of Jamaica High

School and Eleanor Campbell of her staff; Martin Salkin, Chairman of Department of Speech of Forest Hills High School and Millicent Schuker of his staff; Mary Desser, Chairman of the Department of Speech, Martin Van Buren High School; Morton Silverman, Chairman of the Department of Speech of Richmond Hill High School and Irene Clark, formerly of his staff; and Wiley Bowyer of the Mineola Public Schools.

I also acknowledge great obligation to my colleagues in the Department of Speech at Queens College: Dr. Bronstein advised me on the materials in the chapters dealing with philosophy of speech education and with articulation and voice. Dr. Jon Eisenson gave generous assistance in determining the content of the chapter on speech therapy. Dr. Beatrice Jacoby shared her knowledge of teaching voice. Dr. Herman Stelzner and Dr. Hollis White kindly evaluated the chapters on debate and discussion. Dr. Robert Dierlam and Dr. Elizabeth Scanlon made many worthwhile suggestions for the chapters on creative drama and theater. Dr. Dorothy Rambo and Dr. Elizabeth Scanlon gave excellent recommendations for improving the material on oral reading. Dr. Robert Crawford gave wise counsel in the writing of the chapter on television and radio. Dr. Burton Byers and Dr. Florence Santiago made many suggestions of merit for the chapter on managing the classroom. Dr. Wilbur Gilman gave valuable advice on the chapters on philosophy of speech, public speaking, and the career of the speech teacher.

Recognition is also due Dr. Helen Storen of the Education Department of Queens College who gave me constructive criticism on the chapter on managing the classroom and Dr. Samuel Lieberman of the Classics Department of Queens College who made helpful recommendations for the chapter on the career of the speech teacher.

I am also grateful to Alta Bogardus for her care and interest in the typing of the manuscript, to my mother Mary Helen Ogilvie and Marybeth Safrit for the many hours spent in proofreading, and to Joan Fertman, a student teacher at Martin Van Buren High School, for her detailed daily accounts of Mrs. Desser's work in her radio and television course.

Finally I am indebted to the proprietors of the copyrighted materials reprinted with their permission in this book. Acknowledgement to them is made elsewhere.

M. O.

Contents

VIII. THE CAREER OF THE SPEECH TEACHER

I

AIMS AND
METHODOLOGY
OF TEACHING SPEECH

1

Speech Education
for Today's Living

WHEN YOUR STUDENTS become adults, they will find that their
lives with their friends and neighbors, with their colleagues on their
jobs, and with their fellow citizens in a democratic culture demand
skill in oral communication. Much of the satisfaction and stimulation of their social contacts will come from their abilities to talk
easily and effectively and to listen graciously. Their success as job
holders and as citizens depends to a large degree on their abilities
to inquire, to understand issues, to state beliefs, to defend ideas, and
to listen thoughtfully and critically. In each instance as they speak to
gain a response from their listeners or as they listen when others
seek to gain a response, they are engaging in a social activity.

This social aspect makes oral communication complex. This complexity depends on six variables: (1) the participants, (2) the ideas,
(3) the purposes, (4) the patterns for organization, (5) the social
climate, and (6) the physical environment.

In teaching speech you are concerned with the control of these six
variables. You want your participants, the speakers and listeners in
the classroom, to adapt themselves and their ideas successfully and
competently to the purposes and the occasion, to the other participants and their ideas, to the patterns of the ideas, and to the
social and physical environment. By considering the implications of
the six variables for the training of high school students, we may

3

arrive at the aims for speech education. In the following section each variable and its implications will be discussed.

VARIABLES IN ORAL COMMUNICATION AND THEIR IMPLICATIONS FOR SPEECH EDUCATION

Participants

The personal traits and characteristics valuable in a conversation are equally germane to other speaking situations. You want your students to possess such assets as good will toward their fellow men, honesty, kindness, sincerity, tact, a pleasant voice, and acceptable diction and to bring these assets to their speaking whatever its purpose.

In his *Institutes of Oratory,* Quintilian outlines a program of education for the complete training of an orator. He insists that the good orator be a good man speaking well:[1]

Since an orator, then, is a good man, and a good man cannot be conceived to exist without virtuous inclinations, and virtue, though it receives certain impulses from nature, requires notwithstanding to be brought to maturity by instruction, the orator must above all things study morality, and must obtain a thorough knowledge of all that is just and honorable, without which no one can either be a good man or an able speaker.

Similarly, a committee of the North Central Association describes the personality traits and attitudes needed in successful communication:[2]

Speech appropriate to group living is characteristic of the individual who gets along well with others. Personality traits and attitudes seem to be most often revealed in speech, and significant development in speech is usually accompanied by significant gains in personality. Successful communication depends upon the understanding, respect, tolerance, and sympathy which speaker and hearer have for each other. Accordingly, certain attitudes should become intimately associated with speech and speaking situations. They are the attitudes of helpfulness, cooperation, tolerance, inquiry, con-

[1] Quintilian, *Institutes of Oratory,* XII, ii, I, trans. by J. S. Watson (London, H. G. Bohn, 1956).

[2] North Central Association, "A Program of Speech Education," *Quarterly Journal of Speech,* XXXVII (October, 1951), 350. Reprinted by permission of Speech Association of America.

cession, admission, self-reliance, honesty, and conviction. Although some of these may appear more sharply in one speaking experience than in another, they are the attitudinal bases of informal speech and group discussion, of dramatics, and the oral interpretation of literature, and of public speaking and debate. In speaking, as in any other learning experience, such attitudes should be rewarded and reenforced, and anti-social attitudes, such as belligerence should go unrewarded.

Thus, both in 95 A.D. and today speech educators place emphasis on the speaker's being a good man. The role of the personality traits of the participants is necessarily important and suggests this aim: *to develop traits of constructive and ethical group living.*

Besides these traits, an audible, pleasant voice and clear, intelligible articulation are important. The voice and articulation of the speaker should not distract from what he is saying and should be representative of the speech of the educated men and women of the community. The need for the students' speech to be audible and distinct points to this aim: *to speak with pleasant voice and with acceptable articulation.*

Ideas

Your student speaker must also have something of consequence to say. When he has read widely, thought deeply, inquired judiciously, observed keenly, listened carefully, and appraised completely, he has extensive knowledge and understanding and, consequently, a fund of ideas from which to draw. Without ideas he has nothing to say.

In the teaching of speech, paramount importance has always been given to ideas. Plato attacked superficial speechmaking and advocated the philosophy of public speaking based on ideas. Aristotle pointed out that the starting point for all public speaking is the investigation of ideas. Cicero's "ideal orator" was thoroughly familiar with the arts and sciences:[3]

And indeed in my opinion, no man can be an orator complete in all points of merit, who has not attained a knowledge of all important subjects and arts. For it is from knowledge that oratory must derive its beauty and fullness, and unless there is such knowledge, well-grasped and comprehended by the speaker, there must be something empty and almost childish in the utterance.

[3] Cicero, *De Oratore*, I, v, 20, trans. by E. W. Sutton (Cambridge, Mass., Harvard University Press, 1942).

Today Franklin Knower says: "Skill in accumulation and development of ideas as well as analysis and discrimination of the important from related ideas we talk about must be a persistent objective of the student of speech."[4]

In high school classrooms your students search for ideas. They learn to read, listen, observe, investigate, and evaluate the material which they find. When students in a public speaking class explain the principles of harmony in music clearly, or persuade their classmates of the need for a parking lot in their metropolitan center, you recognize that these adolescents are developing mental maturity. As they discuss intelligently their reasons for believing that a play has a particular theme or for their interpretation of a poem, you are glad that they are learning to handle ideas proficiently.

Indeed, one aim of speech education is *to develop sound and meaningful ideas as a result of investigation.*

Purposes

The third variable is the purpose of the speaking activity. The participants express their ideas for the following reasons: (1) to practice the art of good fellowship, (2) to inform, (3) to persuade, (4) to entertain, and (5) to impress.

You and they recognize that no one of these purposes is discrete. There are many illustrations of students' speech activities having more than one purpose: Frequently when they understand a process described in a speech, they are also persuaded that it is the best process to use. They see a play to be entertained but become convinced that the play's theme carries truth for our society. The talk at the dedication ceremony stirs their feelings deeply, but they are also entertained by its humor. As they understand the construction of the latest rocket, they become impressed with the magnitude of the undertaking.

Each activity, nevertheless, has a dominant purpose. Every one of these five forms of speech activity has distinctive characteristics determined by the response which the student speaker desires. Practicing good fellowship requires that the student speaker determine the kind of conversation that will promote pleasant human relationships. Informing requires that he find out what his listeners will

[4] F. H. Knower, "A Philosophy of Speech for the Secondary School," *The Speech Teacher*, I (March, 1952), 82.

comprehend; persuading, what they will accept; entertaining, what they will enjoy; and impressing, what they will honor.[5]

To Practice the Art of Good Fellowship

In their lives at school, students practice various kinds of conversation. Much of it is merely polite phrases. Phrases like "Thank you for the help," "Glad you could come," and "Congratulations" serve little purpose except to create a pleasant social atmosphere. Some conversations, however, are more provocative and intend to inform, entertain, persuade, and impress. For example, the members of a speech fundamentals course, all of whom had seen *Winterset* and were working on improving their conversational techniques, had a stimulating talk about the character Mio and his motivation. Although the primary purpose of the conversation was to further good fellowship, its secondary purposes were to inform and to entertain. When the members of this same class conversed about the Asian situation, the secondary purpose was to inform.

Practicing the art of good fellowship involves knowing how to converse well. Hence this particular purpose moves us to include this aim: *to speak effectively in social life.*

Beyond students' being able to talk with their friends effectively, they must be able to listen courteously. Because they are listening courteously, the conversationalist feels that his listeners are genuinely interested in him and his ideas. Consequently we must include a second aim: *to listen graciously.*

To Inform

In the speech classes of high schools your students are learning to speak and report so that their listeners understand. The listeners are serious about wanting to understand. Since informing is the most prevalent form of speaking in a school, examples are plentiful: A sixteen-year-old boy explains to the members of his drama class the differences between a floodlight and a spotlight. While a dramatic club is deciding which play to produce, one member reports on the theme of a particular play, its structure, and its characters, and another member announces what play is given most frequently in the

[5] W. E. Gilman, B. Aly, and L. D. Reid, *The Fundamentals of Speaking,* (New York, The Macmillan Co., 1951), p. 253. These purposes of informing, persuading, entertaining, and impressing are developed completely in Chs. 15, 16, 13, and 14.

nation's high schools. A seventeen-year-old boy in an oral reading class describes Robert Frost's background so that the members of the class will better understand his interpretation of "Birches." A fourteen-year-old girl in a public speaking class demonstrates the process of cross fertilization of African violets. A thirteen-year-old boy in a fundamentals class defines overtones. A fourteen-year-old reads to the same class an explanation of the differences between tone and noise.

This purpose of speaking implies the skill of imparting information to an audience. Having found and evaluated the necessary information, high school students must be able to disclose it to their listeners in a way that the listeners understand. Consequently this purpose inspires the aim: *to be able to impart information to an audience.*

Your students must be able to receive information as well as to impart it. They must listen carefully to understand a process, a concept, or causes of existing conditions. Consequently this same purpose inspires a second aim: *to listen thoughtfully.*

To Persuade

Informing and persuading often accompany each other. To be persuaded, students must usually first understand. The distinguishing characteristic of persuasion, however, is that the speaker influences the belief and action of the listener. High school students must be able to give arguments and to respond to them.

They persuade their fellow students individually and collectively. Students are persuaded to take individual action. Mary elects to report on the Greek theater; Jack, on the Roman theater. Irving decides to try out for the debating team. Helen chooses to elect public speaking for the coming term. High school students also arrive at collective decisions through persuasion. They decide which play to produce, elect a President, and accept or reject items in a proposed constitution. In a fundamentals class, the boys and girls with their teacher determine the purposes of the course and its content. Members of an oral reading class settle upon a particular interpretation of a poem for choral speaking. In each of these cases, persuasion plays an important part in reaching a decision.

Furthermore, high school students study the theory of persuasion and put the theory to work in class. Since this study and practice is part of every course in public speaking, each student of public speaking makes at least one persuasive speech. In addition a student may read aloud a persuasive speech of a well-known orator so that the students in the class may analyze the orator's techniques of persuasion. Or they may listen to a recording of a persuasive speech for the same purpose.

That the students must at times be competent in persuading others to their way of thinking points to this aim: *to be able to influence the beliefs and actions of others.*

Not only must your students be able to persuade others but they must also attend to and judge the persuasion of the other students. They must be able to detect fallacious reasoning, the use of unfair emotional appeals, and insincerity so that, as they listen, they can accept or reject the ideas of the persuaders judiciously. These abilities help them to be responsible for arriving at their own opinions intelligently and objectively. This responsibility suggests the aim: *to listen critically.*

Beyond being effective persuaders and listeners, students should use the kind of ethical communication needed in democratic behavior. Your students should feel responsible for what they say and for being sure that they are honest in their expression of ideas. Karl Wallace indicates four principles for the ethics of communication in a democratic way of life:[6]

1. A communicator in a free society must recognize that during the moments of his utterance he is the sole source of argument and information, 2. the communicator must select and present fact and opinion fairly, 3. the communicator must reveal the sources of his information and opinion and 4. a communicator will acknowledge and will respect diversity of argument and opinion.

He summarizes with this statement:

It is these four "moralities;" the duty of search and inquiry, allegiance to accuracy, fairness, and justice in the selection and treatment of ideas and arguments, the willingness to submit private motivations to public scrutiny, and the toleration of dissent—which provide the ethics of communication in a free society.

[6] Karl Wallace, "An Ethical Basis of Communication," *The Speech Teacher,* IV (January, 1955), 6.

The need for ethical communication prompts the inclusion of this aim: *to use the kind of ethical communication needed in democratic behavior.*

To Entertain

In high school there are many opportunities for students to entertain. Outside of class, plays, assemblies, and programs of various clubs may serve this purpose. In class, entertaining may take such forms as these: a fifteen-year-old girl's reading of Sandburg's *Chicago*, two fourteen-year-olds' pantomime of a man teaching his wife to drive, two fifteen-year-olds' simulated conversation between a great author and a beginning writer, and a seventeen-year-old boy's amusing talk on the styles of women's dress.

Since entertaining is here defined broadly in terms of amusing, pleasing, and diverting listeners, we may assume that whatever makes speaking dynamic, alive, and interesting makes it entertaining. These qualities help students to get and hold the attention of their listeners no matter what their primary purpose in speaking. With this in mind, we add the aim: *to be able to divert and please one's listeners.*

Besides being able to divert and please listeners, students must be able to receive such experiences with appreciation. Speech education must, therefore, include this aim: *to listen appreciatively.*

Because they are so often exposed to entertainment—neighborhood plays, television dramas, moving pictures, and radio programs—you help your students to be discriminating in their choice of such entertainment. You give them principles upon which to base their selection and find ways to encourage them to listen and respond intelligently to these media. The development of this ability suggests this aim: *to be discriminating in one's choice of entertainment involving speech arts.*

To Impress

It is usually outside of the classroom that high school students hear speeches intended to stir their emotions. A ceremony to initiate members into an honor society, to present a gift to the school from the students, to install student government officials, to welcome a new principal, or to read a notice of the death of a high school leader, would be an occasion for such a speech. Impressive speaking experiences, where students realize the mood of the occasion and communicate it to their fellow students, do occur, however, in speech classes. In public speaking classes, students frequently prepare speeches intended to impress the other students. In other classes, impressiveness may be a by-product of the work. For example, a drama class was stirred by a student's description of a Broadway play and a speech fundamentals class reacted strongly to a short talk called "My Brother Is My Ideal."

In speaking to impress, the speaker reports facts but chooses them carefully to influence his listeners to feel as he does on a subject. In addition, to gain the response he desires, he must express his ideas with simplicity, dignity, and vividness. In other words, the ideas, style, and delivery should be eloquent. The purpose to impress, therefore, points to the aim: *to be able to convey an impression to an audience vividly*.

The listener must be able to recognize and respond to the mood and meaning of the occasion. The purpose to impress, therefore, also points to the aim: *to listen sympathetically*.

Patterns for Organization

No matter what its purpose or occasion, the speaking activity follows a pattern. The ideas are expresssed in a structure and an order which must meet the needs of the speaker, the listeners, the ideas, the purpose of the speaking activity, and the social and physical environment. These needs influence the tightness of the structure of ideas. One student allows a social conversation to be quite loose and leisurely; another maneuvers it so skillfully that it covers the topics in the order which he has chosen. One student, called upon to make an impromptu speech, follows no previously conceived plan; another student reads a speech which follows an extremely careful plan.

As teachers, you stress the similarities and differences in the organization and form of the various speaking activities. You encourage your students to recognize that in every speaking activity, with the possible exception of conversation, the main idea must be clear. Although the main idea may be either implicit or explicit, it should be apparent in the production of a play, the reading of a poem, the telling of a story, in a discussion, a speech, or a debate. You make clear that most speaking activities have an introduction and a conclusion, which may not be essential to the development of the main idea but is helpful in gaining a desired response from the listeners. You point out the differences in the structural organization of the different kinds of speaking activities.

Throughout the teaching of speech you help students to formulate their own patterns for organization and to understand the patterns used by others. As a teacher of public speaking, you teach your students to analyze and outline. As a teacher of oral interpretation, you help your students to understand the sequence of ideas in a selection of prose or poetry. As a teacher of dramatics, you aid them in discerning the play's structure. As a teacher of debate, you assist them in preparing briefs. As a teacher of discussion, you motivate your students to follow the accepted pattern of discussion.

Whatever purpose of speaking your students are to fulfill, they must organize their material so that their listeners understand it and respond favorably to it. They must be able to achieve this aim: *to organize material so that the audience will accept it.*

In addition to organizing their own material, they must be familiar with the patterns of organization used by others. They, therefore, must also be able to achieve this aim: *to identify patterns of ideas in oral communication.*

Social Climate

The participants express their ideas arranged in some kind of a pattern for a particular purpose. These ideas are expressed in a social climate that is friendly, neutral, or hostile. And the social climate within the classroom or auditorium is very much influenced by the social climate without.

Although the conditions in your community and in the world do affect the social climate of your classroom, you can control this climate to some extent. One important principle in this control is that you accept your boys and girls as they are. The boys and girls in your classroom are of different races, nationalities, religions, socioeconomic statuses, and intellectual abilities. They have varying beliefs and attitudes. They speak differently. The example you set of accepting people as they are is significant in developing a desirable social climate in your classroom.

Second, you must foster among your students a feeling of friendliness, of good manners, of courtesy, and of mutual helpfulness. You may do this by conducting yourself in such a way that the students feel respect for and confidence in you. Graciousness, an enthusiasm for the group and the subject, and the setting of reasonable standards and limits of behavior build this respect and confidence. On the other hand, curt commands and criticisms, a lack of a pleasant "thank you" for a favor, an insistence on always being right, and unfavorable comparison of one student's work with another's breed disrespect and lack of confidence.

Lastly, you must give your students chances to participate in group speaking activities. When your students plan and complete group discussions, interviews, and creative dramatic activities, they feel that they belong to the group. As a by-product, they learn socially acceptable behavior. In addition, you and your students will respect each other's status because such consideration is necessary in group situations. As the students have more experience in democratic living and as they become more secure in the group, the social climate of the classroom improves and becomes more favorable to good communication.

In spite of what you achieve in the classroom, your students will often speak in situations fraught with emotion and prejudice because of world, national, and local conditions. Thus you encourage your students to do the necessary research, to think and listen critically, and to recognize their own prejudices. Your students should then accomplish this aim: *to be objective in their views.* When they accomplish this aim and when they have the desirable traits of personality outlined in the section on *participants,* they should be able to make their own points tactfully and listen to the points of others courteously even when the social climate is adverse.

Physical Environment

Physical environment, the last variable, influences oral communication. More and more schools are taking it into account and are providing good-looking, comfortable, and practical classrooms. Such classrooms foster good oral communication. The clean and attractive classroom helps to produce a relaxed and receptive group of students; an unusual bulletin board exhibit and a table with provocative magazines and books provide stimuli for talk. Even the seating arrangement of the classroom makes a difference. Seats screwed to the floor in rigid rows detract from most speaking activities. Flexible seats, that can be moved, provide either for an informal discussion or for a formal presentation.

Students should be aware of the influence physical surroundings have on effective oral communication. They should know what factors of the physical environment stimulate talk. They should be cognizant of the need to adapt their speaking to physical environment. For instance, in a large room they must talk more slowly and distinctly and must use more volume. Students then should fulfill this aim of speech education: *to recognize and respond to the influences of physical environment upon oral communication.*

COMPLEXITY OF THE VARIABLES

Depending on the intricacies of the combination of these six variables, the speaking activity of students may be anywhere from simple to very complex. The following is an illustration of a complex speaking activity. In this case, the purpose of the teacher in a fundamentals class was simple: to show that the acceptable standard of speech is that of the educated members of the community. Although the purpose was a single one, all the other variables were complex. First, the differences among the members of the class were wide. Some had selected the course because of their speaking abilities; others had been advised to choose it because of deficiencies in their speaking abilities. Consequently, some had superior speech; others, substandard speech. Some of the members were working for an academic diploma; others, a vocational one; and still others, a commercial one. As a result, the students' future needs of speech varied. Some were freshmen; others, juniors; and still others, seniors. Thus, the students' levels of maturity were dissimilar. Second, the pattern of the lesson seemed to the onlooker disorganized. Third, the ideas were sometimes unrelated to the aim of the lesson. Students contributed valuable ideas from their study of the history of the English language, from a knowledge of dialects studied in a drama class, from phonics learned in a remedial reading class, and from their acquaintance with different pronunciations as a result of travel, but they also introduced a large amount of inconsequential material having little bearing on the aim of the lesson. Fourth, the climate was influenced by the apathy several members of the class felt toward the substitute teacher. Fifth, the physical environment with seats in rows and with undue street noise was not conducive to discussion. Five of the variables made for a complex speaking situation.

On the other hand, the following illustrates a simple speaking activity. A group of intellectually able high school students, interested in ideas and co-operative, were giving oral book reports on biographies so that the members of the class would know more about a number of prominent American men and women of the theater. The pattern was clear. One student interviewed another who had read the biography and who assumed the role of the prominent man or woman. The interviewer who had planned his questioning beforehand found out pertinent facts about the prominent man or woman. The social climate was a happy one with a warm and friendly teacher. The morale of the class was high. The environment was a comfortable one, well-adapted to the speaking which took place, with the two students doing the interviewing seated in the front of the room and with the rest of the students at tables around the room. This speaking activity was a simple one, for the participants were of similar background and ability, the purpose was to give information, the ideas were stimulating and easily understood by the participants, the pattern was obvious, and the occasion was comfortable and conducive to communication. Most speaking activities lie between these two extremes in complexity.

RELATIONSHIP OF AIMS IN GENERAL EDUCATION TO AIMS IN SPEECH EDUCATION

Since speech plays an important part in an individual's life as a social being, as a job holder, and as a citizen, the aims of speech education should be related to the aims of general education. The need for accomplishing the aims of speech education is implicit in writings published by the Educational Policies Commission, the National Association of Secondary School Principals, and the National Society for Secondary Education.

In 1944, the Educational Policies Commission published *Education for All American Youth*[7] which outlines seven basic purposes of the school. Of these, four are definitely related to the aims of

[7] Educational Policies Commission, *Education for All American Youth* (Washington, D.C., National Education Association and American Association of School Administrators, 1944), pp. 16-17.

speech education as explained in this chapter. One purpose listed by the Commission is to develop the qualities of citizenship: Earlier in the chapter we indicated how being a responsible citizen is tied to being an effective speaker. A second pertains to an understanding of our culture today: Obviously to understand our culture in this age of radio and television, a necessary and important ability is to listen thoughtfully and critically. A third concerns rational thinking: Throughout speech education speakers and listeners are concerned with rational thinking, and particularly when the purpose of the speaking activity is to persuade. A fourth purpose refers to making decisions and taking actions: Persuasion in speechmaking makes a very careful study of the principles involved in arriving at decisions and taking actions. Thus, a strong relationship exists between these four purposes of general education and the aims of speech education.

In 1946 the Educational Policies Commission published *Policies for Education in American Democracy*[8] which states as objectives of secondary education: the objectives of self-realization, of satisfactory human relationship, of economic efficiency, and of civic responsibility. Again a close connection exists between these objectives and those of speech education. For example, under self-realization, "speech" is the objective listed first: "Speech" involves the educated person's speaking the mother tongue clearly. This aim includes all those aims of speech education having to do with the expression of ideas. Under self-realization "sight and hearing" is listed second: "Sight and hearing" involves the educated person's being skilled in listening and observing. This aim quite obviously includes all the aims of speech education that concern listening and the finding of ideas. Throughout, the two sets of aims frequently coincide.

In 1948 the Committee on Curriculum Planning and Development of the National Association of Secondary School Principals published "Evaluating the Curriculum for Provision for Meeting the Imperative Needs of Youth"[9] which lists ten goals of education. Of these, half are related to the aims of speech education. They are related in terms of the role of the speaker as a citizen, as a con-

---

[8] Educational Policies Commission, *Policies for Education in American Democracy* (Washington, D.C., National Education Association, 1946), p. 192.

[9] W. French and W. L. Ranson, "Evaluating the Curriculum for Provision for Meeting the Imperative Needs of Youth," *Bulletin of the National Association of Secondary School Principals*, XXXII (April, 1948), 48-69.

sumer of beauty in literature, as a consumer of entertainment, as "the good man skilled in speaking," and as a reasoning communicator. The connection in this last role is very evident, for the role calls for a youth who can think rationally, express his thoughts clearly and listen with understanding. The aims of the Committee on Curriculum Planning and Development of the National Association of Secondary School Principals correspond closely to the aims of speech education as enumerated in this chapter.

In the 1953 Yearbook of the National Society for Secondary Education, an article[10] describing the characteristics of a secondary school that meets the needs of youth states that secondary education should: (a) satisfy physical and mental health needs, (b) help make students competent for their life work, (c) provide leisure interests and standards, and (d) promote effective group living and successful participation in civic affairs. These requirements again point to the need for abilities in speaking and listening as a social being, as a job-holder, and as a citizen. They encompass all the aims of speech education mentioned in this chapter.

The 1956 Yearbook of the Association for Supervision and Curriculum Development points out that, on the one hand, curricular content may be selected on the basis of categories of life functions and youth needs. In this case the high school curriculum deals with life situations as they are faced by adolescents and makes a direct assault on the problems of living as they are encountered by the youth. The Yearbook indicates that, on the other hand, the curricular content may be selected on the basis of its potential enrichment of lives of students. In this case the program may be a functional one centering around social sciences, natural sciences, and the humanities.[11] No matter which philosophy is basic to the secondary school curriculum, abilities to speak and listen are important. Clearly the life functions and needs of youth require meeting all of the speaking and listening aims described. Just as clearly, a functional program centering around the social and natural sciences and the humanities demand speaking and listening competencies.

[10] W. French, "Characteristics of a Secondary School Meeting the Needs of Youth," *National Society for Secondary Education 52nd Yearbook*, Part I (1953), pp. 300-311.

[11] *What Shall the High School Teach*, 1956 Yearbook of the Association for Supervision and Curriculum Development, p. 104.

The objectives just quoted were drawn up and officially stated by committees reperesenting school administrators of the National Education Association. Some speech teachers say that speech education is not progressing because of the attitudes of school administrators. The organs of these administrators, however, recognize the need for speech education in their goals of general education. These expressed goals of general education are trustworthy evidence to use when you persuade your administrators of the need for speech education.

SUGGESTED READING

ALY, B., "Speech in the Service of Tyranny and Freedom," *The Speech Teacher,* III (March, 1954), 82-88. Gives the relative advantages of tyranny and freedom as a course of action and suggests that the teacher of speech is obligated to advance the doctrines of freedom.

BORCHERS, G. L., "A Reaffirmation in Support of Essentials in Secondary Speech Education," *The Speech Teacher,* VIII (November, 1959), 300-303. Lists eight fundamental laws of speech goals and procedures. Includes a clear-cut and practical definition of speech. An unusually good exposition of the role of the speech teacher in the high school.

GILMAN, W. E., "Unity in Diversity," *Quarterly Journal of Speech,* XXXVIII (April, 1952), 124-132. Discusses challenges to speech education: the independence of speech as a field, its importance, its usefulness, the unity within the speech field, and interest of speech teachers in freedom of speech.

HOCHMUTH, M., "Speech and Society," *The Bulletin of the National Association of Secondary School Principals,* XXXII (January, 1948), 17-33. Discusses speech in industry and in democracy and the relationship of speech to international co-operation.

KNOWER, F. H., "A Philosophy of Speech for the Secondary School," *The Speech Teacher,* I (March, 1952), 79-85. Emphasizes the academic tradition of speech and discusses speech as a dynamic social process and gives its purposes.

————, "Speech Education for All American Youth," *The Bulletin of the National Association of Secondary School Principals,* XXXII (January, 1948), 11-16. Explains the need for effective oral communication in a democracy, interprets good speech as a social activity, and presents the problems of general speech education in the schools.

KRAMER, M., "The Role of Speech in Education: a Re-Evaluation," *Quart-*

erly Journal of Speech, XXXIV (April 1948), 123-127. States clearly the purposes of speech education.

The North Central Association, "A Program of Speech Education," *Quarterly Journal of Speech,* XXXVII (October, 1951), 347-358. Gives basic facts of speech and relationship of speech to society, to leaders, and to the schools in Part I and discusses speech and the learning situations in Part II and speech in specialized education in Part III.

WALLACE, K. R., "An Ethical Basis of Communication," *The Speech Teacher,* IV (January, 1955), 1-9. Explains ethical standards of communication and shows how the speech teacher can help his young communicators to achieve these standards.

EXERCISES

1. Analyze and compare the role of the six variables mentioned in this chapter in these situations which you will observe:

    a. Oral language arts activity in the elementary school.

    b. Speaking assignment in the first speech course in a high school.

    c. Speaking assignment in the first speech course in a college.

2. Visit an elective high school class in speech. Write a short paper on the attitude of the teacher toward his students. Evaluate the part the attitude of the teacher played in the social climate of the classroom.

3. Refute the following criticisms of speech work which were made by students majoring in other departments.

    a. "Speech majors in general are trained to argue. I find they enjoy playing the devil's advocate, finding holes in my argument, winning their point. They should have more work in the humanities and less in argumentation."

    b. "Too much emphasis in speech courses is placed on delivery and not enough on ideas. When anyone knows his subject matter well, he can talk about it."

    c. "Speech is personality. A speaker with a good personality is interesting and persuasive. In training in speech, you ask for changes in personality. You cannot expect much to be achieved."

2

Organizing

for Learning

THE CHAPTER Speech Education for Today's Living includes a discussion of the six variables of a speech situation: the participants, the purposes of speaking, the ideas, the pattern of ideas, the social climate, and the physical environment. Because every teaching situation is a speaking situation, these six variables are present in it. The participants are the teacher and the students; the purpose of speaking, to teach (or to inform); the ideas, the materials of teaching; the patterns of ideas, the plan for learning in the school and classroom; the social climate, the atmosphere of the class; and the physical environment, the classroom itself. The administrators of your school, you, and the students effectively guide the control of these six variables.

This chapter, which has to do with this control, deals with: (1) adolescents in the speech class, (2) the speech curriculum, (3) social climate for the speech classroom, (4) planning for teaching and learning, (5) materials for teaching speech, and (6) managing and equipping the speech classroom.

ADOLESCENTS IN THE SPEECH CLASS

Learning About Adolescents

In your classes in education you have learned much about adolescents. You have studied their sequence of development, their general characteristics, and the wide variations in these characteristics due to heredity, environment, physical traits, and social and emotional problems. You have learned about meeting their developmental needs. You have learned how to know better the adolescents in your class by using sociograms, the study of case histories over a long period, and by analysis of a particular group's mores and attitudes.

In planning a speech curriculum you put some of this knowledge to work; you consider the interests and needs of your adolescents. To find out about your students' interests and their own evaluation of their speech needs, you may ask your students to fill in questionnaires at the beginning of the year. The resulting information helps you to guide their work intelligently. One such questionnaire follows:

NAME .... AGE......

HIGH SCHOOL MAJOR .... GRADE....

Please consider your answers to this questionnaire carefully. They will help your teacher to plan the work for the semester.

1. Have you participated in any of the following extracurricular speech activities in this school? If you have, place a check after the activity in which you have participated.

Debate ....   Theater ....   Discussion ....

Radio Workshop ....

2. Have you within the past three years participated in speech activities such as radio work, discussion, or dramatics in your church or in the community? If so, indicate their nature. ....

3. What high school speech courses have you taken? ....

4. What extracurricular activities do you participate in in this school?

....

5. What do you do for recreation? ....

6. Do you work after school? Yes .... No .... Do you work on Saturdays?
Yes .... No ....

If you do work, what do you do? ....

7. What is your favorite magazine? ....

8. What is your favorite television program? ....

9. What book that you have read do you particularly like? ....
....

10. What is your favorite sport? ....

11. What adults outside of your family do you most admire? ....
....

12. If you have traveled, indicate where. ....

13. If you have decided on an occupation, what is it to be? ....
....

14. If you had a completely free choice of occupation, what would it be?
....

Indicate how you usually feel in each of these speech situations by
writing in the blank the letter corresponding most closely to your
feeling: (a) completely comfortable, (b) fairly comfortable, (c) often uncomfortable, (d) almost always uncomfortable.

Conversing with peers ...... Conversing with relatives ......

Conversing with strange adults ...... Conversing at a formal occasion ......

Telephoning peers ...... Telephoning relatives ......

Telephoning strange adults for particular requests such as a job interview ......

Discussing a problem with peers ......

Discussing a problem in class ......

Discussing a problem in an organization such as student government ......

Reporting in a class ...... Reporting in a club meeting ......

Reporting formally to the entire student body ......

Addressing a class formally ......

Addressing a club meeting formally ......

Addressing a large body formally ......

Acting (playing a part) formally in class ......

Acting in a play before an audience ......

Interviewing a classmate ......

Interviewing a teacher ......

Interviewing a prospective employer ......

Rate yourself 1, 2, 3, or 4 in the following: 1 is excellent; 2 is fairly good; 3 is average; and 4 is poor.

Using voice ...... Pronouncing words ......

Organizing material for a speech ......

Adapting material to an audience ......

Explaining to your classmates ......

Persuading your classmates ......

Holding the interest of the group you are talking to ......

Delivering a speech ......

Finding a topic to talk about ......

Finding material about the topic ......

You may include other questions having to do with acting or reading aloud. From a study of the answers to such a questionnaire you learn something about the interests of your boys and girls, their felt needs in terms of a speaking situation, and their attitudes toward them. This information helps you to adapt your speech material, procedures, and activities to your students.

Meeting the Needs of Adolescents in Speech Class

Other teachers use more informal ways of determining the needs of their students. Mrs. Wilbur, a highly successful young teacher of girls in a vocational high school, said that her students' physical, social and emotional, and intellectual needs became obvious in their actions and conversations in the classroom and that, consequently, she devised ways of meeting these needs. She cited the following examples.

Need for Physical Activity and for Change of Pace

The students' needs for expression of sheer physical exuberance and for change of pace challenged this young teacher who herself had been a quiet, scholarly student. She said that although she had read of the restless energy of adolescents, she was surprised to find this drive so obvious. For her group, creative dramatics proved ideal in meeting this need; her girls played stories based on pictures, a collection of objects, newspaper situations, poems, and short stories. On the other hand, at certain times her girls required quiet, for they had been overstimulated in the previous class. When they were overstimulated, Mrs. Wilbur found that she could calm her girls by reading aloud to them. She remarked, "If my only purpose were to keep my students still and attentive, I'd read every hour of every day of every week." Mrs. Wilbur's use of such activities as creative dramatics and listening to the reading aloud of poetry and stories provided this particular group with needed activity and change of pace.

Social and Emotional Needs

The social and emotional needs of Mrs. Wilbur's group were much like those of any high school group: need for acceptance, for recognition, and for social status. Some of these needs became obvious when Mrs. Wilbur began her required speech course with a unit in which she asked them to express some of their conversational problems. For example, Mary said, "I can't ever seem to talk with my grand-mother about anything without making her angry. And I do try. I'd like to know why she gets so mad at me for nothing." Jane complained, "I have two friends who make fun of my grammar. I'd like to talk right." Maxine remarked, "I get tongue-tied when I'm around boys." Kathleen declared with some asperity, "Somehow neither my friends nor my parents listen when I talk. They listen to others but not to me." Susan murmured, "I'd like to speak just like the wife of my boss—kind of smooth." Such comments gave Mrs. Wilbur insight into her students' social and emotional needs.

Mrs. Wilbur seems to meet with considerable success the social and emotional needs of all of her groups. Her success in meeting them lies first with the fact that she herself is a warm, friendly person who accepts people as they are. Second, her control of a classroom is the kind that breeds respect. Her students know what she expects of them, and at the same time they are free within well-defined limits to make their own judgments and to work in their own way. Third, she is particularly adept with group work. Her skill in group work is due to her direction, which leaves the members of the class free to plan and report their own activities, and to her ability to keep her group homogenous in terms of interest, purpose, and social intent. One of her girls' evaluation of the required speech course gives evidence of Mrs. Wilbur's ability to meet the social and emotional needs of her students: "I was treated like somebody in this class. When our group reported on John Wayne's acting, we did the work ourselves. We reported the way we wanted to. Mrs. Wilbur wasn't prissy when I played an angry, mean, stupid moll in our story."

Intellectual Needs

Mrs. Wilbur took into account her students' varying intellectual interests and abilities. All of her students were devoted to the movies. In Mrs. Wilbur's theater class she, therefore, began with a study of a current moving picture. In another class she started with telephoning. In this unit she took account of the levels of achievement of her girls by giving individual assignments. For instance, she asked one girl, with little intellectual ability, to telephone the adjustment clerk of a department store to ask about a rug which she had ordered but had not received. She assigned another girl the role of the adjustment clerk. She gave the more difficult assignments to the more able girls. One capable girl served as a travel agent, making arrangements by long-distance telephone for a couple to stay at various hotels on their way south. This assignment, involving planning the route, locating the hotels in the various cities, and finding the costs, proved to be a challenge to the girl who received it.

Student Problems Faced by the Teacher

Your students like Mrs. Wilbur's will present varying problems. To help you think about some problems which you may meet, the following are presented. There is no single right solution to any of the three.

Mary Ellen is an exquisite, charming, highly intelligent, sensitive young girl with considerable acting talent. She is the only student whom you have ever had who could conceivably become a professional actress. Her interpretation of a character is sound, imaginative, and mature.

In your classes, fourth-year English and theater, she does brilliantly. She writes as well as she acts—with creativity and originality. Her contributions to the class discussions are always worthwhile and often distinguished. She does her homework well, seems to enjoy doing it, and never misses an English or theater class both of which meet in the afternoon. But the teachers of her other classes, which meet in the morning, report that although she is intellectually superior, she often appears apathetic, does not turn in her homework, and is frequently absent. When they have talked with you about her, their remarks seem to emphasize her lack of a good home background: "Bad environment; can't help her," "Her family situation is deplorable," "No morals in that family," and "Her brother was thrown out of college."

The guidance counselor consults you about her. He tells you that her chemistry and Latin teachers would like her kept from theater activities until she attends class regularly and works somewhere near capacity; he, however, does not agree with their suggestion and has come to you for a recommendation. He notes that Mary Ellen obviously identifies with you, for she copies you in manner of clothes and mode of behavior. How would you respond to this request for help?

The second problem has to do with Alan, a nineteen-year-old senior, who has been somewhat retarded in school because of his inability to write or to speak adequately. In writing he reverses letters, writing *thier* for *their*. In speaking, he substitutes an *f* and *v* for the unvoiced and voiced *th* and *w* for *l* and *r*. On the other hand, his abilities to read silently, to learn facts, and to reason are well above average. He is in school only to pass English, for he has successfully completed his other courses.

He has been retained in your speech clinic class because of his defective articulation. Although he has come regularly for four months, he has made very little progress. He can make all the sounds accurately but he does not incorporate them in his conversation.

One day after school his parents arrive with no appointment. The mother is a high school graduate, attractive, well-groomed, and well-spoken. She is obviously the more dominant of the two. The father is a taxicab driver, very protective of his son and apparently a kind human being. Both ask you to drop Alan from clinic. They say that there is little wrong with his speaking or his writing and that what difficulty he has is due to a series of ineffectual English teachers.

You have samples of both Alan's speaking and writing. You also have an account of how he was taught in speech clinic class in previous years. The account points to sound clinical help. What would you say to these parents?

The third problem concerns Jack, a very bright, likeable, frank, and honest sixteen-year-old senior, who wants to study medicine and who is interested in attending his father's college, a highly respected one. As a member of your public speaking class, he does the best work of anyone in the group. He does not, however, do as well as he could. He relies to too great a degree on his ability to verbalize and on the fund of knowledge that he already has. Since he possesses qualities of leadership, in many ways he sets the pace for the entire class.

During a conference with him you make suggestions for his improving his outlines. He agrees with your suggestions; but he is obviously more concerned over his getting a high grade than improving. He indicates that he has taken the course because he believed that with his abilities he could get a ninety and because he thought that it would not be as time-consuming as another elective he had in mind. He complains that he finds the preparation time-consuming. How would you handle Jack?

THE SPEECH CURRICULUM

The control of the adolescents in your class lies pretty much in your hands; the control of the speech curriculum, however, does not lie there, for when you enter a school as a new teacher, the place of speech in the school curriculum is usually set. In some schools, there are one or two required semesters of speech, usually called Oral Communication, Speech, or Fundamentals of Speech. In other schools part of one or two semesters of required English is devoted to speech. In still other schools no speech is required. Whether speech is or is not required, speech electives are usually offered; these include courses in discussion, debate, public speaking, reading aloud, drama and theater, and radio and television. In addition, the high school frequently offers a remedial speech course or operates a speech clinic for those students defective in speech. Such curricula frequently follow the recommendations advocated by the North Central Association.

Recommendations of the North Central Association

The North Central Association indicates the essentials of a sound minimum program in the following central topics:[1]

1. *Fundamentals:* How speech sounds are made, care and improvement of the voice, the essentials of distinct utterance and acceptable pronunciation, poise and self-management, personality and speech.

2. *Reading Aloud:* The application of principles to a variety of materials and activities, including choral and group reading.

3. *Discussion:* Its values, aims, and chief forms, including procedure adapted to the conference and committee.

4. *Debate:* Its aims, methods, and practices, including its relation to discussion, to parliamentary law, and to the functioning of our society.

5. *Public Speaking:* Its aims, methods, and chief forms.

6. *Drama and Theater:* The qualities of a good play, the conditions and requirements for producing the play, the social and personal values of play participation, acting and role-playing, representative plays, and the creation of one's own play.

7. *Radio, Television, and Motion Picture:* The qualities of an effective broadcast, the differences between radio and television, the demands of radio and television on the speaker and listener, and the functioning of radio and television in our culture; the purposes, chief production methods and techniques, and social effects of the motion picture.

The requirements of the radio medium can be met by the adaptation of the materials and experience included within each topic.

In practice the several topics appear in high school courses in various combinations:

(a) A two-semester course, frequently called Fundamentals of Speech

[1] "A Program of Speech Education," *Quarterly Journal of Speech*, XXXVII (October, 1951), 355. Reprinted by permission of the Speech Association of America.

or Oral Communication, during the junior year and dealing with all the topics.

(b) A two-semester course devoted to fundamentals, discussion, debate, and public speaking, and a semester course devoted to reading aloud and drama and theatre.

(c) A semester course centering on fundamentals and reading aloud, a semester course on discussion, debate and public speaking, and a semester course on drama and theatre.

(d) A semester course dealing with discussion, debate, and public speaking, with some attention to fundamentals and reading aloud.

(e) A semester course dealing with the personal and social implications of radio, television, and the motion picture.

The number and character of the special courses must extend and complement the experiences in speech provided in the general education offerings of the school.

Core Curriculum

In some schools the curriculum is not organized along such traditional subject-matter lines but is organized as "core curriculum." Core curriculum frequently signifies selecting subject matter from two fused areas, such as English and social studies, through student-teacher planning and focusing on areas which relate to the students' needs and interests. According to Storen, the original aim was to help young people solve their immediate problems and satisfy their current needs. She notes that few high schools now have courses which are completely pupil-centered and that the core curriculum of the future might better focus on broad social values. She supports this statement by indicating that content of some units, such as the orientation unit, tends to be thin and uninteresting and that knowing about personal problems does little to change them. The advantages she sees in a core curriculum are that it makes for a less restrictive classroom and builds respect for the uniqueness of each child.[2]

The speech teacher may serve as a core teacher. One teacher[3] describes his experiences of teaching in a core where no basic curriculum is set up and where the school work is the result of teacher-

[2] Helen Storen, "Personal Problems and Social Values in Core Content," *Education Forum* XXI (May, 1957), 397-407.
[3] B. J. Parsteck, "Speech at the Core of the Core Curriculum," *The Speech Teacher,* II (November, 1953), 283-286.

student planning in terms of needs, problems, and interests of the group. He believes that because of his training in oral communication a speech teacher is especially well-equipped to teach in a core curriculum.

Consultant Service

In still other schools the speech teacher acts as a consultant, going into classes to help with particular areas. In addition, he frequently serves as a speech therapist. During a single week one speech teacher worked with the following activities in various English-social studies core classes: (1) She directed a creative dramatics activity for a ninth grade, a dramatization of Dickens' *Christmas Carol*. (2) She taught sophomores how to make papier mâché puppets, how to manipulate them, and how to write a play for puppets that would depict the excitement of the discovery of new lands in America. (3) She guided the evaluation of the juniors' discussion of the problem, "Should our town build a swimming pool?" (4) She showed seniors how to plan reports on the effects of the U. S. government's foreign policy on the coming election. In addition to this teaching, she assisted students in preparing for an assembly, "The News of the Year." She helped them to speak together poetry which they had written for the show, instructed them in the preparation of scenery representing pages of a newspaper, and explained to them how to make several skits in their show more effective dramatically. However, she was able to spend only half her time in working with these curricular and extracurricular speech activities. The other half she spent handling high school students with defective speech. Since another teacher directed debate and still another had charge of the dramatic program, this teacher did nothing in these two areas. Because she was a broadly trained speech teacher with work in theater, oral reading, public speaking, group discussion, debate, speech correction, and radio, she was capable of handling the variety of areas.

Speech Teacher's Role in Curriculum Development

When your school is re-evaluating its curriculum, considering shifting from a subject-matter to a core curriculum, or deliberating on adding new subjects or dropping others, you may take part in the policy-making discussion. As a speech teacher you may serve on a curriculum committee which may be made up entirely of school personnel or may include parents or other laymen from the community. You must be able to explain in terms the members of this committee can understand the need for and the place of speech in the curriculum of your school. You need to know the understandings, skills, and attitudes which the study of speech will give high school students, why these learnings are valuable, and whether they should be taught in an English class, a social studies class, or a speech class. In addition, you should know how the aims of speech education fit in with the aims of general education of your school.

Courses of Study in Speech

Since the speech work in most high schools is organized in terms of subject matter, you will, in all likelihood, teach such courses as Fundamentals, Public Speaking, Discussion and Debate, and Theater. In teaching them you will often follow courses of study made up by former speech teachers and approved by your state education department. In such cases the aims are usually those which you and your students would choose, the content is what you would expect to cover, and the suggested activities are numerous and broadly outlined; consequently, you will find little difficulty in accepting the course's requirements. You adapt, however, the materials of the course in the light of your knowledge about your group, its interests, experiences, level of achievement, and school and community environment. If, on the other hand, you have to plan your own courses, those prepared by others will guide you. Such courses are listed in the Suggested Reading at the ends of the chapters in Parts III and IV, Teaching Public Address and Teaching Interpretative Arts. Although such a course can give direction to your preparation, you will want to meet the special needs and interests of your particular group.

SOCIAL CLIMATE

A course of study is merely a blueprint. From it one teacher can create an autocratic society; another, a democratic society. Your classroom should approach the kind of democratic society in which we believe. This society promotes respect for the individual and for the group, responsibility of the individual for himself and for the group, and the use of discussion in solving problems. To foster these attitudes and habits is your opportunity. One way to take advantage of this opportunity is through your own acceptance of individuals, your own feeling of group responsibility, and your own use of group discussion. A second way is through your students' participation in planning the work for the classroom. Here your students have a chance to assume their share of responsibility for the direction of an area of learning. In this planning they must use the processes of group discussion, must make significant choices, and must set up their own rules and limits. As a result of this procedure, they feel free and valued as individuals.

PLANNING FOR TEACHING AND LEARNING

Student Participation in Planning

The amount of student participation in planning for classes varies widely. The competence of the students, the teacher's training and preference, and the nature of the course account for this variety. For example, the teacher of a group of juniors very proficiently planned with them an entire term's drama course including both the units and the individual lessons. The teacher was a skillful group leader who believed in teacher-pupil planning. On one particular day, groups in her class reported on the Greek playwrights Aeschylus, Sophocles, and Euripides and gave the necessary background of Greek drama. During the next few days, members of the same groups presented several scenes from *Agamemnon, Antigone,* and *Medea.* The lessons achieved important aims, both in terms of developing desirable attitudes and in terms of learning worthwhile content.

On the other hand, members of a high school theater class, who did their own planning, were less successful. This class was made up almost entirely of girls who wanted to make stage careers for themselves. The girls worked very hard on improving their voices, diction, and bodily movements. They studied characterization intelligently. They played all kinds of roles. Their preparation for acting was quite comprehensive and sound. The goal of the course was evidently to develop actresses; and the aim on the part of the students to prepare for an acting career. But in terms of general education in a high school such a goal of students and such an aim of the teacher are too narrow. Although the teacher was meeting certain needs and interests of her students and although the class was ideally permissive, she did not provide satisfactory leadership for carrying out the general education objectives of the school. The teacher must guide the planning.

Another teacher who gave lip service to teacher-pupil planning was equally unsuccessful. After she had worked out her aims, materials, and procedures for a unit in public speaking, she began the unit by asking her students what they hoped to gain from the study of public speaking. She listed these desired outcomes on the blackboard. One boy's comment, "I'd like to be able to make better oral book reports in English class" appeared as "to be able to inform." Another boy's remark, "I'd like to tell jokes well," emerged as "to give after-dinner speeches." In both instances the teacher quite obviously was interpreting the students' responses so that they coincided with her own desires. This same insistence on following her plan was evident when the students discussed procedures in the unit. For example, the boy who wanted to make better book reports said, "I'd like to practice my book reports." The teacher's quick response was, "That belongs in English class. Let's make speeches here that tell us how to build something. Mary, you could tell us how you make those attractive papier mâché puppets." This teacher-pupil planning was not genuine; it followed a tightly conceived plan of the teacher. In your planning you should be prepared with suggestions for three or four courses of action, because your students may choose any one of them.

Another young teacher was struggling with a group who was deciding how to study parliamentary procedure. The students made thirty minutes' worth of all kinds of suggestions. Finally one boy said, "There aren't enough books that contain information on parliamentary procedure to go around. Seems to me the only thing for us to do is to have Mr. Lawrence tell us about the motions, their precedence, and all the business of parliamentary procedure. We need this information. When we have it, we can practice." Although his suggestion solved the problem to the satisfaction of everyone, thirty minutes of class time had been virtually thrown away. Obviously in some circumstances you do just what the boy suggested: give the students the necessary information. You use your own common sense in deciding where teacher-pupil planning is profitable.

To summarize, teacher-pupil planning depends on you, your competence, and your training in leading a group. To be effective it should: (1) follow the accepted goals of general education and speech education, (2) be led by you, (3) be genuinely a co-operative endeavor, and (4) be used only where it is efficient.

The Unit

No matter whether the teacher or the students and teacher plan the work, they plan it in terms of units and sometimes in terms of lessons. Writers use the term *unit* in a variety of ways. Although they generally agree that the unit is centered around a significant area of learning, they disagree on many of its other elements. As just noted some educators believe that the unit should be planned co-operatively by the teacher and students; others, however, that it should be planned by teachers; and still others, that who plans it depends on the focus of the unit. Some declare that the unit should focus on an area of subject matter such as storytelling or discussion; others, that it should focus on the social and personal needs of the students. The first is sometimes called a subject matter unit and the second, an experience unit. In the first the content remains pretty much within an area; in the second it cuts across many subject lines. A written unit may include a variety of parts. For example, it may have a description of the initiating stage (considerations in the selection of the unit), a plan for the developing stage (planning objectives, methodology, and activities), a plan for integrating with other learning areas, a description of the materials and a plan for the culminating stage. Or it may contain a general statement, aims, materials, activities, and a way of evaluation.

When this last scheme is followed, this is the form:

GENERAL STATEMENT

This statement gives a general description of the students in the group, the grade level and the period of time for which the unit is planned, and an explanation of how the unit fits into the overall pattern of the course.

OBJECTIVES

These are the understandings, skills, and attitudes the pupils are to gain.

OUTLINE OF CONTENT

The content may be expressed in terms of subject matter, problems to be solved, or projects to be completed.

ACTIVITIES

Activities include the introductory activity, the activities designed to develop the desired understandings, skills, and attitudes, and the culminating activity or activities.

MATERIALS

The materials are the textbooks, reference books, films, recordings, and other materials such as charts, make-up, lumber, canvas, and paint.

EVALUATION

This statement contains what is to be evaluated and how it is to be evaluated.

The following is a unit on pronunciation:

GENERAL STATEMENT

This unit on pronunciation is part of a course in Fundamentals of Speaking for college-bound seniors. It will last four or five weeks. It is introduced so that the students will understand that although the pronunciation of their language is fluid, it is an important tool which may serve their purposes of communication.

AIMS

Understandings

To understand the different levels of pronunciation.
To recognize the regional differences in pronunciation.
To discern the principles of assimilation.
To know how to use the dictionary as a guide to pronunciation.
To perceive the factors involved in arriving at one's own standard of pronunciation.

Skills

To use the pronunciations of the educated people of the community.

Attitudes

To appreciate the ever-changing quality of our language.
To regard as valid a descriptive rather than a prescriptive approach to pronunciation.
To want to speak as a cultured individual.

CONTENT

   I. Factors in Setting a Standard of Pronunciation.
       A. Levels of Pronounciation.
       B. Regional Differences in Pronunciation.
       C. Assimilation.
   II. Dictionaries as Guides to Pronunciation.

III. Types of Common Mispronunciations Within the Group.

IV. Correction of Pronunciations of Words Commonly Mispronounced by Members of the Group.

ACTIVITIES

Initiating Activity

Discussion centered on the following pairs of pronunciations:

[aɪðɚ], [iðɚ];	(ē′thĕr), (ī′thĕr)
[dontʃʊ], [dontju];	(dōn′chōō), (dont′jōō)
[netʃɚ], [netjɚ];	(nā′chĕr), (nā′tûr)
[ɑrəndʒɪ], [ɔrəndʒ];	(är′ĕnj), (ŏ′rĕnj)
[stetəs], [stætəs];	(stā′tŭs), (stă′tŭs)
[æklɪmet], [əklaɪmet];	(ăk′lĭmāt), (ăklī′mĭt)

Activities to Achieve the Stated Aims

Reading on pronunciation in high school text.

Listening thoughtfully to reports by individual students on the pronunciation guides of various dictionaries.

Committee work involving looking up words in the dictionary.

Group discussion of such problems as: Who sets the standards for our pronunciation? What are the different situations in which we use varying levels of pronunciation?

Listening to records of people from different sections of the country and analyzing them for variations in pronunciation.

Dramatizing situations where formal, informal, and substandard speech are used.

Observing and analyzing a film on pronunciation.

Listening thoughtfully to a talk by the teacher on assimilation, the reasons for its existence, and standards for acceptable and unacceptable assimilations.

Practice on using acceptable pronounciations of particular words.

Compiling a list of words which members of the class mispronounce.

Culminating Activities

A bulletin board showing the areas of regional speech.

A puppet show depicting the levels of usage.

MATERIALS

High school textbook

Hedde, W. G., and W. N. Brigance, *The New American Speech* (Philadelphia, J. B. Lippincott Co., 1957), pp. 87-114.

Films

Improve Your Pronunciation (Coronet, sound, 11 minutes).

Look It Up! Dictionary Habits (Coronet, sound, black and white, 10 minutes).

Recordings
Recordings of speech from various sections of the country.
Recordings of speech of students.

Dictionaries
American College Dictionary
Funk and Wagnall's New College Standard Dictionary of the English Language
A Pronouncing Dictionary of American English by John S. Kenyon and Thomas A. Knott. (Springfield, Mass., G. & C. Merriam Co.).
Webster's New Collegiate Dictionary

Suggested References for the Teacher
ALLEN, H. B., *Readings in Applied English Linguistics* (New York, Appleton-Century-Crofts, Inc., 1958). For its discussion of standards of pronunciation.
BRONSTEIN, A. J., *The Pronunciation of American English* (New York, Appleton-Century-Crofts, Inc. 1960). For its chapters on standards of pronunciation, regional speech, sound changes, and pronunciation.
CROCKER, L., "The Linguist, the Freshman, and the Purist," *The Speech Teacher* III (March, 1954), 129-130. For its account of the struggle between the linguists and the purists.
EISENSON, J., "*The Improvement of Voice and Diction*" (New York, The Macmillan Co., 1958). For its section on standards and for its exercises.
FRANCIS, W., *The Structure of American English* (New York, The Ronald Press Company, 1958). For its chapters on linguistic science, phonemics, the dialects of American English, and linguistics and the teacher of English.
LANGE, P., "Pronunciation and the Dictionaries," *The Quarterly Journal of Speech*, XXXII (April, 1946), 190-193. For its discussion of dictionaries.
THOMAS, C., *Phonetics of American English,* 2nd ed. (New York, The Ronald Press Company, 1958). For its chapters on assimilation, regional variations, and standards of pronunciation.
WEAVER, C. H., "*Don't Look It Up—Listen!*" *The Speech Teacher,* VI (September, 1957), 240-246. For its discussion of the term *cultured speech.*

EVALUATION
Have the students come to an understanding of the forces at work in arriving at the pronounciation of a word?
Do they understand assimilation?

Do they see how pronunciation changes from one generation to the next?
Do they recognize how an editor of a dictionary arrives at a pronunciation?
Do they know how one dictionary differs from another?
Do they know how to use the dictionary as a guide to pronunciation?
Have they arrived at a basis for a philosophy of pronunciation of their own?
Do they realize how their pronunciations will vary in differing situations?
Do they understand why they choose one pronunciation over another?
Are they using the pronunciations of the leaders of their community?

Methods of Evaluation
Test on knowledge.
Listing of students' mispronunciations used throughout the term in their various reading and speaking situations.

Another unit on pronunciation planned for sophomores of average intellectual ability in a general required course followed a different pattern. The aims were to speak with acceptable diction, to know the mechanism of the articulatory organs, to be able to recognize articulatory errors, to use the dictionary to find acceptable pronunciations, and to employ acceptable pronunciations in speaking. The content included the mechanism of articulation, the elements of sound (consonants, vowels, and diphthongs), a study of one particular dictionary and its use of diacritical marks, syllabification and stress, and the problems of unacceptable diction (omission of sounds, substitution of sounds, inversion of sounds, incorrect stress on syllables, and overassimilation). The aims, material, activities, and evaluation of this unit on pronunciation were quite different from the one previously outlined.

The Lesson Plan

Like units, lesson plans vary. In some cases they may be implicit in the unit. In such cases, an individual lesson plan is unnecessary, for the planning has already been done. At other times the lesson plan is a formal one with a stated aim, content, material, suggested activities, assignment, and evaluation procedures. In addition, the complexity of the lesson plan varies. It may be merely a list of material or it may be a carefully planned series of questions designed to elicit specific answers and to develop a clear-cut understanding. Differences in complexity are illustrated in the two lessons subsequently discussed as teacher-planned lessons. Lastly, as in the unit, the lesson may be planned by the teacher or by the teacher and students co-operatively.

Teacher-Planned Lessons

One teacher wanted her group of foreign high school students, newly arrived in this country, to give and receive ideas about food. Consequently, she chose to have ten members of her group bring to class food that was peculiar to their countries and to explain how it was prepared. To help make the explanations clear, she provided the students with measuring cups, spoons, bowls, and different kinds of baking dishes. She selected the activity, because it called for a simple form of communication in terms of ideas and patterns of ideas.

This teacher's written plan contained only a list of the cooking materials to be used for illustration and of the eating equipment such as napkins, paper dishes, forks, and spoons. Although she had not written them down, she had thought of questions she would ask: What foods that you ate today are alike? What are some of the foods you serve in your own home that are similar to these? What are some of the English phrases that you have heard today that you will use? What are some of the English words that you have learned? These last two questions were in reality a simple evaluation. At lunch as she talked about the lesson, she said, "The lesson did bring responses from all members of the group, did clarify vocabulary used in cooking, and did teach certain phrases. But I needed more time. When I try this lesson again, I will reduce the number of students giving explanations to eight. But it's worth trying again."

On the other hand, the outline of development in some lesson plans is quite complex. For instance one teacher was teaching the theme and structure of R. U. R. by Karel Čapek. Since she wanted the students to understand both the structure of the play and the theme in one period, she developed her lesson fully in terms of questions and answers. In such instances a clearly developed plan is almost a requirement. Although she did not ask all of the questions which she had prepared, did change the order and the wording, and did add others, she successfully taught the theme and structure of R. U. R. Her planned questions follow:

INTRODUCTION TO SHOW THAT SIMILAR PROBLEMS EXIST TODAY
What are some of the possibilities of future inventions which will cut down on our own labor?
What could be some of the results of these inventions?
Describe some of the present mechanical men.

TEACHING THE THEME
What is the theme?
(At this point one of the students, who had been asked beforehand, read Edwin Markham's "Man With the Hoe.")
How does the line from this poem, "When this dumb Terror shall rise to judge the world" apply to the theme of this play?
Are the robots stupid? What happened to cause a change in their behavior?
Since this play was written in 1921, what effect did the times have on the theme?
What aspects of our society does Čapek assail?
In *Our Town*, character is very important. Is it as important in this play? If not, why not.

TEACHING THE CLIMAX
Where is the Climax?

TEACHING THE RISING ACTION
What events lead up to the Climax?

SHOWING THE EXPRESSION OF THEME THROUGH CHARACTERS
How does Helena bring about the final action?
Is she a do-gooder? Explain.
How is Mr. Alquist different from the others in the factory?
How does he discover the second Adam and Eve?
What purpose does Nana serve in the play?

INDICATING CONFLICT IN THE PLAY
What conflict or unstable situation is created and then resolved?

FINDING THE USE OF SYMBOLISM AND DRAMATIC IRONY
Symbolism can use character to express abstract ideas.
Does Čapek use symbolism? Where?
Explain how Čapek uses satire and dramatic irony in the play.

POINTING TO THE CONCLUSION
What is Domin's dream for mankind?
How does Somerset Maugham's *The Lotus Eaters* apply to this dream?

Both of these lessons are developmental. In many ways preparing to teach a developmental lesson is like preparing to give a speech. Aly, Gilman, and Reid say that "the outline is a trial run which is changed, rebuilt, and thrown away. . . . It includes supporting ideas. . . . The outline needs authoritative factual support and lively illustration."[4] Instead of explaining to students in a public speaking course how to use an outline, the authors might just as well have been explaining to students in an educational methods course how to use a lesson plan. They also state that "to find material for a speech you observe, talk with others, make inquiries, listen to current speeches and read. . . . You are original . . . You recall your own experiences. . . . Use your own language."[5] Again these statements make as much sense for the students of education as for the students of speech. As a speech teacher, you observe and listen to plays, television discussions, and political speeches. You talk with other teachers to find new ideas and original methods for teaching speech. You go to conventions and listen to ideas of teachers of wider background and experience. You read magazines like *The Speech Teacher, The Quarterly Journal of Speech,* and *The Journal of Speech and Hearing Disorders* and books of methods by such authors as Karl Robinson, Loren Reid, Willard J. Friederich and Ruth A. Wilcox, and Andrew Weaver, Gladys Borchers, and Donald Smith. In the classroom you try to be original, to make use of your own experiences, and to phrase ideas in a way which your students understand. These are but a few of the many likenesses between the two speaking activities.

Teacher-Pupil Planned Lesson

So far the discussion has centered around the lessons planned by the teacher; but, as noted earlier, lessons are frequently planned jointly by the students and the teacher. For instance, a teacher and her students may plan a series of lessons on conversation. What preparation must the teacher give for this teacher-pupil planning? She writes down the problems the students are likely to bring up: how to start a conversation, how to change a subject tactfully, how to find a new topic, how to be friendly, how to disagree, how to

---

[4] W. E. Gilman, B. Aly, and L. Reid, *The Fundamentals of Speaking* (New York, The Macmillan Co., 1951), p. 27.

[5] *Ibid.,* pp. 28, 29, 39.

include everyone in the conversation. She then analyzes ways in which they may want to attack these problems: reading, role-playing, watching films, studying other people's conversation. As a result she locates information in high school texts about conversation, contemplates possible suggestions for role-playing, finds films, and looks for plays that contain suitable conversations. Therefore, when her students ask for a film, she is ready with a suggestion. When they want to read, she is able to recommend books. This kind of lesson plan takes more preparation than the one planned by the teacher alone because of the need to consider several possibilities and to provide a number of resources.

Every lesson should serve a definite purpose. One day its pattern for achieving the purpose is simple; another day, complex. One day you plan the pattern; another, you and the students plan it. Sometimes it resembles a speech; at other times, a group discussion. You choose the kind of lesson wisely to suit its aim. Almost every lesson contains an assignment.

Assignments

First, assignments should carry meaning for the students and, thus, should be adapted to students' individual needs. As indicated earlier, when Mrs. Wilbur gave out assignments for telephoning, she adapted them to particular students. She asked May to work out a route for a couple going south and to make hotel reservations for them at hotels in several cities. May, who wanted to become a travel consultant, worked in a travel agency on Saturdays, so the material on routes, on hotels, their costs, and an evaluation of them was readily available to her. With the permission of her supervisor, she went to work early one Saturday to find the necessary information from the files of the agency. To her this assignment carried meaning.

Sometimes assignments adapted to suit particular students are meaningful. One student reads *The Valiant*; another, *The Potboiler*. One group of students prepares interviews for jobs; another group, interviews to solicit funds. At other times group assignments are meaningful. When all the members of the class say /æu/ for /au/, you may give them the same drill material as an assignment.

Second, assignments should be clear to your students. You word assignments succinctly and explain them carefully. To be certain that the students understand, you use the blackboard, illustrate, and ask questions. Never do you give an assignment in a hurry. If the bell rings, you do not hurl the assignment at the departing students; you wait until you have time to make it clear. That time may be at the beginning or at the middle of the next class hour. Students must comprehend exactly what you expect of them in an assignment.

To help your students comprehend, you make your assignments very definite. A young, inexperienced teacher recently asked her students to read Act I of *Our Town*. Although she gave them no advice on what to look for in the reading, she was surprised when they could not answer some of her questions. An older teacher suggested to her that she tell her students of Thornton Wilder's background, his travels, his education, and his philosophy and that she guide the students' reading. Together the teachers worked out the following questions which were mimeographed and given to the students:

1. Does the title give you a hint about the play's theme?
2. What characters suggest that this play is not a conventional drama?
3. What details does the playwright give about Grover's Corners?
4. Compare Grover's Corners with Central Village.
5. How does the Stage Manager make you feel about the town?
6. How do you know that the Stage Manager is a resurrected character?
7. Is the family life portrayed in this scene like your family life?
8. Compare the actions and attitudes of the young people of Central Village with those of the young people of Grover's Corners.
9. What purpose does the playwright achieve in Act I?
10. Is there rising action in this scene? If so, what is it?
11. What is the conflict in this scene?

This assignment was specific and definite.

Third, you make assignments valuable in terms of learning. Recently a teacher said, "If you don't turn in an analysis of a poem Friday, in preparation for oral reading, you will do a second analysis." This assignment may have been purposeful as punishment, but it did not help the students to learn course materials. On the other hand, in a unit on storytelling, a speech teacher asked each student to tell incidents in the careers of famous persons. She supplied a list of biographies of persons whose careers were those chosen by members of the class. She also gave the students a list of suggestions which would help them to prepare their own performance. This assignment was purposeful in terms of learning.

Finally, you should remember that the learning is for the student and not for you. "I want you to make an outline for your persuasive speech" and "Bring me in two advertisements that represent two different audience appeals tomorrow" suggest that the teacher is the one to gain from the assignment. On the contrary, you must consider the assignment as a task that benefits the *student* in helping fulfill the aims of the course.

In summary, assignments should be meaningful, clear and definite, and purposeful to the students.

Learning Activities

Your decision to use a particular learning activity depends on the area of speech you are teaching, its aims, and your students. For example, when you want to establish quickly the theme and structure of a play, you may well use question and answer, and when you plan with your students, you use discussion. In teaching speech you employ a number of learning activities: lecture-explanation, discussion, question and answer, research activities, creative activities, drill, reading, and studying.

Lecture-Explanation

One high school student remarked, "The course is supposedly a speech course but the person getting the most practice is Mr. Burns. Talk, talk, talk—and always he figures in there somewhere." This complaint exemplifies the method at its worst. On the other hand, one young man said, "My speech teacher never talks. She prides herself on being 'a good listener.' Yesterday John tried to explain the vocal mechanism to us. I wish Miss Best would tell us about it. But I'll read it for myself." Since the explanation of the vocal mechanism is somewhat complex, Miss Best might well have explained it. Lecture-explanation has a place in the high school classroom.

Discussion

After the teaching of the theme and structure of *R.U.R.*, four students formed a panel to discuss the likenesses and differences of the themes of four other plays. The chairman was a strong leader who planned and guided the discussion well. The members of his panel participated effectively. The result was a real learning experience for both the participants and the audience.

Besides using discussion to pool information, students use it to solve their problems. Members of speech classes seek answers to such questions as: What play shall we produce? What topic shall we discuss? What should be our standard of speech? The results of their decisions are actually applied in their classrooms. The problem to be discussed should be a real one which has arisen within the class and which needs a solution.

You must remember that problem solving is a process of obtaining new knowledge. When inquiry has already established knowledge, this learning activity is not applicable. Other methods are then more feasible. Problem solving may also be unsuitable because your students may not have adequate experience to provide the bases for understanding the problem. Before you select problem solving as the learning activity, you should evaluate it in the light of the particular learning to be achieved and your students' experience.

Question and Answer

When children play school, they usually show that their only concept of teaching method is for the teacher to ask questions and the pupils to answer. Question and answer can be used effectively in the teaching of speech when all the students are actively thinking of the answers and when the questions are meaningful and provocative. A casual "What about the character Kurt in *'Watch on the Rhine'*?" brings forth ten or fifteen different answers which lead nowhere. But a well-planned question will elicit information which furthers the desired learning. For example, a teacher who was pointing up the conflicts in this same play placed these categories on the blackboard:

1. Man vs. man.
2. Man vs. himself.
3. Man vs. some phase of his environment.
4. Man vs. beast or machine.

She then proceeded to question as follows:

"Let us think of Kurt's conflicts. Give an example of man versus man." A boy responded with an explanation of the conflict between Kurt and Teck.

"Now give us an example of man versus himself." A girl indicated the conflict of Kurt and fascism.

"Now, man versus some phase of his environment." A boy talked briefly about Kurt's feelings about leaving.

The questions were thought-provoking and motivated discussion.

Research Activities

Research activities grow out of the need for information for speech activities. For instance, the members of a New York State high school group discussing "What can we do about conservation in high schools in New York State" had to find out what the program of teaching conservation in New York State was. *Using Resources Wisely,* put out by the State Education Department of New York in 1956, answered many of their questions. Students should understand the need to find answers to such questions through research. In this age of mass communication a student is likely to support a statement with "Oh, I saw the answer to that on television." Consequently, it is important to make students realize that books and periodicals contain a wealth of informative material of which they themselves must determine the worth.

Creative Activities

Creative activities are an integral part of all speech education. The student may write a poem, help arrange it for choral speaking, and then participate in speaking it. Or he may portray Abe Lincoln. Or he may design a set for *You Can't Take It With You.* Or he may be one of a group who arrange a bulletin-board exhibit tracing the development of language. Or he may summarize a group discussion. Obviously you as a speech teacher have more opportunity than almost any other teacher to encourage creativity. But if you yourself play the role for demonstration purposes, if you set the pattern for choral reading, or if you teach a too rigid structure for the introduction of speeches, you may lessen the students' opportunities to be creative.

Drill

In speech classes there is a place for meaningful drill, but students must understand the need for it and be able to put the results to work. When all the students say /æu/ for /au/, they must comprehend what has happened to the first half of the diphthong, be able to hear the difference between the two diphthongs, be able to produce both of them, and be convinced that the second /au/ is a desirable part of acceptable speech. Drill on this problem may take many forms: the students may write their own stories with many words containing this sound and then read them; they may read loaded material supplied by the teacher; or they may use the sound in conversation contrived to include it. To establish good speaking habits, drill is frequently essential.

Reading, Studying

"I think I'll elect public speaking class. I won't have to study or read for that. I'll just talk." A rude awakening is due this young man about to elect a course in public speaking. He will learn that he has to do research for his speeches. Furthermore, he will soon see that he must study types of speeches, how to deliver a speech, how to prepare a speech, and how to analyze his audience. He may well have to examine speeches made by others. Reading and studying belong to this speech course and to all others.

MATERIALS FOR TEACHING SPEECH

The Textbook

Many high schools use a single speech text; in fact, as a new teacher you may not be able to choose your text, but will have to use one that has already been ordered. If you use it as your only course of study, the point of view and the methods in your course will be those of the author of the text. If, however, you use it as a teaching aid, it can provide a common body of organized knowledge for your students. The ideal plan, however, is to have copies of four or five texts so that you can assign different reading material to different students. You then take advantage of the variety of difficulty, points of view, and methods of organization in the textbooks.

Almost all of the high school textbooks listed below cover all phases of speech; in the lists of suggested readings in the chapters on dramatics and debating you will find high school texts for these specialized areas. If you are to select a single text, choose it carefully in terms of the aims of your course and your students.

ADAMS, H. M., and POLLOCK, T., *Speak Up* (New York, The Macmillan Co., 1956).
BARNES, H., and SMITH, L. W., *Speech Fundamentals* (Englewood Cliffs, N. J., Prentice-Hall, Inc., 1953).

BORCHERS, G. L., *Living Speech,* rev. ed. (New York, Harper & Brothers, 1949).

——, and WISE, C., *Modern Speech* (New York, Harcourt, Brace & Co., 1947).

CRAIG, A., *The Junior Speech Arts,* rev. ed. (New York, The Macmillan Co., 1941).

——, *The Speech Arts,* rev. ed. (New York, The Macmillan Co., 1942).

DODD, C. V., and SEABURY, H. F., *Our Speech* (Austin, Tex., The Steck Company, 1940).

ELSON, E. F., and PECK, A., *The Art of Speaking* (Boston, Ginn & Company, 1955).

FORT, L., *Speech for All* (New York, Allyn and Bacon, Inc., 1951).

GOUGH, H. B., ROUSSEAU, L., CRAMER, M., and REEVES, J. W., *Effective Speech: Complete Course,* rev. ed. (New York, Harper & Brothers, 1948).

GRIFFITH, F., NELSON, C., and STASHEFF, E., *Your Speech* (New York, Harcourt, Brace & Co., 1955).

HEDDE, W., and BRIGANCE, W. N., *American Speech,* 4th ed. (Philadelphia, J. B. Lippincott Co., 1955).

MASTEN, C., and PFLAUM, G. R. R., *Speech for You* (Evanston, Ill., Row, Peterson & Company, 1955).

NELSON, T. F., and ATKINSON, W. K., *Speech and Your Personality* (Chicago, Ill., Benjamin H. Sanborn, 1955).

PAINTER, M., *Ease in Speech,* 3rd ed. (Boston, D. C. Heath & Company, 1954).

RAUBICHECK, L., *Your Voice and Speech,* 2nd ed. (Englewood Cliffs, N. J., Prentice-Hall, Inc., 1954).

SARETT, L. W., FOSTER, W. L., and McBURNEY, J. H., *Speech: A High School Course,* rev. ed. (Boston, Houghton-Mifflin Co., 1956).

SEELY, H. F., and HACKETT, W., *Experiences in Speaking* (Chicago, Scott, Foresman & Company, 1940).

SMITH, H., KREFTING, C. E., and LEWIS, E. E., *Everyday Speech* (New York, American Book Company, 1941).

WATKINS, R., and FROST, E., *Your Speech and Mine* (New York, Lyons and Carnahan, 1945).

WEAVER, A. T., BORCHERS, G., and SMITH, D. K., *Speaking and Listening* (Englewood Cliffs, N. J., Prentice-Hall, Inc., 1956).

Free and Inexpensive Materials

Businesses, public agencies, and private organizations spend millions of dollars on materials to educate and influence the public. These materials are a valuable resource for teaching, but you should be careful to warn your students of their bias. Sponsors of such materials, however, are becoming increasingly aware of their need to refrain from too obvious advertising. In choosing free material, you must make sure that it serves a genuine purpose in your teaching, that it is in good taste, that its bias is minimal, and that its information is accurate.

A unique contribution to our field is a booklet, *Inexpensive or Free Materials Useful for Teaching Speech*[6] which is a carefully compiled list of such materials. It is a comprehensive list containing sections on Fundamentals and the Speech Program in General (including sources for audio-visual aids, tests, and courses of study), Forensics (discussion, debate, speechmaking and parliamentary procedure), Dramatics, Oral Interpretation, Radio and Television, Speech Correction and Improvement, and General Lists of Free Materials. For example, on dictionary and word study alone, Dr. Santiago has included the following items: *A Guide to Dictionary Study, Dictionary Word Power Builder, How Words Get Into the Dictionary, Inside the ACD, Interesting Origins of English Words, Levels of Usage Chart, New Word News, Picturesque Word Origins, Four Star Collegiate Word Power, Our Language, Growth and Changes, Mark My Words, Word Power Made Easy, Words and What They Do to You, Words Are Important, Word Resources, Word Study,* and *Michigan Vocabulary Profile Test.* She has annotated each item clearly so that you are well aware of its content.

Audio-Visual Methods

Audio-visual methods are those methods that do not depend upon reading to convey meaning. Because these materials offer many opportunities for improving learning, speech teachers have been using them for years. They have used models, dramatic experiences, demonstrations, field trips, displays, motion pictures, still pictures, radio and television, recordings, charts, and cartoons. When these aids help to explain a process or build a concept, when they supply a meaningful experience, they are of value to your students. You must, however, first satisfy yourself that the aid does have definite value and then decide whether it has more value than some other activity.

[6] F. M. Santiago, compiler, *Inexpensive or Free Materials Useful for Teaching Speech: A Source List for Secondary Schools* (Ann Arbor, Mich., Brau, Brunfield, 1959).

In *Audio-Visual Methods in Teaching* Edgar Dale gives these criteria:[7]

Do the materials give a true picture of the ideas they represent?

Do they contribute meaningful content to the topic under study?

Is the material appropriate for the age, intelligence, and experience of the learners?

Is the physical condition of the materials satisfactory?

Is there a teacher's guide available to provide help in effective use of the materials?

Do they make students better thinkers, critical-minded?

Do they tend to improve human relations?

Is the material worth the time, expense, and effort involved?

Models

Models are used quite frequently in the speech class. For example, in explaining the vocal mechanism you may illustrate with a professionally-made model of the larynx. In making clear the principles of sound, you may use a cigar box with various kinds of strings or bottles filled to different levels with water. Although the box and bottles oversimplify the ideas of sound, they do serve as bases for understanding. Furthermore, students frequently make stage models in a theater class, to learn the principles of stage design. The stage is particularly appropriate for representation in a model, for the construction can be accurate when made to scale.

Dramatized Experiences

Obviously the speech teacher makes much use of plays, puppetry, and role playing. Since these are discussed in the chapter on theater, they will not be discussed here.

Demonstrations

Demonstrations are particularly useful in the theater course. You must make sure, however, that your demonstration is clear and interesting and that you prepare your students for it. For example, you may well demonstrate the use of stage makeup. You first write on the blackboard the names of the materials which you intend to use and the steps in putting on makeup:

[7] Edgar Dale, *Audio-Visual Methods in Teaching*, rev. ed. (New York, The Dryden Press, Inc., 1951), p. 83. Reprinted by permission of the publishers, Holt, Rinehart and Winston, Inc.

1. Remove makeup with cold cream.
2. Use foundation or base paint.
3. Use liners to darken eyebrows, eyelashes, and as eyeshadow. (Diagram indicates where the liners are used around the eyes.)
4. Put on rouge. (Diagram indicates where it is to be placed.)
5. Put on powder.

You make sure that everyone in the class can see and do not hurry the demonstration. You summarize as you proceed and you encourage your students to ask questions.

The blackboard is readily available for all kinds of demonstrations. You and your students use it for such purposes as summarizing a discussion on the elements of effective conversation, indicating parliamentary steps in a business meeting, drawing attention to the likenesses and differences in pronunciation in various geographical areas, diagraming the vocal mechanism, or showing relationships of characters in a play.

Field Trips

Probably the first field trip that comes to mind is to attend a play. Speech teachers have, however, other opportunities for field trips. For instance, one speech teacher takes her foreign accent group to the United Nations. She precedes the trip with an explanation of its functions and a description of the work of the committee which they are to visit. Before she goes, she works out with her students what they are to see and how they are to act. Other trips valuable in speech courses are visits to a city council, to a town lecture, to a moving picture, to a radio station, to a college play rehearsal, to a college speech clinic, to a college forum or debate, and to a ballet. On such trips you plan for more than the learning and behavior of your students; you prepare for their safety. For example, you may ask your students to walk or ride in pairs; or you may invite the student teacher to go along. Although the planning and the responsibility for a field trip may seem onerous, the results are usually worth the effort.

School Displays

In one school a committee from each speech class was responsible for the bulletin board in the speech classroom. Pinned up on it at various times were: (1) news stories that could be dramatized; (2)

stick figures with printed speeches (written as they are in comic strips) showing ways to introduce guests to an audience; (3) a series of cartoons depicting frequent mispronunciations; (4) costume plates for *The Importance of Being Earnest*; (5) designs for stage settings for *The Taming of the Shrew*; (6) play bills with reactions to the plays written by the students who had seen them; (7) jackets of biographies of actors and actresses; (8) a series of pictures with captions showing the differences between debate and discussion. To provide direction for the committee the teacher mimeographed suggestions for preparing a bulletin board. She advised that the bulletin board, like a speech, have a main idea, attract attention and convert the attention to interest, inform, entertain, persuade, or impress its audience, be arranged neatly, and have a lively style.

Motion Pictures

The film cannot replace the teacher, for the students need a guide to make the experience meaningful. For example, the C and B Educational film, *Speech Preparation,* establishes the importance of research, of purpose, of organization, and of adaptation to occasion and audience in the preparation of a speech. But unless you prepare for the film in some way, such as asking that your students list the steps in preparing a speech, the experience is one of passive watching and listening. To teach public speaking you must augment this film with information, with an evaluation of the students' research and outlines, with direction in speaking and listening, with practice, with suggestions for improvement, and with an opportunity to practice the suggestions. The film, however, helps make clear the need to determine the purpose of a speech to secure information, to adapt the material to the audience and occasion, to narrow the subject and be selective in choosing information, and to organize and outline the content.

Still Pictures, Illustrations, Film Strips, Opaque Projection

Pictures can be put to many uses in a speech course. A picture that suggests a story is an excellent beginning for creative drama. In fact, theater classes find many uses for pictures. Those depicting characters suggest makeup projects. Those representing scenes from Broadway plays show different styles of scenic design. Those showing period costumes are sources for costume design. Pictures are also used in public speaking classes: advertisements would be excellent illustrations of basic appeals in persuasive speechmaking.

Opaque projectors can hold material up to 10" x 12" and can project photographs, illustrations, charts, and handwritten materials. One teacher of public speaking finds that an opaque projector is a valuable aid in studying outlining. She throws one of the student's outlines on the screen so that the students may evaluate its form and content.

Filmstrips, series of colored or black and white pictures, help illustrate many explanations. The International Film Bureau has available filmstrips on designing a set, acting problems, makeup for girls, for boys, and for characters, and managing a show. These are very useful in a play production class. Stanley Bowman of Valhalla, New York, puts out one on preparing a speech, which gives the steps in finding, selecting, and arranging material for a speech. It is useful in a fundamentals class or in a public speaking class.

Recordings

Recordings help students to acquire skill in using voice and articulation, in reading, in speaking, and in discussion. Recordings also illustrate ideas you wish to convey. For instance, one teacher herself recorded two paragraphs using acceptable pronunciations, unacceptable pronunciations, and variable pronunciations. This recording served as a basis for a discussion of pronunciation. Almost all speech teachers record speaking and reading for evaluation. From recordings students can often determine for themselves their strengths and weaknesses. For classroom use tape recording is simpler, more convenient, and less expensive than disc recording.

Commercial recordings can be employed in a variety of ways in the speech classroom: After a boy has prepared his reading of Frost's "Stopping by the Woods on a Snowy Evening," he may compare his interpretation with that recorded by the National Council of Teachers of English. Records show the differences in speech in various sections of the country and how pronunciation has changed over the ages. For instance, the four National Council of Teachers of English records of H. M. Ayres, which contain selections from Beowulf, Chaucer, Shakespeare (in the Elizabethan manner), and the Gettysburg address (as spoken in Lincoln's time) illustrate changes in pronunciation. Recordings provide background material for interpretation. For example, the National Tape Repository has 31 taped recordings, *Rhyme and Reason Over the Coffee Cups,* that are panel discussions analyzing the poetry and prose of such writers as Frost, Keats, Shelly, and Shakespeare. The National Council of Teachers of English recording *The Golden Age of the Theater* shows the similarities and differences in modern styles of acting. Such recordings bring to the class illustrations not otherwise readily available.

P. A. System

One radio workshop of a school presents ten-minute programs three times a week during home-room periods. The students make the necessary announcements for the school, advertise the school plays, concerts, and athletic events, and sometimes enact short plays for entertainment. They always give a short digest of the day's news, both local and national. These performances give meaning to their study in the workshop.

Charts, Cartoons, and Sketches

One teacher prepared a series of charts showing the vocal mechanism, the consonant and vowel sounds, ways of supporting a speech, methods of makeup, and the precedence of motions in a meeting. She found that the charts saved time, for otherwise she would have placed the material on the blackboard.

Managing and Equipping the Classroom

Part of the daily work in the classroom is to take attendance, adjust ventilation, direct seating arrangements, secure needed material, and take care of other such necessary tasks as returning papers. Students can handle many of these chores. For instance, one high school student can take attendance. Another can open and close the windows as needed. Another two or three can arrange the seats to suit the speaking situation and replace them at the end of the period. Still another student can hand out necessary materials.

There are other ways of using students to take care of routine matters. One teacher employs the procedures of parliamentary procedure to run her class. She has a student chairman who conducts the business of the class and a student secretary who takes roll and keeps an account of the activities of the group. When decisions are to be made, they take place in a parliamentary way under the leadership of the chairman. The secretary's minutes include these decisions and other items such as the committee reports of the group. At the beginning of each period, the secretary reads the minutes from the preceding day and in this way reviews the work of the day before.

A routine which you must organize is the collecting and returning of papers. One speech teacher spent twenty minutes of a class period with this routine. As each child's name was called, he came to the desk. Some children made as many as five trips to receive five different papers. As a result, the teacher and the students wasted twenty minutes. To avoid such waste, one teacher keeps a manila folder for each student on her desk. As the student enters the class, he slips his paper into its proper folder; when the paper is corrected, he takes it from the folder. This folder also contains a record of criticism given him on speeches and of the grades which he has received on oral and written work. Another teacher has a student collect the papers in the order in which the students are seated. Since the teacher keeps them in the same order, they are easily returned. Some such system of collecting and returning papers saves time.

Your Physical Environment

Classroom conditions such as lighting, ventilation, seating, neatness, and color of the walls affect the work of all students. In addition, the speech classroom has particular needs: room for small group work, areas for construction of material such as flats for a stage set, space to put on a show, a place to give a speech or to hold a panel discussion, and a spot for recording. When your classroom is large, with a flexible arrangement of seats and tables, effective soundproofing, and a small raised platform, you will have an adequate environment for teaching speech effectively.

MOTIVATION

Some teachers refer to motivation as a separate matter. Actually it is closely related to all the ingredients of the teaching situation: the students, the aims, the ideas or content, the pattern in which the ideas are presented, the social climate, and the physical environment. The following account illustrates this statement. Mrs. Maxwell, about to start a unit on announcing in Radio Workshop, was happy to find a cartoon[8] depicting a gentleman telling his class of announcers, "You did fairly well with Krispy-Krunchy and now we'll take up m-m-m-good. I want you to pay particular attention to the rolling *m*," for she knew she could use it to motivate her students. However, all six ingredients of Mrs. Maxwell's teaching situation were favorable to learning and would help to create strong motivation in that classroom. The students, who had completed at least one course in speech, had elected Radio Workshop, because they were particularly interested in learning about radio. Since Mrs. Maxwell had spent three years working in commercial radio and had an excellent academic background in the area, she was a competent guide in this teaching-learning situation. Furthermore, she enjoyed adolescents and learned to know her students well so she was able to adapt her material to them. Under Mrs. Maxwell's direction, the students set their goals and planned many of their units and lessons; as a result a friendly feeling and an attitude of intellectual curiosity prevailed. Her classroom was a well-equipped small radio station. All of these factors motivated learning. Her motivation did not come from the cartoon but rather from her students' desire to learn, co-operative planning, her adaptation of material to them, and the social and physical environment of the class.

The desire to learn is normal in most adolescents. When it is absent, you may assume that some factor in the learning situation has thwarted the desire. It may be that your goals are not clear or are unrealistic. Or your methods may be inappropriate; your unit, your lessons, or your assignments may be faulty. Or your material may not be geared to the students and their interests. Or the social climate may cause the slow learning. Students may feel that they are not accepted; they may even dislike or resent you. A particular student may have an emotional or physical disturbance that limits his effectiveness. Or the physical environment may detract from the learning situation. Instead of finding a motivation gimmick, observe your students and their achievements; and analyze the aims, methods, and materials of your own teaching. When necessary, modify your aims, your content, your activities, and your evaluation.

[8] H. T. Webster, *The Best of H. T. Webster; A Memorial Collection* (New York, Simon and Schuster, Inc., 1953), p. 220.

Study the social climate and the physical environment. Do what you can to improve them.

Motivation is that which makes the student want to work hard at learning. Since it is necessary for all learning, the means of motivation have been implied in all sections of this chapter.

You adapt your speech curriculum to the adolescents in your group; for one group, you achieve one kind of learning; for another group, a different kind. The materials and methods which you use to achieve these learnings may vary in two sections of the same course in the same school. There is no single recipe which works with all students. Some of the ingredients and possible combinations have been suggested in this chapter, but in no instance will you be able to follow a recipe slavishly. You add an ingredient, take one away, and prepare the mixture differently. A large part of the excitement of teaching lies in trying new combinations and in achieving good results.

SUGGESTED READING

ALCORN, M. D., HOUSEMAN, R. A., and SCHUNERT, J. R., *Better Teaching in Secondary Schools* (New York, Holt, Rinehart and Winston, Inc., 1954), Chs. 3 and 4. Includes a discussion of long-term planning in Ch. 3 and of daily planning in Ch. 4. Gives examples of units and lesson plans.

BLANCHARD, B. E., "Tentative Criteria for the Selection of Textbooks," *The High School Journal*, XXXVIII (May, 1955), 293-296. Gives principles for choosing a textbook. Contains a checklist for rating a textbook.

BOSSING, N. L., *Principles of Secondary Education*, 2nd ed. (Englewood Cliffs, N. J., Prentice-Hall, Inc., 1955), Chs. 4, 5, 6. Discusses the nature of the secondary school pupil, the nature of our democratic society, and the nature of problems facing youth in our democratic society.

BUSH, R. N., *The Teacher-Pupil Relationship* (Englewood Cliffs, N. J., Prentice-Hall, Inc., 1954). Reports on a long-term study of the complexities of teacher-pupil relationships.

CANTOR, N., *The Teaching-Learning Process* (New York, The Dryden Press, Inc., 1953), Ch. 4. Tells about the teacher's place in establishing the right classroom social climate.

COLE, L., *Psychology of Adolescence*, 4th ed. (New York, Holt, Rinehart, and Winston, Inc., 1954). Discusses phases of adolescent growth.

COOK, L. A., and COOK, E. F., *A Sociological Approach to Education*, 2nd ed. (New York, McGraw-Hill Book Co., 1950). Suggests the implications of social status in community to work in the school. Ch. 5 deals with the small city community and Ch. 6 with the urban community.

CROW, L., and CROW, A., *Adolescent Development* (New York, McGraw-Hill Book Co., 1956).

DALE, E., *Audio-Visual Methods in Teaching*, rev. ed. (New York, The Dryden Press, Inc., 1954). Gives the theory of audio-visual instruction, materials for audio-visual instruction, and classroom applications of audio-visual methods. Chapter 25 deals with audio-visual materials in English and reading.

FRIEDERICH, W. J., and WILCOX, R. A., *Teaching Speech in High School* (New York, The Macmillan Co., 1953), Ch. 2. Describes the speech teacher's approach to his class.

GESELL, A. L., and others, *Youth: The Years From Ten to Sixteen* (New York, Harper & Brothers, 1956) .

GRAMBS, J. D., and IVERSON, W. J., *Modern Methods in Secondary Education*, rev. ed. (New York, Holt, Rinehart and Winston, Inc., 1958). Discusses democratic behavior in the classroom (Ch. 5), group techniques in the classroom (Ch. 10), unit and lesson plans (Ch. 6), and managing the classroom for effective learning (Ch. 12).

HANSEN, K. H., *High School Teaching* (Englewood Cliffs, N. J., Prentice-Hall, Inc., 1957), Chs. 1, 4, and 6. Deals with the high school in its social setting (Ch. 1). Tells how to organize the classroom learning environment (Ch. 4). Gives the elements of good unit plans (Ch. 6).

———, *Public Education in American Society* (Englewood Cliffs, N. J., Prentice-Hall, Inc., 1956), Ch. 13. Suggests ways in which teachers can grow professionally.

HYDE, E. B., "A Speech Program in a Central School," *The Speech Teacher*, IV (January, 1955), 53-55. Describes the speech program in a public school system of 1600 pupils.

HURLOCK, E. B., *Adolescent Development* (New York, McGraw-Hill Book Co., 1954) .

JERSILD, A. T., *The Psychology of Adolescence* (New York, The Macmillan Co., 1957).

JOHNSON, J. L., "Minimum Speech Program for the Small High School," *National Association of Secondary School Principals Bulletin*, XXXIX (May, 1955), 121-125. Tells about the kinds of programs for three groups: those with impediments, average, and gifted.

KELLELKAMP, G. C., *Teaching Adolescents* (Boston, D. C. Heath & Company, 1949). Includes a chapter on counseling by the classroom teacher (Ch. 19) and one on directing learning activities of pupils (Ch. 6).

KLAUSMEIER, H., *Teaching in the Secondary School* (New York, Harper

& Brothers, 1958). Includes a chapter on adolescents (Ch. 2), and one on democratic living in the school (Ch. 4), one on unit and daily planning (Ch. 6), and one on conducting group and individual work (Ch. 10).

LONGERICH, E. B., and LONGERICH, M. C., "The Junior High School Speech Teacher," *Quarterly Journal of Speech*, XXX (April, 1944), 216-221. Suggests speech units that will meet the needs of adolescents.

MACOMBER, F. G., *Teaching in the Modern Secondary School* (New York, McGraw-Hill Book Co., 1952). Includes a checklist for self-evaluation of teaching (pp. 248-254) and a section on unit planning (Chs. 4 and 5).

The North Central Association, "A Program of Speech Education," *Quarterly Journal of Speech*, XXXVII (October, 1951), 347-358. Describes in Part III the amount and kind of speech in the school curriculum.

OLSEN, E. G., (Editor) *School and Community*, 2nd ed. (Englewood Cliffs, N. J., Prentice-Hall, Inc., 1954), Ch. 3. Gives the effect of the social structure of the community on the school.

PARSTECK, B. J., "Speech at the Core of the Core Curriculum," *The Speech Teacher*, II (November, 1953), 283-286. Tells how a speech teacher taught in the core curriculum. Shows the similarities in teaching speech and in teaching core.

RASMUSSEN, C., and WALSH, G., "Wisconsin's Speech Curriculum Committee," *Quarterly Journal of Speech*, XXXIV (October, 1948), 367-368.

REID, L., *Teaching Speech*, (Columbia, Mo., Artcraft Press, 1956), Ch. 5. Tells how to manage students in the speech classroom.

RIVLIN, H. N., *Teaching Adolescents in Secondary Schools: The Principles of Effective Teaching in Junior and Senior High Schools*, 2nd ed. (New York, Appleton-Century-Crofts, Inc., 1961). Gives sound guidance to the high school teacher.

ROBINSON, K. F., *Teaching Speech in the Secondary School*, (New York, Longmans, Green & Co., 1954), Chs. 7, 8, and 9. Tells about the relationship of speech to other departments, planning the speech program, and gives the basic principles of getting started in teaching.

WEAVER, A. T., BORCHERS, G. L., and SMITH, D. K., *The Teaching of Speech* (Englewood Cliffs, N. J., Prentice-Hall, Inc., 1952), Chs. 3 and 5. Explains clearly and in detail the scope and purpose of the high school curriculum. Describes classroom procedures.

WHITEHILL, B., "Speech Education in Pennsylvania," *The Speech Teacher*, II (January, 1953), 33-37.

WILES, K., *Teaching for Better Schools*, (Englewood Cliffs, N. J., Prentice-Hall, Inc., 1952), Chs. 6 and 8. Includes a chapter on planning (Ch. 8), and one on the organization of classroom groups for learning (Ch. 6).

WILCOX, H. F., "The Siamese Twins," *The Speech Teacher*, IV (September, 1955), 176-182. The siamese twins are speaking and thinking. Describes the speech activity program of a high school.

EXERCISES

1. Prepare a unit for teaching a particular area of speech in the fundamentals course to a particular group.
2. Read at least four high school speech texts. Write a report assuming that you must recommend two texts for adoption for your particular high school and that you have to justify your recommendations.
3. Read carefully a course of study for an elective speech course. Assume that it is the course which has been given you in a particular school for a particular group of students. Indicate what modifications you would make in this course.
4. Prepare a developmental lesson plan to accomplish a specific aim. Prepare for a teacher-pupil planned lesson to accomplish the same aim.
5. Write a criticism of the following assignment for a class in beginning theater. The assignment is based on a lesson which suggested sources of material for dramatization and which gave principles for the selection of the material. Each row in the class was given a different assignment.

   Row A: Write a story, which we can later play in class, based on the words *ugly* and *beautiful*.
   Row B: Find a ballad to dramatize.
   Row C: Find a story to dramatize.
   Row D: Find two pictures to use as bases for dramatization.
   Row D: Find material from a book or journal on folklore to dramatize.

6. Describe a lesson where you may well lecture; one where you may lead a discussion; and one where you may use drill.
7. Start a file on free and inexpensive materials for a fundamentals course. Prepare labels for various areas and their subdivisions. Send for some of the material suggested in Florence Santiago's booklet.
8. Prepare a bulletin board depicting some aspect of speech. For example, you may depict levels of usage, purposes of speaking, or audience appeals.

II

TEACHING
THE FUNDAMENTALS
OF SPEAKING

II

3

Fundamentals

of Speaking

THE HIGH SCHOOL fundamentals course, usually the first course in speech, tries to meet all the aims of speech education listed in Chapter 1. It stimulates interest in ideas, develops ability to organize these ideas and to recognize the patterns of organization in the ideas of others, stresses the positive attributes of the personality of the speaker and listener, and teaches the students to speak, read aloud, and listen effectively.

AIMS

Acquiring Ideas

As a teacher of the fundamentals course, you constantly stress the importance of ideas. You encourage your students to acquire knowledge purposefully. One speech teacher found that his homogeneous group of slow students were to a large degree unaware of their surroundings. As a result, he took them to the airport, to the United Nations, to a garment factory, and to a college play; he encouraged them to find out what their city offered and to talk about its offerings. Furthermore, he introduced the members of the group to interesting reading materials at their own level. For instance, one ardent baseball fan spoke on the invention of baseball in 1839 by

General Doubleday. As a source of information, he used Robert Holzman's *General "Baseball" Doubleday* (New York, Longmans, Green & Co., Inc., 1955). Later this same boy, having read *Base Burglar* by Jackson Scholz (New York, William Morrow & Co., Inc., 1955), entertained his group with the tale of Cliff Connor's crashing the gate at spring training camp. He based his oral book report on Richard Hubler's *Lou Gehrig: the Iron Horse of Baseball* (Boston, Houghton Mifflin Co., 1941). The teacher's skillful guidance made this young baseball fan realize that books contain worthwhile and useful ideas. In addition to trips, books, and magazines, you may use television shows as a source of ideas in a variety of units: theater, discussion, debate, and oral interpretation. During the entire course, you encourage your boys and girls to broaden their intellectual horizons.

Organizing Ideas

Knowledge, however, is almost useless unless it is organized. Throughout the fundamentals course, you, therefore, place emphasis on stating the main and subordinate ideas of a reading, speech, or play, and on establishing the relationship of one idea to another. Mrs. Kirchman, Chairman of the Speech Department, Jamaica High School, Jamaica, New York, suggests to the members of her staff that they use the analogy of the organization of an explanation of a theorem by a geometry teacher to the organization of material for a speech. She further advises that they have the students observe the organization in a social studies lesson—that they ask the students to note the aim of the lesson and how it was developed.

Developing Effective Personalities

Since you want your students to possess more than organized knowledge, you are also intent on developing desirable assets of personality. You emphasize sincerity and honesty not only because the sincere, honest speaker is more effective but also because he is a better member of a group. You help your students to reject the speech or reading that deliberately distorts to make a point and to respect the need for adequate evidence, logical reasoning, and good sound appeals. In addition to placing stress on the ethics of speaking, you place it on being a co-operative member of a group. You want your students to be intellectually honest and to be assets to the group.

Improving Voice and Diction

Closely related to personality are voice and diction. Many teachers make use of this close relationship in the fundamentals course. For instance, one teacher asks her students what they know of the person who says, "That there fella tole me he donno. He ain't gonna go wit us." Similar approaches are described in the chapter on voice and articulation. Throughout the course you help your students, no matter what the speaking activity is, to keep their voices pleasant, audible, and flexible and to use the articulation of an educated individual.

Achieving Purposes of Speaking Competently

The purposes of the speaking activity influence your aims in the fundamentals course. Most fundamentals courses emphasize the informal speaking situation. The students learn to converse more effectively whether with their friends or elders, whether the situation is a social or a business one. In addition, they learn to impart information, to persuade others to their way of thinking, and to divert and please their listeners. All kinds of activities further these aims.

Listening Effectively

To all the speaking in a fundamentals course, listening is important. When they speak themselves, your students will understand the need for a lively sense of communication and may be encouraged to listen themselves. You should, however, always keep in mind that the speaking situation involves speakers who speak or read *and* listeners who must respond. You will probably need to provide some motivation for this response, particularly if you wish to achieve the five listening aims noted in Chapter I.

To listen graciously
To listen thoughtfully
To listen critically
To listen appreciatively
To listen sympathetically

Where may these aims be achieved in the fundamentals course?

First, gracious listening may be encouraged in the units on informal speaking, such as conversation and telephoning. In conversation, students can note attitudes and responses which are indicative of gracious listening. "He looks as if he is really interested," "His response showed delight," and "She smiled at my joke" are all evaluations that point to gracious listening.

Second, thoughtful listening should occur when information is being given. Opportunities exist in listening to informative talks, to the explanation of background for oral interpretation, to the description of the setting for a story, or to the questions of the interviewers; they also occur in group discussions, debates, and parliamentary procedure. Teachers motivate this listening. For example, one high school student said, "My speech teacher is insistent about our getting the main idea and finding the supporting statements in speeches given in our class." Or when a complicated process is explained, students may ask the speaker questions. Or the speaker may turn the tables and ask questions of members of his audience. You will find many other techniques which encourage your students to listen thoughtfully.

Third, critical listening as a response to persuasion, should be encouraged. Your insistence on detecting false reasoning, unsound evidence, and unfair appeals leads to critical listening. One boy became very adept at argumentation. He came to class smiling and saying, "I may lose my happy home. My father says that our home is now a court of law." When his father met the teacher, he said that for the first time his boy was listening to him and thinking critically. He quipped, "To think his thinking began in a speech class."

Fourth, appreciative listening should be the response to creative dramatics, oral reading, and storytelling. If you are careful of your students' choice of material, if you make sure that your students understand their material and do their best to present it well, the listeners in the class are more likely to listen appreciatively. In addition you develop the attitude that sharing is important. One student declared, "For the first time I'm appreciating poetry. Mary's reading of Emily Dickinson today makes me realize what I've been missing." This comment points to appreciative listening.

Fifth, oportunities to listen sympathetically occur infrequently in a fundamentals class. When, however, you teach speaking to impress, it should be present. Encouraging students to listen for unusual wording and creative ways of expressing ideas fosters this type of listening. For example, one group of students were asked to view a televised memorial service for Oscar Hammerstein and to list the striking ways in which the quality of the man's work and the strengths in his character were portrayed. The students' list included such items as the use of particularly appropriate lyrics composed by Oscar Hammerstein, phrases and sentences that vividly described the man, and anecdotes told by well-known theatrical personalities.

REASONS FOR DIFFERENCES
IN FUNDAMENTALS COURSES

Basic Philosophy of Speech Education

The basic educational philosophy of speech teachers is more alike than different. Undoubtedly you agree with most of the aims noted in Chapter I; you may, however, disagree with some. Such differences will influence your teaching of the fundamentals course. For instance, one young teacher remarked, "I do not like the moral emphasis of these aims." She further explained that she did not believe that the speech teacher should try to develop "ethical group living" or "the kind of ethical communication involved in democratic behavior." She said, "My job is to teach speech, not ethics. I am willing to admit that the persuader should be sincere and honest and that the discussant should co-operate to his fullest with his fellow discussants. But I will not buy the philosophy behind 'the good man speaking well.' I feel my responsibility is to teach my student to use his body well, to speak clearly and distinctly, to be poised, to have worthwhile ideas, and to organize them effectively."

Another young woman thought that the philosophy explained in Chapter I did not go far enough in developing "the good man." She would give more attention to the adjustment of one individual to another in a group situation, to the adaptation of the speaker to his audience, and to the importance of good human relationships in all speaking situations. She said, "I like the idea of 'the good man speaking well.' I want this goodness to be the central focus. I want the speaker to sit at a conference table, contribute worthwhile ideas, organize them effectively, present them well but most of all I want him to be a truly co-operative, honest, and ethical human being."

A young man noted that for him these aims did not put enough stress on utilizing the creative talent of each individual or on developing his natural style of speaking. He held the opinion that in the first course, the teacher should give the student with a dramatic flair opportunity to act and the one with persuasive ability a chance to be a successful advocate. He said, "I may have a Helen Hayes or a Clarence Darrow in my class." He was also convinced that each speaker has a style natural to him that should be encouraged. He illustrated this statement with an extreme comment, "Sometimes even a stutter may be part of a style that is effective."

The basic philosophies of speech education of these three individuals will affect the designs of their fundamentals courses. Even though they plan their courses with their students, their basic philosophies will influence the course strongly. For example, the girl who objected to the "good man speaking well" may well design a course with emphasis on basic processes. She will give careful attention to correcting articulatory errors, to improving voice, to assisting the speakers in finding ideas and patterns. She will not be as concerned with his relationship to others. On the other hand, the girl who applauded the "good man speaking well" will construct a somewhat different course. It may well be that she will start with a unit on group discussion and give considerable emphasis in it to the interaction of human beings. Although the young man may have some difficulty with the structure of his fundamentals course, he will tailor it strictly to meet the needs and talents of his students.

Thus, your basic philosophy of speech education affects the design of the course. Two other causes for differences in fundamentals courses are: (1) the teacher's training and (2) the needs and abilities of the students.

Teacher's Training

Your training influences the blueprint of your basic course. For example, one young woman did her practice teaching in a core curriculum, the main purpose of which was to meet the social and intellectual needs of the adolescent students. This training affected her subsequent teaching of a fundamentals course. When she planned it with her students, their first unit was "The Teen-Agers Speak," involving group discussion of the problems of many teenagers: money, dating, families, and choice of career. A study of contemporary magazines comprised another unit in her course. Individual students read aloud stories and poetry to illustrate the content of various magazines (oral reading), compared and analyzed reports of national affairs in different magazines (informative speaking), and gave the advantages of one magazine over another (persuasive speaking). A panel of four analyzed humour in today's magazines, showing its shortcomings and making suggestions for its improvement (group discussion). Not many teachers of speech care to teach fundamentals in this way. But if the proof of success is in the eating, the members of this particular group ate enthusiastically and voraciously.

Furthermore, your major interest in a specialized area of speech reflects itself in your scheme of teaching. One effective teacher of fundamentals is a man who majored in theater and who, as a result, devotes one third of his basic course to theater activities. From their participation in theater activities, his students, however, become proficient in most of the basic elements of oral communication. The prime purpose of the course is to teach students to speak and listen effectively, and this may be achieved in a variety of ways.

Needs and Abilities of Students

Lastly, the speaking needs and abilities of your students dictate to a large extent the purposes of your fundamentals course. For example when almost all the members of your group use substandard pronunciation, meagre vocabularies, and hesitant speech, your goals will be quite unlike those for students with excellent voice and diction, adequate vocabularies, and fluent speech. If your group is made up of college-bound students, you arrange for one set of learnings; if your group is to end its formal education with high school, you arrange for a somewhat different set. Even courses in two vocational high schools vary. If you teach in a vocational high school with an emphasis on printing, you plan one kind of course, but if you teach in a vocational high school with an emphasis on aviation, you plan another kind of course.

Thus, your philosophy, your training, and particularly the needs and abilities of your students influence your planning of the fundamentals course.

Fundamentals courses, however, are more alike than unlike. Admittedly, whether the course is elective or required, whether it is taught early or late in the high school years, whether it is a one-term or a two-term course, and whether it receives credit as an English course will influence the content. To show the similarities and differences in content, several courses of study will be examined.

CONTENT

The Secondary School Interest Group of the Speech Association of America proposes the following units:[1]

Introduction	1 week
Bodily Action	2 weeks
Informal Speech	1 week
Voice and Diction	2 weeks
Listening and Speaker-Audience Relationships	1 week
Preparation and Delivery of Talks	3 weeks
Parliamentary Procedure	2 weeks
Oral Reading	3 weeks
Discussion	3 weeks

This course is a required one proposed for a single semester with one-half unit academic credit. It is interesting to note that this syllabus contains no unit in theater although in the unit on bodily action the teaching of pantomime is suggested. Even though discussion is included, debate is not. No mention is made of radio or television.

A syllabus for a fundamentals course from a New York City high school contains the following units:[2]

Voice and Diction
Getting Along with Others (Conversation, Listening, Manners, Interviewing)
Speaking in Public
Group Discussion
Debate
Parliamentary Procedure
Oral Interpretation
Dramatics
Story Telling
Mass Media

[1] Secondary School Interest Group, "Fundamentals of Speech: A Basic Course for High School," *The Speech Teacher*, VIII (March, 1959), 94.
[2] Martin Salkin, Chairman Department of Speech, Forest Hills High School, Forest Hills, New York, *Syllabus for a Basic Course in Speech*.

This syllabus is organized by areas of speech. It was prepared for a term course for college-bound students in an academic high school of superior standing. The course is an elective one, selected in the main by the more able students.

The differences in choice of units between this course and the one recommended by the Secondary Interest Group of The Speech Association of America are noteworthy. The New York City high school syllabus contains no units on introduction (definition of effective speech and its values), bodily action, or listening. A look at the content of its units, however, will show that these aspects are taught indirectly. Furthermore, in addition to those units suggested in the Secondary Interest Group Syllabus, the New York City High School Syllabus possesses units on debate, dramatics, storytelling, and the mass media.

A high school located in Mineola, Long Island, recommends the following materials for study:[3]

Speech Arts—Definition
Poise
Voice and Diction
Spontaneity
Conversation
Business Interviews
Usage
Vocabulary
Speechmaking
Speeches for Special Occasions
Impromptu Speeches
Informal Class Discussion
Parliamentary Procedure
Debate
Oral Reading
Choral Reading
Storytelling
Radio and Television
Mock Trial

This syllabus obviously provides training for students of widely varying abilities. The introduction states,[4] "General speech is taught on the high school level and is open to all students from the ninth

[3] *Syllabus for General Speech*, Mineola High School, Mineola, New York.
[4] *Ibid.*, p. 1.

to twelfth grades. Students who have slight defects and students who are self-conscious are encouraged to take the course, although all students who elect it are included." This syllabus again omits theater. The reason for this omission may be that the school offers two elective courses in theater: Dramatics and Advanced Dramatics.

Somewhat different selections of units are suggested by Seabury and Reid. Seabury advises the following:[5]

Oral Interpretation of Prose
Explanatory Speeches with Visual Aids
Phonetics, Spelling, Pronunciation, Articulation
Informatory and Expository Speeches on Speech Content
Oral Interpretation of Poetry
Discussion
Parliamentary Procedure
Radio Plays
Individual and Group Pantomimes
One Act Plays
Extemporaneous Speeches on Timely Topics
Argumentative Speeches

Reid gives two possible sets of units and includes a timetable.[6]

Set A

Orientation	1 week
Voice and Articulation	1 week
Informal Speech	3 weeks
Parliamentary Procedure	2 weeks
Speechmaking	5 weeks
Group Discussion and Debate	4 weeks

Set B

Orientation	1 week
Articulation	3 weeks
Voice	3 weeks
Pronunciation	2 weeks
Vocabulary	2 weeks
Informal Speaking	3 weeks
Speechmaking	2 weeks

[5] H. Seabury, "Objectives and Scope of the Fundamentals Course in Speech in High School," *The Speech Teacher,* III (March, 1954), 117-120.

[6] L. Reid, *Teaching Speech* (Columbia, Mo., Artcraft Press, 1956), p. 71.

Certain trends in content in fundamentals courses are discernible. Most of the fundamentals courses incorporate units on voice and articulation, informal speaking situations, preparation and delivery of talks, parliamentary procedure, oral reading, and group discussion. Listening and bodily movements may not be separate units, but they are usually part of the study in other units. Or they may be taught indirectly; for example, the teacher may give attention to them in the processes of criticism and evaluation. Theater may or may not be included. Even though theater is not a separate unit, pantomime may be a technique used in teaching bodily movement and creative drama may be used in a unit on informal speaking activities such as conversation or interviewing. The study of radio and television and debate are frequently omitted.

That discussion is included and debate omitted does not seem logical. Both processes are often needed to reach a decision. Both play an important part in the conduct of personal, local, state, and national affairs. Discussants propose the solution; debaters advocate it. Finding a solution is important, but if those proposing it can not persuade others of its worth, the search for the solution is rather futile.

In a study of the fundamentals courses taught in Missouri, Reid and Roberts[7] say that certain patterns emerge clearly. They state that in a full-year course public speaking is always included and comprises about a fourth of the course, that theater either receives considerable emphasis or is excluded, and that oral interpretation and voice and diction get more emphasis than the remaining areas of speech. On the other hand, they note that the semester course tends to concentrate on a few aspects of speech. The larger schools devote almost 42 per cent of the course to public speaking, slightly less than 15 per cent to other areas of public address, notably discussion, debate and parliamentary procedure, and the remaining time to different areas, particularly voice and diction and oral interpretation. The smaller schools tend to concentrate on what teachers call "everyday speaking experiences" as voice and diction, conversation, standards of pronunciation, and vocabulary development. Emphasis

[7] R. R. Reid and R. A. Roberts, "A Survey of Fundamentals of Speech Courses in Missouri Public High Schools," *The Speech Teacher*, VII (November, 1958), 321, 322.

is placed on informal speech situations rather than the formal speech situations.

Similarities and differences in content also exist within units. A comparison of the units on voice and diction and the units on giving talks in the syllabi prepared by the Secondary Interest Group and in the one prepared for a New York City high school follows:

In the units on voice and articulation both syllabi contain material on the vocal mechanism, on the attributes and characteristics of voice, on the pronunciation of particular words, and on the recording of these pronunciations by dictionaries. The New York City syllabus has, however, additional material on standards, on strong and weak forms, and on assimilation. A more academic approach is evident in the New York City syllabus; a more personal approach is advocated in the Secondary Interest Group syllabus. Both approaches may be equally effective in dealing with voice and articulation, but some teachers prefer to include more linguistic background than others.

In the unit on making speeches, both syllabi suggest teaching types of speaking, purposes, preparation (including selection of materials, research for a speech, and outlining), and delivery. But the New York City high school syllabus specifically recommends a study of the audience in terms of its attitudes, knowledge, and human appeal. The Secondary Interest Group syllabus does not. Undoubtedly those who use the Secondary Interest Group syllabus will teach adaptation to audience indirectly through suggestion and criticism. The author of the New York City syllabus, however, prefers to attack the problem directly.

Fundamentals courses with quite different approaches can be equally successful. The emphasis in some is on formal speaking situations; in others, on informal speaking situations. In some, on theater; in others, on public speaking. In some, on aspects of speech almost entirely personal; in others, on aspects more academic. The approach which you select depends upon you, your training and, most important of all, upon your students.

Problems in Content

You will face problems regarding the content in each unit. You must make a decision whether to teach bodily action and listening directly or indirectly in relation to speaking activities. You either include or omit material on telephoning. One teacher remarked, "Any four-year-old uses the telephone and usually effectively. Why waste time on telephoning?" Another teacher refuted the argument by "high school students don't know how to talk on the telephone. Their business telephone conversations are inefficient and disorganized. Just try asking them to make travel reservations to a specific place." Other problems emerge. Do you teach the vocal mechanism in the unit on voice or do you not? One highly successful teacher of voice says that teaching the vocal mechanism is a waste of time and that the time should be spent in teaching students to listen to their voices. In your unit on articulation do you teach phonetics? One teacher asserts that the study is not very difficult, that it trains students to hear accurately and efficiently, and that it is an absolute necessity for improving articulation. But another teacher says that she teaches only the phonetics that is absolutely essential— a minimal amount. Do your students give speeches of all four kinds? Many teachers emphasize informative and persuasive speaking and ignore impressive and entertaining speaking. Others give considerable emphasis to the impressive and entertaining speeches usually calling them speeches for special occasions. Such problems you resolve. You weigh the advantages and disadvantages of each solution and arrive at your decision as wisely as you can.

PROBLEMS IN MANAGING THE FUNDAMENTALS COURSE

Other problems in teaching the beginning course arise. They include the allotment of time to the course and its units, the size of the classes, how to start the course, the order of the units, and the evaluation of the work.

Allotment of Time

The administration of the school almost always decides for or with you whether the fundamentals course is a one-semester or a two-semester course, whether it is required or elective, in what year it is to be taught, and what the size of your class is to be. Such decisions are usually made before the new teacher arrives at the school. Most administrators are, however, amenable to suggestions for the future. You recommend what seems desirable to you and support your recommendations soundly. When you do a superior teaching job and when your students and their parents believe that the fundamentals course is needed, your task of persuading the administration to expand speech work is easier. The administration considers these opinions sound evidence.

The size of the classes in fundamentals courses affects the amount of time of performance for each student. When the class is large, you and the students have too little time for listening to each student and for evaluating his performance. If a fundamentals course is to provide opportunities for performance in speaking activities and for the evaluation of these performances, your class should contain no more than twenty-five students.

Another problem related to time is what proportion of the course to allot to the various units. Here again the needs and abilities of your students influence your decision. When your students are in obvious need of oral reading, you give more time to it. When their articulation is poor, you devote considerable time to that. One young teacher asked, "But what if no one speaks clearly and no one seems to have any ability at all to communicate?" At the other extreme another young teacher of an honor class said, "My students are unusually able. They already speak well. I don't know how much time to spend on units in the prescribed course, for I feel sure they don't need all the suggested work." In such cases you decide what seems to you to be most essential to your students. Many times their own evaluation of their needs helps in this decision. You use the time given you to the best advantage for your students.

Beginning the Fundamentals Course

During the first week you should take into consideration the six variables in any speaking activity: the participants, ideas, purpose, patterns for organization, social climate, and physical environment. You must get to know your participants, find out their backgrounds and motivate them to develop constructive group living and to speak effectively. You give your students an understanding that ideas are important and that they must be organized. You help to establish a friendly climate. You make sure that the physical environment is conducive to communication.

The unit you begin with is important since it should help you to know your students and to establish the right atmosphere. One teacher starts with creative dramatics, for she believes that she and her students get to know each other quickly in this speech situation. As they participate in this activity she is able to observe their personality traits and has opportunities to evaluate their speaking assets and liabilities. In addition this activity establishes good group feeling and an atmosphere of friendliness. For the same reasons, another teacher begins with conversation, using topics like ghosts, fortune-telling, or present-day comedians which stimulate talk. Still another teacher starts her course with interviews. As one student interviews another, he learns about the interviewee's early life, his hobbies, his scholarly interests, his ways of earning money, and his vocational plans. Whatever way you choose, it should set the climate for the rest of the course and help you and your students to become acquainted.

TEACHING OF AREAS OF FUNDAMENTALS COURSE

Many of the areas that you will cover in the fundamentals course are later treated more fully in specialized courses. High schools often offer advanced courses in voice and diction, public speaking, discussion, debate, oral interpretation, theater, and radio and television. The discussion and debate courses frequently include a unit in parliamentary procedure; the oral interpretation, one in storytelling. Therefore you must make sure that the same material and methods are not used in the fundamentals course and in the specialized courses. The fundamentals course provides the broad base from which specialized courses grow. Rose Kirchman in the syllabus which she and her staff prepared for their fundamentals course describes this broad base:[8]

Students will be expected to stand up with good posture and ease, face an audience, speak intelligently, think coherently, listen critically, evaluate their own performances and those of their classmates, and develop a high regard for the function and value of spoken language. All the students will be given the opportunity to learn better speech habits and skills through specific instruction and speaking experiences.

On the other hand, the aims of learning in the specialized courses are much more pointed.

[8] R. Kirchman, *Syllabus for Oral English,* required course in Jamaica High School, Jamaica, New York, 1960, p. 1.

One area, however, belongs uniquely to the fundamentals course, that of informal speaking. Informal speaking comprises all forms of conversation—introducing people, sharing personal experiences, interviewing, informal discussion, giving brief reports or directions, and telephoning. Since this area is unique to the fundamentals course, it will be included in this chapter. The other areas will be discussed in separate chapters; you will take from them those materials and methods which will be suitable for your particular fundamentals course.

Conversation

Students should be encouraged to make their topics of conversation more significant and their participation more effective. One teacher begins her unit by asking her students what problems they have faced in conversing. Typically these answers include:

Forgetting to introduce people.
Not being able to put people at ease.
Forgetting names.
Not being able to speak easily with adults.
Continuing a conversation after an introduction.
Being at a loss for words.
Giving the impression of being snobbish.
Answering with just "yes" or "no."
Finding out the interests of the other person.

After the students have analyzed these problems, they talk about the purposes of conversation. Generally they agree that they talk together to acquire information, to share ideas, to modify or change opinions, and to entertain. They list situations in which conversation occurs: telephoning, social gatherings, business interviews, interviewing for information, and television conversations.

After they have analyzed their own problems in conversation and determined when they converse and why, they agree on the topics that they will cover in their unit on conversation. They may include:

What makes for good conversation?
How do you start a conversation?
How do you change the subject?
What subjects do you avoid?
How do you find something to interest the other person?
How do you show consideration for the other person?

When do you keep still?
How do you encourage others to enter a conversation?
How do you handle conflict?
How do you differ tactfully?

The students first read and report on the theory of conversation found in high school textbooks on speech. This theory contains answers to some of their problems. With this reading as a basis, they then analyze conversation. They may use the five conversations found in *Speaking and Listening*.[9] Or they may use sections of a play. They discuss these questions: What is the speaker like? What is the worth of his ideas? How does he affect others? Finally they evaluate him as a conversationalist. This study is followed by practice in social conversation, in interviewing, and in telephoning.

The practice in social conversation frequently includes practice in making introductions, in informal discussions, in requesting and giving information, and in apologizing to and congratulating others. Chapter 1 of the high school text *Your Speech*[10] contains an excellent bibliography of teen-age etiquette books and a series of exercises where students play different roles in introductions. The high school text *Speech: A High School Course*[11] offers unusually good suggestions for topics for informal discussions ranging from whether to refuse an assignment to room 13 in a hotel to whether to leave a tip for a waitress. Chapter 5 of *Your Speech* gives a series of requests for information designed for criticism and many assignments on asking information and making announcements; Chapter 6 deals with apologizing and congratulating. These exercises stimulate the imagination of the high school student.

The practice in interviewing usually involves role playing with one student interviewing another for a job, for information about an exciting experience, for guidance in selecting a career, or for some other purpose. The high school text *Speak Up*[12] gives many alternatives for practice on interviews.

[9] A. T. Weaver, G. L. Borchers, and D. K. Smith, *Speaking and Listening* (Englewood Cliffs, N.J., Prentice-Hall, Inc., 1956), pp. 312-317.

[10] F. Griffith, C. Nelson, and E. Stasheff, *Your Speech* (New York, Harcourt, Brace & Co., 1955).

[11] L. Sarett, W. T. Foster, and J. H. McBurney, *Speech: A High School Course* (Boston, Houghton Mifflin Co., 1947), p. 255.

[12] H. M. Adams and T. C. Pollock, *Speak Up* (New York, The Macmillan Co., 1956), Ch. 5.

Almost all of the high school texts suggest a wide variety of assignments for telephoning. In addition, the telephone company in your area will probably be glad to supply you with a tele-trainer and with materials for teaching telephoning. A tele-trainer consists of two telephones and a unit which controls the ringing of the telephones and the giving of a busy signal. A telephoning lesson[13] follows:

At the opening of the class, its members summarized the theory of conversation. One student pointed out that people must understand one another in a face-to-face situation. Another indicated that the speaker must get his ideas across successfully and that the listeners must respond to these ideas. Still another noted that the conversationalist creates the impression of himself through his appearance, voice, articulation, pronunciation, gestures, and the content of his ideas.

They then went on to carry out the assignment, a series of telephoning situations, which had been given the previous day. Before they began their speaking activity, they talked about the special aspects of telephoning: the necessity for early identification, the revelation of personality through voice, the obligation to create the right kind of atmosphere, the organization of ideas for telephoning, and the desirable effects to be created by both persons involved. After this preliminary discussion, the following telephone conversation took place:

Mrs. C. Hello, This is Mrs. Carlson speaking.

Mrs. B. This is Mrs. Brunbridge. I would like to inform you that your dog Rover has been in my flower beds.

Mrs. C. But he was inside all day yesterday. How did you know it was my dog?

Mrs. B. Because I saw his dog tag.

Mrs. C. It might have been my sister's dog. What did he look like?

Mrs. B. A greyish mongrel—part police, part collie.

Mrs. C. That's my sister's dog. She lives down the street.

Mrs. B. I'm sorry. I'll call her.

An evaluation then took place. One student complimented the participants on their dialing, holding of the telephone and on identifying themselves. Another said, "Mrs. B. should have been more careful. Mrs. C. could have blown her top." Still another questioned Mrs. B.'s getting close enough to see the dog's tag. Still another

[13] Taught by Wiley Bowyer, Mineola High School, Mineola, New York.

said the conversation needed more smoothness. Another pointed out that Mrs. B.'s apology was inadequate. They then talked about how Mrs. B. could have approached Mrs. C. more tactfully.

Two other conversations followed: one an inquiry into printing programs for the school show and one to make plane reservations for three for a return trip to Bermuda. Both were evaluated carefully.

EVALUATION

All of the work in the fundamentals course, including listening, must be evaluated soundly. The principles of evaluation discussed elsewhere are applicable in the evaluation of a student's work in a fundamentals course. The purposes for which you will use evaluation in this course are (1) to diagnose, (2) to guide learning, and (3) to record achievement.

In a first speech course diagnosis is particularly important, for here you are dealing with the basic factors of communication. Both you and your students must be aware of their assets and liabilities. For example, you must evaluate such items as clarity of your students' voice and articulation, extent of vocabulary, success in finding topics to talk about, in developing them, and in presenting them, in discovering material that reads aloud or plays well, skill in reading aloud, in playing parts, and in participating in discussions and argumentative situations, and ability to listen in all of the speaking activities.

The second purpose, to guide learning, is equally important, for a student's ability to set his own goals and to evaluate his own progress toward them are important phases in the development of speaking ability. One student's query of her classmates, "Did my introduction interest you this time?" and another student's remark, "I am supporting my statements more soundly," reveal the importance of evaluation to their speaking progress. This attitude comes about through your guidance.

The last purpose, to give a grade, is probably the least important. You must be sure of what you are evaluating as well as how you evaluate. You take into consideration the aims of the course, students' abilities to achieve them, their natural abilities, and their degrees of improvement in relation to themselves and to other members of the class. You use short-answer questions to test fact and problem-solving questions to test concepts and their relationships. For example, the knowledge of the vocal mechanism responds well to multiple-choice or matching questions. Ability to outline a speech, however, where relationships and insight into the main idea and the subordinate points are important, is more readily tested in an essay question.

You make your decision on how to evaluate for the term. You may count the final examination for very little, because you may be grading largely on ability to participate effectively in speaking situations. Or you may wish to give considerable emphasis to the understanding of the theory in the course; in this case the written final weighs more heavily in your final grade. In this matter you must be guided by the philosophy and the practices of the school in which you teach.

SUGGESTED READING

BARNES, H. G., "The Fundamentals of Speech: Basic Concepts for the High School Teacher of Speech," *Quarterly Journal of Speech,* XXX (October, 1944), 340-43. Lists the aims of the high school fundamentals course.

——, "Teaching Fundamentals of Speech at the College Level," *The Speech Teacher,* III (November, 1954), 239-251. (Although this article deals with a college course in fundamentals, much of its content applies to high school teaching of fundamentals.) Answers some of the frequent questions concerning a fundamentals course

FRIEDERICH, W. J., and WILCOX, R. A., *Teaching Speech in High School* (New York, The Macmillan Co., 1953), pp. 62-96. Tells how to gain poise, develop free bodily action, improve one's voice and diction, comprehend language and meaning, acquire a speech style, and listen creatively.

McNESS, W., "An Orientation Course in Creative Skills for First Year Junior High School Students," *The Speech Teacher,* I (November, 1952), 279-287. Includes units on meaning through language, meaning through bodily action, and meaning through voice.

MERCER, J., "Listening in the Speech Class," *The Bulletin of the National Association of Secondary School Principals,* XXXII (January, 1948), 102-107. Outlines the listening activities of a fundamentals course.

MERSAND, J., "Developing Competence in Listening in Secondary Schools," *The Speech Teacher,* VII (November, 1958), 289-301. Reviews literature on listening.

NICHOLS, R. G., "Listening Instruction in the Secondary School," *The Bulletin of the National Association of Secondary School Principals,* XXXVI (May, 1952), 158-174. Tells how to teach discriminative listening to informative speeches.

NILES, D., "Teaching Listening in the Fundamentals Course," *The Speech Teacher,* VI (November, 1957), 300-304. Discusses methods of helping high school students to listen.

PARSTECK, B. J., "Speech at the Core of the Core Curriculum," *The Speech Teacher,* II (November, 1953), 282-286. Compares the objectives of the core curriculum with the objectives of speech education. Shows how various speech activities fit into the pattern of the core.

PHELPS, W. W., "The Panel-Forum as a First Assignment in the Secondary School Speech Fundamentals Class," *The Speech Teacher,* I (September, 1952), 162-166. Describes in detail an assignment which allows students with differing speech abilities to experience a feeling of success while, at the same time, challenging all the students in the class to do their best work.

REID, L., *Teaching Speech* (Columbia, Mo., Artcraft Press, 1956), 43-73. Makes clear how to begin the first course, the units to teach, and how to teach them.

RENWICKE, R., Jr., "A Listening Course for High School Seniors," *The Speech Teacher,* VI (January, 1957), 59-62. Explains how students may acquire skill in listening comprehension and how they may learn to listen critically.

RIDGWAY, J. M., "The Teaching of Speech in High School Through Examples," *Quarterly Journal of Speech,* XXVII (February, 1941), 74-78. Describes a plan of teaching public speaking in high school through the use of published speeches.

ROBINSON, K. F., "Getting Started in the High School Fundamentals Course," *Quarterly Journal of Speech,* XXX (October, 1944), 343-346. Tells how to get acquainted with students and how to begin the fundamentals course wisely.

———, "Teaching Listening Through Evaluation and Criticism," *The Speech Teacher,* II (September, 1953), 178-180. Suggests how to teach listening for recognizing and discrimination, for information, for pleasure, for making intellectual judgments or evaluating ideas, and for appreciation.

———, *Teaching Speech in the Secondary School* (New York, Longmans, Green & Co., Inc., 1954), pp. 75-231. Includes discussion of basic principles in getting started, evaluation, poise, teaching communicativeness, bodily action, voice and articulation, language, speech preparation, listening, and choosing a fundamentals textbook.

SEABURY, H., "Objectives and Scope of the Fundamentals Course in Speech in High School," *The Speech Teacher*, III (March, 1954), 117-120. Gives good advice on preparing the fundamentals course.

Speech in the Secondary School Interest Group of the Speech Association of America, "Fundamentals of Speech: A Basic Course for High Schools," *The Speech Teacher*, VIII (March, 1959), 94-113. Outlines a course of study for a high school fundamentals course. Contains many excellent suggestions.

WEAVER, A. T., BORCHERS, G. L., and SMITH, D. K., *The Teaching of Speech*, (New York, Prentice-Hall, Inc., 1952), Chs. 1, 2, 3, 4, and 12. Tells how to develop effective action, voice, language and meanings. Ch. 12 has to do with conversation.

WOLFE, D. M., "Students' Problems," *English Journal*, XLIV (April, 1955), 218-225. Lists problems of high school students: school, social, family, boy-girl, money, recreation, appearance, moral and ethical.

AUDIO-VISUAL AIDS

Anthony and Cleopatra (Parthian Productions, Young America Films, black and white, 33 minutes). Adapted for senior high school students.

Cyrano de Bergerac, read by Walter Hampden (The National Broadcasting Company, available from the National Tape Repository, 30 minutes, *tape*).

How to Read Poetry, Ruth Strang, collaborator (Coronet, black and white, color, 11 minutes). Advises students to learn something about the poet, to discover what the poet saw or felt or what experiences he wishes to share, and to look for poetic devices. Examples taken from poets such as Lindsay, Poe, Shelley, and Thoreau.

Macbeth, acted by Maurice Evans, Judith Anderson, and others (The National Broadcasting Company. Available from the National Tape Repository, 60 minutes, *tape*).

Speech-Conversation (Young America Films, black and white, 10 minutes). Gives examples of good and bad conversation. Shows bits of conversation interspersed by the commentator's observations.

Telephone Courtesy (American Telephone and Telegraph, black and white, 25 minutes, *free loan*). Shows the use of the telephone in a business organization. Suggests how to dial properly, call the right number, identify yourself, use a pleasant conversational approach, transfer calls properly, have vital information at hand, indicate your whereabouts to the switchboard operator, answer properly, and end a call courteously.

Telephone Technique (International Film Bureau, black and white, color, 9 minutes). Tells the story of a family attempting to purchase a gift for Mother by telephone. Give examples of good and bad techniques in retail telephone sales. Stresses the importance of good telephone manners and the need to know your job of selling by telephone.

Why Study Speech (Young America Films, black and white, 12 minutes). Emphasizes competency in speech in school and in later life.

You and Your Voice (Bell Telephone Company, black and white, 20 minutes, *free loan*). Deals with telephone voices in terms of operators and their training. Shows how feelings are conveyed through a telephone voice.

Your Voice (Encyclopedia Britannica Films, black and white, 10 minutes). Covers respiration, phonation, resonation, and articulation. Presents motion picture photography of the vocal folds in operation.

EXERCISES

1. Find ten biographies which would appeal to high school students and which could be used in some way in a high school fundamentals course. Indicate how each biography could be used.
2. Select one television program which could be used in teaching appreciative listening and one which could be used in teaching critical listening. Explain how you would use each program.
3. Make clear how your own training may affect your teaching of a fundamentals course.
4. Explain how the needs and the abilities of the following groups would affect the teaching of the fundamentals course:
   a. The fundamentals of Speech course is replacing the fifth term of English. All of the 25 students in your class expect to go to college where they are to prepare for a variety of professions. All except four are girls and all of them have unusually good scholastic records. Four of them are timid and quiet whereas eight of them are unusually verbal and fluent. About half of them are likely to substitute their ability to verbalize for hard work. Half of them have had wide theater-going experiences. Three of them have traveled abroad. All of them have read widely.
   b. The students, half of them male, and half of them female, are all of low intelligence. None will go on to college. The class includes six students whom the administration calls "delinquents" and who often stay away from school. Four of the students are repeating the course.

Some of the students are noisy and sometimes rude; others are quiet and apathetic. From the inventory you learn little except that all of the boys and most of the girls are enthusiastic baseball fans and that all of them spend considerable time watching television. You know that they do almost no reading except the required school reading.

5. Plan a developmental lesson on telephoning.

4

Articulation

and Voice

MOST HIGH SCHOOL students prefer to believe their articulation meets their needs adequately and that their voices are pleasant. Generally they welcome criticism of neither. Teachers of speech collect evidence of this attitude quickly. One director of high school dramatics tells the following story: A play casting committee, made up of students and faculty, passed by a young Thespian because it found her voice thin, rasping, metallic, and entirely unsuitable for the part she wanted. When the aspiring actress came to the director to find out why the committee had not chosen her, he told her quite frankly that her voice was inadequate for the stage. Whereupon she assured him that several members of the committee liked her voice. When he questioned them, they said that they were loathe to tell her why she wasn't chosen and had thought that since he was a teacher of speech, he could tell her more tactfully.

A second incident concerns the substandard diction of a high school valedictorian. The speech teacher tried various means of motivating him to sound "educated." Very honestly the valedictorian said that he was satisfied with his speech as it was and, furthermore, if he changed his articulation, his friends in his neighborhood would accuse him of being "high-hat."

Such anecdotes point to the necessity of making apparent to your students the values of pleasant voice and clear articulation. Our society as a whole considers them important. And since the desire for social approval is a powerful motivation for high school students you may help them to change their speech patterns by showing them the social need for pleasant voice and clear articulation. Many high school teachers start their work in this area with a study of standards.

CONTENT

The content of a course or a section of a course in voice and articulation may include:

Standards of Speech
   Levels of Standards of Speech
   Regional Differences
   Changing Nature of Language
   Definition of Acceptable Speech

Pronunciation and the Dictionary
   Types of Dictionaries
   Purposes of Dictionaries
   Using a Dictionary

Sounds of Speech
   Articulatory Mechanism
   Kinds of Sounds
      Vowels
      Consonants
      Dipthongs
   Assimilation
   Weak and Strong Forms

Types of Articulatory Errors
Incorrect Production of a Sound
   Substitution of One Sound for Another
   Omission of a Sound
   Addition of a Sound
   Transposition of a Sound

Improving Articulation

Voice
   The Vocal Mechanism
   Importance of Critical Listening

Characteristics of Voice
    Quality
    Pitch
    Volume
    Rate

Improving Voice

AIMS

From the study of voice and articulation the teacher hopes that his students will achieve the following aims:

Understandings
    To recognize levels of standards of speech
    To be aware of regional differences
    To understand the place of dictionaries in pronunciation
    To know the parts of the articulatory mechanism
    To define kinds of speech sounds
    To comprehend assimilation
    To identify types of speech errors
    To perceive how voice is produced
    To discern the characteristics of voice

Attitudes
    Appreciation of the ever-changing quality of our language
    Acceptance of a descriptive rather than a prescriptive approach to pronunciation
    Appreciation of the voice and articulation of cultured persons

Skills
    Ability to use the pronunciations of the educated people of the community
    Ability to use a pleasant voice

STANDARDS OF SPEECH

Your students must understand several concepts of standards of speech: (1) levels of standards of speech, (2) regional differences in pronunciation, and (3) the changing nature of language.

Levels of Standards

One young woman teaches the levels of standards of pronunciation (formal and informal and substandard) by role-playing. For instance, to represent formal speech one of the girls who speaks well assumes that having been crowned Miss America, she is to accept the honor. Or a boy pretends that having been elected the chairman of a state legislature, he is to call the meeting to order and announce its purpose. To illustrate informal speech, three members of her group make believe that they are a committee who are meeting to determine a school policy. One time the group discussed what to do about the small attendance at athletic contests; another time, the degree of emphasis on the school's oratorical contest; and at still another time, the policy of admitting no one but students of the school to the school dances. Finally, to typify substandard speech, two members of the class pretend that they are working in a forest with an illiterate lumberjack. To be accepted by the workman, they must talk as he talks.

After the three demonstrations, the students list the characteristics of the three levels of standards of speech: formal, informal, and substandard. Usually they indicate that formal speech belongs to a formal occasion and is used infrequently. Typically they say persons using formal speech speak more slowly and utter their vowel sounds more distinctly. On the other hand, they agree that informal speech is the level used most frequently and that it occurs in the conversation of educated persons in everyday living. Lastly, they note that substandard speech, a real and useful part of our language, is typical of the speech of persons with little education.

In teaching levels of speech, another high school teacher uses the analogy of the suitability of different types of shoes. She brings to class pictures of high-heeled evening shoes, of everyday casual shoes, and of sloppy camping shoes. As she shows the pictures, she asks about the occasions when such shoes are appropriate. She then discusses with her group comparable speaking occasions, showing that people of good sense adapt their levels of speech to particular situations.

Still another teacher uses words and their synonyms to demonstrate the three levels. First she explains the three levels, indicating that they are not completely discrete and that they frequently overlap. Then using a word like *drunk, tired,* or *poor,* she asks students to note which synonyms they would use in formal speech, which in informal, and which in substandard. Finally, she suggests that they use the synonyms in sentences illustrating the three levels. These utterances serve as a basis for an understanding of the characteristics of the three levels.

In such discussions some of the conflicts in students' minds about acceptable speech become apparent. As members of a tenth grade fundamentals class talked about the speech of Franklin Delano Roosevelt and Dwight Eisenhower as represented in two recordings, their teacher noted the following comments:

"I like the way Roosevelt sounds. But I wouldn't want to sound like him. Imagine my saying [aɪðɚ] (ī'thẽr)."[1]

"Me either. I think he sounds like an egghead."

"I like Eisenhower's speech better. He doesn't wear his education on his shirt sleeve."

"Eisenhower probably sounds better than he once did. But I'm sure that when he was at West Point and when he went back home, he sounded like the rest of the guys."

These comments suggest two conflicts in the minds of the students: (1) They want more education but at the same time disparage intellectual achievement. (2) They desire to rise from one social level to another but to retain their friends from the lower social level. Class discussions uncover these conflicts which influence the students' acceptance of their need for changes in their speech.

Regional Differences in Speaking

The amount of information concerning regional speech that high school teachers of speech expect their students to understand varies. Since the dialectal differences in American English are relatively few, some teachers do not believe that their students must even recognize that regional differences exist. Most teachers of speech, however, at least allude to these differences. A few give considerable emphasis to regional variations in speech, even relating it to their students' work in social studies—showing the economic, social or cultural forces of which these speech differences are the result.

In one instance, an unusually brilliant twelfth-year speech class spent an entire term studying regional differences. Since this class was made up of sons and daughters of scientists from many parts of our country, differences in pronunciation were evident. As a result

[1] Pronunciations will be transcribed in phonetics in brackets and in diacritical markings in parenthesis.

of the interest engendered, the teacher of the course taught his students to use the International Phonetic Alphabet so that the students could transcribe the speech of the members of the class. The students then worked out a scheme for exchanging recordings with high school students in nine different areas of the country. They then analyzed the pronunciation of these students. Next they studied some of the factors underlying dialectal distribution in the United States and the historical development of some of the sounds. Through these activities they came to understand that some factors work for uniformity in our language and others for variety. Such study could only occur in a very exceptional class.

Furthermore, many teachers of speech find it necessary to dispel false notions. For example, students are likely to explain differences in Southern speech with the notion that the heat causes Southerners to be slow-moving and, consequently, to drawl. They are surprised to learn that in Bengali, which has a far hotter temperature, the speech is rapid and clipped. Southern students, on the other hand, remark on the nasality of Northerners, due, they are sure, to the cold climate. They, too, are astonished to learn that nasality is not characteristic of all Northern speech.

Almost all teachers of speech point out that people in the United States speak many patterns of speech, each with its own peculiarities, and that no individual ever speaks exactly as the other people in his region do.

Teachers use this study of regional differences and of levels of usage to develop the attitude that in every locality there are those whose speech is regarded by members of the community and by outsiders as being the best speech of that locality. They point out that this speech does not draw attention to itself and does not detract from the expression of ideas.

The Changing Nature of Language

Most teachers of speech help their students to realize that the speech of one generation is never exactly the same as that of the preceding generation, for the forms and meanings of words, pronunciations, and grammatical structures change.

Some teachers provide a systematic study of the changes. One teacher traces the change in meaning of the word *pretty* from sly, to clever, to good-looking. She explains how meanings of other words have been broadened, raised, or lowered. By references to Chaucer and Pope she indicates how spelling and grammar have altered. Speech teachers, however, usually give most emphasis to changes in levels of standards of pronunciation.

During the discussion of historical changes you may well point to changes in levels. For example many of the forms, words, and pronunciations of substandard speech are much older than their more formal counterparts. Chaucer on occasion used a double negative. In the eighteenth century "you was" was acceptable. *Comin'* for *coming* is a remnant of an original participial ending. *Hussy* is a contraction of *housewife* and used to be applied to respectable women. Old English *stincan* from which *stink* is derived meant to give forth a good or a bad odor; sometimes it meant to smell sweet. *Clumb* for *climbed, catched* for *caught, deef* for *deaf* are all relics of earlier pronunciations.

Slang

High school students like the novelty of slang. As they tend to pepper their writing with exclamation points, they pepper their speaking with slang. They believe that it adds vividness. In addition, they like the idea of revolting against adult standards of speaking. Therefore, your study of standards of speech may well reveal that slang has been current in all ages. Shakespeare's comedies are a rich source of such Elizabethan slang as "knotty-pated fool" and "eel-skin."

Sometimes students want to know about the linguistic origin of slang. You may well explain that it results at times from modifying the form of a word as *enthuse* for *express enthusiasm, prom* for *promenade, home ec* for *home economics,* and *TV* for *television.* You show that it also derives from the unconventional metaphor such as *dimwit* or *good egg* or from shop talk such as *in the limelight, a ham actor,* or *a flop*—all from the theater. You point out that such phrases have added color and variety to our language. You may well instill the attitude that educated speakers do not scorn slang altogether but that they use it with discretion. Conversely, you must make sure that your students realize that when slang is used too frequently, it is meaningless.

TEACHING PRONUNCIATION

Your students tend to consider their dictionary the Supreme Court of pronunciation. You must, therefore, help them to use it judiciously. They should know that the pronunciations given in a dictionary are generalizations of the way many educated people say a word and that no current dictionary claims to be the "absolute authority." One dictionary's stated aim is "to record as far as possible the pronunciations prevailing in the best present usage rather than to attempt to dictate what usage should be."[2]

You yourself should study the introduction to the dictionary which your students use so that you can help them understand its levels and procedures. You should learn whether the dictionary adapts for representation the style of formal platform speech or of informal speaking, whether its first listed pronunciation is the one held to be more prevalent or not, and whether it uses diacritical markings, phonetic symbols, or a combination. This information influences your teaching of the use of the dictionary. For example, when formal speech is the standard employed by a dictionary, students who follow the pronunciations in this dictionary slavishly will sound pedantic. In conversational speech the sounds are different from what such a dictionary indicates. Your students must be aware of the procedures of the dictionary which they are using.

Although dictionaries are imperfect guides to pronunciation because it is difficult to record all the acceptable pronunciations in a country as large as ours, the dictionary does give your students help in determining syllabification, accent, and pronunciation of sounds of vowels, diphthongs, and consonants. For instance, the student who says *ath-e-let-ic* is aware of his mispronunciation as he examines the syllabification in the dictionary. He recognizes that *impious* must be [ɪmpiəs] (ĭm′ pĭ.ŭs) when he sees the accent mark on *im*. Lastly he knows that his pronunciation of caffein [kæfin] (kăf′ēn) is acceptable when he finds the *ei* represented by a long *e*.

Your students, however, will probably learn more about pronunciation from listening than they will from a study of their dictionaries. You encourage them to listen carefully to educated

[2] *Webster's New Collegiate Dictionary* (Springfield, Mass., G. and C. Merriam Company, 1956), p. ix.

speech. As a result of their listening, you will frequently be called on to be the arbiter in disputes concerning pronunciation. You must justify the stands you take by a thorough knowledge of American English. The more information you have concerning the structure of our language the better able you are to present and to discuss information on pronunciation.

You must, in addition, be careful to be objective about the pronunciation of your students. Supervisors of speech teachers have reported the following instances of teachers' prescriptive attitudes: the acceptance of ['drɪrɪ] ('drēr'ĭ) and not ['drɪrɪ] (drĭr'ĭ), of [kætʃ] (kăch) and not [kɛtʃ] (kĕch), and insistence on the inclusion of *t* in *nests* and of the first *r* in *surprise*. When a supervisor questioned the teacher about [sə'praɪz] (sŭ·prīz'), the teacher quickly explained that the loss of the *r* was due to dissimilation. Although she had some knowledge of phonetics, her conclusion was questionable.

Your attitude should be one of "let's listen to what educated persons say." When students listen critically to pronunciations around them, they tend to make judicious use of the dictionary. One young speech teacher teaching parliamentary procedure used the pronunciation [pri'sidns] (prē·sēd'ĕns). Whereupon a student asked whether a variant pronunciation ['prɛsədəns] (prĕs'·ĕ·dĕns) was acceptable. The teacher quickly replied "no" and explained the difference in *precedent* as a noun and as an adjective. To her amazement, one of her students arrived next day with a dictionary listing both [pri'sidns] (prē·sēd'ĕns) and ['prɛsədəns] (prĕs'ĕ·dĕns). She took the opportunity to explain to the members of her class that her attitude toward the pronunciation of this word was one that was far too prevalent, The next year in teaching parliamentary procedure she purposely used both pronunciations. When one student asked which was acceptable, she explained that the word has equally acceptable variant pronunciations.

SOUNDS OF SPEECH

Your students, who are to improve their speech, must understand the structure of the sounds of the vowels, the diphthongs, and the consonants of American English. First, they must think in terms of sounds and not in terms of letters. One teacher furthers this skill by asking her students to give the spellings of a sound such as [ɪ] (ĭ); the boys and girls list words like *city, women, guild,* and *myth.* Second, the students should know how each sound in American English is made and the possible influence of one sound upon another.

Teachers use both the International Phonetic Alphabet and diacritical markings as a tool to teach the sounds. Some teachers prefer the International Phonetic Alphabet, for they believe that it makes the study of articulation and pronunciation more meaningful and orderly and that it emphasizes listening for sounds. They discover that teaching the International Phonetic Alphabet is not too difficult. Other teachers prefer to use diacritical markings as their tool. They justify this choice because of the widespread practice of employing diacritical markings in dictionaries and in classes of English.

Vowels and Consonants

Almost all teachers of speech teach the vowels as front, middle, or back and as high, mid, or low. They explain to their students that in the front vowels the highest part of the tongue is forward in the mouth and that in high vowels the tongue is held high. Most teachers add the concept of tenseness and laxness and of rounding and unrounding the vowels. Much of this teaching is accomplished by the students' making the vowel sounds and analyzing how they make them. After students have learned about the sounds of individual vowels, they go on to learn about the diphthongs.

Many teachers claim that the most difficult vowel sound to make clear is the *schwa* [ə]. The first difficulty is the use of many different diacritical markings for the same sound. When students discover that the same sound is represented by eight different symbols, in words like *about, circus, sofa, condition, slacken, button,* and *martyr,* they are confused. To simplify this problem some dictionaries use the schwa. A second difficulty is that the schwa is often interchangeable with [ɪ] (ĭ) as in *heeded, creases, beneath, develop, prevent,* and *horrid.* A third difficulty is caused by the tendency of students to stress words which they are analyzing phonetically. As they say a word slowly, they may change the [ə] to [ʌ] (ŭ) as in the last syllable in *circus* or the [ə] to [ɛ] (ĕ) as in the last syllable in *development.* That students learn to hear the schwa is particularly important, since it often provides the differences in emphasis, essential in effective communication.

Teachers usually place the consonants in categories of plosives, fricatives, glides, and nasals. Each sound is then examined to determine whether it possesses voice and/or nasal resonance and to find out what articulatory agent is working on what other articulatory agent. One teacher begins the study by a determination of differences among the sounds *p, b,* and *m;* this investigation serves as a basis for showing the four factors involved in any consonantal sound: (1) manner of articulation, (2) articulatory agents involved, (3) presence or absence of voice, and (4) presence or absence of nasal resonance.

A knowledge of how sounds are made helps high school students to understand assimilation and the use of strong and weak forms in our language.

Assimilation

Students should learn that we tend to modify pronunciation in the direction of simplicity and economy of effort. For example, the past tense of *tipped* and *begged* have two different final sounds. When students know that *p* is voiceless and *g* is voiced, they can deduce the reason for the use of the final unvoiced *t* and the final voiced *d*. Finding the reasons for changes in pronunciations of other words like *nature, handkerchief,* and *captain* can be a challenge to high school students. They should know that some of these accidental mispronunciations within words or phrases become acceptable and some remain unacceptable. Listening for assimilations in educated speech is one way of finding out which assimilations are acceptable.

Strong and Weak Forms

Partly as a result of poor teaching of oral reading in their early education many of your students will read *the* as [ði] (thē) and *a* as [e] (ā). These students need to be aware that in ordinary conversation and in reading almost all material we use the weak forms of pronouns, prepositions, articles, auxiliaries, and conjunctions.

FAULTS OF ARTICULATION

Usually the faults of articulation fall into one of five categories: (1) the incorrect production of sounds, (2) the substitution of one sound for another, (3) the omission of sounds, (4) the addition of sounds, and (5) the inversion of sounds.

Incorrect Production of Sounds

Some of your students will approximate a given sound but distort it. For example, they may dentalize their *t*'s and *d*'s making them with the tips of their tongues on their teeth instead of on their gum ridges. Or they may raise the height of their tongues on the [æ] (ă) sound in *man* so that it sounds somewhat like [mɛən] (mĕăn). Many Americans, however, do dentalize their *t*'s and *d*'s and do raise the sound of [æ] (ă).

When a large majority of the members of the community dentalize *t* and *d* and raise [æ], you will have difficulty deciding whether or not to accept these sounds as they are generally uttered. Your decision may well be based on such factors as the total effect of these faults on the communicative processes of your students and their needs in terms of their futures. For example, in a small community where most of the students remain all of their lives, the elimination of their localisms may be a deterrent to their success as businessmen and as citizens. On the other hand, some of these people, because of their industry, intelligence, or higher education, will leave their community and represent it in places where their speech will attract attention to itself. You will do well to remember that educated speech of any area does not detract from the communicative process.

The correction of unacceptable dentalization and raising of the [æ] (ă) sound takes place in the high school speech classroom. But the correctionist and not the teacher of speech works with children whose distortions of sounds are definitely speech difficulties. For example, the girl whose distorted *s* is due to an open bite may have to make compensatory movements in order to achieve an acceptable *s*. The speech teacher in a fundamentals class surely does not have the time for this kind of teaching; sometimes she does not have the training for it. This difficulty needs specialized help given individually or in small groups.

Substitution of Sounds

Again the speech therapist works with those substitutions of sounds which are definitely speech difficulties, whereas the classroom teacher of speech works with those substitutions which are more easily corrected. Such substitutions corrected by the teacher are [trə'di ʃən] (trà·dēsh'ŭn) for [trə'dɪʃən] (trà·dĭsh'ŭn), [wʌnt] (wŭnt) for [wont] (wōnt) [lɛnθ] (lĕnth) for [lɛŋθ] (lĕngth), and [hos] (hōs) for [hoɔs] (hoăs) and voicing and unvoicing errors or the substitution of a voiced sound for an unvoiced sound or of an unvoiced sound for a voiced sound. You must remember that in some instances the substitutions are acceptable. For example both the *American College Dictionary* and the *Pronouncing Dictionary of American English* list absorb with an *s* and a *z*.

Omission of Sounds

When your students consistently omit a sound like *r*, they usually need the concentrated help of a speech therapist. But you help your students to correct such unacceptable omissions as ['lɛm: əgo] (lĕm ĭ gō) for ['lɛt mi go] (lĕt mĭ gō), [ol] (ōl) for [old] (ōld), and ['rɛkənaɪz] (rĕk'ŏ·nīz) for ['rɛkəgnaɪz] (rĕk'ŏg·nĭz). You do well, however, to investigate before you insist on the inclusion of a sound. One teacher was chagrined to find that Kenyon and Knott note that the first *n* in *government* is omitted by leading statesmen in both America and England even in formal address.[3]

Addition of Sounds

Once again you must make sure that you are not too demanding. Some dictionaries now record such pronunciations as *almond* with an *l*, *often* with a *t*, and *forehead* with an *h*. Many additions, of course, exist which are not acceptable. Obviously you will not approve such pronunciations as [wɪʃt] (wĭsht) for [wɪʃ] (wĭsh), [ɛfn̩] (ĕfn) for [ɪf] (ĭf), ['sɪŋgɪŋ] (sĭngg·ĭng) for ['sɪŋɪŋ] (sĭng·ĭng), and ['æθəlit] (ă th'ă·lēt) for ['æθlit] (ăth'lēt).

Transposing Sounds

Boys and girls frequently transpose sounds. Here, too, dictionaries record that educated persons use some of these transpositions. *A Pronouncing Dictionary of American English* lists ['tʃɪldrən] (chĭl'drĕn) and ['tʃɪldɚn] (chĭl'dûrn) and ['hʌndrəd] (hŭn'drĕd) and ['hʌndɚd] (hŭn'dŭrd). Cultured persons, however, do not use some transposi-

---

[3] J. S. Kenyon and T. A. Knott, *A Pronouncing Dictionary of American English* (Springfield, Mass., G. and C. Merriam Company, 1944), p. 188.

tions. Examples of these undesirable transpositions are [plə'bɪsɪtɪ] (plŭ·bĭs'ĭ·tĭ), [madrɪn] (mŏ'drĭn), and ['rɛvələnt] (rĕv'ĕ·lănt).

Unacceptable speech can include any one or all of these faults. For example the pronunciation of the word *little* may involve four of them: the incorrect production of a sound, the substitution of one sound for another, the omission of a sound, or the addition of a sound. The *t* and *l* may be both dental with their incorrect production clearly denoting a foreign speaker. *W* may be substituted for *l;* a weakly articulated *d* or a glottal stop may be substituted for *t.* The *t* may be omitted altogether. The schwa [ə] may be inserted between *t* and *l* resulting in [litəl] (lĭt'ĭl), a form of overcareful speech that draws attention to itself. In most instances you encourage your students to make the *t* and *d* with the tip of the tongue on the teeth ridge, to avoid the glottal, and to make the final *l* syllabic; your guide is the pronunciation of the educated people in the community in which you teach.

CORRECTING FAULTS OF ARTICULATION

The correction of these faults of articulation involves four steps for your students:

1. Understanding the diagnosis.
2. Learning to make the sound acceptably.
3. Practicing making the sounds acceptably in words.
4. Carrying the acceptable sounds over into conversation.

Understanding the Diagnosis

To understand the diagnosis, the student must hear his articulatory errors. But most high school students do not listen to sounds carefully. For these students training to listen is necessary. For example, on a rainy day one teacher talked with her students briefly about the sound that the rain was making—a gentle pitter-patter. The teacher then asked the boys and girls to listen for three days to the sounds of the weather and to describe them as accurately as they could. At the end of the three days they found that the rain had pitter-pattered, plunked, and swished, that the wind had roared, whizzed, and sizzled along, and that the hail had played a staccato rhythm on the window pane.

Following this listening activity they talked about other sounds: those that represented the four seasons, those used in radio production, those on the street early Sunday morning, and those in the very center of town on a busy Saturday. Still other activities stressed hearing sounds. The students pointed out that they enjoyed the sounds of many of their classmates names: Robert Amodeo, Carmellita DeLucia, and Theresa Marie O'Reilly. In addition, they analyzed how the repetition of particular sounds in poems helps communicate their feeling. For this purpose they used Wallace Stevens', "Ploughing on Sunday," e e cummings', "in just spring," William Wordsworth's "Written in March," T. S. Eliot's "New Hampshire," and Walter James Turner's "Romance."

This general training in listening prepares your students to hear their own and others' errors. You must, however, help each student to hear specific faults. Many teachers believe that a study of the International Phonetic Alphabet helps to accomplish this purpose. They find that in phonetic analysis children stop thinking in terms of visible symbols and listen for the various sounds. Although this analysis of individual errors may or may not be based on the phonetic alphabet, it usually takes five or six lessons and accomplishes two purposes: (1) it helps students to listen to sounds of speech, and (2) it makes each student aware of his own errors.

To prepare students to hear their own errors, one teacher lists on the blackboard the probable faults of the group. She then demonstrates by saying words with the faults and without them. In addition, she explains each fault, giving the reasons for its existence.

After she has made clear the probable unacceptable articulatory patterns, she asks each student to read certain material. Her prerequisites for the material are two: (1) that its content and style stimulate the adolescent reader to do his best to communicate and (2) that it contain in various positions and in different blends those sounds which are frequently made inaccurately by the members of this group. This material she has collected all year, clipping it from such sources as *Harpers, The Atlantic Monthly, The Saturday Evening Post,* the school newspaper, and the daily newspaper.

After each performance, the students and the teacher diagnose the reader's articulatory errors. When the material is recorded on tape, the articulatory faults can be analyzed more carefully, since the reading can be repeated exactly as it was spoken. By listening for the errors, students learn to hear them in each others' and their own speech. The teacher in the meantime has noted them on her own checklist. Such a checklist follows:

ARTICULATORY DIAGNOSIS

NAME.............................. CLASS..........................

Type of Error	Vowels	Diphthongs	Consonants
SUBSTITUTION	[gɪt] (get) [kɛəndɪ] (candy) [ros] (rose)	[tɒɪm] (time) [hɒɪ] (high) [tɒɪd] (tide) [dævn] (down)	[kʌmɪn] (coming) [sɪdɪ] (city) [bəkɔs] (because)
DISTORTION			*t, d* dentalized *s,* over-aspirate
OMISSION			[lɒɪbɛrɪən] (librarian) [prɑblɪ] (probably)
INVERSION			[mɑdrən] (modern)
ADDITION	[fɪləm] (film)		

Learning to Make Sounds Accurately

No one of the four steps of correcting a sound is entirely discrete. During the diagnostic period, many of your students, who are adept at imitating, will make the sounds accurately. Conversely, although you have tried to make sure that each student hears the unacceptable sound, some few will continue to have difficulty recognizing the differences between the acceptable and unacceptable articulation. You, therefore, may need to repeat the ear training when students are learning to make the sounds accurately.

In teaching how to make a sound, you may work with the entire class or with groups. Often you will find working with the entire class more profitable even though only half of its members make the particular error upon which you are concentrating, for the ability of the other half to listen will be sharpened. At other times you may have one group practicing on one sound; another, on a second sound; and still another, on a third sound. The chairmen, selected because of their ability to hear the sounds, to make them accurately, and to help others correct their sounds, conduct the practice of their groups while you are guiding one of the other groups.

Your approach is a multiple one. You teach your students to make the acceptable sounds through imitation of a correct sound, through telling them where to place their articulatory agents, and through having them watch how these agents work. You make sure that each individual can make the sound accurately. To be sure, you may ask the members of the class who make the sounds well to direct the others, or you may ask the students to work in pairs with one correcting the other, or you may have them record their efforts. After they can make the sound by itself, they are then ready to incorporate it in words.

Practice in Making Sounds in Words

You should provide practice periods for including difficult sounds in words. Drill must always be made as interesting and stimulating as possible. Some teachers use games like baseball, football, card games or parlor games, such as the one involving sentences like "I am thinking of a word that begins with *r;* it may lead nowhere." Students will reply with words like *road* or *route.* Still other teachers give to their students frankly loaded reading material. Or they ask their students to make up loaded material. Students can be quite ingenious at this composition as the following paragraph stressing the blend *sn* shows:

Have you heard of our sneezing Sam Snerd? Mr. Snerd is a snooty, snarling snob! He snaps at the postman; he snaps at the milkman; and he snaps at his wife Sally. Poor long suffering Sally! Sally puts up with his snapping, with his sulking, and above all with his snoring. For how he can snore! Even when he snoozes, he sort of snorts. And when he really sleeps, he roars. Today, however, his surly, testy, peevish brother Saul arrives. Saul too snarls and growls. Sally loves the visitor Saul, for the two brothers somehow vent their rages on each other. As each snaps at the other with more venom, each surveys the world more kindly. And as each sneers at the snores of the other, even the snoring diminishes. Long may newly arrived brother Saul Snerd remain with Sam and Sally!

Students enjoy making up such paragraphs at home, and they also like to write loaded sentences in class and then read them aloud. The one who writes the longest sentence with the largest number of the desired sounds is proud of his accomplishment.

Carry-over into Conversation

After making the sound in isolation and incorporating it into words, the student must learn to use the acceptable sound consistently. The speech teacher must give the student opportunities to use the newly acquired sound in such activities as conversation, oral reading, and dramatization. By providing the topic of conversation, the subject of the telephone call, or the story to be dramatized, you can make sure that your students gain practice in particular sounds. For example, one group is working on the *s* sound. You, therefore, ask that a student call the manager of the adjustment department of Seeley's store to tell him that the Salisbury mattress, which was purchased on sale last week, has two large stains on it. The resulting conversation gives practice on the *s* sound in a variety of positions. In a similar activity you give your students a topic that will provide practice in two sounds in conversation. In such cases you suit the topic to the students. In one class two students who had difficulty with their *s*'s and *t*'s were enthusiastic Latin scholars. A conversation group was made up of them and two others talking about the thesis: Latin, including a study of Caesar and Cicero, should be required of all high school students.

VOICE

The voice of your students depends on a variety of factors: (1) physical characteristics, (2) psychological elements, and (3) the mores of the group. Voice is contingent upon the physical characteristics, on the structure of the vocal cords, on the size, shape, and texture of the resonators, on the muscular co-ordination, and on the central powers of discriminating pitch, loudness, and quality. Secondly, it depends on psychological factors that are closely related to personality. Jane may be dull of mind and personality with a resulting monotonous voice. Jack may be overly aggressive with a too loud voice. Jim may be disgruntled with a whining voice. Thirdly, voice reflects the mores of the group. In one high school English class, all the girls spoke with too little volume. Because the leader of the group spoke with little more than a whisper, the others in the class followed suit. Had the leader spoken with sharp tones, the girls would have spoken piercingly. Had she spoken with too much voice, they would have spoken too loudly.

Traditionally teachers begin their explanation of voice with an analysis of sound and its dependence on the vibrating body, the source of energy which produces the vibration, and the resonation. You make clear how these three factors affect the resulting sound either by the use of musical instruments or by a film. You then show the relationship of this knowledge to the vocal mechanism. You explain and demonstrate how breathing provides the motivating force, how the vibrating body is the vocal bands, and how the resonance may be pharyngeal, oral, or nasal. As you study the attributes of voice, quality, pitch, volume, and duration, you associate them with the vocal mechanism and its operation.

On the other hand, many teachers give little emphasis to the vocal structure, stressing instead students' critical analytical listening to their own and others' voices. Trying to divorce the voice from its owner, students write down the attitudes and feelings evoked by particular voices. Their comments are similar to these:

"Mike sounds angry; he shouts his ideas."
"Kathy makes me feel weary. She sounds exhausted."
"Sheila's voice is pleasant. It gives me a happy feeling."

Admittedly you may be detecting how a student feels about himself and others, for to an extent voices identify individuals who are assured or timid, aggressive or self-effacing, and whose feelings toward others are apathetic or interested, sympathetic or antagonistic. But when a student wishes to improve his voice, he must face up to what he sounds like and learn how to make his voice suit his purpose. Critical listening to ascertain one's vocal assets and liabilities is the first step.

Obviously, in either approach, students listen for effects of quality, pitch, volume, and duration.

Quality of Voice

Although we agree that a pleasant speaking voice is important, although we are usually conscious that the voices of our friends and associates affect us, and although we believe that voice and personality are interrelated, we do not always agree on the characteristics of an effective voice. On paper we say that we like clear, well-modulated, and resonant voices. But a voice may possess these characteristics for one person and not for another. Recently ten of twelve persons commended the husky voice of a woman who possessed vocal nodes. For this group of ten her smile, her enthusiasm, and her love of living seemed to mask the husky voice quality. Or they were loathe to admit that they didn't like her voice. Her voice did disturb the other two because of its "harsh" quality.

. You must strive to make your study of voice as objective as possible. As indicated earlier, relating this study of quality to the study of the mechanism is one way of achieving a degree of objectivity. Another way is through analytical, critical listening.

Breathing and Its Relation to Quality

Most students control their breathing for speech unconsciously and do it well; for example, most of them can sustain a hum from about twenty to thirty seconds. If they cannot, they need to learn that in breathing the muscles of the abdomen relax in inhalation and contract in exhalation and that they must direct the contraction. By these means they avoid wasting breath.

Some high school girls like the sound of a breathy and husky voice. To make them realize that their laryngeal mechanism does not tolerate breathiness and tension is sometimes difficult. However, when they do recognize the fatigue resulting from the strain, they are more ready for help. Furthermore, often other members of the class by their frank discussion can change this unhealthy attitude toward a breathy and husky voice.

Producing Clear Tones

You also discuss the relationship of tones to resonance, showing how quality enables you to discriminate between two sounds alike in pitch, duration, and loudness. You explain the importance of the original tone and the selective modification of this tone through resonation. One teacher illustrates this concept by the use of his trombone. He first blows the mouthpiece and then shows how the tone changes as he cups his hand over it to form a kind of resonator. He is illustrating how varying resonating chambers present tones somewhat different in quality on the same pitch level with the same degree of loudness and duration.

After some such exercise, you explain the relationship of clear tones to the resonators in human beings. You show how the voice becomes strident when excessive tension exists in the walls of the throat and in the muscles of the soft palate. You demonstrate how the voice sounds denasal when you cut down nasal resonance by holding your nose. You illustrate the guttural quality that results when you hump the back of your tongue blocking the pharyngeal passage.

With this information as background you go on to investigate the quality of the voices of the members of the class. After you have made sure that each student is prolonging his tones long enough for his mechanism to achieve good quality, you may record all the voices so that each student can hear his own. You then analyze the voice of each student, explaining to him what makes for his particular quality. For example, in the case of excessive nasality, you find out whether the cause is functional or organic. When you have diagnosed the difficulty, you help the student to hear his nasality and to control it when it is excessive. When classroom work fails, the student needs clinical help.

Pitch

When the voice is thin or husky, it is advisable to check the optimum pitch. Boys and girls are interested in the explanation of this aspect of voice and its application to themselves. Almost all high school children like to take tests that concern themselves and that do not evaluate their classroom work. When you are in doubt about the optimum pitch of some members of your class, you may well take time to test the whole group.

Widening the Pitch Range

Persons tend to speak at the lower end of their pitch range. Research shows that superior speakers use a wider pitch range than do average or poor speakers. Whatever you can do to help students widen their pitch range upward is helpful. Sometimes work on inflection and intonation in which students associate words and sentences with meaning and feeling provide stimuli for widening the pitch range.

Teaching Inflection

Inflection should be taught in relationship to meaning. You may start with a single word and ask your students to express its different meanings. You use words with explanations as indicated in the following:

Him   You mean that you have chosen him—him of all people?
Idiot   You're foolish but pleasantly so. I don't really disapprove.
Come   You come here right now. I've called you for the last time.
What?   You can't make me believe that!
Yes   You may be right but I doubt it very much.

After this exercise, you may suggest that your students attach a situation to each of the following words, writing a sentence to indicate the situation:

well	what	where	rot
fun	can't	good	shoot
fine	go	bad	write

The students then say the word expressing the meaning which they have indicated.

Teaching Intonation

You may teach intonation by following a similar procedure using sentences like:

I'm going home. I'm really going to go home soon!
Are you going to Washington or Baltimore? 1. Which place are you going? 2. Are you going to either place?
Are you going to Washington? I want a yes or no answer. Your going doesn't concern me but I do want to know whether you are going.
Were you late? Same as the preceding explanation.

After a study of the pitch movement on such sentences, you and the members of your class generalize on what statements and questions take downward inflections and which upward inflections.

You and the members of your class may also analyze the use of inflection and intonation in a series. First, you ask a student to look at and then list five items on your desk. Second, you request another student to recall what he had for breakfast. Third, you have still another student list articles as you show them to him. You record on tape the answers and the members of the group analyze the pitch changes on the recordings of the three series. From this analysis the group makes generalizations. In one instance the speaker knows exactly what is on the desk and lists the first four items with an upward movement and the last with a downward one. In another instance the student is not certain what he did have for breakfast and is trying to recall, so each item has an upward movement. In the third instance he doesn't know what the teacher is going to produce; as a result each item has a downward inflection.

Volume

Students should realize that the degree of loudness depends on: (1) the energy with which the breath stream vibrates the vocal cords and (2) the amount of amplification or reinforcement of the vocal tone by the resonators. You must, therefore, teach your students that *both* factors are important and that force or energy is not the sole factor.

They should also recognize that adequate loudness means being heard easily by their listeners. If they are leading cheers in a football game, they need more voice than if they are conversing in a small room. Furthermore, they should also know that articulation and rate of speaking are important in being heard.

Variations in Loudness

Your students' listeners also receive the speakers' color and meaning through variations in loudness. Combined with changes in pitch, quality, and duration, changes in force add variety to speech. One teacher begins by having her students say, "Watch it; watch it; watch it!" In these phrases the effect of force is quite obvious. She then gives them sentences in which they must change the stress on words to achieve different meanings. From here they go on to sentences with subordinate phrases. Her students discover that the subordinate phrase is read less loudly than the main phrase. Finally, they put what they have learned about loudness variations to work in reading a paragraph.

Rate

Students should learn to speak and read at a rate that is readily understood and should suit the rate to the material to be read or spoken. Generally students use a fast rate in depicting excitement and a slow rate for solemnity or sadness. In addition students read or speak material that is difficult to understand slowly and material readily understood faster. Changes in tempo should match the emotional and intellectual content of what the student is reading or speaking.

Today more and more students are reading and speaking too quickly. One way to point this out is to time the number of words read or spoken. Usually adults speak about 130 words per minute and read about 160 words per minute. When students read and speak considerably faster than these rates, they should be taught to read and speak more slowly. Frequently a recording dramatizes a student's speed. One student's comment, "Sounds like movies running double tempo," showed her awareness of her problem. To slow down their speaking or reading students must understand the factors in rate: the duration of the individual sounds, the length of the pauses, and the speed with which phrases are uttered.

PUTTING THE ARTICULATORY AND VOCAL SKILLS TO WORK

Your students may articulate clearly and may use pleasant voice and still not communicate mood and meaning effectively. Throughout this study you must, therefore, point to the necessity of a thorough and vivid understanding of the content and a lively sense of communication. The skills indicated in the chapters on giving talks and on oral reading deal with these matters.

SUGGESTED READING

AKIN, J., *And So We Speak: Voice and Articulation* (Englewood Cliffs, N. J., Prentice-Hall, Inc., 1958). Contains chapters on the linguistic environment, the structure of American English sounds, the anatomy of the speech mechanism, and voice.

ALLEN, H. B., *Readings in Applied English Linguistics* (New York, Appleton-Century-Crofts, Inc., 1958). Contains an excellent discussion of the standards of pronunciation and grammar.

BRONSTEIN, A., *The Pronunciation of American English* (New York, Appleton-Century-Crofts, Inc., 1960). Contains a particularly good section on the standards of American English. Includes a complete and thorough analysis of all the sounds of American English.

CROCKER, L., "The Linguist, the Freshman, and the Purist," *The Speech Teacher*, III (March, 1954), 129-130. Points out that the constantly changing usage is difficult to teach. Depicts the struggle between the linguists and the purists.

EISENSON, J., *The Improvement of Voice and Diction* (New York, The Macmillan Co., 1958). Contains material on voice, articulation, and the mechanism of speech. Much of the exercise material can be adapted for high school use.

FRANCIS, W. N., *The Structure of American English* (New York, The Ronald Press Company, 1958). Includes chapters on language and linguistic science, phonetics, phonemics, morphemics, grammar, the dialects of American English, and linguistics and the teacher of English.

HAHN, E., and LOMAS, C. S., HARGIS, D. E., and VANDRAEGEN, D., *Basic Voice Training for Speech* (New York, McGraw-Hill Book Co., 1958). Contains material on critical listening, articulation, and integrating the vocal skills. The selections for practice could well be used with many high school students.

KENYON, J. S., "Levels of Speech and Colloquial English," *English Journal*, XXXVII (January, 1948), 25-31. Distinguishes between "cultural level of English" and "functional varieties of standard English." Points out that it is impossible to draw a strict dividing line between the colloquial and the literary or formal diction.

KENYON, J. S., and KNOTT, T. A., *A Pronouncing Dictionary of American English* (Springfield, Mass., G. & C. Merriam Co., 1944). Provides the best source for the pronunciation of American English words. Based on the pronunciations of educated speakers in America.

KONIGSBERG, E., "Making Drill Functional," *The Speech Teacher*, I (March, 1952), 128-130. Suggests ways of making drill on articulation and voice interesting to the students. Shows the need for teaching voice and articulation.

LAMPORT, F., "Dictionaries—Our Language Right or Wrong," *Harper's Magazine*, CCXIX (September, 1959), 49-54. Describes the history of dictionary publishing. A witty and amusing article.

LANGE, P., "Pronunciation and the Dictionaries," *The Quarterly Journal of Speech*, XXXII (April, 1946), 190-193. Describes a study of six dictionaries. Indicates the need for standardizing symbols of pronunciation. Gives suggestions for improving dictionaries.

MAYNARD, N., "Poor Reading, Handmaiden of Poor Speech," *The Speech Teacher*, V (January, 1956), 40-46. Reviews the relationship between reading and speaking difficulties. Shows that poor reading can be caused by poor speech on three reading levels: the readiness level, the primary or beginning level, and the intermediate reading level.

THOMAS, C. K., *Phonetics of American English*, 2nd ed. (New York, The Ronald Press Company, 1958). Deals with the pronunciation of English in the United States. Includes chapters on the mechanism of speech, the vowels, the consonants, stress, length of sounds, assimilation, regional variations, and standards of pronunciation.

WEAVER, C. H., "Don't Look It Up—Listen!" *The Speech Teacher*, VI (September, 1957), 240-246. Points out the constant shifts in the pronunciations of words. Discusses the use of the term *cultured speech*. Indicates that the dictionary is a guide, not a refuge, in matters of pronunciation.

EXERCISES

1. Find a series of quotations about which boys and girls can make impromptu speeches for drill on *s, r, l,* and *th.* Examples are:

   "Liberty means responsibility. That is why most men dread it."—*G. B. Shaw.*

   "Expedients are for the hour; principles are for the ages."—*H. W. Beecher.*

2. Find seven poems which high school boys and girls will like and which emphasize particular sounds.

3. Prepare a lesson to show how dictionaries are alike and how they differ.

4. List phrases which could be used in teaching intonation. Explain how you would use them.

III

TEACHING
PUBLIC ADDRESS

III

5

Public Speaking

HIGH SCHOOL STUDENTS give talks in classes, in meetings of their organizations, and in assemblies before their student bodies. In classes the topics of their talks vary. In an advanced mathematics class, a student may explain the gambler's interest in the theory of permutations and combinations. In an elementary science class, he may define the process of osmosis. In an English class, he may share with his fellow students his pleasure in reading *Vanity Fair*. In a social studies class, he may persuade his classmates of the values of the city manager system for municipal government. Much of the students' learning in classes involves giving and listening to talks.

During the course of school meetings, students make many short speeches. The winner of the county cow-judging contest may explain to his fellow Future Farmers of America the basis for his judgment. At a meeting of the home economics club, one of its members may make clear the principles of design in early American furniture. The President of Broadcasters may express regret at the loss of the secretary who is moving to another state. Almost no high school meeting passes without a speech being presented.

Students deliver different kinds of speeches before the student body. They electioneer for a particular person for president of their student organization. The president of the senior class presents the class gift to the school; the president of the student body accepts it. At assemblies, the student chairmen introduce the speakers of the day, or students make strong pleas for support of athletic and dramatic events. At commencement the valedictorian and the salutatorian deliver addresses. Student speeches before large groups of their fellow students are commonplace.

COMPETENCE IN PUBLIC SPEAKING

To make effective informative, persuasive, entertaining, and impressive speeches, students should acquire the necessary speaking understandings, attitudes, and skills. In addition, in order to listen to speakers thoughtfully and reflectively students should gain the required competence in listening. To be effective speakers and listeners students should have the following abilities:

1. To select a topic that is appropriate to the speaker, the audience, and the occasion.
2. To find the necessary material for a talk and to organize and adapt it so that the audience will understand and respond.
3. To make the speech interesting to the audience.
4. To understand the factors involved in speeches to inform, to persuade, to entertain, and to impress.
5. To listen attentively to respond to the content, and to evaluate the ideas of these four types of speeches.
6. To have a vivid realization of the meaning of the words as they are uttered.
7. To possess a lively sense of communication.
8. To deliver the speech with adequate voice and diction.

CONTENT OF THE PUBLIC SPEAKING COURSE

So that students may develop these abilities, the high school course of public speaking may include the following material:

Importance of Public Speaking

Selecting the Topic
   Influence of the Speaker
   Influence of the Audience
   Influence of the Occasion
   Influence of the Purposes of Speaking

Preparing Material for a Speech
   Personal Observation
   Interviews
   Library Research
   Taking Notes

Organizing the Speech
  Purposes of Speaking
    Informing
    Persuading
    Impressing
    Entertaining
  Factors of Organization
    Divisions
    Subdivisions
    Introduction
    Conclusion
    Development of Ideas

Principles of Composition
  Unity
  Coherence
  Concreteness

Making the Speech Interesting

Delivery
  Methods of Delivery
  Requirements for Effective Delivery

Supporting Material
  Information
  Examples
  Comparison
  Testimony

SELECTING THE TOPIC

Students feel that the term *public speaking* connotes a weighty topic or at the very least an unusual experience. As a teacher, you hear such remarks as: "I don't know what to talk about." "Nothing exciting ever happens to me." "How can I make a topic interesting when I cull the information from the encyclopedia?" You, therefore, help your students to work out sound criteria for selecting a topic and then to follow these criteria.

One teacher started her discussion of the selection of a topic for giving talks the day after Carl Sandburg delivered his celebrated address on Lincoln before the joint session of Congress. She illustrated its effect by reading parts of an account of the experience from the daily newspaper which indicated that down on the floor of the house the spell of poetry and legend took hold, that a senator leaned forward and cupped his ear, that two representatives broke off a whispered chat and stared wonderingly at Carl Sandburg, and that when he finished, the members of the Congress broke into a thunder of applause. She then gave some of the background of the author of the six volume Pulitzer-prize-winning life of Abraham Lincoln. Finally, she read part of the speech to the group.

After this preparation, she led a discussion of Carl Sandburg's selection of the topic *Lincoln*. The students pointed out that Sandburg understood and appreciated his topic well. He had interviewed persons who knew Lincoln personally. He had been thorough in his research. They indicated that, in addition, Sandburg had a deep respect for and a kind of reverential feeling toward Lincoln. Moreover, they noted that since the speech was made before the joint session of Congress on Lincoln's birthday, the topic was particularly appropriate. Finally they said that since all legislators supposedly believe in the democratic tradition, they should surely always be interested in the truly democratic Lincoln, the lover of liberty.

Criteria for Selecting a Topic

As a result of this analysis, the students set up five criteria for their own selection of a topic:

1. We must have some information about our topic to start with and must proceed to learn more and more about it.
2. We must choose a subject in which we are absorbed and one that we wish to share with our classmates.
3. Our topic should be interesting to our classmates or one that can be made interesting.
4. Our topic must not be incongruous with the mood of the occasion.
5. Our topic should be such that we can cover it in the time allotted to us.

After the students set up the criteria, the teacher then asked them to suggest topics which they might be able to handle effectively in speeches of about five minutes. One girl said that in early February an appropriate topic might well be "The Legend of St. Valentine's Day." She went on to say that because she had bought a valentine which explained the legend, and because she enjoyed looking at a collection her aunt had made, she would like to learn more about the day and its customs. The students decided that this topic met well the five criteria upon which they had agreed and that if the speech were to be delivered shortly before or on Valentine's Day, the topic would be particularly appropriate.

Another girl, a daughter of two teachers, announced that she would like to speak on the advantages of teaching as a career. She stated that since education had been undergoing a barrage of criticism and since people tend to feel sorry for teachers, she would like to present the other side of the coin. She began to compare her parents' choice of profession with that of her uncle's, a doctor. One student suggested that she might better save her fire for her speech and indicated that he was enthusiastic about her topic. Her interest in the subject, her almost dedicated attitude toward the teaching profession, and her obvious serious thinking made this topic appropriate for her.

Still another girl had just read a short story which dealt with the difficulty a ten-year-old had in finding a place to read alone and undisturbed. This child had used the jail as a reading spot until other boys and girls discovered it. The student then related that she herself had the same difficulty: her sisters and brothers came trooping into her room, wanting help with their homework or just teasing. She explained that after trying the garage, a bench in the park, and the attic, she found a neighbor with no children, who was perfectly willing for her to curl up in the big chair in the den, and that there she read to her heart's content. Her classmates chuckled at her predicament. But some of them questioned whether she had enough material for a significant speech. Before they declared her topic suitable, they wanted to know how she would develop it.

Contributing to the Group's Knowledge

Not every student is immediately able to suggest topics upon which he wants to talk. You, therefore, add the criterion that every speaker should contribute to the knowledge of the group. One teacher points out that since each student is a specialist in some area, he should share his specialty with his classmates. In one class, for example, one student's speeches were based on some aspect of music. As a result of them, almost all of the members of the group listened to Leonard Bernstein's televised broadcasts. On a Monday morning after one of the broadcasts, this teen-age expert on music answered the students' questions arising from the broadcast. At the end of the term, one of the students remarked that he had received a general education from the talks of his classmates, noting that he had learned something about such widely varying areas as aviation, medicine, the study of Latin, music, and even Mother Goose rhymes.

Beyond helping students to recognize their specialized areas, you recommend that students think about topics related to school organization, both curricular and extra-curricular, places they have visited, and special experiences which they have had. After students have suggested a number of possible topics from these sources, you may ask your students to recommend other sources. They frequently respond with these: publication of a book, presentation of a television program, a local, state, or national controversy, or a need for reform in the city, state, or nation.

Students then decide which of these topics will best suit their classmates, for they must think in terms of their audience. The more suitable, the more successful will be the speech. For example, one of the talks which most interested the members of a high school public speaking class was one which persuaded that going steady was healthy for adolescents.

Adapting a Topic to the Purposes of Speaking

After the students have suggested many topics and have completed an assignment in which they list a number of possible topics with reasons for their choices, you then suggest that these topics imply different purposes of speaking. Later in the term the group will study purposes more thoroughly but you define them at this time. One reason for defining them here is that you may want the first speaking assignment to be giving informative talks.

The teacher who read Carl Sandburg's speech to her group asked what purpose Sandburg had in speaking. The responses of the students were that he was celebrating Lincoln's birthday, that he was giving the members of Congress a feeling for Lincoln's concept of democracy, and that he was providing an inspirational experience. At this point, the teacher explained the meaning to *impress* as a purpose of speaking.

The teacher then asked what purposes their proposed topics would serve. When one boy said that some of the topics served the purpose of argument, the teacher asked, "Why do we argue?" The responses varied: "to win a point," "to persuade," "to convince," "to get your own way," "to make others see your point of view," "to get something done." The teacher then told the group that the terminology generally used in public speaking is "to persuade." They agreed that the topics about teen-agers going steady, the advantages of a teaching career, the need for an expanded town library, and the requirement of two years of Latin for all high school students suggested talks designed to *persuade*. Some students thought, however, that explanations would occur as these topics were developed. The teacher made clear that giving facts and information is often a necessary part of persuasion.

Next, they talked about speeches which only give facts. They cited as examples talks about Valentine's Day, the basic principles of harmony, and the relationship of the Secretary of State to Congress. Whereupon one student made the point that the speech on Valentine's Day could be persuasive, because if we knew the meaning of Valentine's Day, we might be more likely to send cards. Another student remarked that explaining Valentine's Day might even be an advertising device of printers of cards. Again the teacher demonstrated the interrelationship between informing and persuading. She noted, however, that the main purpose of many speeches is to *inform*.

Lastly, the students decided that to *entertain* was still another purpose. They noted that the girl's topic, about finding a place to read peacefully, was amusing. One student indicated that an expansion of this girl's comments could make an amusing after-dinner speech.

The teacher then summarized the criteria for selecting a topic. She noted the dependence of the topic on the purpose of speaking as well as on the speaker, the occasion, and the audience.

PREPARING MATERIAL FOR A TALK

Sources

In helping your students to find material for their talks, you suggest that (1) they make use of personal observations and experience, (2) they interview persons, (3) they study current documents and reports, (4) they avail themselves of the resources of the library, and (5) they listen to relevant broadcasts.

Many students think that a talk can only be compiled from information gathered in the library. They forget that to interest their audience, they should choose a topic about which they know something and have real enthusiasm. In selecting the topic and in finding material for it, students should use their own experience and their own observation. For instance, one girl, who was going to be an elementary teacher, spoke on creative play for children. Before she went to the library to read, she observed children in her neighborhood playing store, fire, and hospital. She found that this background made her reading more meaningful. Still another girl wanted to make a plea for keeping our national parks free from commercial influences. She used her own disappointment with the commercial aspects of Yellowstone as the starting point for gathering material and as a focus for her speech.

Students may well interview people for information. Frequently members of their own family, their neighbors, their minister, the town librarian, or a businessman can give them worthwhile information or opinions on a particular topic. Quoting a well-known local personality adds interest to a speech. You should make sure, however, that the student knows how to interview. He should be taught to plan the interview by determining its purpose carefully and preparing thoughtful questions beforehand. He should be courteous and able to conclude the interview graciously. He should also be taught not to impose on the good nature of city authorities or to ask them for the impossible.

Frequently students may obtain current documents or reports. Material sent out by such organizations as the National Education Association, the United Nations, the United States Chamber of Commerce, and by the various agencies of the United States Government often give valuable information useful to the speaker. Suggestions for such material can be found in the source list of free and inexpensive materials listed in the bibliography of Chapter II.

You must also teach or review for the student the use of school library resources. The student should be well acquainted with the card catalog and the purpose of the author, title, and subject cards. He should know how to use the various reference books—encyclopedias, dictionaries, atlases, almanacs, reference works in special fields, and bibliographies. In some instances the librarian prefers to teach these facts to the students; in other instances you yourself will teach them.

Finally, students can often listen to broadcasts on radio and television that have to do with their topic. By investigating the week's program carefully, they can discover such broadcasts. Telecasts often deal with personal problems, school situations, and state and national affairs. Radio discussion groups are concerned with many contemporary affairs.

Taking Notes

One aspect of the preparation for a talk which you yourself must give to your students is instruction in taking notes. One teacher gives out the following pages of mimeographed material, for she has found through her years of teaching that the students continue to be careless in recording bibliographic material, to take many useless notes, and to work in a highly inefficient way. After she has distributed the material and explained it, she asks the students to turn in to her, before they begin their outlines, the notes which they have taken on a particular topic. She returns them with comments, thus helping her students to record material more efficiently.

Instructions for Taking Notes

1. Use 4″ x 6″ cards for both note-taking and bibliography cards. Keep *separate* files for each.
2. Include on the bibliography cards the following information:
   For a Book: author, title underlined, place of publication, publisher, date of publication and pages. If you have not read the entire book, indicate the pages you have used.
   For an Article: author, title of article in quotes, title of magazine underlined, volume number, date, pages.
   In both instances write a one-sentence or sentence fragment annotation indicating the usefulness of the book or article to you or your topic.
3. Follow these directions for inclusion of material on note-taking cards:
   a. Use direct quotations when the ideas are concisely expressed or stated with unusual skill so that you may use them as quotations. Include the page number.
   b. In paraphrasing, express ideas as concisely as you can, without distorting the meaning of the author. Include the page numbers.
   c. Write the subject of each note on the right hand side of the card.
   d. By reference to your bibliography card, write the source of your quotation on the left hand side. Use a numbering and lettering

system for this notation. For example, if the author's last name begins with *C,* you put a C_1 on both the bibliography and note-taking cards. For a second author whose name begins with *C,* you use a C_2.

Examples

BIBLIOGRAPHY CARD (MAGAZINE)

C_1
Cleveland, Harlan, "The Pretty Americans," *Harpers,* 218 (March, 1959), 31-36.
Describes and explains the problems of the American wife who is living abroad.

BIBLIOGRAPHY CARD (BOOK)

S_1
Shoenburn, David, *As France Goes* (New York, Harper & Brothers, 1957).
Describes the influence of the past on France of today and tomorrow.

NOTE CARD—PARAPHRASING OF IDEAS (from magazine article by Harlan Cleveland)

C_1—p. 35   Tips for Wives of Business Men and Diplomats Living Abroad.
1. Decide you really want to go.
2. Learn what you can about the country you are going to visit.
3. Brush up on your American history and current events.
4. Expect poor physical conditions.
5. Be curious.
6. Learn the language of the country you expect to visit.
7. Learn about health and school facilities right away.
8. Don't try to shield your children.
9. Be yourself.

NOTE CARD—QUOTATION (from magazine article by Harlan Cleveland)

C_1—p. 36   Very Important Person
                                               Feeling

"And indeed, there are so many distinguished circuit riders these days
that you are much more likely to meet a Senator, the Secretary of
State, a "name" newspaper writer—or even Louis Armstrong or Bob
Hope—in Tunis or Tokyo than in New York."

ORGANIZING THE SPEECH

You must teach your students to organize their ideas clearly in
relation to their audience. To accomplish this purpose, students
must understand the importance of exact phrasing of the main idea,
making an outline with its divisions and its subdivisions, and opening and closing a speech appropriately.

To introduce the problem of arranging material for a speech, one
teacher uses the analogy of the organization of a supermarket. She
begins with a discussion on the likenesses between opening a supermarket and preparing a speech. She poses the question, "If you were
a businessman in this community thinking of opening a supermarket
on 175th Street, what are the facts that would influence your
decision?" The responses of her students usually are about as follows:

1. Does Central Village need another supermarket?
2. Has it ever had one on 175th Street before?
3. What do I know about running a supermarket?
4. What are my limitations in this project?
5. What do I know about my potential customers?
6. What will I need to stock?

The first two questions indicate the need to find out the history
of the retail grocery business in the community; in planning a speech
there is a similar need to find out the interests of the listeners on a
particular topic. The third question concerning the owner's knowledge of the market business corresponds to the speaker's analysis
of his own knowledge of the topic upon which he is to speak. The
fourth question on the limitations of the potential supermarket
manager points to his financial status, his managerial capacity, and

his ability to hire other people; in terms of the student speaker it points to his ability to find material and to handle the topic within a specific time limit. The fifth question, dealing with potential customers, requires a study of their income level, their age and the age of members of their families, and their known preferences in food. A corresponding question dealing with listeners requires a study of their likenesses and differences in terms of information, beliefs, interests, and modes of action as related to the topic. Answers to the last question depend on the customers' eating habits and needs. Answers to a speaker's corresponding question, "What shall I say?" depend on his listeners, on the occasion, and on his purpose.

After the owner has purchased the store and the stock, he must organize his stock and induce his potential customers to buy. His supermarket has a sign which indicates the purpose of the store; similarly the speech has a main idea which indicates its purpose. The store proprietor decorates his window attractively to catch the attention of his potential customers, for he hopes to convert this attention to interest. This attention-getting device corresponds to the introduction of a speech. After the customers enter the store, they discover that it has a dairy department, a meat department, a fresh fruit and vegetable department, a frozen goods department, and a grocery department. Within these departments merchandise is organized. For example, in the canned fruit department fruits are separated one from the other. A shelf may include several sizes, varieties, and brands of peaches placed side by side so the shopper may pick out the size, variety, and brand which he prefers. The divisions and subdivisions in a speech are similar to the organization of the supermarket shelves. Furthermore, the grocery store contains markers in the aisles to guide customers to the food they want to buy. In a speech the markers are the transitions. Finally the proprietor of the store hopes his customers will be satisfied when they have made their purchases; the speaker hopes his audience will be satisfied at the conclusion of his speech.

Main Idea

Various terms are used to express the formal phrasing of the central idea of a speech or composition. Terms frequently used are *main idea, central idea, statement, subject sentence,* and *thesis.* Members of English and speech departments in a high school do well to use the same term consistently. No matter what the terminology, students should be able to express the main idea accurately. It should be complete, represent one idea, be tied to the purpose, be clear, direct, concise, and should serve the function for which it is intended.[1]

One teacher approaches the task of teaching the main idea through a study of the Gettysburg address. After she has read the address to her students, she asks them to tell her its main idea. Sometimes a student will quickly note that the main idea is that we should dedicate our lives to the cause of liberty and equality. Other times a boy or a girl will respond with the statement: "Our father founded a nation, conceived in liberty and dedicated to the ideal of equality." When a pupil makes such a statement, the teacher points out that he is confusing the introduction of the speech and the main idea. She shows that the introduction frequently does not include the main idea; rather it provides a satisfactory approach to it.

Her assignment then consists of asking her students to phrase in single sentences the main ideas of three speeches which they may make during the term. The members of the class evaluate these sentences, changing them where they are not complete, unified, linked to the purpose, clear, direct, concise, and functional.

Purposes of Speaking

At this time you may review with your students the definitions of the four purposes of speaking: to inform, to persuade, to impress, and to entertain. After this review, you may ask the members of the group to phrase four main ideas about a topic, such as the school newspaper, representing each of the four purposes. The choice of the topic the school newspaper was particularly appropriate for one group, since the class included three staff members of the paper and since the paper had just won a journalism award from Columbia University. The group phrased the following four main ideas:

1. *To inform.* Setting up the front page of *The Centralite* involves three steps.
2. *To persuade.* You should try out for a position on *The Centralite*.

[1] See W. E. Gilman, B. Aly, and L. D. Reid, *The Fundamentals of Speaking* (New York, The Macmillan Co., 1951), p. 47.

3. *To impress.* Winning the Columbia University Award is a worthy accomplishment for *The Centralite.*
4. *To entertain.* Setting up copy for *The Centralite* is both enjoyable and amusing.

After such preliminary work, you proceed to develop the concepts of the four purposes more thoroughly.

To Inform

You point out that students speak to inform more often than for any other purpose; they give information when they make announcements, review books, explain processes, devices, and policies, and give reports. You make clear that informing is the method of the reporter or the teacher who tells what something is, how it works, what purpose it serves, or what its real nature and limits are; and you show that in all instances the account has resulted from inquiry and its end is clarity and understanding.

You may then ask students to bring to class two main ideas expressed clearly in sentences. The main ideas are for informative speeches which may be given later. The following are representative:

> Dr. Hans Selye believes that all illness is related to chemical imbalance in the body caused by stress.
>
> Rhythm is an important element in most Latin American dances.
>
> Graphology is the deduction of a person's character from lines, spaces, curves, and the formation of letters of the handwriting.
>
> The Bar Mitzvah Ceremony is an important step in the maturation of a Jewish boy.

To Persuade

Although a high school public speaking course is concerned with the problems and techniques basic to all four purposes of speaking, some additional knowledge of the method of the advocate is of practical value to the high school student, for he often attempts to influence the beliefs and conduct of his classmates, parents, and others.

High school students should know that persuasion involves three factors: (1) reasoning, (2) disposing, and (3) accrediting.[2] In reasoning, students should be able to distinguish the issues involved.

[2] *Ibid.,* p. 317.

To teach finding issues you may again use a problem related to the school. One high school group, who believed that the high school gym should be open evenings, found the three issues of the problem:

1. Is there a demand for its facilities?
2. Do other agencies fail to provide these facilities?
3. Would the cost of opening the gym from seven to nine o'clock on Monday through Saturday be reasonable?

In addition, students should use evidence wisely and reason well. They should be able to recognize fallacious reasoning; Stuart Chase's book, mentioned in the bibliography, provides some excellent teaching material in this area.

Disposing has to do with the selection of appeals that will gain a favorable hearing for the student's argument. You must, therefore, teach the student speaker to select and phrase his supporting ideas so that they will carry weight with his classmates. Most high school students enjoy analyzing the basic attitudes and interests of the members of their groups.

In accrediting, the student is concerned with the personal impression he makes on his classmates. Here you can emphasize the importance of the character of the speaker. You point out that Quintilian believed that the speaker must be a good man and that the audience will not honor a bad man. You and the students analyze how they arrive at the impression of a student speaker. They usually point out that the speaker should be sincere, accurate, fair, gracious, and show respect for his listeners.

Students should also be aware of the different kinds of persuasion. One teacher teaches them by illustration. She exemplifies the persuasive speech of fact by this main idea: Outsiders were responsible for the vandalism on the subway last year on our trip to the basketball finals; the speech of value by: The best room to use for the school newspaper room in our building is the discarded men's lounge; the speech of policy by: The honor system should be adopted as the system most likely to eliminate cheating in our school.

The following are main ideas of persuasive speeches developed by students:

Going steady is a healthy practice for teen-agers.
The citizen of today should invest in mutual funds.

The students of Central High School should support their literary magazine, *The Quill.*

The United States Government should control and dispense narcotics.

To Impress

Students rarely give speeches to impress. Some teachers omit them altogether, for they think that the student will have little opportunity to give impressive speeches in the future. They further think that much of the value of impressive speeches lies in the interest of well-chosen language and in the selection of particular facts and ideas to produce a desired effect, and that these abilities are not so important to the student as the clarity of expression taught in informative speaking and the reasoning taught in persuasive speaking.

Examples of main ideas developed by students in speeches to impress include:

Franklin Delano Roosevelt was a noble man.

As Irishmen we honor St. Patrick.

To Entertain

High school students must realize that all kinds of speeches may, to some extent, entertain. When the student informs or persuades an audience, his vividness of expression, a factor in entertainment, keeps its members interested. Just as every speech possesses some element of entertainment, no speech is entertainment alone. It must contain interesting, unusual, or significant ideas. A description of Madame Curie's discovery of radium, an unusual tale of deep sea diving, a story of the life of a racketeer, a travelogue to an unusual country are all topics that can be entertaining. Bryant and Wallace indicate that "the end of entertainment is a glow of friendly satisfaction in the listeners—satisfaction with the speaker and with themselves."[3]

High school students rarely give speeches to entertain. For this reason many teachers omit teaching the entertaining speech altogether. They think that if the student can make an informative speech and a persuasive speech interesting, alive, and vital, he does not need to make the entertaining speech. Other teachers do in-

[3] D. C. Bryant and K. R. Wallace, *Oral Communication: A Short Course in Speaking,* 2nd ed. (New York, Appleton-Century-Crofts, Inc., 1954), p. 239.

clude them. Main ideas for high school speeches of entertainment may well be:

> The life of a bell boy at a summer hotel is filled with amusing incidents.
> A younger brother can be the bane of one's life.
> This political campaign contained many malapropisms.

Forms of Organization

You teach different forms of organization such as categories, space, time, causal relationship, similarities, differences, and problem-solution.[4] You may use as an illustration some of your own teaching. For example, if you employed the idea of the organization of a supermarket's being similar to the organization of a speech, you may point out that the pattern of this teaching was based on bringing out similarities. Or you may show varying patterns of organization appropriate for developing different main ideas based on a single topic. For example, using as a topic the radio station of the school, you may point out that the layout of the radio station might be explained according to space, that the radio program for one day might be described by following a time sequence, that a persuasive speech advocating that every high school should own and operate a radio station might be based on reasons, and that a student's speech on how to improve the radio programming in the school might first describe the causes of the unsatisfactory conditions and then suggest the remedy. Such study helps boys and girls to establish and follow appropriate plans of organization.

Divisions and Subdivisions of Outlining

Whether you teach topical or sentence outlining depends upon the members of your group and upon you. Some high school teachers think that their students can use the topical outline more satisfactorily than they can the sentence outline. Others believe that a sentence outline shows more effectively the logical relationships of the ideas in the speech. Whichever you prefer, you must teach some form of outlining, for the outline is the foundation of a successful speech.

You include, in your teaching of outlining, the parts of the outline, the symbols which show the relationships between supporting

[4] See W. E. Gilman, B. Aly, and L. R. Reid, *The Fundamentals of Speaking* (New York, The Macmillan Co., 1951), p. 59.

statements and subsupporting statements, the importance of sub-supporting statements' dependence on supporting statements, and the discreteness of each phrase or statement.

Outlining by Entire Group

One of the most frequent means of teaching outlining is to have members of the entire group develop an outline based on a main idea. For instance, the members of one class made an outline of their visit to LaGuardia Airport:

MAIN IDEA: A visit to an office and a plane showed us the workings of an airport.

Visit to Sections of Airport

I. American Airlines office.
   A. Network of communication with planes.
   B. Network of communication with passengers.
   C. Bookkeeping for planes taking off and arriving.
   D. Bookkeeping for passengers' reservations and departures.

II. American Airlines plane.
   A. Facilities for passengers.
   B. Facilities for controls of flying.

To teach sentence outlining, you may well outline an informative talk explaining the kinds of extracurricular activities offered by your school. The main idea may be: The extracurriculur activities of Central High School are related to its curricular activities. The categories of the activities then fall into those represented by departments within the school. Or the main idea may be: The extracurricular activities are based on areas of interests of students in our school. Then the categories may include science, speech, photography, writing, athletics, homemaking, agriculture, and self-government. The subdivisions follow quite naturally; for instance, writing includes working for the school newspaper, for the literary magazine, and for the annual; speech includes debating, discussion, dramatics, and oral reading. Part of such an outline follows:

MAIN IDEA: Our school offers extracurricular activities based on the in-interests of the students of the school.

I. Central High School takes account of the interests of the students who wish to write.

A. *The Centralite,* a weekly newspaper, offers several such opportunities.
   1. It offers opportunities for beginning reporters to report activities of such organizations as minor clubs.
   2. It offers opportunities for those specializing in drama, athletics, music, or dance, to report these events.
   3. It offers opportunities for the more experienced students to write editorials.
B. *The Quill,* the literary magazine, offers several such opportunities.
   1. Students may submit stories to this magazine.
   2. Students may submit poetry to this magazine.
   3. More experienced and talented students can put their editorial abilities to work on this magazine.
C. *The Blue and Gold,* the annual, offers several such opportunities.
   1. (Developed as in IA and IB)

II. Central High School takes account of the interests of students who wish to participate in athletics.
A. (Developed as in I)

This experience gives students the principles of building an outline. They find out that the outline brings order to the talk and makes it easier to present the talk to their particular audience.

Introducing the Speech

Your students must recognize that the introduction of their speech accomplishes two purposes: (1) preparing their classmates to listen and (2) leading them to the main idea.

In preparing their classmates to listen, students must catch their attention and convert the attention to interest. In this process they must recognize that the speaker must make his listeners like him for what he is and that he must associate his listeners' own knowledge, feelings, or interest with the main idea.

Some teachers teach the purpose of the introduction by an analysis of introductions of well-known speeches; others, by helping students to prepare effective introductions for their own speeches. They explain that the introduction can be a question, a quotation, a personal reference, or an illustration. They indicate that at times it may be a simple announcement such as: Today I propose to show that our high school should sponsor an honor society for students who attain unusual academic excellence.

In helping her students to determine what makes an effective introduction, one teacher used the following introductions to two students' speeches as examples:

MAIN IDEA: The Bar Mitzvah Ceremony is one of the most important institutions in the life of a Jew.

INTRODUCTION: Last week excitement reigned in our house. My brother Jack, dressed in a new blue suit, white shirt, polished shoes, and with his hair neatly plastered in place sat nervously waiting for the rest of us. You see, last Sabbath, the first Saturday after Jack's thirteenth birthday, was one of the most important days in his whole life—Bar Mitzvah Day. To my brother and to us, the ceremony meant that Jack was no longer a boy but a man.

After hearing this, one student indicated that the girl who was to make the speech was using a personal experience to catch the attention of her audience. Another student noted that Jennie, the girl giving the speech, was a person whom all the members of the group liked and respected and that the students were, therefore, interested in learning more about her beliefs. Some thought, furthermore, that the transformation of a boy to an adult interested all teen-agers. Finally one student pointed out that in the last two sentences Jennie had led her audience to the water and they were about to drink.

The second introduction served to introduce a speech whose purpose was to tell the members of the class of some of the unsavory practices of the press. The introduction follows:

William Allen White calls the American Press "a peddler of news rather than a leader of the public." He also says that the press has become "a commercial enterprise along mercantile lines."

The students responded quickly with the idea that a quotation introduced the speech. One student then questioned the use of the writing of William Allen White, for he had never heard of him. Another declared that most of the class did know of William Allen White and that a speaker cannot possibly anticipate the knowledge of every member of his audience. Still another said that they were more apt to listen to Kennie, the boy giving the speech, talk on this subject, because he had served as assistant editor on the school paper and because he intended to become a newspaper man.

After this discussion, the students entered in their notebooks the purposes of the introduction and the various techniques of introducing a topic.

Concluding the Speech

You indicate that the conclusion must leave the audience favorably disposed to the speaker and to his subject and purpose and that it must focus the attention of the listeners on the ideas and feelings that the speaker wishes them to remember.

At the beginning of the discussion of conclusions, most teachers find that their students think of the conclusion primarily as summarizing the main ideas in the speech. Students do not realize that the conclusion must emphasize the central idea and must secure favorable reaction to it. You will, therefore, stress these purposes of the conclusion and indicate that a final example, illustration, anecdote, or quotation are effective provided that they do emphasize the essential idea and do secure favorable reaction to it.

Here too teachers frequently analyze the speeches of well-known orators or of their students. When the conclusions belong to speeches which the students have already studied or heard, the purpose of conclusions become clearer. For example, the conclusion to the speech on the Bar Mitzvah Ceremony was:

> This last Sabbath was an exciting, momentous day of Jack's life—the day when he became a man.
> Jack is now a part of his ancient ancestral heritage which he will always maintain.

Students pointed out that this conclusion, which was related to the introduction, did emphasize the essential idea and did secure a favorable reaction to it.

Developing Ideas

Whether the student is to explain, prove, or make entertaining or stimulating his main idea, he must support it. For support, he uses such aids as statistics, example, authority, definition, illustration, stories, personal experiences, visual aids, comparison, and contrast. The high school student must be taught to use these aids, for he too frequently believes that making generalized statements, giving two or three details, or stating a single example develops his main idea adequately. You must help your students to develop their ideas more completely.

One teacher asks her students to watch two half-hour news programs on television and to look for means used to develop news items. In the discussion that follows, students point to the use of various techniques. For example, the weather girl uses a visual aid, a map, to help her explain weather, because the complexity of weather prediction becomes simpler through its use. After the announcement of the reopening of the Geneva Conference, an authority on foreign affairs is quoted as stating that the resumption of the Geneva Conference indicates some measure of success in furthering peace. Or the reporter elaborates on the strange story of a woman kidnapper. Or he shows examples of the waste of water in the opening of too many fire hydrants on a hot day. Many of the means of development are present in broadcasts of news.

Another way of teaching the developing of ideas is to show ways of supporting a main idea such as "Central high school has varied offerings in its extracurricular program." You may explain the general nature of the talk, list on the board the means of development, and then ask the students to indicate how each can be used. Students point out the use of such support as statistics in giving the number of students in the various activities, definition in using words like *workshop* as applied to the drama and radio work, comparison in showing similarities and differences of extracurricular work in their schools and neighboring ones, and authority in stating the principal's philosophy of extracurricular education.

This teaching may be part of a larger project. After members of the class have talked about ways of developing ideas and have completed an outline, one member may deliver the speech on the extracurricular activities of Central High School. The class may then wish to tape it to send to a public speaking class in another section of the country who will then return the tape with an explanation of its extracurricular activities.

Still another method of teaching the development of ideas is through an analysis of well-known speeches. By using *Vital Speeches* or speeches in *The New York Times*, a teacher can find a paragraph or two to exemplify each means of development. The students then list the means of development in their notebooks, adding the definitions which they themselves have devised.

You may either give assignments on developing ideas or you may expect your students to apply the knowledge in the speeches which they are to give. Some teachers ask their students to prepare and give short speeches using means of developing ideas like charts, maps or models, or statistics. For instance, they ask that students explain a weather map or show with a diagram the percentage of students in the school in the various curricula. Or they suggest that students use a quotation in a speech; one teacher saves the "Outstanding Quotations" given in *The New York Times* each day and then assigns these to particular students to use in making a speech. Or teachers have their students make a speech in which the students give three examples pointing to a main idea. As such procedures are time-consuming, many teachers think that the application of the theory of support can better be incorporated in speeches centered around topics in which the students are vitally interested.

PRINCIPLES OF COMPOSITION

You encourage your students to prepare their speeches in such a way that they will be unified, coherent, and concrete. Here again you frequently reinforce the teaching of the English instructor. You may well find out how the English instructor has taught unity, coherence, and concreteness; at times you repeat what he has taught for emphasis.

Students must know that a clear statement of the main idea and a good outline are prerequisites for unity. You can teach them to check their main ideas and their outlines just as they check a mathematical problem. In checking they make sure that every idea directly or indirectly supports the main idea. If they are not reminded to check their supporting ideas, many students tend to ramble or to bring in extraneous matter.

By requiring clear outlines, you help your students to make their speeches coherent, for the outlines should reveal plainly the relation of each part of the speech to every other part. To achieve coherence, your student speakers must, in addition, make the transitions between the sequence of thought clear. You may ask your students what words they use to show transitions in English composition. They usually suggest words like *next, to continue, to conclude, again,* and *an example is.* Frequently they volunteer that the

English teacher suggests that transitions should refer back and look ahead and not merely string ideas together. You advise students to avoid *well, now* and *and*.

Similarly you re-emphasize the English teacher's demand for concreteness. You may show the value of concreteness by reading to your students speeches such as Thomas Dewey's *The ABC of Racketeering*. Students listen to this speech deeply enthralled. When they give their reasons for their interest, they almost inevitably include among them that the speech described racketeers in considerable detail. The need to be concrete must be called to the attention of students often.

MAKING THE SPEECH INTERESTING

Many high school teachers use advertisements, either those found in magazines or those given over television or radio, to show how the writers and artists have interested their audiences. When you do, however, you must make sure that the advertisements cover both general interests such as the novel and the familiar and human interests such as prestige and preservation of life and health.

One teacher showed advertisements representing varied human interests. For example, one booklet contained the statement, "Get your polio shot now." The students indicated that most of us want to live and that we have a fear of contracting polio. The teacher then held up a picture of a man and a boy—an appeal for funds for Big Brother Week. The caption was, "No man ever stands as straight as when he stoops to help a boy." Youngsters quickly discerned this appeal to pride. Another advertisement, a Samsonite Silhouette, pictured a lavish hotel, a bell boy, and a well-dressed man and woman. Students noted that this appeal was to the satisfaction of prestige. A picture of a beautiful banana pie with the wording, "Help yourself—Eatabanana," brought sighs and "It's too near lunch time." An Arthur Murray dance advertisement appealed to the desire of all for popularity. The picture of a little girl, quite sad, saying, "I wish Grandma would call today," called for sympathy. A Fieldcrest advertisement indicating the bed with "the withdrawing personality" aroused curiosity. A picture of a mother in a decidedly disordered kitchen with three youngsters demanding attention bore the caption, "You need an extra phone," and brought smiles to the faces of the members of the class.

As an assignment, the teacher asked each member of the class to indicate how he could use two of the appeals in a speech which he planned to give.

DELIVERY

Methods of Delivering Speeches

Students may memorize their speeches, read them aloud, give them impromptu, or deliver them extemporaneously. Although most teachers place major emphasis on extemporaneous delivery, students do sometimes give declamations, read their speeches aloud, or make an impromptu speech. When a student memorizes a speech, you make sure that he recreates the ideas as he utters them. Such training is of value in teaching the student techniques of oral delivery. A similar value lies in having the student read a speech: he learns the techniques of reading aloud. In giving memorized speeches or in reading speeches, students use exact language. On the contrary, in impromptu speeches, they speak as they think. Occasions often arise when students must speak briefly without preparation; answering questions in class falls into this category. Here the problem of organizing their thoughts and following a specific plan is particularly important.

In a public speaking class students will, however, usually make extemporaneous speeches in which they think their thoughts, find the words, and make them into phrases and sentences as they talk. Their language comes with their utterance. They do, however, make very definite preparation, for they know the content of their outlines thoroughly, and they have planned their transitions. They should go over their speeches as many as ten to fifteen times. Admittedly some of the phrases and some of the sentences will become fixed; the student speaker, however, has not consciously memorized them although he is aware of their repetition. He recreates his thoughts each time he speaks.

Bases for Good Delivery

There are two basic requirements for good delivery:

1. The speaker has a vivid realization of the ideas and their meaning as he is uttering them.
2. He has a lively sense of communication with his listeners as he is speaking.[5]

You may compare speaking in public to speaking in conversation. You explain that as your students converse with their friends, they get an idea and put it into words. Their pitch and stress patterns, their rate of speed, their vocal quality all help to interpret their thought. Their speaking is spontaneous, and their listeners are listening not to the way they are speaking but to what they are saying. The listeners understand what they are saying. You emphasize that this same vivid realization of the idea at the moment of utterance that usually occurs in conversation should be an aspect of good delivery of a speech.

How can you help your students to attain this vivid realization of the idea at the moment of utterance? You must make sure that they know their material thoroughly and that they have a real interest in it. This understanding and interest depends to a large extent on the choice of a topic. As was indicated in earlier sections in this chapter, the teacher's responsibility is to see that the student selects and develops a topic so that he will enjoy sharing his ideas with his audience and that the audience in turn will respond to them. Beyond this care in selecting and developing a topic, the student should rehearse his speech often enough to be sure of the content, and he must keep his mind constantly on the full meaning of what he is saying.

A lively sense of communication means an awareness that the listeners are reacting to the speaker, that there is an interplay of thought and feeling. This reaction is often evident in smiles, nods of the head, an intense moving forward to catch the next word, or expressions of annoyance at an interruption. Some student speakers achieve this lively sense of communication easily and readily; in fact, some of them tend to substitute it for content. For those, however, who do not have it, experience before the group with attention to some of the details that help communication promotes better interaction with the audience.

What are these details? The student who walks to the platform

[5] See J. A. Winans, *Speech-Making* (New York, Appleton-Century Crofts, Inc., 1938), pp. 11-40.

indirectly and slowly with a slouched body almost says, "Why listen to me?" whereas the student who walks there directly with his body alert says, "I'm worth listening to." Students quickly recognize that this second type of behavior is appropriate to the speaker before a group.

Similarly the student who speaks to the acorn on the oak tree outside his classroom window is not likely to get a response from it or from his classmates. Somehow you must convince the student that keeping his eyes on his audience makes it easier for him to speak to them. You may point out that he does look at his listeners in conversation. After the student has once kept his eye contact with his audience, he usually will not revert to fixing on the acorn in the oak tree. Sometimes telling him to use the style of direct address or to name students in the class in his speech will help him build his contact with his audience. When necessary, the teacher may quietly say, "Look at us, John." This is one of the few times when an interruption of a speech is justified. In some instances the teacher may need to point out that the student is merely glancing at his listeners rather than directing his attention to them to get a real response.

Lastly, a student must learn that his customary posture and movements are not always appropriate on the platform. He must eliminate any mannerisms which, like bad articulation, call attention to themselves. In addition, he must stand comfortably erect with his feet not too far apart and with his balance in weight placed equally on both feet. Until he is ready to use them to help in communication, the best place for his arms and hands is at his sides. By his bodily stance and movement, he should show that he wants his audience to listen.

EVALUATION

Evaluation of public speaking activities is complex, for you are measuring many different abilities: to chose a topic, to do research, to organize a speech, to recognize the organization in others' speeches, to compose a speech, to make it interesting, to select supporting materials appropriate for the audience, to deliver it, and to listen to other speeches. Teachers employ many ways of measuring achievement in these areas: short-answer questions, essay questions, evaluation of written materials handed in for various assignments, oral and written answers to questions, evaluation sheets, and oral and written critical reviews of speech performances.

Written Tests

The short-answer question is used frequently to test understanding of the theory of a public speaking course. Knowledge of such content as criteria in selecting a topic, in judging opinion, in detecting fallacious reasoning, kinds of appeals, and types of support are readily examined by this method. On the other hand, ability to organize or to recognize the pattern for organization in the speeches of others is best tested through essay questions. Frequently, however, teachers scramble an outline, requiring that students arrange its parts in the best sequential order. Or they present the students with a mimeographed speech asking them to give the main idea and the supporting ideas of the speech. In addition, they may base questions for testing understanding of such theory as kinds of support, means of interesting the audience, type of introduction and conclusion, and the purpose of the speaking on the same mimeographed speech.

Written Assignments

Second, you use written assignments on research and on outlining both for diagnosing students' difficulties and for evaluating their understanding of these areas. You examine the students' bibliographies and the notes which they have taken. As a result, you make suggestions to some students for more authoritative bibliographies and for more competent note-taking. Furthermore, since a student's outline gives you insight into his ability to organize, you advise him on how to outline his material more appropriately. Admittedly such evaluation is time-consuming but it does bring worthwhile results.

Questions and Evaluation Sheets

Third, you want to make sure that your students are learning to listen intelligently. When they know that they are to be held responsible for what is said, they are more likely to listen with care. Moreover they can be taught to listen purposefully. For example, one time you and the speaker may ask questions about the main idea of the speech and about the supporting material; another time, you may query the students on the worth of the ideas in the speech. Or you ask students to write answers to specific questions. Or you prepare an evaluation sheet which can also be used as a base for a critical review of the speech. Students respond to the items on this sheet.

The evaluation sheet helps the new teacher to keep specific items in mind and gives direction to students' critical analyses of speeches. Admittedly, the experienced teacher can do as well with or without it. The chapter on evaluation contains a sample sheet for the in-formative speech.

Critical Review

The criticism based on the evaluation sheet or on certain prede-termined items is given after each speech or after a group of speeches. Sometimes it is written; sometimes it is given orally. One teacher uses a carbon on a note pad; she retains the original for her record and gives the copy to the student.

Since students learn from the criticism of speeches by other people, you do well to discuss the assets and liabilities of many speeches. Bryant and Wallace[6] suggest that impromptu speeches can lay the foundation for good criticism. They give a series of patterns for evaluating subject matter, information and choice of ideas, delivery, speech organization, and interest devices that could be used to advantage in a high school class.

You and your students should stress the positive rather than the negative aspects of criticism. To stress the positive aspects of criti-cism, one teacher tries to have her good speakers speak first on the initial speaking assignment. Hypothesizing which students will be the better speakers, she calls on them first. She has found that she is usually able to pick out the better speakers and that the less able speakers profit from the positive criticism given those who speak well.

When your students know that you accept them as they are, that you recognize their worth, that you are sincerely interested in them, their ideas, and their progress, they are then glad to accept your counsel. Furthermore, such an attitude on your part sets an example

[6] D. C. Bryant and K. R. Wallace, *Oral Communication* (New York, Appleton-Century-Crofts, Inc., 1954), p. 151.

for the attitudes of the members of the group. With this positive social climate, criticisms in the class can be penetrating and helpful. Consequently students make constructive use of the criticism given. They themselves have a sense of achievement as they improve and the other members of the class are proud of the achievement.

SUGGESTED READING

BAIRD, A. C., *General Speech* (New York, McGraw-Hill Book Co., 1949). Focuses on fundamental speech principles and techniques from viewpoint of social adaptation. Covers the speaker, his delivery, speech content, structure, oral interpretation, voice and articulation improvement.

BRIGANCE, W. N., *Speech: Its Techniques and Disciplines in a Free Society,* 2nd ed. (New York, Appleton-Century-Crofts, Inc., 1961). Includes getting started, the audience, the speech, the speaker, occasions and forms, and dynamic persuasion in an industrial democracy.

————, *Speech Communication: A Brief Textbook,* 2nd ed. (New York, Appleton-Century-Crofts, Inc., 1955). Emphasizes clarity in organization and language. Contains material on delivery, voice and diction, group discussion, persuasion, listening, organization and radio-television techniques.

BRYANT, D. C., and WALLACE, K. R., *Oral Communication: A Short Course in Speaking,* 2nd ed. (New York, Appleton-Century-Crofts, Inc., 1954). Emphasizes the practical aspects of public speaking and group discussion. Includes chapters on basic processes, stage fright, subjects, materials, organization, development, delivery, use of voice, persuasion, language, occasional speaking, group discussion, and parliamentary procedure.

CARLILE, C. S., *Brief Project Text for Public Speaking* (New York, Harper & Brothers, 1957), Contains 38 excellent speaking projects. Stresses the act of speaking, the use of reliable source materials, and the use of the complete sentence outline. Assignments are organized according to the nature of the assignment, possible topics for speeches, how to pick a topic, how to prepare a speech, and how to present a speech.

CHASE, S., *Guides to Straight Thinking* (New York, Harper & Brothers, 1956). Focuses on commonplace applications of logic. Contains a readable discussion of "13 common fallacies." Explains logic in an informal and easily understood way by giving many examples.

CROCKER, L., *Public Speaking for College Students,* 3rd ed. (New York, American Book Company, 1954). Contains four sections: the speaker, the speech, the audience, and the occasion. Includes many illustrations which your class will enjoy.

CROMWELL, H., and MONROE, A. H., *Working for More, Effective Speech* (Chicago, Scott, Foresman & Company, 1955). Designed to be used with Monroe's *Principles and Types of Speech*. Contains a series of projects in such areas as improving delivery, understanding the audience, listening, types of speeches, and group discussion.

DICKENS, M., *Speech: Dynamic Communication* (New York, Harcourt, Brace & Co., 1954). Conceives of a public speaking course as a dynamic process of communication between speaker and listener.

Dow, C. W., "Teaching Listening Comprehension of High School Seniors and College Freshmen." *The Speech Teacher,* IV (November, 1955), 239-246. Contains a listening test which a teacher might well administer to his students. Scores cannot be considered standardized since the sampling was limited to one high school and to college preparatory students only.

EHRENSBERGER, R., and PAGEL, E., *Notebook for Public Speaking,* 2nd ed. (Englewood Cliffs, N. J., Prentice-Hall, Inc., 1956). Outlines materials of public speaking. Provides space for notes, outlines of speeches, instructor's criticism, and outside listening reports.

FESSENDEN, S. A., *Designed for Listening—A Speaker-Listener Workbook* (Dubuque, Iowa, William C. Brown Co., 1951). Gives primary attention to listening proficiency. Guides students through group activity speaking, socio-drama, oral reading, and public speaking.

FESSENDEN, S. A., and THOMPSON, W. N. *Basic Experiences in Speech* (Englewood Cliffs, N. J., Prentice-Hall, Inc., 1958). Stresses activities approach. Material is presented in a functional setting.

GILMAN, W. E., ALY, B., and REID, L. R., *Fundamentals of Speaking* (New York, The Macmillan Co., 1951). Includes sections on the speech, the speaker, the purpose, the audience, and the occasion. Gives a comprehensive, complete, and thorough treatment of all phases of public speaking. Excellent chapters on analyzing and organizing material and purposes of speaking.

GRAY, G. W., and BRADEN, W., *Public Speaking Principles and Practices* (New York, Harper & Brothers, 1951). Gives techniques of public speaking from point of view of today's world.

HALLADAY, L. S., *Making Speeches: Necessary Information and Activity Workbook for Beginners* (Minneapolis, Burgess Publishing Co., 1955) A workbook designed for high school and junior high school classes of speech. Contains four sections: aims of speech, parts of speech, kinds of speeches, and speech activities for beginners. Emphasizes content and organization. Includes work and criticism sheets for each suggested speech and numerous written exercises. The teacher will probably not want to use this as a text but will find many practical suggestions within it.

Hance, K., ed., "Public Address in the Secondary School," *The Bulletin of the National Association of Secondary School Principals*, 36 (May, 1952). Contains a section on the philosophy of public speaking, one on types of experiences in public speaking, discussion and debate, and a third on listening, extracurricular activities, and experimental studies on debate, discussion, and public speaking.

McBurney, J. H., and Wrage, E. J., *The Art of Good Speech* (Englewood Cliffs, N. J., Prentice-Hall, 1953). Includes three parts. Part I and II deal with the speaker as a person and with voice and delivery. Part III deals with exercises in discussion, debate, occasional speaking, and radio and television speaking.

———, *Guide to Good Speech* (Englewood Cliffs, N. J., Prentice-Hall, Inc., 1955). States principles of good speech in a shorter, more precise form than *The Art of Good Speech*.

Mersand, J., "Developing Competence in Listening in Secondary Schools, *The Speech Teacher*, VII (November, 1958), 288-301. Reviews a large portion of the printed material on listening. Tells how to achieve the various purposes of listening.

Monroe, A. H., *Principles of Speech*, brief rev. ed. (Chicago, Scott, Foresman and Company, 1958). Contains an excellent chapter on listening.

Nichols, R. G., and Stevens, L. A., *Are You Listening?* (New York, McGraw-Hill Book Co., 1957). Explains the need for teaching listening and the benefits of effective listening. Gives suggestions on how to teach listening.

Oliver, R. T., Dickey, D. C., and Zelko, H. P., *Communicative Speech*, rev. ed. (New York, The Dryden Press, Inc., 1955). Contains three sections. The first two deal with standards, delivery problems, listening, finding materials, purpose, organization. The second deals with informative, persuasive, and entertaining speeches, discussion, parliamentary procedure, conferences, and interviews.

Powers, G. D., *Fundamentals of Speech* (New York, McGraw-Hill Book Co., 1951). Emphasizes social, semantic, vocal, and phonetic training in public speaking, discussion, and speech arts.

Robinson, E. R., "What Can the Speech Teacher Do About Students' Stage Fright," *The Speech Teacher*, VIII (January, 1959), 8-14. Stresses that a feeling of anticipation is a natural and desirable state, that the appearance of confidence and poise, regardless of inner tensions can be readily acquired, and that confidence in itself is no substitute for good preparation and practice.

ROBINSON, K. F., "Teaching Listening Through Evaluation and Criticism," *The Speech Teacher,* II (September, 1953), 178-180. Tells how to teach listening for these purposes: for recognition and discrimination, for information, for pleasure and entertainment, for criticism or evaluation of ideas, and for appreciation.

SOPER, P., *Basic Public Speaking,* 2nd ed. (New York, Oxford University Press, 1956). Stresses composition of speeches. Treats informative and persuasive speaking well.

THOMPSON, W., *Fundamentals of Communication: An Integrated Approach,* (New York, McGraw-Hill Book Co., 1957). Includes material for a college freshman course in general communication. Contains information on choice of topic, selection of material, source of ideas, development of topics, analysis of reader and listener and forms of discourse, research papers, and written usage.

THONSSEN, L., and GILKINSON, H., *Basic Training in Speech,* 2nd ed. (Boston, D. C. Heath & Company, 1953). Includes units on nature and importance of speaking, basic skills, speech composition, forms of speaking, and research in speaking.

WEAVER, A. T., and NESS, O. G., *An Introduction to Public Speaking* (New York, The Odyssey Press, Inc., 1961). Gives basic materials on public speaking. Excellent explanations and illustrations.

————, *The Fundamentals and Forms of Speech* (New York, The Odyssey Press, Inc., 1957). Contains two sections dealing with (1) fundamentals of speech which include particularly good chapters on listening and stage fright and (2) the forms of speech including public address.

COLLECTIONS OF SPEECHES

BAIRD, A. C., ed., *American Public Addresses* (New York, McGraw-Hill Book Co., 1956). Includes texts of 38 speeches by 26 outstanding speakers. Some of the speakers are Jonathan Edwards, Patrick Henry, Webster, Lincoln, Emerson, Henry W. Grady, Samuel Gompers, Franklin Delano and Theodore Roosevelt, Harry Emerson Fosdick, Eisenhower, and Stevenson. Provides short biographical notes for each speaker and an introductory statement for each speech.

————, *Representative American Speeches* (New York, H. W. Wilson Co., Published each year). Gives excellent brief introductions to each speech. Contains biographical notes of speakers.

COPELAND, L., and LAMM L., eds., *The World's Great Speeches,* 2nd ed. (New York, Dover Publications, 1958, paperback). Contains 255 speeches of which 114 are abridgements.

HARDING, H. F., ed., *The Age of Danger: Major Speeches on American Problems* (New York, Random House, 1952). Contains over sixty addresses. Classified under "The World Outlook in the Atomic Age," "The United States and Foreign Affairs," and "The United States and Home Affairs." Orators include Churchill, Toynbee, Acheson, Truman, Dulles, Eisenhower, Hutchins, Conant, and Bunche.

PARRISH, W. M. and HOCHMUTH, M., *American Speeches,* (New York, Longmans, Green, & Co., Inc., 1954). Contains 28 speeches by 17 American speakers including Jonathan Edwards, Patrick Henry, Jefferson, Emerson, Henry W. Grady, William Jennings Bryan, Woodrow Wilson, Webster, Franklin Delano Roosevelt, and Lincoln. Each speech is prefaced by biographical information, comments on the occasion and the speaker.

Vital Speeches (New York City, City News Publishing Company, published twenty-four times a year). Contains outstanding speeches made during the publishing period.

AUDIO-VISUAL AIDS

Better Choice of Words (Coronet, 1952, sound, black and white, color, 10 minutes). Shows how a group of high school students improved their vocabularies. Gives examples of overworked words. The group studied how to choose the best words for the occasion, purpose, and the audience.

Better Use of Words, Paul Wendt, ed. (Coronet, sound, black and white, 20 minutes). Shows high school students' need for effective expression in various situations.

Build Your Vocabulary (Coronet, 1948, sound, black and white, color, 10 minutes). Indicates how students can build workable vocabularies and discourages them from using ineffective words.

Find the Information (Coronet, 1948, sound, black and white, 10 minutes). Covers the basic types of library research.

Fundamentals of Public Speaking (Coronet, 1950, sound, black and white, color, 11 minutes). Shows the need for public speaking in real-life situations. Offers suggestions for the selection and arrangement of material and for delivery.

How to Give and Take Instructions (Coronet, 1953, sound, black and white, color, 10 minutes). Gives the steps of giving and taking instructions.

How to Judge Facts (Coronet, 1948, sound, black and white, color, 10 minutes). Emphasizes need to look for irrelevant facts, wrong analogies, and false assumptions. Based on a high school reporter's "hot scoop" about the principal.

How to Prepare a Class Report (Coronet, 1953, sound, black and white, color, 11 minutes). Tells how to supplement personal experience by library research, interviews, and observations and how to organize materials for a specific audience.

Learn to Argue Effectively (Coronet, 1951, sound, black and white, color, 11 minutes). Tells when to argue and how to present sound arguments. Story of Jeff who learns to test arguments and the fundamental rules for argument in everyday life.

Let's Pronounce Well (Coronet, sound, black and white, 11 minutes). Emphasizes sense of communication with listener. Junior high school level.

Look it up! Dictionary Habits (Coronet, sound, black and white, 10 minutes). Shows high school students' need for effective expression in and speak.

Making Yourself Understood (Encyclopedia Britannica Films, 1954, sound, black and white, 14 minutes). Introduces the listener to the field of communication. Shows the need for communication in all facets of life and discusses it in terms of medium, content, listener and response sought.

Speech: Planning Your Talk, E. C. Buehler, technical supervisor (Young America Films, 1949, sound, black and white, 11 minutes). Explains the fundamentals of planning and organizing a speech. Shows how to plan an introduction, to tell the listeners why the topic is important, to organize the speech around a main idea in a logical manner, to get down to facts, examples, and reasons and finally to conclude the speech.

Speech: Stage Fright and What to Do About It (Young America Films, 1949, sound, black and white, 11 minutes). Tells the story of a young man who has faced the problem of stage fright and how he solved the problem. Gives five steps in the control of stage fright.

Watch That Quotation (Coronet, 1949, sound, black and white, color, 10 minutes). Opens with students playing the game "whispering." Goes on to consider how inaccurate quoting can result in misunderstanding.

EXERCISES

1. Read the section on teaching organization for composition in a book that deals with methods of teaching English. Indicate what part of this teaching you can use in teaching organization in speaking.
2. Find five speeches which could be used to illustrate particular points for a high school group. Justify your selection in terms of the particular point and the probable interests of the adolescent student.

3. In your methods class, demonstrate how you would teach sentence outlining.
4. Devise an evaluation chart for a persuasive speech.
5. Find ten advertisements which you could use to show different appeals.
6. Preview a public-speaking film. Indicate how you can use the film in your teaching.
7. Compare the advice given about delivery in Aristotle's *Rhetoric,* in Cicero's *de Oratore,* and in a high school text.

6

Parliamentary
Procedure

MANY HIGH SCHOOL students believe that parliamentary procedure adds to the confusion of a meeting and that it consists of a bag of tricks. They are quick to say that the motions become entangled and that people use parliamentary procedure for their own ends. When they express these attitudes, you show them the values of parliamentary procedure.

VALUES

You demonstrate to your students that the rules of parliamentary procedure are logical and that they apply common sense to getting business transacted easily and quickly. The rules do not hinder but rather expedite business. You point out that since all argument pertains to the motion on the floor, only one subject is taken up at a time. If a member does introduce extraneous matter, he is ruled out of order. Because the members attack one subject at a time, they organize their thinking around one topic. Such orderliness of procedure aids them in getting their business done efficiently and expeditiously.

Second, you make clear that parliamentary procedure provides for the full and democratic expression of opinions of every member of the group. Advocates of both sides have a chance to make their arguments known. They can debate until they have exhausted their ideas or until two thirds of the assemblage calls a halt. Furthermore, by arguing for and against the motion and by the use of subsidiary and incidental motions, the minority makes its voice felt. Frequently compromises in the form of amendments to the main motion are effected. But the majority rules and votes for what it feels is best. This procedure is the essence of democracy.

AIMS

The aims of parliamentary procedure provide for the attainment of certain understandings, attitudes, and skills.

Understandings
   Ways of organizing a body for managing its business
   Writing a constitution
   Election of officers
   Order of business
   Types of motions
   Precedence

Attitudes
   Respect for the right of the majority to rule
   Respect for the right of the minority to make itself felt
   Respect for the right of all to be heard
   Acceptance of the importance of compromise

Skills
   Ability to conduct a parliamentary meeting effectively
   Ability to participate in a parliamentary meeting successfully
   Ability to take minutes
   Ability to give reports of a committee or an officer

CONTENT

To accomplish these aims you may include such content as the following:

Procedure for Organizing a Group
   Accomplishments of First Meeting
   Election of Officers
   Drafting of Constitution

Duties of Officers
  President
  Vice-President
  Secretary
  Treasurer
Methods of Voting

Order of Business

Presentation of a Motion
  Gaining Recognition
  Proposing a Motion
  Seconding a Motion

Kinds of Motions and their Precedence
  Privileged
  Subsidiary
  Renewal
  Main

GENERAL PROCEDURES

You may approach the teaching of parliamentary procedure in two ways, either directly or by organizing your class into a club which conducts its affairs according to the rules of parliamentary procedure.

Teaching Parliamentary Procedure Directly

When you teach parliamentary procedure directly, you present the theory and then put it systematically to work in the classroom. For example, you may ask all your students to prepare a constitution for a mythical organization, to participate in a series of hypothetical meetings, and to prepare minutes of these meetings. Frequently you use nonsense motions to give practice in presenting and recording many different motions. Some teachers start with just a few motions, then add more until they have included all of them.

Organizing Your Class into a Club

On the other hand, when you organize your class as a club, the learning is gradual and based on the needs of the group in conducting its business. In successive meetings the boys and girls learn more and more of the forms. When parliamentary procedure is taught in this way, many teachers feel that its effects are more lasting than when a unit of two or three weeks is included in the course. Many others, however, believe that they teach parliamentary procedure in a more orderly and thorough fashion by the direct method.

In both instances your role is one of a teaching parliamentarian. You make sure that your students make no errors in parliamentary law, that they use all its forms correctly, and that they employ the different kinds of motions when they need them.

ORGANIZATION OF THE GROUP

In the direct teaching of parliamentary procedure you call the meeting of the class to order and preside until a chairman is elected. At this time you teach your students how to nominate and elect officers. After the newly elected chairman has taken over, the other officers are elected. You point out the duties of each of them. Then the chairman chooses or the group elects a committee to draft the constitution. The constitution is presented to the class whose members probably accept some sections, reject others, and make changes in still others. After the committee has revised it according to the dictates of the class, the teacher may mimeograph it so that students have a copy for future reference.

A similar organization occurs when your class is an actual parliamentary body. You usually ask, however, that opportunities be provided to allow different members of the class to serve as chairman and secretaries during the term. Under the leadership of the various chairmen the members of the group carry on the business of the class. For example, they plan with you the units of learning and the activities of the group such as taking trips, viewing films, giving committee reports, preparing bulletin boards, and arranging exhibits of books, materials, and equipment. As a guide for this teacher-student management, you and your students write a constitution. In this process students learn not only how to write a constitution but they also become aware of the purposes of the class, the respective responsibilities of the students and the teacher, and the rules applicable to running the group.

DUTIES OF OFFICERS

Again students learn through your teaching and through practice the duties of the various officers. For instance, you prepare the President for being responsible for the order of the group and for being an impartial judge. This preparation frequently involves conferences outside of class. While he presides over the group, others learn from watching him.

Whereas you may teach one individual at a time to preside, you may teach all the members of your group to take minutes accurately. One teacher gives her students this form:

Suggested Form for Taking Notes for Minutes

DATE: 2-26-59   TIME WHEN MEETING WAS CALLED TO ORDER: 2:05

PLACE: Room 301.   TIME OF ADJOURNMENT: 2:50

PRESIDING OFFICER: Helene.

MINUTES: Accepted as read.

REPORTS:
Officers: John asked that all members pay this week's dues.

Committees: Mary reported for the theater-going committee that arrangements with the theater were made to see *J.B.*, Thursday matinee. May 14, 1959 and that the Assistant to the Principal approved the outing.

UNFINISHED BUSINESS: None.

NEW BUSINESS:
Class to go to see Kings College play, *Prometheus Bound.* (Jay) Carried.

Amend—strike out *Prometheus Bound,* insert *Pygmalion.* (Frank) Carried.

Lay on table. (Helen) Lost.

Class to do bulletin board to show settings and costumes of *J. B.* (Irving)

Refer to a committee ·to be appointed by teacher to report next Thursday. (Helen) Carried.

Appointed: Frank, Marvin, Joan.

PROGRAM:

Group pantomimes and their evaluation. (Program attached.)

ANNOUNCEMENTS:

The teacher announced that the members of the class were invited to the lighting rehearsal for *Prometheus Bound* on March 2nd at the College Auditorium.

She also asked the members of the class to read Chapter 12 in the text and to write the answers to the questions listed on the mimeographed sheet.

The teacher then asks four or five different students to take secretary's notes on the board. From these notes the group writes the minutes.

In cases where the class is run as a club the minutes serve as a record of what has happened during the semester, for the secretary records what occurs daily. The following is an example of such minutes prepared by a member of a high school class.

Minutes of Drama 43 XH

March 10, 1959

Jane called the regular meeting of Drama 43XH to order at 2:05 P.M. in Room 308. Those absent were Kay and John.

The minutes of March 9th were read and approved.

Mrs. Kirchman gave out consent slips for our parents to sign to permit us to go to see *J.B.* She also gave out reduction rate tickets for *The Disenchanted, West Side Story,* and *The Cold Wind and the Warm.*

Helene moved that the class accept March 22nd as a date to see the college production of *The Importance of Being Earnest.* Seconded and carried.

Jane announced that since there was no more business, we would begin the program of the day, a discussion of *An Enemy of the People* which we saw on Sunday. The discussion included the following:

The Press: Can it be bought? According to the play, it can.

Truth: Does a man who stands for truth stand alone? This question we found difficult to answer but most of the members of the class think that he does stand alone.

Moderation: This word suggests a character who is afraid and is always trying to please those in authority. He will not go against anyone or anything. We discussed whether Nasser comes under this category.

Majority: The majority is not always right. Ibsen makes this point emphatically. A compact majority is an unthinking one which follows power and authority indiscriminately.

Liberal: Ibsen shows that a liberal wants radical changes as long as they do not affect him.

At this point Mrs. Kirchman asked a very thought-provoking question as to whether or not we knew someone who would be as courageous as Dr. Stockman. One student answered, "President Roosevelt." But members of the class pointed out that he did not have to make the sacrifices that Dr. Stockman did. Other students told briefly the stories of neighbors and friends who are heroes in their own less spectacular ways.

Mrs. Kirchman gave us our assignment: to write a study of a character in the play we are studying. We are to include the character's background, motivation, the author's attitude toward him, the character's appearance, and his personality. We are to suggest acting techniques which will help us to portray this character.

The meeting was adjourned at 2:45 p. m.

Respectfully submitted,
Paula Winkler.[1]

Some teachers give out mimeographed sheets containing information on the order of business. It includes material on calling the meeting to order, acceptance of minutes, giving reports, introducing business, putting the question, requesting information, rising to a point of order, and adjourning. Other teachers teach the order of business as a mock or real meeting progresses. In either case, students actually learn to run a meeting through participation in one.

MOTIONS

You will teach your students the various kinds of motions. Normally you teach main, subsidiary, incidental, and privileged. One high school teacher, however, found that the addition of *renewal motions*[2] made the types of motions dealing with renewal of business easier for high school students to understand.

One way to teach the kinds of motions is to ask students for a

[1] Paula Winkler, Drama 43XH, Teacher, Mrs. Rose Kirchman, Chairman Speech Department, Jamaica High School, Jamaica, New York.

[2] This term is used by W. Gilman, B. Aly, and L. Reid in *The Fundamentals of Speaking* (New York, The Macmillan Co., 1951), p. 565.

definition of the word that represents the type of motion and then relate the definition to the purpose of the motion. A second way is to teach a particular motion as the need for it arises. When the students have acquired knowledge about a considerable number of the motions, the teacher then categorizes them.

Teachers usually try to show students that the precedence of motions and the answers to other parliamentary questions make sense. They may place on the blackboard four or five motions and without studying the table, students decide which should have first, second, third, and last priority. They also decide which motions can be amended, which are debatable, which need two-thirds votes to pass, and which may be introduced while another has the floor. They find that such decisions are logical.

Nonsense motions are frequently used as a means to teaching parliamentary procedure. The teacher may structure this teaching by asking one student to amend, another to amend the amendment, another to refer the motion to a committee, another to reconsider, and still another to limit debate. On the other hand, some teachers prefer to conduct their class like an assembly. Students elect a chairman, present resolutions to various committees who discuss them and who finally present them to the group often in a modified form. The resolutions are then changed through amendment and finally are accepted or defeated. As the need arises, various motions are introduced. When the resolutions have to do with matters important to the students, this procedure has real value and carries decided interest with it. One class dealt with resolutions concerning cheating, scheduling of examinations, providing trips of educational value to students, and inaugurating a high school summer session. The final resolutions as passed were sent to the Administrative Council of the High School the members of which did consider the suggestions of the class seriously.

In such instances as this students learn the basic procedures of parliamentary procedure and prepare for arriving at a clear-cut decision on a controversial problem. Through this activity they have been taught to formulate the proposal as a resolution and to test it by vote. They have also found out how to modify and change the proposal so that it may be acceptable to all. They discover that when the prosposal is clearly acceptable to some and unacceptable to others, parliamentary procedure makes a decision with majority and minority opinions feasible.

SUGGESTED READING

Auer, J. J., *Essentials of Parliamentary Procedure,* 3rd ed. (New York, Appleton-Century-Crofts, Inc. 1959). Includes in abbreviated form the rules of parliamentary procedure.

Bridge, L. W., *The Funk and Wagnalls Book of Parliamentary Procedure* (New York, Funk & Wagnalls Co., 1954). Systematically presents the rules of order. Contains six model meetings.

Gilman, W., Aly, B., and Reid, L., *The Fundamentals of Speaking* (New York, The Macmillan Co., 1951), Ch. 27. Explains parliamentary law in simple clear terms.

Mason, P., *Mason's Manual of Legislative Procedure* (New York, McGraw-Hill Book Co., 1953). Contains parliamentary procedure for legislative groups.

Menderson, M. F., *Parliamentary Procedure Simplified,* 3rd ed. (Cincinnati, Dale Press, 1957). Includes material on forming a new organization, writing by-laws, duties of officers, and an explanation of all motions and parliamentary terms.

O'Brien, J. F., *Parliamentary Law for the Layman: Procedure and Strategy for Meetings* (New York, Harper & Brothers, 1952). Includes relationship between parliamentary procedure and democratic processes, a formulation of four basic principles of parliamentary discussion, a presentation and explanation of the code of rules, a discussion of parliamentary strategy, organizing a meeting, order of business, duties of officers, and means of election.

Powers, D., *Fundamentals of Speech* (New York, McGraw-Hill Book Co., 1951), Ch. 21. Contains ideas that will be helpful in teaching parliamentary procedure.

Robert, H. M., *Rules of Order,* rev. ed. (New York, Scott, Foresman & Company, 1951). Contains the complete rules of parliamentary procedure adapted to the use of organizations. The official authority on all matters not contained in the constitutions or by-laws of organizations.

Shryock, R. O., *Parliamentary Procedure Made Easy* (New London, Arthur C. Croft Publications: a Division of Vision, Inc., 1955). Contains handy usable presentation of rules of order. Questions of parliamentary procedure readily found and answered in this book. Loose-leaf pad of 16 pages bound in hard covers.

STURGIS, A. F., *Learning Parliamentary Procedure* (New York, McGraw-Hill Book Co., 1953). Tells how to make use of parliamentary procedure. Discusses organization of a club and kinds of motions. Shows how organizations function in their meetings and when they use parliamentary procedure.

SUGGESTED READING FOR HIGH SCHOOL STUDENTS

BAILARD, B., and McKNOWN, H., *So You Were Elected* (New York, Whittlesey House, 1946). Contains a discussion of parliamentary procedure. Includes the order of a meeting, duties of officers, reports of the treasurer and secretary, and adoption of the constitution.

JONES, O. G., *Senior Manual for Group Leadership,* rev. ed. (New York, Appleton-Century-Crofts, Inc., 1949). Contains a fairly complete treatment of parliamentary procedure with motions indexed for easy usage.

AUDIO-VISUAL AIDS

Parliamentary Procedure (Coronet, black and white, 11 minutes). Demonstrates the order of business of a meeting. Tells how to obtain the floor, make a motion, rise to a point of information, put the question, make an amendment by striking out and inserting.

Parliamentary Procedure in Action (Coronet, black and white, 16 minutes). Shows how to use parliamentary procedure; to make and second motions, amend them, arise to a point of order, and table motions. Setting is a high school club.

EXERCISES

1. Organize your class into a club. While one student serves as the teacher, the others make different types of motions. Indicate the kind of planning that would make this activity meaningful for a high school class.
2. Prepare a developmental lesson plan for teaching the types of motions.
3. Observe a high school club in action. Evaluate the members' use of parliamentary procedure.

7

Group Discussion

TEACHERS, OTHER than speech teachers, have different concepts of the term *discussion*. Some of them define discussion as group deliberation to solve a problem under the guidance of a leader. Others consider any interchange of ideas, discussion. Still others call communication which stresses advocacy discussion. Obviously some of these teachers should be more discriminating in their use of the term and at times should be using the terms *conversation, debate,* or *argument.*

Along with these different impressions of the meaning of *discussion* come different attitudes. Many teachers believe that whereas a place exists in the high school for discussion, none exists for debate. These teachers do not realize that both debate and discussion are necessary in our high schools and that whereas the discussant is reflective, co-operative, and seeking truth, the debater is assertive, argumentative, and seeking support.[1] The unhealthy attitude of such persons is expressed in the following comparison of debate and discussion:[2]

DISCUSSION	DEBATE
Purpose: To find out the facts.	To prove you are right.
Method: Asking questions.	Making dogmatic statements.
Characteristics: Cool and collected.	Hot and bothered.
Results: New knowledge, valid opinion.	Strengthened prejudices, bloody noses, and black eyes.

[1] R. H. Wagner and C. C. Arnold, *Handbook of Group Discussion* (Boston, Houghton Mifflin Co., 1950), p. 7.

[2] M. F. Emerson, "Discussion vs. Debate," *Social Education*, XVI (December, 1952), 382.

You show teachers who are convinced of the accuracy of such a comparison that to prove one is right is sometimes necessary. That when people cannot agree, when issues are clearly drawn, and when circumstances seem plainly to point to the wisdom of a particular action, they must resort to debate. When they as teachers have reached the limits of discussion, the only reasonable recourse is debate. They may prefer co-operative, reflective discussion, but they must be realistic and recognize its limitations. You point out that the question is, Shall the decision be made by the vote of the majority or shall it be made in an autocratic way by the person in charge?

The opinion that to debate, is to make "dogmatic statements" is equally fallacious. You indicate that although debate is a competition between two opposing results of thought and inquiry, it does not imply "making dogmatic statements." It does imply logical, reasoned argument to achieve majority rule. You may emphasize that frequently debate occurs in a parliamentary group where its members make motions, debate them, and arrive at compromises through amendments.

Lastly, you point out that the "hot and bothered" characteristic may sometimes be healthy. Surely when the study of a problem and the resulting judgment indicate that one position is strongly advantageous, its advocates should be enthusiastic about it.

You must convince your colleagues and your administration that our country and our schools need both discussion and debate and, most important, that students must be trained in both. Many writers support you in this statement. Paul W. Keller indicates that "if by some ingenious device a person were able to take the lid off a community and to observe the individuals, Lilliputian-like, going about their complex of activities, he ought to be able, before long, to pick out those who had received training in discussion."[3] J. Walter Reeves writes that "it is highly desirable that all societies, clubs, and organizations of any kind in a democracy should follow the same basic rules of open consideration—rules governing the conduct of argumentation and debate. It should be the purpose of a course to set forth these rules . . . and it is to be hoped that an

[3] P. W. Keller, "A Secondary School Course in Discussion," *The Bulletin of the National Association of Secondary School Principals*, XXXVI (May, 1952), 45.

understanding of them will enable participants to start at a precise point, to proceed with little or no confusion, and to arrive at a conclusion which is similarly precise and meaningful."[4] James McBurney states, "We can no more dispense with legislative and forensic debate in a democratic society than we can take a walk to the moon . . . The worst we can do is to deny our students the proper kind of training for this important democratic activity."[5]

AIMS

Having convinced your colleagues of the need for a study of discussion and debate, you make clear the aims to be accomplished by a study of group discussion. In a study of group discussion, students should acquire certain understandings, attitudes, and skills.

Understandings
  Kind and amount of preparation for a discussion
  Steps of reflective thinking
  Bases of belief
  Content of a discussion outline
  Responsibilities of leader and discussant

Attitudes
  Fairness and objectivity
  Open-mindedness
  Spirit of co-operation in working with others
  Concern for the development of group thinking

Skills
  To reason clearly
  To think reflectively
  To lead effectively
  To participate fully in group discussion

CONTENT IN GROUP DISCUSSION

To accomplish these aims the teacher may well include in her work on group discussion:

[4] J. W. Reeves, "A Secondary School Course in Argumentation," *The Bulletin of the National Association of Secondary School Principals*, XXXVI (May, 1952), 57.

[5] J. McBurney "The Role of Discussion and Debate in a Democratic Society," *The Bulletin of the National Association of Secondary School Principals*, XXXVI (May, 1952). 26.

Nature of Group Discussion
  Definition
  Differences between Discussion and Debate
  Values

Topics
  Classification
  Factors in Selection

Forms and Types
  Informal
    Study Groups
    Policy Determining Groups
  Formal
    Panel
    Dialogue
    Symposium
    Case-Conference

Bases of Belief
  Evidence
    Facts
    Opinion
  Reasoning

Preparation
  Gathering Information
  Processes of Thinking for the Problem
  Making an Outline

Process
  Formulating Questions
  Steps of Reflective Thinking
  Analysis of Accumulative Group Thinking
  Analysis of Co-operative Group Thinking

Participation
  Responsibilities of the Leader
  Responsibilities of the Participants

Evaluation
  Information
  Orderliness of Thinking and Participation
  Communicative Abilities of Leader and Participants
  Thinking
  Spirit of Co-operation of Entire Group
  Degree of Success in Solving the Problem Discussed

NATURE OF GROUP DISCUSSION

One way to teach the definition and values of group discussion is through the analysis of a taped group discussion, preferably one by high school students on a timely and important problem. You arrive at a definition as exemplified by this discussion, and you talk about the values of discussion in solving the particular problem involved. On the other hand, you may begin by using one of the definitions given by an authority like McBurney or Arnold.

When you begin, however, with a definition by an authority, you must then show the purposes and values of group discussion. After you and the students have defined the term and distinguished discussion from conversation and debate, you and the students talk about discussions in various classes, organizations, and at home in which they have participated. Here you use their examples of discussion to show that discussion serves two purposes: (1) to disseminate information, (2) to solve a problem. The first may be clarified by such an example as four students' reporting on exporting policies of four different South American countries. The second may be illustrated by a social studies class discussion of, "What should be our State Department's attitude toward South American countries run by dictators?" At this time you also point out to the students the importance and values of both group discussion and debate. You may do this by analyzing procedures of our democratic form of government which appear in any good newspaper. Attempts to reconcile differences and to solve conflicts through discussion and debate are reported every day.

TOPICS FOR HIGH SCHOOL DISCUSSION

Many teachers begin their study of group discussion with case-conference discussion. They make sure that the case, which they are to use, is the kind of problem-incident for which the students can formulate principles that can be applied in similar cases. For example, one case presented in a high school class was that of a brilliant student who did well in all her subjects but who began to bring answers to examinations with her. She announced that since other members of the class brought answers, she believed that in order to compete successfully for a scholarship, she must do likewise. At the same time she felt guilty and unhappy about the procedure.

A similar case-conference discussion revolved around a high school social studies class where the teacher gave short-answer quizzes which students exchanged and corrected. One boy felt all alone because no one would exchange papers with him. He explained that no one would exchange with him, because he marked the paper exactly as it was given to him. Furthermore, although he did not want to report the dishonest activity of the other students, he did not like the feeling of being left out.

After the students have discussed such a case under the leadership of the teacher, you may suggest that they form committees to choose problems for solution. You advise, of course, that the topics meet the criteria usually given in discussion texts. In addition, however, you must make sure that the topic is within the range of experience of high school boys and girls and is important to them. For instance, one high school group discussed the problem of beautifying the school grounds. "What kind of landscaping?" "Who should do it?" and "How can it be financed?" were real and provocative questions to these boys and girls. In addition, you will likely find that questions of policy are the most practical for high school discussion. Such questions as "What should be done to control inflation in our town?" "What should be done to improve the academic rating of our school?" "What should be done to improve the quality of our high school yearbooks?" "How can we improve testing procedures in this school?" are subjects which require the group to think co-operatively and to decide upon a course of action important to them.

PHRASING THE PROBLEM

Just as you and your students analyzed the phrasing of the main idea of a speech, you analyze the phrasing of the question for discussion. The question should be so phrased that it helps the students to give attention to the problem honestly and objectively. For example, "Should our school tax each person so that all will be able to attend extracurricular activities, since attendance at football games is too small?" is badly phrased. Students may well discover why it is badly phrased. They should recognize that the framer of the question has an obvious bias, that the phrase "our school" may represent the administration of the school or the student body, that "each person" may mean all students or all students and all faculty, that the clause "since attendance at football games is too small" is part of the analysis and does not belong. In addition, they should note that the question excludes from discussion all solutions except the imposition of a school-wide tax. Finally, they must note that the attendance may be as large as could be expected even though the proposer of the solution indicates that it is too small. Your group, however, may profit more from an analysis of those questions which are well phrased.

FORMS OF DISCUSSION

After the students have brought in their topics, have evaluated their worth, and have phrased their questions, the teacher points out that in some instances a particular form of discussion may be better than some other form. For example, two students who were experts on makeup wanted to discuss the makeup of actors and actresses in the Kabuki Theater which they had recently visited. The teacher explained that here one student might question the other as to the purpose of the makeup in the Kabuki Theater, its materials, and its use. She gave them the name of the form of discussion, *dialogue*. Two other questions called for a symposium. In one the students were to explore the possibilities of teaching as a career on the various levels; elementary school, high school, and college. In the other students were to discuss the proposed changes in curriculum from the viewpoints of the principal, the teachers, and the students. On the other hand, some teachers teach the forms of discussion more formally. They name the terms and see that the students understand the concepts and the uses of the various forms.

BASES OF BELIEF

The study of evidence and of reasoning wherein each member tries to establish the facts and to refine his inferences is especially important to high school students, for such study helps each individual to think more effectively.

Fact and Opinion

In emphasizing that facts are data collected by those skilled in observing and reporting, one teacher makes use of her own experiences as a Gallup Poll reporter and of the research which she did for her Master's thesis. After this introduction, she has members of her group ascertain certain facts like the average age of members of the class, the birth places of eight of the teachers, the vocational plans of all the members of the group, and the date when the school was constructed. After such preliminary study, the members of the group examine an editorial to see whether the facts included should be accepted at their face value. They examine the source of the facts, their recency, their consistency with each other, and their completeness.

She then emphasizes that when facts are scarce or when they require interpretation, the authority becomes our chief source of opinion. They talk about the members of the class who are more or less authorities in various areas. After this preliminary study, she asks students to listen to a particular news broadcast or discussion for opinions, to note who gave the opinions, and to indicate whether those giving them were well-informed persons and competent judges.

Reasoning

Students must see the relationships among facts and opinions both in debate and discussion. Many teachers spend considerable time on this unit. J. Walter Reeves suggests that it include the following material:[6]

Inductive Reasoning
  Generalizations
  Analogy
  Causal Relations
    Cause to Effect
    Effect to Cause

Deductive Reasoning
  Major Premise

[6] J. Walter Reeves, "A Secondary School Course in Argumentation," *The Bulletin of the National Association of Secondary School Principals*, XXXVI (May, 1952), 63-69.

Minor Premise
Conclusion

In teaching reasoning, you do well to use examples close to students' lives, for they unconsciously reason and infer every day. For instance, one teacher uses the following example in explaining generalization. In her groups most of her boys and girls are college bound. She then indicates that since Mary, John, Jim, Ken, Bennie, Lanie, Elsa, and Maxine are all college bound, most of the members of the class are probably college bound. She then gives them the tests for generalization. At this point the students analyze several other generalizations which the teacher presents. For example, she says that Miss Marlow, Mr. Brown, Mr. Kane, Mr. Ludlow, and Miss Bray are all New Englanders and that, in fact, the school is full of New Englanders. The students quickly point out that she is not giving a sufficient number of cases and that there are too many exceptions.

This same teacher teaches the meaning of analogy by an illustration which is always vital to students. She gives an account of John who wanted to enter Yale; he was industrious, received superior grades, and was a leader in his high school. He was admitted. She then explains that Jim from the same school with similar habits of industry, slightly superior grades to John, and even more of a leader can well expect to be admitted to Yale. On one occasion, one student pointed out that perhaps John's father was a Yale graduate and that this factor would make a difference.

You do well to use examples that are related to school activity. For instance, in teaching reasoning from cause to effect, one teacher said that a basketball team was made up of five unusually skillful players, intelligent and well-co-ordinated, who spent a large number of hours practicing to perfect their game under the direction of a very able coach. The effect of these multiple causes was a team that won almost all of its games. In this instance the causes were adequate to explain the result. The team, however, in the last part of the season lost three of its games. Here the causes were not able to produce the expected result. She asked for some plausible reasons. One student indicated that another school might have equally able and industrious players, a coach who was almost a genius and that in addition, the players of this other school might have re-

ceived all the breaks of the game. A second student said that three of
the players might have been stricken with influenza. The teacher
noted that in this last instance a known cause prevented the producing of the desired effect; the good team failed because of the
loss of some of its vital players.

Throughout you try to make your teaching of reasoning meaningful by showing that ability to reason well is important in the management of our daily lives.

PREPARATION

Almost every teacher teaches the steps of reflective thinking.[7] You
phrase these steps according to the ability of your students. For a
bright class, you may use the same phrases as are used in a college
text on discussion. For others you state the steps more simply as:

1. What do we need to explain in attempting to understand our problem?
2. What is the nature of the problem? Why do we want to talk about
   it? Is it important? What will happen if we do nothing about it?
   What caused it?
3. What can we do about it?
4. What had we best do about it?
5. How can we put into effect what we want to do?

One teacher taught the preparation and techniques of discussion
by having the entire group work on the question, "What can we do
in our town to reduce juvenile delinquency?"

After the students had stated their problem, they did some research to find out whether the problem was a significant one in their
town. They went to the newspaper files of the town and listed for
the period of the current year the articles which pointed to the
problem of juvenile delinquency. They then investigated files of
the same newspaper for a similar period twenty years ago. They
found that the increase in reported incidents was significant. Another group interviewed the Chief of Police who stated that the
increase in juvenile delinquency was meaningful. They talked about
the significance of the problem of juvenile delinquency to themselves and others in the town. The members of the group believed

---

[7] J. Dewey, *How We Think* (New York, D. C. Heath & Company, 1933), p. 107.

that the amount of juvenile delinquency posed a threat to them and other inhabitants of the town and that its presence gave a bad name to all teen-agers. They also talked about the significance of the problem to the juvenile delinquents themselves and the likelihood of their delinquent acts marring their chances for successful and happy adulthood.

After this study indicated the problem's significance, they began to read and to take notes on material that dealt with juvenile delinquency. From this reading and from their statement of the problem, they made a list of words which needed defining. Such words included *juvenile delinquency, slum area, public training school, work camp, juvenile detention, juvenile probation,* and *juvenile parole.*

From here they went on to find out about the causes of juvenile delinquency. An understanding of the causes required that they know some of the personality factors of the typical juvenile delinquent. They also read about the environmental conditions of home, school, and community which seem to be influential in developing juvenile delinquents. They read about world conditions and their effects on juveniles. They related this reading to conditions in their own community.

Next they set up the criteria by which they would judge their solutions. They indicated that the solution should be capable of controlling delinquency, effective in rehabilitating the delinquent, and within the budget and possible resources of the town.

They then suggested solutions. These included getting at the causes of the difficulty in terms of housing and economic factors, providing services in club and community to keep juveniles occupied in worthwhile activities, instituting a work camp to provide healthy activity for those already pronounced delinquent, and establishing a bureau which hires trained personnel to work with the delinquent youths.

Teachers have many other ways of teaching the process of discussion. Students listen to taped discussions determining the pattern which the discussion follows, finding out whether the discussion group deals with one issue at a time, and analyzing the co-operative thinking that occurs in the discussion. Quite obviously they cannot listen for all aspects at one time; one group of students may listen for one aspect; another group, for another. In addition, small groups work on preparing discussion outlines which follow the accepted form. These outlines are excellent preparation for the actual discussions.

PARTICIPATION

You encourage your students to think critically, to speak clearly, succinctly, appropriately, and logically and to listen accurately, thoughtfully, and reflectively. These abilities mean that the student must be constantly attentive, must be thinking carefully with an inquiring mind, and must be responding objectively to what the other discussants are saying. Your own attitudes and your own discussion leadership abilities are important in fostering these attributes, for students will emulate you. For example, your own open-mindedness helps students to give weight to an idea and not to who presented the idea. When you show that you respect those whose opinions differ from yours, you motivate your students to adopt a similar attitude.

In addition to motivating your students to speak and listen well, you assist them in developing good human relationships within the group. Your own friendliness, your own interest in what is said, and your own acceptance of all class members and their ideas again are important. You must, moreover, help your students to see the difference between democratic and autocratic leadership, between group-centered and leader-centered leadership. A few members of one discussion class reported on the study of group-centered and leader-centered leadership by Richard W. Wischmeier.[8] Other members studied and reported on ways of reducing unnecessary conflict. They made distinctions between those conflicts which are necessary and those which are not.

DISCUSSION LEADER

Some of your students stand out almost immediately as leaders. Usually these are the students who can most successfully conduct a discussion. You help them and the others to be effective leaders by encouraging them to find out as much as they can about their topics and their group and to plan for the discussion well. In addition,

[8] R. W. Wischmeier, "Group-Centered and Leader-Centered Leadership: An Experimental Study," *Speech Monographs,* XXII (March, 1955), 43-48.

you advise them on how to open and close a discussion and on how to develop group thinking and good human relationships.

EVALUATION

Group evaluation in discussion is particulary important, for students learn from each other their strengths and weaknesses. This is unusually true for the evaluation of the human relations exhibited. Sensitivity to other members, objectivity in presenting ideas, willingness to listen to and accept different ideas, strength of group participation, encouragement of group thinking, and the quality of the leadership are all areas which a student group can evaluate well. You as a teacher guide the evaluation tactfully and sympathetically.

The students and you also evaluate other areas: knowledge of the problem, the thinking processes, and clarity and skill in the use of voice, articulation, and language.

The authors of the high school text *Speaking and Listening*[9] offer some excellent suggestions on evaluation. On page 241 and 242 they call student discussants by the names "Mr. Conclusion Jumper," "Mr. Issue Changer," "Mr. Gloom and Doom," "Mr. Irrelevant," and "Mr. Problem Solver." These apt names point to successful and unsuccessful approaches to problem-solving. On page 254 are listed sound questions for evaluating the participation of the high school discussant and discussion leader.

Some teachers devise charts for recording the evalution of criticism. Others place the items on the board and the members of the class criticize the discussion as a whole mentioning the performance of specific individuals. In all instances you make sure that students start with the positive aspects and that they attack the negative aspects courteously.

The following are examples of charts used to evaluate discussion. The first two require students to give an evaluation and then to support their stand. These two charts require careful attention to the discussion and a thorough understanding of discussion procedures. They test the person doing the evaluating as well as the person being evaluated. The second two are checklists which guide the evaluation specifically.

[9] A. T. Weaver, G. L. Borchers, and D. K. Smith, *Speaking and Listening* (Englewood Cliffs, N.J., Prentice-Hall, Inc., 1956).

GROUP DISCUSSION EVALUATION

DISCUSSION GROUP ....DATE..............

TOPIC ....

GENERAL EVALUATION: ....Superior ....Good ....Average ....Poor

Give your reasons for your evaluation under the following categories:

CHOICE OF TOPIC: (Indicate the value and importance of the problem to the group and the topic's appropriateness for discussion.)

PREPARATION: (Give evidence of preparation or the lack of it.)

PROCESS OF DISCUSSION: (Outline briefly the process, giving attention to the steps in reflective thinking.)

LEADERSHIP: (Indicate the leader's ability to state the problem, to motivate participation, to guide the discussion, and to develop good human relationships.)

PARTICIPATION: (Indicate in general how widespread participation was, the quality of the comments, and the value of the participants' contributions in helping to solve the problem.)

EVALUATION OF DISCUSSION LEADER

NAME .... TOPIC............. DATE...........

EVALUATION: ....Superior ....Good ....Average ....Poor

Support your evaluation by your answers to the following questions:

1. How did the leader introduce the problem?

2. How did he keep the discussion on the track and how did he move it forward?

3. What types of questions and comments did he make?

4. How often and how well did he summarize?

5. How skillfully did he handle tensions, controversies, and interruptions?

6. How well prepared was he in terms of information?

7. How did he bring the discussion to a close?

LEADER'S EVALUATION

NAME .... DATE...................

TOPIC ....

NUMBER OF SUMMARIES	
Scoring	
Total	
KNOWLEDGE OF TOPIC	
Good	
Insufficient	
SOCIAL ATTRIBUTES	
Respectful of others	
Interested in responses	
Tactful	
Tolerant	
Impartial	
Not respectful of others	
Not interested in responses	
Unresponsive	
Intolerant	
Partial	

Role in Furthering Progress of Discussion	
Moved discussion forward	
Allowed discussion to meander	
Followed steps of reflective thinking	
Leadership	
Totalitarian	
Democratic	
Strong	
Weak	

SUGGESTED READING

Anderson, K. E., and Polisky, J. B., "The Application of the Symposium-Forum to Contest Discussion," *The Speech Teacher*, IX (March, 1960), 131-134. Lists criticisms aimed at contest discussion. Suggests a symposium-forum-discussion contest with the integration of the co-operative investigation of group discussion and the sharpness of critical procedures characteristic of debate.

Baird, A. C., *Argumentation, Discussion and Debate* (New York, McGraw-Hill Book Co., 1950). Gives the principles of argumentative discourse, oral and written, and applies them to discussion and debate. Includes material on subjects for argument, research and collection of materials, definition and analysis of the subject, development of ideas by logical and motivating methods of proof, supporting material, organization and outlining, language usage, and presentation-delivery.

Barnlund, D. C., "The Use of Group Observers," *The Speech Teacher*, IV (January, 1955), 46-48. Suggests that two observers are useful in the evaluation of group discussion: one to concentrate on matters of thought, the other on matters of interpersonal feelings. Notes the areas each observer is to judge.

Behl, W. A., *Discussion and Debate* (New York, The Ronald Press Com-

DISCUSSANT'S EVALUATION

TOPIC .... DATE..................

NAME	Mary	John	Jane	Harold	Helen
NUMBER OF PARTICIPATIONS					
Scoring					
Total					
INFORMATION					
Sound, sufficient evidence					
Dated, unsound, or insufficient evidence					
Irrelevant evidence					
Good use of authority					
Questionable use of authority					
Logical reasoning					
Illogical reasoning					
ATTITUDE TOWARD OTHERS					
Co-operative					
Objective and fair					
Dogmatic					
Argumentative					
Hostile					

pany, 1953). Includes material on topic analysis, evidence, reasoning, organization, logic, audience analysis, speech composition and delivery. Devotes one chapter to discussion and types and one to types of debates and evaluation.

BRADEN, W. W., and BRANDENBURG, E. S., *Oral Decision Making: Principles of Discussion and Debate* (New York, Harper & Brothers, 1955). Includes three parts: nature and materials of oral decision making, reaching decisions through discussion, and reaching decisions through debate. Includes material on the dynamics of the group and on understanding language.

CROWELL, L., "Rating Scales as Diagnostic Instruments in Discussion," *The Speech Teacher*, II (January, 1952), 26-32. Talks about evaluation of group discussion. Good suggestions for the teacher.

DEBOER, J. J., "Implications of Group Dynamics for English Teachers," *English Journal*, XLI (May, 1952), 239-244. Talks about the origin of group dynamics, composition of groups, types of group leadership, and problem members of a group.

EWBANK, H. L., and AUER, J. J., *Handbook for Discussion Leaders,* rev. ed. (New York, Harper & Brothers, 1954). Contains material on the nature of group discussion, the problem, the listener, discussion, debate, and interpersonal relations. Excellent explanation of the purposes of discussion. Includes practical, usable suggestions for exercises in locating and defining the problem and for research on the problem.

————, "Decision Making! Discussion and Debate," *The Bulletin of the National Association of Secondary School Principals,* XXXII (January, 1948), 34-49. Gives the differences between debate and discussion. Defines discussion. Lists forms of group discussion and public discussion. Contains an evaluation ballot for discussion.

FRIEDERICH, W. J., and WILCOX, R. A., *Teaching Speech in High Schools* (New York, The Macmillan Co., 1953), Ch. 5. Gives specific goals, a proposed syllabus, and suggested methods and procedures in teaching discussion.

GULLEY, H. E., *Essentials of Discussion and Debate* (New York, Holt, Rinehart and Winston, Inc., 1955). Contains a discussion of skills needed by both debaters and discussants, essentials of both activities, and ethics in deliberation.

HANCE, K. G., ed., "Public Address in the Secondary School," *The Bulletin of the National Association of Secondary School Principals,* XXXXVI (May, 1952). Contains articles by many authorities in the field on the role of discussion and debate in a democratic society and gives types of experiences—both curricular and extracurricular—in public speaking, discussion, and debate.

Howell, W. S., and Smith, D. K., *Discussion* (New York, The Macmillan Co., 1956). Contains excellent chapters on reasoning—both inductive and deductive, interpersonal relationships, and language in discussion. Aims to combine critical thinking and sound human relationships. Includes excellent material on evaluation techniques in discussion and a syllabus for a thirty-meeting college course.

Keltner, J., "The Laboratory Method of Discussion Training at Kansas State College," *The Speech Teacher*, VII (September, 1958), 199-208. Describes a method of teaching discussion which stresses human relationships in group discussion.

McBurney, J. H., and Hance, K. G., *Discussion in Human Affairs* (New York, Harper & Brothers, 1950). Parts I and II cover background and theoretical aspects. Parts III and IV are a systematic manual in discussion procedure for both participants and leaders.

Phelps, W., and Dobkin, M., "Problem Solving Discussion in High School Civics," *The Speech Teacher*, VI (November, 1957), 305-318. Reports findings of a study on high school civics students' ability to phrase a problem, define terms, outline, and summarize as a result of problem-solving panel forums.

Robinson, K., *Teaching Speech in the Secondary School*, 2nd ed. (New York, Longmans, Green & Co., Inc., 1954). Contains excellent suggestions for units on group discussion.

Robinson, K. F., and Keltner, J., "Suggested Units in Discussion and Debate for Secondary Schools," *Quarterly Journal of Speech*, XXXII (October, 1946), 385-390. Gives an outline for units in debate and discussion.

Shepard, D. W., "Some Observations on High School Discussion," *The Speech Teacher*, IV (September, 1955), 191-195. Discusses four errors of group discussion: failure to exercise reasonable selection in reading, failure to evaluate the material, failure to evaluate the contributions of others, and failure to follow the discussion formula.

Utterback, W. E., "Evaluation of Performance in the Discussion Course at Ohio State University," *The Speech Teacher*, VII (September, 1958), 209-215. Describes a method of evaluating discussion which shows its weaknesses and strengths. Problems and a number of solutions are prepared by the teacher and discussed in class. Choices among these solutions or of other solutions are recorded.

Wagner, R. H., and Arnold, C. C., *Handbook of Group Discussion* (New York, Houghton Mifflin Co., 1950). Contains chapters on the nature of discussion, the bases of belief, subject problems, preparation, the process, leadership, participation, speech and language, and types and forms. Includes specimens of college students' discussions. Could be used advantageously by the bright high school student. One of the best references for the high school teacher of discussion.

WEAVER, A. T., BORCHERS, G. L., and SMITH, D. K., *The Teaching of Speech* (New York, Prentice-Hall, Inc., 1952), Ch. 14. Includes materials on types of discussion and advantages and disadvantages of discussion. Particularly good explanation of human relationships in discussion.

AUDIO-VISUAL MATERIALS

Conducting a Meeting (Young America Films, black and white, 10 minutes). Depicts a confused meeting. Narrator shows correct procedure.

Discussion in Democracy (Coronet Films, black and white, color, 10 minutes). Shows function of discussion in democracy and need for thorough preparation and good organization. Indicates the necessity for preparing an outline for discussion.

Discussion Techniques (United World Films, Castle Films Division, black and white, 30 minutes). Demonstrates the various types of discussion and effective and poor ways of leading discussion. Done in an army setting.

Do Words Ever Fool You? (Coronet Films, black and white, color, 10 minutes). Explains to junior high school students the importance of correct word usage.

Group Discussion (Young America Films, black and white, 10 minutes). Explains and demonstrates the basic techniques of leadership and participation in group discussion. Shows a high school boy and his family discussing the problem of college entrance.

How to Conduct a Discussion (Encyclopedia Britannica Films, black and white, 25 minutes). Explains the qualities of good leadership and the requirements of good discussion.

How to Judge Authorities (Coronet, black and white, color, 10 minutes). Establishes criteria for judging authorities in terms of an audience.

Learning from Class Discussion (Coronet, black and white, color, 10 minutes). Shows the value of discussion as a learning tool in the classroom. Brings out some of the basic principles of leading and participating in discussion. Demonstrates the value of exchange of students' thoughts through discussion.

Organizing Discussion Groups (Encyclopedia Britannica Films, black and white, 25 minutes). Tells how to organize a discussion group. Shows how discussion breaks down the barriers between people.

Room for Discussion (Encyclopedia Britannica Films, black and white, 25 minutes). Motivates the student to participate in group discussions. Points out its usefulness in practical situations.

Speech: Group Discussion (Young America Films, black and white, 12 minutes). Demonstrates and explains some of the basic techniques of group discussion. Gives the five steps of reflective thinking.

EXERCISES

1. Prepare a paragraph or two as a topic for a high school case-conference discussion.
2. Phrase six questions for discussion that might well appeal to high school students.
3. Discuss: What are the principal difficulties of high school discussion?
4. What are the advantages and disadvantages of using the discussion method to teach speech content?
5. Show how you yourself follow the steps of discussion in a pupil-teacher planning session.
6. View one of the suggested films. Explain how you could use it in discussion class.
7. Prepare a lesson plan for teaching the steps of discussion.

8

Debate

GETTING READY to debate is in many ways like getting ready to discuss. In both, students determine the causes and histories of the problem and define terms. Both discussion and debate require that the students learn to find and weigh evidence—to discover and evaluate facts and opinions, to reason logically and to detect fallacious reasoning. For this reason, some high schools, instead of having separate courses in discussion and debate, have a single course. Students are first taught the principles of argumentation, of presenting argumentative speeches, of determining causes and histories of problems, and of defining terms. The students then hold discussions on certain problems. After some of the discussions, the need for debate becomes obvious. At this time the teacher turns attention to the principles of debate.

DEFINITION

Regardless of whether debate is a separate course or a part of a debate and discussion course, you help your students to define debate. When through discussion, they have proposed a definite solution of a problem, you explain that it now takes the form of a motion, a bill, a resolution, or an indictment and that opposing sides openly advocate the acceptance or rejection of the proposed solution. Each advocate tries to persuade others to his point of view through evidence, arguments, and appeals.

VALUES

Students must be as aware of the values of debate as they are of the values of discussion. Debating methods help students to weigh evidence, to use their own best judgment, and to arrive at their own decisions carefully. Not only will debating aid students in arriving at their own decisions wisely, but it will enable them to influence others to agree with their decision, to be an advocate for it. In our society everyone is an advocate at some time, although admittedly leaders are advocates most frequently. The lawyer in the court of law makes a case for his client. The incumbent senator argues for his being returned to the United States Senate. The sales manager strongly urges the expansion of territory to his salesmen. The teacher pleads for a curricular change. For such leaders to be able to use evidence, arguments, and appeals effectively is particularly important.

Advocacy proves attractive to the intellectually able in the high school community. H. L. Ewbank records that the mean I.Q. of 218 debaters representing twenty-five high schools was 119.[1] In addition, one half of these debaters had all *A* records. Since debate does appeal to the gifted, ample opportunity should be given them for training in it. This training seems almost imperative, for the gifted are likely to become the leaders in their communities.

AIMS

The aims of teaching debating include the acquiring of understandings, attitudes, and skills.

Understandings
    Methods of finding and organizing material
    Different types of debate
    Ways to analyze the background of a problem
    Tests of evidence

    Principals of rebuttal
    Contents of a brief
    Principles upon which a debate is judged

[1] H. L. Ewbank, "What's Right with Debate," *Quarterly Journal of Speech*, XXXVII (April, 1951), 197-202.

Attitudes
  Respect for a search for truth
  Tolerance of different points of view
  Courteous spirit of fair play in an argument

Skills
  To ascertain truth and advocate it
  To marshal the best evidence clearly
  To argue effectively
  To listen objectively and critically
  To analyze arguments under pressure
  To rebut arguments
  To weigh alternatives judiciously
  To speak clearly and succinctly

CONTENT

A unit on or a course in debate may contain the following material:

Definition and Values

Selecting and Phrasing the Debate Proposition

Types of Debate

Getting Ready to Debate
  Finding Facts, Opinion, and Appeals
  Reasoning
    Inductive Reasoning
    Deductive Reasoning
  Writing the Brief
    Analysis
    Body of Proof
    Conclusion
  Preparing the Case
    The Constructive Speech
    The Rebuttal Speech

Presenting the Debate
  Good Human Relationships
  Effective Communication

Evaluating Debate
  Understanding the Proposition

Understanding the Issues
Adapting to the Opposition
Refuting
Maintaining Effective Communication
Promoting Good Human Relationships

SELECTING AND PHRASING THE DEBATE PROPOSITION

Selecting the Proposition

Just as many teachers of discussion begin their study of discussion with a vital, personally important case-conference, so do many teachers of debate begin with a vital, personally important proposition. A proposition like "A course in typewriting should be required in the eighth grade" meets this requirement. Using such a proposition, teachers present to the whole class many of the techniques of preparing for and holding a debate.

Students next break into groups and debate propositions that arise from school, local, state, and national problems. The proposition should be one about which they feel strongly, should be timely, and should be intellectually challenging.

School propositions include:

Two years of mathematics should be required of all high school students.
Credit toward graduation should be given for extracurricular activities.
Our school should establish an employment agency.
A driver-training course should be instituted in our school.

Possible local propositions are:

A junior college should be established in our town.
John Street should be made a one-way street.
A public parking area should be provided on the site of the old railroad station.

State propositions that prove stimulating are:

All employees of our state government should be under civil service.
Advertising billboards should be prohibited from being erected on grounds within 500 feet of our state highways.
The Governor should serve a six-year term.

Propositions involving national issues are:

The President of the United States should hold office for one term of six years.

The United States should adopt uniform traffic laws.

Diplomats' salaries should be doubled.

The United States Government should establish a college for training men and women for foreign service.

National Proposition

The Committee on Discussion and Debate Materials of the National University Extension Association helps schools formulate a proposition for use during each year and provides materials on the problem. The Committee sets up the machinery for state leagues to agree on a common problem. It also prepares two volumes: one containing articles by leaders in the area especially prepared for the high school students and one containing articles reprinted by permission from current sources. This same group distributes pamphlets and articles bearing on the topic. This service of providing material is particularly helpful to schools which contain meagre libraries.

Phrasing the Proposition

You must teach your students to phrase the debate proposition well. You tell them that, like the main idea in a speech, the proposition must be only one idea and should be phrased affirmatively. You further indicate that it must be simply, clearly, specifically, and concisely stated and that it must be susceptible of proof. Often you will illustrate with a well-worded proposition such as: "*Resolved* That the administration of Central High School should give credit for work in extracurricular activities." Or, "*Resolved* That the administration of Central High School should permit the formation of sororities and fraternities."

After you have made clear the requirements for wording a proposition, you may present the class with one which violates most of the rules. The following is an example: "Since the athletic program needs more funds, should we begin to have night games or ask for more money from the Board?" Obviously this proposition possesses more than one idea, is phrased as a question, and is not clear.

Athletic program, night games, and *we* all need to be more specific. "Since the athletic program needs more money" is part of the analysis. The proposition is not susceptible to two-way argument, for it gives two concrete suggestions. Accordingly students revise it to read: "*Resolved* That the administration of Central High School should inaugurate night football games."

TYPES OF DEBATE

After your students have learned to find topics for debate and to phrase the proposition, they may study the types of debate. Most high school students begin with formal debating and then, as they become more proficient, take part in other types such as cross-examination debating, a legislative session, mock trial, problem-solving, and direct clash. For advanced students participation in a legislative session and in a mock trial are worthwhile. On a recent telecast of an interview with the former members of a school legislative conference, one now training for the law said that he felt that his experience in the legislative conference helped him to think clearly and to detect fallacious reasoning. Another who is a premedical student indicated that he found that his debating experience in the legislative assembly helped him to make himself understood in his college classes. The mock trial, also for experienced debaters, creates the necessity for students to think quickly on their feet. Problem-solving debate is popular with some teachers, for they believe that it prevents debaters from taking sides too early. You suggest the kind of debate that fits your students and your situation.

PREPARING TO DEBATE

Following this preliminary study, your students analyze the need for the debate, the history of the problem. They define terms, decide what to admit, to waive, or to exclude as irrelevant. They discover the main issues. In most high school classes of debate you use the terminology used here. In other classes, you simplify the language but keep the concepts. You may use such language as the following:

What is wrong with the situation now?
What caused the difficulty?

What terms must we make clear?

Do we need a change?

Is what we are proposing practical?

Do the advantages of our proposed changes outweigh the disadvantages?

Are there any other changes that would be better than the one proposed?

Much of this material of analysis has likely been taught in discussion just as the material on evidence has been taught there. Surely students have determined causes of problems, have found out their history, have defined terms. New concepts, however, are admitting, waiving, and declaring material irrelevant. Frequently you can teach them by using a proposition on a subject on which the students already have considerable information. For example, you may use the proposition, "*Resolved* That the administration of Central High School should permit the formation of sororities and fraternities." You then ask, "Is there really anyone who believes that all students should be admitted to all organizations?" Students usually make the point that if they can't sing, they either have sense enough not to try out for the chorus; or if they do try out, they surely are not accepted. You and the group then deduce that they must admit in a debate that societies do have the right to be selective in certain matters.

You use a similar attack in showing that some material is irrelevant. For instance, you may indicate that the doubling of the school population has no immediate bearing on the problem since need for fraternities or the objections to them do not depend on the size of the school population.

Lastly you make clear the need to waive certain material. Again using the proposition concerning secret societies, you demonstrate that even though the student body does agree that fraternities and sororities are desirable, students may find that the administration of the school will not permit them. You, therefore, agree not to argue the hypothetical question of whether the administration will permit fraternities and sororities. In other words, the students waive this point.

This analytical material is placed in a brief. In a debate, a brief, like an outline of a speech or a discussion, is the foundation for speaking. You, therefore, emphasize that it is important and that students must prepare it carefully. An example of a good brief is found in the high school text *Speak Up* on pages 177-180.[2]

At this point one teacher makes use of a recording of a debate from a previous class. She first gives the students copies of the brief. She then asks that as they listen to the debate they find out what parts of the brief were used, how much attention was given to each part, and how the debaters made their constructive speeches and rebuttals interesting. After a discussion of these, she divides the members of the class into groups for a second listening experience. One group is to decide whether any of the issues overlap and whether they were introduced in the best order; another is to look for unsupported assertions; another is to evaluate the reasoning, paying particular attention to generalizations; still another is to indicate where the refutation is adequate and where it is inadequate. The groups then report their findings.

The committees of students who have planned and executed briefs are then ready to prepare their cases. The students again work in committees agreeing how to make use of their briefs and how to present their cases effectively. In this instance the choice of chairmen is particularly important. The chairmen must be able to stimulate thinking, to synthesize ideas and information, and to foster co-operation. Consequently, you do well to set up the criteria for their selection with especial care. This choice is even more important when your class is large and when you cannot give each group the guidance that you would like.

PRESENTING THE DEBATE

You make sure that all that the students have learned in presenting informative and persuasive speeches is applied in presenting a debate. In addition to having a clear understanding of what they are saying and a vivid sense of communication with their audience, the debaters must be particularly careful to establish and maintain good human relationships. To be reasonable and to be unfailingly courteous are essential in a debate.

[2] H. M. Adams and T. C. Pollock, *Speak Up* (New York, The Macmillan Co., 1956), pp. 177-180.

EVALUATION

In the evaluation of debate, a group of your class members may serve as a jury and you may serve as a judge. The jury indicates its collective opinion on the ability of each team to understand the proposition, to discover the issues, to adapt to the opposition, to refute, and to communicate ideas. You, however, give the expert analytical criticism which the jury has not given. Through the evaluation of the jury and the judge, the debaters learn their strengths and their weaknesses; their classmates learn the principles of debate.

Two forms are helpful in this evaluation. One is for the use of the jury in analyzing the number of shifts of opinion, because the jury may consider the shift of opinion a factor in deciding which side made the better case. The other form guides the critic in his analysis of the debate. The forms follow:

SHIFT OF OPINION BALLOT

Please do not sign your name.

Before the debate, I was undecided. ...

        I believed in the affirmative side. ...

        I believed in the negative side. ...

After the debate, I was undecided. ...

        I believed in the affirmative side. ...

        I believed in the negative side. ...

DEBATE BALLOT

PROPOSITION: ....

....

Indicate abilities by rating from 1 to 5. 1, Very poor. 2, Poor. 3, Average. 4, Good. 5, Excellent.

	1st Aff. Speaker	2nd Aff. Speaker	1st Neg. Speaker	2nd Neg. Speaker
ANALYSIS OF PROPOSITION	....	....	....	....
CONSTRUCTIVE SPEECH	....	....	....	....
REBUTTAL SPEECH	....	....	....	....
USE OF EVIDENCE AND REASONING	....	....	....	....
COMMUNICATIVE ABILITY	....	....	....	....
ADAPTING TO OPPOSITION	....	....	....	....

DECISION: ....

COMMENTS: ....

....

....

....

....

Signed ....

EXTRACURRICULAR DEBATING

Your first activity is to publicize the advantages of a debating organization. If no team existed before, you give information to a school newspaper reporter, plan a demonstration for assembly on Organization Day, make announcements on the public address system, and prepare posters. To insure having enough students for your organization, you recruit members from your own classes and from the classes of other teachers. The social studies teachers are usually interested in the debating program of the school and can often suggest students who may want to participate in debate. Such preparation insures a good turnout for your organization meeting.

When debate is already part of the activities in the school, you try to promote it. You may indicate in your publicity the names of debaters, the record of the past season, and attendance at various debate tournaments. Instead of your giving announcements on the public address system yourself, the debaters make the announcements. You encourage the school newspaper to review the history of debate in the school.

Organization Meeting

An organization meeting is important. At this meeting you and your students explain the purposes of the debate organization. The program may include talks on the study groups that work for the debate teams, on the preparation for debates, and on attendance at tournaments. Students explain the philosophy of the group—its standards, ethics, and practices. They may even put on a short debate.

Tryouts for Debate

After this organization meeting, you and your committee hold tryouts for the team. Some schools have senior and junior teams—much like first and second string football teams. Your tryout material may consist of a short talk on one or another side of a problem. The length of the talk depends on the number of tryouts you must hear and the time available; it probably should be no longer than three minutes. In order to keep the preparation the same for all who try out, you may supply the research material and give each person the same amount of time for preparation.

Responsibilities of the Director

As a director of debate you have certain responsibilities.

1. You promote in your students courteous and honorable treatment of each other and of their opponents. You stress that they debate fairly, that they respect officials, and that they co-operate with one another. Before they go on a trip, you tell them that their behavior is representative of their school and community. On the trip, you insist that they conduct themselves like ladies and gentlemen.

2. You help them to be objective and to find stimulation in argument. You stress the importance of intellectual curiosity and the fun of debating. Bright students are naturally intellectually aware and the mental stimulation that comes from argument is exciting to them.

3. You make sure that they have an abundance of evidence to use

in debate. You yourself provide materials such as *The Reference Shelf* and *The Debaters Handbook*. You encourage them to work hard to provide superior bibliographies. You assist them in their selection and evaluation of evidence and in their argumentation.

4. You help them in their development of critical thinking and in their anticipation of arguments from opponents.

5. You schedule meetings, often with the help of a student committee.

6. You superintend the selection of judges and the running of debate tournaments.

DEBATE TOURNAMENTS

Frequently you will teach in a school where debate is a going concern and where, during your first year, you will be expected to participate in a debate tournament. In some subsequent year your school may serve as host for the debate tournament. Where debate is not an established activity, you may wish to initiate a debate tournament. Frequently you can get suggestions and assistance in initiating a debate tournament from a debate coach in a neighboring college. Or you can invite other speech teachers in the area to serve with you as a committee to plan a tournament.

Planning the Tournament

In planning such a tournament you need to keep in mind several factors: available dates, administrative approval, invitations to teams to participate, managing of the tournament, and the securing of judges.

Before you begin to plan a tournament, you make sure that your school administration approves of the idea. You talk over with the head of your department or your principal the feasibility of a tournament, possible dates, necessary facilities, the assistance of other staff members, and finances. In each instance you must be specific. You arrive with several tentative dates, with an outline of the school facilities you will need and the times when you will need them, with a detailed explanation of needed help from other staff members, and with a provisional budget.

After you have secured approval, you choose your date. You discover which date is the best from the standpoint of your own school and of the participating schools. You are then ready to issue letters of invitation. Either a committee issues the letters or you do it alone in the name of your school. You include in the letters the place, date, hour, the kind of debate, probable number of rounds, awards, a tentative list of the judges, and an entry blank.

After this, more thoughtful and detailed plans will be required. First, you must make certain that the auditorium and a specific number of the rooms in your building are available for that particular time. Second, you must provide meals and lodging when the students are to stay overnight. Frequently churches or the school will prepare meals inexpensively. Sometimes visiting students are housed with your debating students; other times they are housed at a local inn or motel. The invited students should know before they arrive where they will stay and eat and what the cost of the lodging and meals will be. Third, you should have the necessary materials for conducting the tournament handy. These include judges' folders with their ballots, the timekeepers' stop watches and time sheets, and the certificates or trophies which are to be awarded. You also provide a supply of note paper and pencils. Students can assist you in this planning.

The organization of the activities of the day also requires careful preparation. First, at the first general meeting you see that the group is welcomed and that procedures are explained. You may well invite your principal to welcome the group. One of the judges may explain the evaluation procedure. You yourself make clear the programs of debates. Second, you post the schedule of rounds with their times, judges, and timekeepers. You see that no judge judges a group from his school and that no judge judges the same group twice. Third, you prepare for the closing session, a banquet, reception, or an assembly meeting, where the awards are presented, with close attention to all of its detail.

Judging the Tournament

Before you tell the opposing team who your judges will be, you write and invite them to serve. You tell them the date, the kind of debate, what is expected of them as judges, the schools likely to participate, and the fee which you can pay. In addition, you make clear whether expenses to and from your school will be paid and what they include. When at all possible, you should pay your judges. Just as umpires in football games are paid, so should debate judges be paid. Judging a debate is as onerous and time-consuming as umpiring a football game. The responsibility of giving valid criticism and of making a decision requires professional training, expert listening, and effective speaking. Such professional service deserves payment. When you have received the judges' notes of acceptance, you may list them as judges.

You prepare for the judging by supplying your judges with folders containing ballots. Your committee may have agreed upon the content of the ballots or you may decide on it yourself.

Second, you ask the judges to give critiques: as a result the students participating and the audience gain knowledge of an evaluation of a debate. Since most judges are teachers, they give their criticisms tactfully and in such a way that the experience is a valuable one.

SUGGESTED READING

See bibliography at the end of the chapter on discussion for books and articles that deal with both discussion and debate.

BRADLEY, B. E., Jr., "Debate—A Practical Training for Gifted Students," *The Speech Teacher,* VIII (March 1959), 134-138. Focuses attention on the values of debate.

CAPP, G. R., HUBER, R., and EUBANK, W. C., "Duties of Affirmative Speakers—A Symposium," *The Speech Teacher,* VIII (March, 1959), 139-149. Explains the duties of the first and second affirmative speakers in the constructive and rebuttal speeches.

CARMACK, P. A., "The Development of State High School Speech Leagues," *The Speech Teacher,* III (November, 1954), 264-268. Describes typical management of a state contest or festival.

DONALDSON, A., "Experimenting in Debate," *The Speech Teacher,* I (January, 1952), 42-45. Tells about the use of debate in high schools.

FREELAY, A. J., "An Anthology of Commentary on Debate," *The Speech Teacher,* IX (March, 1960), 121-126. Quotes the opinion of leaders in our country on the values of debate.

FRIEDMAN, R. P., "Purdue University High School Debaters Conference and Student Legislative Assembly," *The Speech Teacher,* VII (September, 1958), 226-232. Tells about debate events, legislative assembly, special events, fiscal and physical facilities, and personnel of the conference.

FRIEDERICH, W. J., and WILCOX, R. A., *Teaching Speech in High Schools*

(New York, The Macmillan Co., 1953), Ch. 6. Contains goals, proposed syllabus, and methods and procedures for teaching debate.

FUGE, L. H., and NEWMAN, R. P., "Cross-Examination in Academic Debating," *The Speech Teacher*, V (January, 1956), 66-70. Explains cross examination in debating clearly. Contains a sample cross examination from a high school debate.

GILMAN, W. E., ALY, B., and REID, L. D., *The Fundamentals of Speaking* (New York, The Macmillan Co., 1951), Ch. 26. Defines debate and the kinds of debate. Explains the principles of preparing and presenting a debate.

GILMAN, W. E., "Debate," in MULGRAVE, Dorothy, *Speech: A Handbook of Voice Training, Diction and Public Speaking* (New York, Barnes & Noble, Inc., 1954), Ch. 6. Gives uses of debate, types of debating, requirements for wording the proposition, explanation of issues and of the preparation of a brief. Contains a sample brief.

MILLER, N. E., "Some Modifications of Contest Debating," *The Speech Teacher*, II (March, 1953), 139-140. Offers criticisms of conduct of forensic programs. Suggests better ways to conduct them.

MILLS, G. E., "Audiences and Tournaments; Two Forms of Overemphasis," *The Speech Teacher*, IX (March, 1960), 95-98. Refutes some of the criticism made of high school debate, particularly that of debate without an audience. Emphasizes importance of a thorough oral critique and of participation in both tournament and audience debate situations.

REID, L., *Teaching Speech* (Columbia, Mo., Artcraft Press, 1954), Ch. 12. Gives clear directions on how to debate. Includes a section on tournament debating.

ROBINSON, J. L., "Are We 'Over Legalizing' School Debate," *The Speech Teacher*, IX (March, 1960), 109-115. Lists the malpractices in school debate. Suggests that the item *ethics* be placed on evaluation sheets.

ROBINSON, K. F., *Teaching Speech in the Socondary School* (New York, Longmans, Green & Co., Inc., 1954), Chs. 20 and 21. Gives explicit directions on running a debate tournament. Contains material on evaluation of debates. Describes in detail a training program in debate.

SMITH, C. C., "Practical Procedures in Coaching High School Debate," *Quarterly Journal of Speech*, XXIX (April, 1943), 222-234. Lists the types of debate. Tells how to select the squad. Gives suggestions for the coach on debate strategy and management. Includes a timetable for getting a debate ready.

WATKINS, L. I., ed., "Ethical Problems in Debating," *The Speech Teacher*, VIII (March, 1959), 150-156. Discusses causes for problems that exist. Suggests types of constructive behavior for the coach.

WEAVER, A. T., BORCHERS, G. L., and SMITH, D. K., *The Teaching of Speech* (New York, Prentice-Hall, Inc., 1952), Ch. 15. Contains an excellent discussion of when debate is appropriate. Explains clearly how to teach material on debate.

WINDES, R. R., Jr., "Competitive Debating: The Speech Program, the Individual and Society," *The Speech Teacher,* IX (March, 1960), 99-108. Shows the values of debating to our society. Makes a case for tournament debating. Refutes arguments against tournament debating. Tells how to promote the cause of ethical debating.

AUDIO-VISUAL AIDS

How to Judge Authorities (Coronet, black and white, color, 1 reel). Gives criteria for judging an audience's acceptance of authorities.

How to Judge Facts (Coronet, black and white, color, 10 minutes). Shows how materials may have double meanings. Tells how to guard against false analogies, unfounded assumptions, and platitudes.

Learn to Argue Effectively (Coronet, black and white, 11 minutes). Contrasts serious use of argument with irrelevant, purposeless use.

EXERCISES

1. Phrase four debate propositions that might well interest high school students.
2. Write a paper entitled, "The Role of Debate in High School Social Studies Classes."
3. Refute the statement, Discussion has a place in democratic society but debate does not.
4. List ways in which you would foster good human relationships in debate.
5. Listen to a high school debate. Indicate the high school students' abilities in handling facts, opinions, and appeals, and in reasoning.
6. Make a checklist of items that must be planned for an interschool debate. It will be similar to the checklist on assemblies in Chapter XV.

IV·

TEACHING
INTERPRETATIVE ARTS

9

Oral Reading

SINCE MOST HIGH SCHOOL STUDENTS believe they know how to read aloud, you must motivate them to be critical of their reading aloud. Then, you show them how they can become more effective oral readers. You, therefore, teach either a course or a unit in reading aloud. Usually this work comprises a unit in a fundamentals course.

AIMS

The aims of this unit consist of the acquisition of certain understandings, attitudes, and skills. These are:

Understandings
  Definition of oral reading
  Purposes of oral reading
  Factors in choosing a selection for oral reading
  How to arrive at the meaning of a selection
  How to arrive at the mood of a selection
  Principles of imparting meaning
  Principles of imparting mood

Attitudes
  Appreciation of the literary value of a selection
  Recognition of the importance of reading aloud in giving information

Skills
  To select material appropriate for oral reading
  To impart meaning and mood of selections to an audience
  To listen thoughtfully, appreciatively, sympathetically, and critically

To accomplish these aims you may include the following material:

CONTENT

Definition

Purposes of Oral Reading

Selection of Material for Oral Reading
  Interests of the Reader
  Interests of the Audience
  Literary Value
  Adaptability to Reading Aloud

Understanding Meaning
  Significance of the Title
  Finding the Main Idea
  Looking up Meaning of Unfamiliar Words
  Looking up Allusions to Names and Places
  Looking up Historical and Geographical Background
  Learning the Influence of the Author's Background
  Comprehending the Relationship of Punctuation and Grammar to
    Meaning

Understanding Mood
  Influence of Literary Devices
  Feelings and Attitudes Evoked by Selection

Imparting Thought
  Highlighting Important Ideas
  Subordinating Dependent Ideas
  Indicating Units of Thought
  Showing Causal Relationships
  Introducing New Ideas
  Highlighting Ideas Repeated for Emphasis
  Relating Thoughts in a Series
  Building Climax
  Contrasting Ideas
  Comparing Ideas
  Indicating Parallel Attention
  Noting Concession

Imparting Mood
  Using Attributes of Voice
    Quality

You define oral reading as the communication of the meaning and mood of a selection to listeners who respond to its ideas and feeling. Some high school boys and girls define oral reading in the same way; others, however, have preconceived false notions. They may visualize a girl with a beautiful voice intoning, "In Scarlet town, where I was born, There was a fair maid dwellin'," or a boy with sweeping gestures declaiming, "Curfew shall not ring tonight." You help such students to arrive at a usable definition of oral reading.

DEFINITION

One teacher talks with her boys and girls about the kinds of oral reading in which they engage. At one class session, various members noted the following experiences in oral reading:

A thirteen-year-old girl told of reading a recipe for cherry cobbler to her mother who was preparing the dish.

One fourteen-year-old boy described reading ghost stories to his young charges at camp, explaining that they liked the eerie, uncanny quality of the stories.

A twelve-year-old boy said he read the scriptures at the opening services of Sunday School last Sunday.

A thirteen-year-old boy, Herman, reminded the group that when Joan spoke on achieving creative peace in the world, she concluded her speech by reading two verses of Oppenheim's "Create Great Peace." Herman remarked that everyone in the class had been still, impressed with Oppenheim's idea of a peace of discipline and justice.

From these examples, the students listed what the readers did and what happened to the listeners. They included:

What the Reader Did	*What the Listeners Did*
Read words.	Understood the words.
Read ideas to reinforce his own point of view.	Understood the story.
Read a story.	Understood the directions and followed them.
Felt the eerie quality of the story.	Stopped to think about what was being read.
Entertained his charges.	Felt frightened by the ghost story.
Knew what he was reading and why.	Was impressed by another's ideas.

The analysis of the common elements of the above lead to these general assertions about oral reading: You understand what you are reading and you make it clear to your listeners. You also are sure of what you feel about your material and make your listeners feel as you do. The members of the class, with these concepts as a basis, arrived at this definition: Oral reading is understanding the meaning and feeling of the author and conveying both this meaning and feeling to the listeners so that they react to what has been read.

PURPOSES

After formulating the definition, these same boys and girls talked about the purposes of reading aloud. One boy told of his English teacher's sensitive reading of Frost's "The Death of the Hired Man" and the resulting pleasure of the members of the class. This purpose, to share delight in a piece of literature, is the most important one. It is further exemplified by a sixteen-year-old boy's reading aloud the section from the *Autobiography of Lincoln Steffens* which tells of the closeness of the relationship between Steffens and his six-year-old son Pete; Steffens includes a ditty that he and Pete made up: "Pete and Papa are wonderful: Mamma and Anna (the maid) are absurd." This boy, in communicating effectively the intellectual and emotional significance of his selection, was giving an oral reading at a quite complicated level.

The second purpose is the one illustrated in the reading of the recipe: to give information. This communication was oral reading at a simple level, for the ideas in the recipe were not complex and the feeling engendered was not involved.

Boys and girls are always surprised to find how often they use oral reading. John, a high school sophomore, kept an account for one day of his activities in oral reading. At breakfast he read the weather report from the newspaper to his parents. On his way to school he read aloud an address from a slip of paper for a stranger who had forgotten his glasses. In various classes during the school day, he read aloud a problem in algebra, an editorial on labor unions, and the part of Mio in *Winterset*. The only class in which he did not read aloud was his speech class. Students read aloud more frequently than they realize.

MATERIAL FOR ORAL READING

The choice of literature for oral reading by high school students depends upon: (1) the interests and capacity of the reader, (2) the interests of the audience, (3) the literary value of the material, and (4) the adaptability of the material for reading aloud.

Interests and Capacity of the Reader

Original Material

One way to make sure that the student reads material in which he is interested and which he is capable of reading is to have him read what he himself has written. Consequently, you may well encourage your boys and girls to write material that reads aloud well. One particular teacher had her students talk about the various sounds that are part of a day's living. As a result of this discussion, a seventeen-year-old girl, wrote:

Music of the Masses

A deep fog lay over the bay—the kind that shuts out the world, leaving only heavy gray. Through the thick air the horn sounded as though it were being choked by the smoke-like fog. The low moan came. How Columbus' crew would have welcomed it. Paul Jones' crew stood on deck and listened for it. A Cape Cod fisherman turned his craft because of it and headed in for land.

Yes, for centuries, the men at sea heard and were thankful for the fog horn's music.

* * *

They fought hard and long but now liberty was theirs! Here was a song for all the world to hear. But how could they carry this song of freedom to all the world. How?

They shouted, shot muskets, sang until they were hoarse. But no, that was not enough. Their voices were not enough. The bronze bell! The great bronze bell would ring out their song. The voice of all the people calling to all mankind in its single tone the words inscribed in its crown:

"Proclaim Liberty Throughout All the Land Unto
All the Inhabitants Thereof."

The music of that bronze bell fills the heart of every American.

* * *

So this was it. It had finally come. He lay very still; the least move might warn the enemy and that warning might mean death to a great many men. Black—everything was pitch black. No sound came. No sound except the thud of his own pulse and his own unsteady breathing. No sound. He began to wonder whether he had fainted or could he have been. . . . Suddenly sound came. All about him he heard the dread music: the loud tympany, the snare drum roll, cymbal crashes and the rapid staccato. In high school he had been a drummer but never had he known drums like these. His first big fight.

He, like a million others, heard the hateful symphony of war.

* * *

The room was bright and sunny. Gran liked rooms that way. She lay looking very small in the large oak bed. It was strange to see Gran still. Gran whose house always shone, who belonged to the Ladies' Aid and the Red Cross, who ran the church suppers, who helped everyone and anyone who needed help and those who didn't too, who baked wonderful cakes, and who raised six ordinary but awfully nice children. My Gran—still— it was ridiculous—but it was true. The kettle as always was sitting on the kitchen stove and now it began to hum as the water boiled. Pete, the canary, joined in. How many times I have heard those sounds; but now they didn't seem the same. Pete soon stopped. He felt that one of the trio was missing.

The symphony of Gran's life had come to its close. It was a beautiful symphony though not perfect. Kindness and love brought beautiful tone coloring; laughter added brightness; sorrow made it more mellow than a thousand cellos. Trouble placed a discord here and there; anger gave it vividness. Children lavished joy and strength. Cleanliness supplied sparkle.

And throughout hope and faith furnished continuity. Happiness was its theme. Gran's symphony ended as it had been played throughout the years—the finale calm and quiet; the last chord a sigh.

Grace Gilbert

The reward of this seventeen-year-old girl was rapt attention on the part of her audience followed by a moment of silence.

Another student who had just spent a year in Chile shared the following poem with his classmates:

> Majestic, pure, tall and clear
> The Andes soar, steep and sheer,
> A blaze of light from dawn to dark
> Above a land, lonely, stark,
> A skyward stretch of shining snow,
> God's glorious eternal show.
>
> *Richard P. Lange*

Sometimes the sharing goes beyond the classroom. For instance, an English teacher of a New York City high school selected several bits of creative writing from her classes and invited their authors to read them over the local radio station. The following was composed and read by a fourteen-year-old girl:

The many-headed monster sleeps fitfully on the cluttered ground. It stirs, awakening with a singular discord, stretches, yawns, and idly looks around; when one identical countenance, more perceptive than the rest (or, perhaps, just more the fool), spots, nearby, a shining object, swoops down upon it, and raises it aloft with such a roosterish pride, to convince them all (as he himself is convinced) that here before them is the current hero-idol.

And now we find that he, who could succeed, at most, in raising a mild dislike in the breasts of his fellows, is quite capable of stirring passions, running the gamut from hate to a sort of awe (which has to serve as love for most of these) and—always—envy.

But soon, with that unexcelled boredom which is only born of dimmed fervor, the many-headed monster lies sleeping once again.

Lydia Razran, September, 1958.

Material to Meet Interests of Students

The subject matter of a selection for oral reading should be related to the students' interest and experiences. In one class, a boy intending to become an architect read from Frank Lloyd Wright's *The Future of Architecture;* a would-be comedian, from Fred Allen's *Treadmill to Oblivion;* a future ballerina, from Agnes G. DeMille's *Dance to the Piper;* a student journalist, from William Allen White's *The Autobiography of William Allen White.* A speech teacher had suggested these books as possible sources and guided the students in their selection of particular parts of the books. In addition, this teacher made other recommendations based on the students' experiences. For instance, she encouraged one boy in her group to read Robert Frost, because he had spent the summer in New England. He enjoyed reading some of Robert Frost's poems to his classmates and explaining how similar his impressions of New England were to Frost's. In each of these illustrations, the selections chosen were related to a student's interest or experience.

Level of Difficulty of Material

Even though the content may interest the student, some material is more difficult to read aloud than others; the level of the material should be matched to the pupil. In a speech class, one fourteen-year-old boy, struggling to read aloud Shakespeare's "When in Disgrace with Fortune" clearly did not understand what he was reading. When the teacher asked him why he had chosen this particular poem, he replied, "I thought if I read Shakespeare, I'd get a *B;* but if I read something I liked, I'd get a *D* or maybe an *F.*" This lad had difficulty getting the meaning of what he read. The teacher, therefore, decided to interest him in reading tall tales. He fully appreciated their humor; and when he read "They Make Excellent Pets,"[1] the story of the rattlesnake who became a pet, he brought out all its wry, dry humor. From this tall tale, he graduated to short cowboy stories; and from these, to ballads. Finally he read aloud with obvious comprehension and considerable feeling Robert Frost's "Stopping by Woods on a Snowy Evening."

On the other hand, some of your group may well begin by reading material that appears difficult to interpret. They will be able to look up the allusions in: "The bright-haired Vesta long of yore/ To solitary Saturn bore;" understand the line's implications, and

[1] B. A. Botkin, *Treasury of American Folklore* (New York, Crown Publishers, Inc., 1944), p. 622.

read the poem with acceptable meaning and appropriate feeling; furthermore, they will appreciate the magical effect of the words, the sounds, and the images. They may go on to read still more difficult poetry. You begin with the prose and poetry your boys and girls can understand and appreciate, and as the term progresses, you motivate them to read poetry with more difficult ideas, words, and images. But they must make sure that the selection with the more difficult ideas, words, and images appeals to their audience.

Interests of the Listeners

Just as the speaker considers his audience in selecting a topic, so does the reader in choosing his selection. He takes into account his listeners' likes, dislikes, and prejudices. Sometimes the particular occasion or time of year influences the listeners' attitudes toward material. For example, one day just before Christmas vacation, the teacher of a fundamentals of speech class asked various students to prepare Christmas material for reading aloud. A twelve-year-old boy read the Christmas story from the Bible. A thirteen-year-old boy read Dickens' *Christmas Carol*. A twelve-year-old girl read a little known Christmas poem, "Christmas Morning," by Elizabeth Madox Roberts. This program was appropriate for the Christmas season.

At other times factors in the environment play a part in the listeners' interest in material. You find poems for your students to read on snowy days, on foggy days, or on rainy days. Or perhaps you are teaching in New York City. If you are, Walt Whitman's *Mannahatta* is an ideal selection for some member of your group to read. The interest soon extends beyond one borough of New York City to Whitman the man, to his wanderings, to his changes of personality, to his striving for success, and to the concepts expressed in his poetry.

One speech teacher even found herself the stimulus for a selection. She always insisted on accuracy, making sure that each quotation was exactly right, that the word used expressed the meaning precisely, and that a paraphrase of a quotation was correct. One lad seemed always to misquote slightly or slant his sources to prove his point. After a rather sharp rebuke from the teacher, he selected the following poem to read aloud:

The Purist[2]

I give you now Professor Twist,
A conscientious scientist.
Trustees exclaimed, "He never bungles!"
And sent him off to distant jungles.
Camped on a tropic riverside,
One day he missed his loving bride.
She had, the guide informed him later,
Been eaten by an alligator.
Professor Twist could not but smile.
"You mean," he said, "a crocodile."

Ogden Nash

Both the teacher and students enjoyed this appropriate bit of humor.

Importance of Literary Value

In selecting material for oral reading, you consider not only its interest to the reader and his audience, but also its literary value. You relate your teaching of literary value to that of the teachers of English in your school. You find out how you can reinforce their teaching.

One teacher listed these three criteria for literary value: universality, imaginativeness, and suggestibility. She then asked her students to describe in one sentence a train's rushing through their town. The writings included:

The train makes a shiny silver streak at midnight.
The train goes madly through the middle of our town.
Dash—dash—dash—and it's gone!
A whistle—a whiz—the Empire State has whisked by.
The train goes quickly through our town each night.

The students talked about the different words used to express the same idea and about the feelings evoked by them.

After this discussion, the teacher read her students two poems about trains.

[2] From *Verses From 1929 On* by Ogden Nash by permission of Little, Brown, & Co. Copyright 1935 by The Curtis Publishing Company.

I Like to See It Lap the Miles[3]

I like to see it lap the miles,
And lick the valleys up,
And stop to feed itself at tanks;
And then, prodigious, step

Around the pile of mountains,
And, supercilious, peer
In shanties by the sides of roads;
And then a quarry pare

To fit its sides, and crawl between,
Complaining all the while
In horrid, hooting stanza;
Then chase itself down hill

And neigh like Boanerges;
Then, punctual as a star,
Stop—docile and omnipotent—
At its own stable door.

Emily Dickinson

Still Life[4]

Cool your heels on the rail of an observation car
Let the engineer open her up for ninety miles an hour.
Take in the prairie right and left, rolling land and new hay crops, swaths
of new hay laid in the sun.
A gray village flecks by and the horses hitched in front of the post office
never blink an eye.
A signalman in a tower, the outpost of Kansas City, keeps his place at a
window with the serenity of a bronze statue
on a dark night when lovers pass whispering.

Carl Sandburg

Since the teacher had already set up three criteria of literary value: universality, imaginative writing, and suggestibility, the members

---

[3] Reprinted by permission of the publishers from *The Poems of Emily Dickinson*, Thomas H. Johnson, Editor, Cambridge, Mass., The Belknap Press of Harvard University Press, Copyright 1951, 1955 by the President and Fellows of Harvard College.

[4] From *Cornhuskers* by Carl Sandburg. Copyright, 1918, by Henry Holt & Co. Inc. Copyright 1946 by Carl Sandburg. By permission of Holt, Rinehart and Winston, Inc.

of the group then discussed their own writing and the two poems in terms of these three criteria. They first talked about universality. All the students agreed that almost everyone thinks about trains, where they go, and what they are all about. One of the boys made the point that people like to dream of riding on trains.

The most interesting statements were on imaginative writing. One sixteen-year-old boy remarked, "Dickinson and Sandburg make us look like what we are—amateurs." Another seventeen-year-old girl observed that whereas all of the members of the class had written their sentences from the point of view of the train's being an inanimate object traveling through the village, that Emily Dickinson had written her poem from the point of view of the train's being animate and that Sandburg had written his from that of a rider on a train. Another boy indicated that he particularly liked the idea of the train lapping the miles and licking the valleys up. Another boy volunteered that some of the class might not know who Boanerges was and explained that he was the son of thunder. Another girl noted that you could almost fit Emily Dickinson's train into a painting by Grant Wood. Still another boy said that he liked the way Emily Dickinson halted the train. At this point one of the group read Emily Dickinson's poem.

After the reading, one eighteen-year-old said that he preferred Carl Sandburg's poem, because there was something inane and simple about a train's crawling and complaining; but that he could readily visualize a man about town cooling his heels on the rail of the observation car, looking out over all the countryside. This statement started an argument over which was the better poem until the teacher remarked that our tastes in poetry differ just as our tastes in clothing differ. She pointed out that two men might both be equally well dressed but that she would prefer the man in the cream colored suit with a blue necktie, whereas Joan might prefer the one dressed in navy blue with a bright red necktie. Jack remarked that Carl Sandburg didn't say that the man was the "about-town" type. Again the teacher intervened, explaining that this interpretation is an example of the poem's suggestibility and pointing out that most of us do read into poetry some of our own concepts and ideas.

You may well use a completely different approach. Many of you will do no direct teaching of literary quality at all. You will, however, guide the students in their selection of poetry and by this guidance develop their taste. You develop appreciation for literary value in the way you find most suitable.

Adaptability of Material for Reading Aloud

Besides being of interest to the reader and his listeners, and having literary value, material must be the kind that reads aloud well. One new teacher found that her students chose selections from *Reader's Digest, Coronet,* and *Saturday Evening Post,* many of which did not read aloud well. She recognized at once that the difficulty lay in her assignment. Although she had taught the students to obtain the meaning and to arrive at the feeling of a selection, she had not worked with them individually or in groups on the selection of material. She had simply asked them to prepare a three minute reading for class. She, however, made constructive use of her poor assignment by showing how several of the articles were obviously not intended for reading aloud. Their sentence structure was long and cumbersome and they did not have a conversational sound. She made "conversational sound" clear by reading to them the first three paragraphs of "Aunt Jean's Marshmallow Fudge Diet."[5]

Fred Allen used to talk about a man who was so thin he could be dropped through a piccolo without striking a single note. Well I'm glad I never met *him*. I'd hate to have to hear about *his* diet.

I can remember when I was a girl—way back in Truman's administration and No-Cal was only a gleam in the eye of the Hirsch Bottling Company. In those days it was fun to go to parties. The conversation used to crackle with wit and intelligence because we talked about ideas—the aesthetic continuum in Western culture, Gary Cooper in Western movies, the superiority of beer over lotion as a wave-set, and the best way to use left-over veal.

Go to a party now and the couple next to you won't say a word about the rich, chocolate texture of their compost heap or how practical it's been to buy bunkbeds for the twins. They won't talk about anything except their diets—the one they've just come off, the one they're on now, or the one they're going to have to start on Monday if they keep lapping it up like this.

Jean Kerr

The students contrasted this piece of material with the unconversational one. The students agreed that conversational sound might well be one criterion for selecting material.

You are well aware that your students must understand the meaning intended by the author. They should comprehend the significance of the title and the main idea of their selection. They should also know the meaning of the words in the selection, the allusions to names and places, and sometimes the historical and geographical background. Frequently students must be aware of the author's purpose in writing and his background. Sometimes their study of punctuation and the grammar of the selection helps them to get a clearer idea of the meaning of the selection. You encourage your students to take into account all the factors that influence meaning.

TEACHING THE UNDERSTANDING OF MEANING

Significance of the Title

Sometimes boys and girls explain in their introduction to their oral reading the significance of the title of the poem or bit of prose that they are to read. Even when they have taken the material from part of a book, they do well to give the selection a title. For example, the boy who read from Lincoln Steffens' autobiography entitled his reading "Papa and Peter," since the selection was about these two characters. The girl who wrote the paragraphs on sounds in the world called the collection "Music of the Masses." She wanted to show that sounds have meaning to all people in all ways of life.

A sixteen-year-old boy read Edwin Arlington Robinson's "An Old Story," a short poem in which the narrator regrets that he has never known the worth of a friend until he has died. In his explanation of the title, this student wrote: "All of us have acted and felt as this man did. It *is* an old story." He used this idea in the introduction to his reading.

Finding the Main Idea

Admittedly when students spend too much time analyzing and studying a poem, they may lose interest in reading it aloud. But to read aloud well the boy or girl must know the main idea of his selection. In some selections the main idea is obvious. For example, the lad who read Ogden Nash's "The Purist" surely knew exactly what Ogden Nash's central idea is. So did the boy who read part of Steffens' autobiography. When, however, the student appears unsure of the main idea, or not to have realized it in his reading, you encourage him to discover it. You may question him about it or ask him to write it in his own words. For example, of Walt Whitman's "I Hear America Singing," a poem that tells of the mechanic, carpenter, mason, shoemaker, wood-cutter, and mother singing, one student wrote: "The main idea is that America is made up of all kinds of happy working individuals each singing his own particular song. It is similar to the *Ballad for Americans*."

Finding the Meaning of Unfamiliar Words

You should encourage boys and girls to find the meaning of unfamiliar words. For instance, one boy decided that he would like to read Robert Burns' "To a Louse on Seeing One on a Lady's Bonnet at Church." The first verse is:

> Ha! whaur ye gaun, ye crawlin ferlie?
> Your impudence protects you sairly:
> I canna say but ye strunt rarely,
>   Owre gauze and lace:
> Tho', faith! I fear ye dine but sparely
>   on sic a place.

The boy deduced the meanings of some of the Scottish dialect. He decided that *sic* meant *such.* When he came to the word *ferlie,* however, he was completely at sea. One of his classmates with a Scotch mother said, "My mother always tells me to come watch the ferlies. She means to come watch the excitement." Jack then had some concept of the meaning of *ferlie;* when he looked for the meaning in the dictionary, he found "something amazing or a wonder." By using the word in context, Jack's friend had helped Jack to gain a clearer meaning of the word than if he had just looked it up in the dictionary. Jack felt fairly certain that *strunt* meant *strut,* but to be sure he consulted his dictionary again. He found that he was right. Such a study of words is essential to an understanding of meaning.

Allusions to Names and Places

To understand the meaning of a selection, students must not only know the meanings of all the words, but also the allusions to names and places. Sometimes the allusion becomes clear in an incidental way. In the example cited earlier, the group member who knew who *Boanerges* was, was delighted to share his knowledge with his classmates. But usually students must look up the unknown allusion. One girl who was to read Wordsworth's "The World Is Too Much With Us" discovered that the last two lines contain references to Proteus and Triton. In order to understand this poem, she, therefore, first looked up the words in the dictionary and then found out more about them from a book on mythology.

Historical and Geographical Background

For full understanding a knowledge of the historical and geographical background is also necessary. One quite sophisticated sixteen-year-old senior chose to read this particular poem written by Suckling in 1643:

Song

Why so pale and wan, fond lover?
    Prithee, why so pale?
Will, when looking well can't move her,
    Looking ill prevail?
    Prithee, why so pale?

Why so dull and mute, young sinner?
    Prithee, why so mute?
Will, when speaking well can't win her,
    Saying nothing do't?
    Prithee, why so mute?

Quit, quit for shame! This will not move;
    This cannot take her.
If herself she will not love,
    Nothing can make her:
    The devil take her!

Sir John Suckling

He proceeded to learn something about Sir John Suckling and the group of court poets of the seventeenth century. Admittedly, elegance, grace, and gaiety of these fashionable gentlemen are revealed in every line. Because they are so obvious, you may feel that Bob did not need to learn what was happening in England in 1646. That Bob did, however, aided him in reading the poem well; furthermore, his summary of the historical background of the time helped his classmates to appreciate the poem more completely.

Author's Background

To read a biography of a poet before reading one of his poems is not necessary. Admittedly many poems speak for themselves. But a knowledge of the background of the writer frequently aids the reader in understanding the poem more thoroughly and in interesting his audience in it. Boys and girls like to know that Carl Sandburg tried his hand at truck driving, scene shifting, delivering milk, and going to college. This information helps them to appreciate some of the universal appeal of his poetry. Whether you ask the student to find out the writer's background depends to a large extent on the kind and content of the selection to be read.

Relation of Punctuation and Grammar to Meaning

Students have been taught from time immemorial to stop at the commas and the periods and to raise their voices at the question marks. We usually do stop at a period, for the period indicates the end of a thought group. The meaning, however, dictates whether we stop at commas or raise our voices at question marks. You can help students understand the relationship between punctuation and meaning by an analysis of written lines. For example, one teacher gives to her students cards, large enough to be read by the group, containing sentences. In the first group punctuation influences meaning decidedly.

Woman without her man would be a savage.
Woman! Without her, man would be a savage.

Some girls I know are always giggling.
Some girls, I know, are always giggling.

The second group contains identical questions with the same punctuation but with different intended meanings. Here the punctuation influences the meaning very little.

Are you coming, John? (meaning—Come quickly, John.)
Are you coming, John? (meaning—Are you coming with us this time?)
Are you coming, John? (meaning—Is John as well as Jack coming?)
Are you coming, John? (meaning—Are you coming rather than going?)

From such a study, boys and girls recognize that punctuation is more to the reader than a long stop or a short stop, that it should not be considered a reliable guide to oral reading, but that it is useful.

The same principle applies to grammar. As it helps your student to see which words belong together and the relationship of these words to other words or thought groups, it is useful. The students' concern with grammar is not with nouns, pronouns, kinds of sentences and clauses, but with which words belong together to make the meaning of the selection clear.

Written Assignments on Understanding Meaning

To make sure that your students do understand the meaning of a selection, you frequently ask them to turn in written material. The following are examples of material written by two different high school students in the same third year speech class.

TITLE: "On First Looking Into Chapman's Homer"
SIGNIFICANCE OF TITLE: The title indicates the subject matter of the poem.
AUTHOR: John Keats. John Keats lived in the early 1800's. His father kept a livery stable. Keats was the oldest of four children. His closest friend was Charles Cowden Clarke, the son of the master of the school that Keats attended. Clarke introduced Keats to Chapman's *Homer*.
MAIN IDEA: Keats was so excited about reading Chapman's *Homer* that he compared this excitement to that of an explorer or astronomer when he makes a new discovery.
MEANINGS OF UNKNOWN WORDS:
   demesne—estate or land of which the owner is in possession.
   fealty—faithfulness as a duty.
EXPLANATION OF IMAGES OR FIGURES OF SPEECH:
   Traveled—read widely.
   Realms of gold—good reading material.
   Goodly states and kingdoms—authors and their books.
   Western islands—literature of Europe and England.
   Bards—poets.
   Wide expanse—world of story-telling literature.

ALLUSIONS:

Cortez—Keats really meant Balboa who discovered the Pacific.

Darien—Isthmus of Panama.

FEELING: The feeling in this poem is one of wonder and amazement.

The second paper was written by a less able student.

TITLE: "The Little Turtle."

SIGNIFICANCE OF TITLE: This title indicates the subject matter of the poem.

AUTHOR: Vachel Lindsay. Vachel Lindsay was born in Springfield, Illinois in 1879. He attended college and an art school. He traveled to awaken in people a response to beauty. He was very patriotic. He was very high-spirited.

MAIN IDEA: The turtle caught the mosquito, flea, and minnow but not me!

MEANING OF UNKNOWN WORDS: *minnow*—a small fish.

EXPLANATION OF IMAGES OR FIGURES OF SPEECH: Self-explanatory.

ALLUSIONS: None.

FEELING: The feeling in this poem is a mixture of pride and fun.

TEACHING THE UNDERSTANDING OF FEELING

After you have helped your students to determine the author's intended meaning, you help them determine his intended mood. In English classes students have studied meter, rhyme, and the use of such figures of speech as alliteration. You can reinforce this teaching and at the same time help the high school student to understand the mood of what he is to read. For example, if a student is to read from Alfred Tennyson's *Sir Galahad*, you may well point out to him Tennyson's use of alliteration in the lines:

> The shattering trumpet shrilleth high.
> The hard brands shiver on the steel.

You then may well indicate how this use of alliteration helps to create mood in this poem.

Using Other Arts

For less-advanced students, you must make evident the important part that emotion and feeling play in writing. For instance, you may ask them to either paint, draw, or find a picture that illustrates Elinor Wylie's "Velvet Shoes." As they look at the pictures, the students absorb their whiteness, calmness, quiet, and peace. Using a different technique, a teacher, whose group had already studied creative drama, asked one student to portray the speaker in Wordsworth's "The World Is Too Much With Us" and another student, his friend. Two indignant young men spoke:

JOHN: Too many people in the world today are too busy being successful—earning money.

HARRY: Yes, everybody wants to own electric dishwashers and Cadillacs.

JOHN: How many people stop to look at a tree—like that one over there with its reds and yellows?

HARRY: Or to listen to the howling winds.

JOHN: Or to the splashing of the waves at sea.

HARRY: No—all of us are out to become millionaires.

Beginning with Materials about Familiar Experiences

Still another teacher working in New York City starts with a familiar subject, the subway. She begins by asking her students to express their own feelings about the subway. The boys' and girls' responses are as varied as:

"Boredom."
"Interest in watching the people."
"Uncomfortable because it's dirty and hot."
"I would have hated to build a subway."

She then reads Sandburg's "Subway" and the boys and girls contrast their feelings with his.

TEACHING IMPARTING OF THOUGHT
TO THE AUDIENCE

Using Original Material

Again one way to teach students the techniques of imparting thought is to start with their own. One teacher has the group write a short paragraph, guiding the writing of the paragraph to make sure that it has a conversational sound and that it contains material which requires use of various techniques of oral reading. The students read as they write. From this exercise she lays the foundation for reading aloud with meaning.

For example, this teacher, on one occasion, started with the word *grandpa*. She explained that this word alone did not make a thought group but that if they described Grandpa, it would. One girl submitted *sweet*. The teacher then suggested that they describe him with another word which was quite different from *sweet*. Joe chose *bossy*. Whereupon *grandfather* became "the sweet but sometimes bossy grandfather." This phrase, the teacher told her students, was a thought group. She then asked that they indicate what grandfather did. A boy thought of *ran*. Therefore, "The sweet but sometimes bossy grandfather ran." The teacher then called for two clauses, one beginning with *who*, that would describe grandfather still further and another that would tell why grandpa was running. The students produced: "The sweet but sometimes bossy grandfather, who thought his word law, ran as fast as he could across the fields, because he saw his three-year-old grandson Mickie heading for the brook."

As the students read this sentence aloud, they brought out the contrast between *sweet* and *bossy*, they subordinated the clause, "who thought his word law," and made clear the causal relationship in "because he saw his three-year-old grandson Mickie heading for the brook." The teacher explained that in reading aloud one indicates contrast and causal relationships and that one subordinates the less important ideas. They talked about how they showed contrast, causal relationships, and subordination in their reading aloud of this particular sentence.

At this point the teacher asked that for emphasis they repeat what Grandpa was doing. The following sentence resulted: "Grandpa ran and ran and ran, but three-year-old Mickie ran faster and faster and faster." The student who read this sentence failed to highlight the running. Another student showed how the repetition of *running* and *faster* should be highlighted. The teacher then explained the principle of highlighting when the writer has repeated for emphasis.

As a result of the teacher's request to carry the story forward, the students added two more sentences: "As Grandpa ran, he shouted, 'Come here, ye little monkey. Come here!' Might as well have saved his breath."

The teacher remarked that Grandma might well enter into the picture here. Grandma did with: "Grandma calmly looked on from the window. Finally she called, 'Mickie, ice cream's ready.'" The teacher emphasized that Grandma and her action were new ideas which needed to be highlighted.

The teacher then advised them to tell the most exciting part of the story. It was: "Mickie stopped dead in his tracks." The teacher then asked what else Mickie did. "Mickie stopped dead in his tracks, turned, headed right into Grandpa's arms." One of the boys volunteered to read the sentence. Here the teacher pointed out that the boy who read the sentence made clear that it was the most important part of the story by reading it more slowly and more loudly. Although he did both without thinking about it, the teacher told the group exactly what he had done. She also showed the group that in reading "stopped dead in his tracks, turned, headed right into Grandpa's arms," the boy was reading a series and that he had raised his voice on the first two phrases and lowered it on the last.

Several of the boys and girls then read the completed paragraph:

> The sweet but sometimes bossy grandfather, who thought his word law, ran quickly across the fields, because he saw his three-year-old grandson Mickie heading for the brook. Grandpa ran and ran and ran, but three-year-old Mickie ran faster and faster and faster. As Grandpa ran, he shouted, "Come here, ye little monkey. Come here!" Might as well have saved his breath. Grandma calmly looked on from the window. Finally she called, "Mickie, ice cream's ready." Mickie stopped dead in his tracks, turned, headed right into Grandpa's arms. Grandpa, spluttering, carried Mickie to Grandma.

From the writing, reading, and analysis of this material, the teacher laid down the principles for highlighting the important ideas, subordinating dependent ideas, indicating units of thought, showing causal relationships, introducing new ideas, highlighting ideas repeated for emphasis, relating thoughts in a series, building ideas to a climax, and contrasting opposite ideas.

On another day, still using as a base the story of Grandpa, this teacher taught techniques for making clear ideas that are compared, that are parallel in attention, and that note concession. She asked the students to compare grandpa to an animal. One of the students chose to compare him to a bull. He contributed, "Grandfather roared like a bull." The parallel attention took care of itself, for another student suggested that he ought to do more than roar like a bull. He, therefore, suggested: "Grandfather roared like a bull. He charged like a bull. He champed his food like a bull."

"But," the teacher interposed, "Remember you are very fond of Grandpa. He is a sweet old man."

Whereupon one of the girls submitted: "But he remained sweet, kindly, lovable. For all his quirks, he was our favorite relative." They conceded the point that although he was stubborn and bull-headed, they still liked him, and they read the material to indicate the concession. The teacher made them aware of how they had read the material to indicate parallel attention, concession, and comparison.

Assignment on Imparting Thought

The assignment following this teaching included an analysis of readily understood prose and poetry which contained the need for such techniques as highlighting important ideas, subordinating, indicating parallel attention, building the climax, and showing causal relationships. The students were asked to indicate which parts of the material called for such techniques. One of the poems included was Vachel Lindsay's "To a Golden-Haired Girl in a Louisiana Town." The students were quick to recognize the need for indicating parallel attention, contrast, the dependence of the clauses, the building of a series, and the climax in the line "You are my love."

In the following poem the students pointed out the need for emphasis due to repetition and for indicating parallel attention:

Old Roger

Old Roger is dead and gone to his grave,
He, Hi, gone to his grave.
They planted an apple-tree over his head,
He, Hi, over his head.
The apples grew ripe and ready to drop,
He, Hi, ready to drop.
There came an old woman of Hipertihop,
He, Hi, Hipertihop.
She began a picking them up,
He, Hi, picking them up.
Old Roger got up and gave her a knock,
He, Hi, gave her a knock
Which made the old woman to hipertihop,
He, Hi, Hipertihop.

Anonymous

Finally, she asked a student to read a carefully selected piece of prose. To read this selection well, the student had to highlight important ideas, subordinate dependent thoughts, build a series, indicate comparison, highlight new material, and note parallel attention.

HELPING STUDENTS TO IMPART MOOD

Using Original Material

Again an effective way to help students to interpret mood to an audience is through material written by the group. One teacher uses as his theme the different kinds of weather in the fall. One boy mentioned that he liked "the gentle kind of rain that went pit, pat, pit, pat." He spoke the words softly, slowly, and with a kind of mellow quality. Another boy said that he enjoyed "lying in bed at night, hearing the wind rage past his windows—wooh—woooh— wooooh." He used more voice, talked more quickly, and gave his hearers the feeling of angry wind. One of the girls noted that she liked "the first snowfall, coming so quietly, so gently—and just barely covering the ground with white fluff." She spoke softly and rather slowly. Another girl announced that she liked "the gay, crisp weather of the fall with the leaves rustling and whirling around you." She spoke quickly with a gay, joyous quality in her voice. At this point they wrote a poem together called "Fall Comes." After the reading of the poem, the members of the class analyzed the effects of volume, tempo, pitch, and quality on expressing the feeling of different ideas in the poem.

Assignments in Imparting Mood

As an assignment this teacher gave the students mimeographed poems asking the students to describe briefly the feeling that each poem or bit of prose evoked. Her list included:

Sara Teasdale's "The Coin"
Robert Frost's "After Apple Picking"
Edgar Allen Poe's "The Bells" (two verses)
Lew Sarett's "Four Little Foxes"
"Yaller Bread" (A Pioneer tale from Botkin's *Treasury of American* Folklore.)
"The Hyphen" (A Peacocks on Parade tale from Botkin's *New York City Folklore.*)
Excerpt from Charles Lamb's *Dream Children.*

On the next two days the students read the poems and bits of prose. The teacher recorded some of the readings and the members of the class evaluated them in terms of their ability to evoke the feelings intended by the author.

CHORAL SPEAKING

Introducing Choral Speaking

Usually high school students have spoken poetry together in elementary school. When they have not, you teach them the nature of choral speaking. You may ask them to listen to a record such as *The Verse Choir of the College of Chestnut Hill, Philadelphia* (Linguaphone Institute). Or you may prefer to use recordings of choral speaking made by your former classes. After listening to the record, the students point out the characteristics of choral speaking. Some compare it to choral singing. Others liken it to the antiphonal reading carried on at church. Still others say that it is rather like children chanting a popular ditty.

Members of one group noted the following characteristics of a recording of choral speaking:

The readers begin together.
They stay together.
They blend their voices.
Their words are clear.
They sound conversational.
They make you feel with them.
Their voices are expressive.
They make you understand what they are saying.

The next step is for the boys and girls to speak together. For this purpose one teacher used the poem about the weather that they had written together. Almost all the members of her group agreed that "The gentle rain goes pit-a-pat, pit-a-pat" needed light voices. Whereupon the girls said the line together softly and quietly. The boys interpreted, "The raging wind goes wooh-woooh-woooh." The teacher helped each group to start and stay together.

Division Into Light and Heavy Voices

From this discussion and participation, the students realize that they must divide themselves into two groups: heavy and light voices. You explain that the light voices are the higher-pitched, finer, and more delicate voices whereas the heavy voices are the lower-pitched, heavier, and fuller ones. Since one particular senior class had more girls than boys and since there was a wider variation in the voices of the girls, the teacher suggested three groups: I, Light; II, Medium; and III, Heavy. After each girl gave her name and address, the group decided whether she belonged in I or II. Where they were not certain, the girl tried her voice with both group I and group II. The boys made up group III.

Deciding on the Type of Choral Speaking

As the students speak together some of their own writing, they try at least one type of choral speaking. For example, in reading the poem on weather the boys read the parts that required heavy voices and the girls read the parts that required light voices. You, however, can help your boys and girls to recognize how the different kinds of choral speaking may enhance the meaning or feeling of the selection. You may well introduce the different types of choral speaking as the need for them arises. These types include: unison, antiphonal, refrain, cumulative, solo, and part speaking.

Types of Choral Speaking

Unison Speaking

Some poems maintain one mood and one theme throughout. When they do, they should be read in unison. You can teach your students to recognize such poems. Quite clearly the following poem needs to be read either by an individual or in unison, for it is a nonsense poem about one beast told by one person.

The Rhinoceros[6]

The rhino is a homely beast,
For human eyes he's not a feast,
But you and I will never know
Why nature chose to make him so.
Farewell, farewell, you old rhinoceros,
I'll stare at something less prepoceros!
Ogden Nash

[6] From *Verses From 1929 On* by Ogden Nash, by permission of Little, Brown, & Co. Copyright 1933 by Ogden Nash.

Antiphonal Speaking

In antiphonal speaking, two types of voices talk to each other. Thus boys and girls identify poetry suitable for this kind of choral speaking easily. The division of voices in such a poem as the following is quite obvious:

Whistle, Whistle

"Whistle, whistle, auld wife, and you'll get a hen."
"I wouldn't whistle," said the wife, "If you could give me ten."
"Whistle, whistle, auld wife, and you'll get a cock."
"I wouldn't whistle," said the wife, "If you gave me a flock."
"Whistle, whistle, auld wife, and you'll get a gown."
"I wouldn't whistle," said the wife, "for the best one in town."
"Whistle, whistle, auld wife, and you'll get a man."
"Wheeple, whauple," said the wife, "I'll whistle if I can."

Anonymous

The only problem that arises in choosing the type of reading for such selections is whether the voices questioning and answering should be light and heavy or two variations of the light or the heavy.

In the following poem some members of a class thought that the poem needed two groups of heavy voices whereas other members were quite sure that it could be done with light and heavy voices. One boy said, "Imagine girls reading Bret Harte."

Relieving Guard

Came the Relief, "What, Sentry, ho!
How passed the night through the long waking?"
  "Cold, cheerless, dark—as may befit
  The hour before the dawn is breaking."
"No sight? No sound?"
                "No; nothing save
  A plover from the marshes calling,
  And in yon western sky, about
  An hour ago, a star was falling."
"A star. There's nothing strange in that."
"No, nothing; but above the thicket.
  Somehow it seemed to me that God
  Somewhere had just relieved a picket."

Bret Harte

Refrain

In refrain speaking, the members of the class speak the refrain while one student or a group of students tell the story. Students quickly recognize that the following poem adapts well to refrain speaking.

The Holly and the Ivy

The holly and the ivy
Now both are full-well grown,
Of all the trees that are in the wood
The holly bears the crown.

   Refrain:
O, the rising of the sun,
The running of the deer,
The playing of the merry organ,
   Sweet singing in the choir.
   Sweet singing in the choir.

The holly bears a blossom
As white as lily-flower!
And Mary bore sweet Jesus Christ,
To be our Sweet Saviour.
   Refrain:

The holly bears a berry
As red as any blood:
And Mary bore sweet Jesus Christ,
To do poor sinners good.
   Refrain:

The holly bears a prickle,
As sharp as any thorn;
And Mary bore sweet Jesus Christ,
On Christmas day in the morn.
   Refrain:

The holly bears a bark
As bitter as any gall;
And Mary bore sweet Jesus Christ,
For to redeem us all.
   Refrain:

The holly and the ivy
Now both are well full grown,

Of all the trees that are in the wood
The holly bears the crown.

Refrain:

Anonymous

Cumulative Speaking

Choral reading achieves a cumulative effect with a small group reading one section, the original group and an additional one reading the second section, and the original group and two others reading the third section. Usually no more than five groups build the cumulative effect. You will need to show your boys and girls that this type is effective in poetry when the intensity must increase. In the following poem, cumulative choral speaking helps the excitement of Hannibal crossing the Alps to mount.

When Hannibal Crossed the Alps[7]

Hannibal crossed the Alps!
Hannibal crossed the Alps!
    With his black men,
    His brown men,

        His country men,
        His town men,
With his Gauls, and his Spaniards, his horses,
    and elephants.

Hannibal crossed the Alps!
Hannibal crossed the Alps!

Hannibal crossed the Alps!

    For his bowmen,
    His spearmen,
        His front men,
        His rear men,
With his Gauls, and his Spaniards, his horses,
    and elephants

Wanted the Roman scalps!
And *that's* why Hannibal, Hannibal, Hannibal,
    Hannibal crossed the Alps!

Eleanor Farjeon

[7] Eleanor Farjeon, *The Children's Bells* (New York, Henry Z. Walck, Inc., 1960). Copyright © 1960 by Eleanor Farjeon. Reprinted by permission of the publisher and Harold Ober Associates Incorporated.

Solo Part Speaking

In solo part speaking individual boys or girls speak different lines. In the following poem all the "I remembers" may be spoken by individual pupils; but the whole group may speak the "I have one remember, two remembers, etc."

New Hampshire Again[8]

I remember black winter waters,
I remember thin white birches,
I remember sleepy twilight hills,
I remember riding across New Hampshire
    lengthways.
I remember a station named "Halcyon,"
    a brakeman calling to passengers
    "Halcyon! Halcyon!"
I remember having heard the
    gold diggers dig out only
    enough for wedding rings.
I remember a stately child telling
    me her father gets letters
    addressed "Robert Frost, New
    Hampshire."
I remember an old Irish saying,
    "His face is like a fiddle and
    everyone who sees him must
    love him."
I have one remember, two remembers,
    ten remembers; I have
    a little handkerchief
    bundle of remembers.

One early evening star just over
    a cradle moon.
One dark river with a spatter of
    later stars caught,
One funnel of a motorcar head
    light up a hill,
One team of horses hauling a
    bobsled load of wood,

[8] From *Good Morning, America,* copyright, 1928, 1956 by Carl Sandburg. Reprinted by permission of Harcourt, Brace & World, Inc.

One boy on skis picking himself
up after a tumble—
I remember one and a one and a
one riding across New Hampshire lengthways; I have a little handkerchief bundle of
remembers.

Carl Sandburg

In one class a boy with a heavy voice that had some anger in it spoke the first line; a girl with a soft melodic voice the second line; a boy with a quiet resonant tenor voice the third line. Each line was spoken by someone who seemed able, partly because of voice, to interpret the line well. The members of one class took real pleasure in matching voices to the lines of this poem.

Part Speaking

You tell your students that part speaking is the type of choral speaking in which each group of the class speaks a portion of the selection. You stress that when a whole section expresses a slightly different emotion or theme, a different group may well speak it. Students enjoy dividing Lew Sarett's "Four Little Foxes" into groups. The first and third verses talk to Spring and the second and third to March. You may decide with your group that the whole poem should be spoken quietly but that the second and fourth stanzas lend themselves well to the heavier, more mellow voices whereas the first and third stanzas respond better to lighter, more delicately toned voices.

Selecting Material for Choral Speaking

Principles

All the criteria that apply to the choice of material for oral reading also apply to the choice of material for choral speaking. When your students select material for choral speaking, however, they should make sure that the thought is not open to many differ-ent, individual interpretations and that the poetry is adaptable to choral speaking. You guide your students not to try to read as a group poems like Edgar Lee Master's "Silence" or Elizabeth Barrett Browning's "How Do I Love Thee?" You make clear that these poems are too delicate and introspective for choral reading. If you do not make this fact clear, some members of the group will be adamant about accepting their particular interpretation.

You also help your students to make sure that the form of the poem is adaptable to choral speaking. You may have to explain that choral speaking needs strongly rhythmical poetry and poetry where variety in tempo and volume can express its different feelings. You will likely have to illustrate this principle with different bits of poetry.

Using a Theme

Material for choral speaking may be built around a theme. For example, one group used the theme of Abraham Lincoln; another, the theme of storm; another, the theme of cities; and still another, the theme of railroads and bridges. Still another group chose to read poetry and prose by Carl Sandburg. This particular group had within it two or three members who were modern dancers. With the help of the physical education instructor, they interpreted some of the Sandburg poetry in dance. In this same group another student was an able musician who liked to compose. He composed background music for some of the selections. Because the students were proud of their Sandburg program, they decided to share it with the rest of the school. The resulting program, presented before the student body, was well received.

Deciding on the Interpretation of the Poem

It is as necessary to understand both the ideas and the mood of the poem for choral speaking as for individual oral reading. Here, you should discuss with the members of the class all the elements of the poem. Individuals try reading lines in different ways, giving their reasons for their choices. Through questioning, you bring out the important ideas of the poem which the students have not mentioned. You must guard against boys and girls' arriving at the bizarre or unusual reading and substituting novel effects for an interpretation which sincerely imparts meaning and feeling. Just as their taste in clothing is not always mature neither is their taste in reading aloud. You help them to develop good taste.

One group of high school sophomores decided to read:

Nostalgia[9]

"Through pleasures and palaces"—
Through hotels, and Pullman cars, and steamships . . .

Pink and white camelias
    floating in a crystal bowl,
The sharp smell of firewood,
The scrape and rustle of a dog stretching himself
    on a hardwood floor,
And your voice, reading—reading—
    to the slow ticking of an old brass clock.

"Tickets please!"
And I watch the man in front of me
Fumbling in fourteen pockets,
While the conductor balances his ticket-punch
Between his fingers.

Amy Lowell

The students arrived at the main idea rather quickly: that here was someone sitting in a train daydreaming of all the pleasant events in his life when his dreaming was disturbed by the conductor's collecting his tickets. But the discussion from here was diverse. One girl was sure that the speaker was female, for only a woman would remember the pink and white camelias and that, furthermore, a man would not call attention to the fourteen pockets. One rather artistic boy said that he recalled a flower arrangement of lilacs and tulips from when he was a very little boy. The students agreed that actually whether the speaker was a man or a woman made little difference. They decided that different individuals would read lines one and two, three, four, five, and six, and that the recurring theme was the recollection of a very pleasant experience.

One boy asked that the conductor be a burly soul rudely shouting, "Tickets please," and that the disturbed daydreamer, who resented the intrusion, say the last few lines in an annoyed fashion. Another boy took the position that there was nothing in those lines to show annoyance. Finally the group decided that the whole class would read these lines in a way that would indicate that the narra-

[9] From *Pictures of the Floating World* (Boston, Houghton, Mifflin Co., 1919). Reprinted by permission of Houghton, Mifflin Co.

tor felt a remnant of nostalgic feeling mingled with slight amuse-
ment at the man hunting through all his fourteen pockets.

Teacher's Direction

Your direction involves having your students start together, stay
together, and speak with approximately the same interpretation.
You give the signal to start and to end and indicate the rhythm of
the poem. The rhythm can be revealed through onward flowing
motions of your hand; your response should be not to the beat of
the poem but to its meaning. You lead lightly so that the pupils
respond first to the meaning and then to the rhythm. You also
designate the pauses which the boys and girls and you have agreed
on earlier. You may reveal an increase or decrease in tempo and
in volume by the use of your other hand. After the students have
worked with you, they need little direction except indications of
where to begin and to stop. Often one of your students can give
whatever direction is necessary.

EVALUATION

Individual Oral Reading

At the end of each individual reading you and the students
evaluate the performance. You may have already criticized the preparation before the actual reading, for you may have gone over
the written analysis with the student. You and the students, however, talk about the reader's choice of material for reading, his
introduction to it, his evident understanding of the meaning and
feeling of the author, and his ability to communicate this meaning
and feeling. You consider other factors that have helped or hindered
the communication such as the reader's use of voice, of articulation,
of pronunciation, and of bodily movements. Finally you talk about
the total effect of the reading upon the audience.

You and the students may use a chart to guide this evaluation.
As in other areas of speech, the chart may take the form of a rating
sheet or of a form on which you and the students make comments.
Such forms follow:

ORAL READING EVALUATION CHART

NAME			
CHOICE OF SELECTION			
Appropriate for audience			
Of literary worth			
Inappropriate for audience			
Of doubtful literary worth			
EVIDENCE OF UNDERSTANDING MEANING AND MOOD			
Introduction revealed understanding			
Main idea clear			
Subordinate meanings clear			
Mood well portrayed			
Introduction showed meagre preparation			
Main idea hazy			
Subordinate meanings not always clear			
Mood inadequately portrayed			
TECHNIQUES OF CONVEYING MEANING AND MOOD			
Important ideas highlighted well			
Phrasing appropriate			
Volume appropriate			

Pitch appropriate			
Rate appropriate			
Acceptable articulation			
Important ideas not highlighted well			
Phrasing inappropriate			
Volume inappropriate			
Pitch inappropriate			
Rate inappropriate			
Substandard articulation			
AUDIENCE REACTION			
Interested			
Somewhat interested			
Uninterested			

Group Oral Reading

The evaluation of individual readings is fairly easily accomplished, for you have a room full of listeners. In choral speaking, however, your students are all participating. In this case, you may select two listeners, who do not participate, to criticize the reading. Or you may record the reading and after listening to the recording, you and the students evaluate it. In this method different groups of students may listen for different things. The following form may help in the evaluation of choral speaking:

ORAL READING EVALUATION SHEET

NAME .... DATE ....

SELECTION ....

CHOICE OF SELECTION:

INTRODUCTION OF SELECTION:

UNDERSTANDING OF MEANING:

UNDERSTANDING OF FEELING:

PROJECTION OF MEANING:

PROJECTION OF FEELING:

BODILY ACTIVITY:

VOICE AND ARTICULATION:

AUDIENCE RESPONSE:

SIGNED ....

EVALUATION CHART FOR CHORAL SPEAKING

SELECTION: ....

UNDERSTANDING OF MEANING:

UNDERSTANDING OF FEELING:

PROJECTION OF MEANING:

PROJECTION OF FEELING:

CONTRIBUTION OF ARRANGEMENT OF VOICES TO MEANING AND FEELING OF POEM:

BALANCE OF LIGHT AND HEAVY VOICES:

TECHNIQUES OF CHORAL SPEAKING:

Blending of Voices:

Clarity of Articulation:

Beginning Together:

Staying Together:

Moving Along:

DATE...................   SIGNED............................

EXTRACURRICULAR ACTIVITIES IN ORAL READING

Your school may engage in an oral interpretation festival. For the festival you select one, two, or three readers to represent your school at the city or regional meeting. You and your interpretation group may choose the readers by selecting them yourselves or by having a contest with a judge deciding on the winners. After you have chosen the readers, they go to the regional festival where critiques are made of each reader and where, in some cases, awards are made to those considered best.

Material for Reading

Usually there is broad scope in the choice of materials for a festival. Your students may choose either prose or poetry from a wide variety of sources using the same criteria as were discussed earlier. You make sure, however, that the selection can be read within the time limits announced by the festival chairman. The following are the titles of selections read by high school students at a festival sponsored by New York University on April 18, 1959:

"The Suicide" by Edna St. Vincent Millay
"Renascence" by Edna St. Vincent Millay
"The Hemp" by Stephen Vincent Benét
"Ash Wednesday" by T. S. Eliot
"Home Burial" by Robert Frost
Selections from "Paradise Lost" by John Milton
"Song of the Open Road" by Walt Whitman
Excerpts from "John Brown's Body" by Stephen Vincent Benét
"The people—Yes!" by Carl Sandburg
"The Murder of Lidice" by Edna St. Vincent Millay
"The Ship of Death" by D. H. Lawrence.

This program, a varied one both in terms of themes and poets, is made up of material with literary value. Too often, however, students read material chosen not for its literary worth but for its bizarre effects or its highly sentimental quality. You can break with such a tradition and introduce a run of quite different selections. One high school teacher of speech helped a boy pick one of Stephen Leacock's essays and a girl, one of Frost's poems. When both placed in the regional contest, teachers and students of the school reported such comments as, "It was unfair to read a poem," "Imagine reading something funny," "He sounded as if he were talking and not reading." Next year came a rash both of poetry and of conversational quality in reading.

At reading festivals conversational quality and not an exhibition of skills needs to be stressed. Too many elocutionists are still performing at these events. Perhaps one way is to make clear to all entrants the fundamental differences between reading and acting. You may well advise your own students to look at the chart in *Communicative Reading*[10] which shows the relationships of the interpretative speech arts and which does make clear the differences among acting, impersonative reading, and interpretative reading. It also clearly delineates the place of impersonation. Another way is to make sure that the judges are trained speech teachers. The local lawyer or a former opera singer may be a very worthy citizen but may have quite different values of oral reading from those trained speech teachers have.

Managing the Festival

Usually one school serves as host and representatives of the faculty from other schools serve as the committee for the festival. The committee or its chairman decide on the date, the place, the judges, and in some instances, a theme. Usually the chairman receives the titles of the selections well ahead so that no two readers from different schools read the same selection. Sometimes the group decides on a theme like "Spring," "Seventeenth Century Prose and Poetry," "Our Country—America," "Struggle for Justice," "War and Peace," "Personal Relationships." With a theme the resulting program is more unified.

The person who presides at the festival may be the principal of the host school, the winner of the previous year's contest, or the chairman of the committee. His introduction and transitional material should be brief and to the point. The chairman frequently conducts the discussion of the performance with the entering students, their teachers, and the critics. When awards are made, either the chairman of the festival or the presiding officer may present them.

[10] O. J. Aggertt and E. R. Bowen, *Communicative Reading* (New York, The Macmillan Co., 1956), p. 9.

The Critics' Evaluation

Again, as in other speech contests and festivals, it is more important for the experience to be a learning one than a winning or losing one. Careful evaluation of the readers' performances helps the students to read better another time. The critiques, therefore, should be thoughtfully prepared. When the critic can take time to discuss the performance with the contestants and their coaches, everyone learns from the experience.

Rating sheets are provided for the critics. These sheets are similar to the evaluation sheet for oral reading included in this chapter. In some cases critics are asked to award first, second, and third places to the contestants. As a result, they may rank the readers, may assign percentages, or may use a combination of both methods. The use of the percentage method alone is not valid. For instance, in one contest where the percentage method alone was used a boy, who was given two firsts and a third, placed third; another with one first and two thirds placed first; and one with three seconds placed second. This resulted from a spread of from 25 per cent to 100 per cent in one judge's scores with spreads of from 81 to 94 per cent in the other two judges' scores. The scoring follows:

	CONTESTANT A		CONTESTANT B		CONTESTANT C	
	Rating	Percentage	Rating	Percentage	Rating	Percentage
Judge X	1	.94	3	.88	2	.90
Judge Y	1	.89	3	.85	2	.87
Judge Z	3	.76	1	1.00	2	.90

Since the awards were made on the basis of percentage, contestant *B* with an average of 91 per cent placed first; contestant *C* with an average of 89 per cent placed second; and contestant *A* with an average of 86.3 per cent placed third. If, however, the awards had been made by adding the ratings, contestant *A* would have been given first place; contestant *C*, second place; and contestant *B*, third place.

Participation in an oral reading festival carries with it many benefits: It focuses attention on the values of oral reading and on the interest in it as an activity. It provides students with an opportunity to listen to superior readers from other schools. It gives them a chance to become acquainted with literature which they may not

know. And the superior readers benefit from the advice given by
the critics.

SUGGESTED READING

Oral Interpretation

AGGERTT, O. J., and BOWEN, E. R., *Communicative Reading* (New York,
The Macmillan Co., 1956). Contains many suggestions for teaching oral
reading in the high school. Includes selections that high school students
can understand and will enjoy.

CROCKER, L. G., and EICH, L. M., *Oral Reading* (Englewood Cliffs, N. J.,
Prentice-Hall, Inc., 1947). Contains a series of lessons dealing with
various aspects of oral reading.

DOLMAN, J., JR., *The Art of Reading Aloud* (New York, Harper & Brothers,
1956) .

DUNCAN, M. H., "Localizing Individual Problems in Oral Interpretation,"
Quarterly Journal of Speech, 32 (April, 1946), 213-216. Explains two
devices in teaching: use of standard personality inventories and a test
of expressiveness.

FLEISCHMAN, E. E., "Another Look at Interpretation," *Quarterly Journal
of Speech*, 35 (December, 1949), 477-483. Discusses the role of oral interpretation in today's education.

HARGIS, C. N., and HARGIS, D. E., "High School Literature and Oral Interpretation," *The Speech Teacher*, 2 (September, 1953), 205-208. Shows
the use of oral reading in the teaching of literature.

HENNEKE, B. G., *Reading Aloud Effectively* (New York, Holt, Rinehart
and Winston, Inc., 1954).

LEE, C. I., *Oral Interpretation* (New York, Houghton Mifflin Co., 1952).

MOUAT, L. H., "The Question Method for Teaching Emphasis in Oral
Reading," *Quarterly Journal of Speech*, 35 (December, 1949), 485-488.
Shows how emphasis (stress, pitch change, and pause) can be taught by
means of the teacher's questions. Good illustration of this kind of
teaching.

PARRISH, W. M., *Reading Aloud*, rev. ed. (New York, The Ronald Press
Company, 1941).

WOOLBERT, C. H., and NELSON, S., *Art of Interpretative Speech*, 4th ed.
(New York, Appleton-Century-Crofts, Inc., 1956).

Choral Speaking

ABNEY, L., *Choral Speaking Arrangements for the Junior High School*
(Boston, Expression Company, 1939). Gives the educational values of
choral speaking and suggests procedures. Contains many selections.

ADAMS, H., and CROASDELL, A., *A Poetry Speaking Anthology* (Boston, Expression Company, n.d.) Book III.

GULLAN, M., *The Speech Choir* (New York, Harper & Brothers, 1937). Presents the history and theory of choral speaking.

HAMM, A., *Choral Speaking Techniques* (Milwaukee, Wisc., Tower Press, 1946).

SWANN, M., *Many Voices* (London, General Howe, 1934). Suggests poems for high school students.

AUDIO-VISUAL AIDS

Appreciation of Poetry, Vol. I, *Great Themes;* Vol. II, *Our American Poetry;* Vol. III, *Speeches and Documents from American History* (National Council of Teachers of English Recording, Columbia Recording Company).

Dramatic Sketches by Judith Anderson (Victor Red Seal). Includes *Letter to Mrs. Bixby,* John La Touche's *The Fog* and *The Statue of Liberty.*

How to Read Poetry (Coronet, sound, 10 minutes). Demonstrates techniques of reading poetry aloud.

The Lady of the Lake (Coronet, black and white, color, 11 minutes). The narrator reads *The Lady of the Lake* while the viewer sees Scott's home, his working environment, and the locale of the poem. Emphasizes the importance of understanding the background of a poem to its interpretation.

Let's Read Poetry (Bailey Film Co., black and white, 10 minutes). Shows members of a class learning to read poetry.

Literature Appreciation: How to Read Poetry, Ruth Strang, ed. coll. (Coronet, black and white, color, 11 minutes). Indicates the importance of understanding a writer, sharing his experiences, and learning poetic devices in reading poetry.

Our Common Heritage, Great Poems Celebrating Milestones In the History of America, Louis Untermeyer, ed.; original music and sound effects composed by Victor Young and Lehman Engel with the Jean Neilson Verse Choir; read by Brian Donlevy, Agnes Moorhead, Frederic March, Walter Huston, Pat O'Brien, and Bing Crosby (Decca Album no. 536, 78 RPM). Complete on eight ten-inch records. Includes poems that "trace the course of our history from the very beginning through a series of crises to unity. They memorialize the milestones in the life of a nation." Includes such poems as Whittier's *Barbara Frietchie,* Emerson's *Concord Hymn,* Holmes' *Old Ironsides,* Markham's *Lincoln, the Man of the People,* and Lindsay's *Abraham Lincoln Walks at Midnight.*

Poet's Gold, read by Helen Hayes, Raymond Massey, and Thomas Mitchell (RCA—Victor, no. LM 1813, one 12″ disc, 33⅓ RPM. Available in album no. ERB 27, 45 RPM EP). Includes the reading of such poems as Keats' *Ode to a Grecian Urn,* Millay's *The Ballad of the Harp-Weaver,* Keats' *On First Looking into Chapman's Homer,* Browning's *My Last Duchess,* and Kipling's *Recessional.*

Poet's Gold: Verses of Today, read by Geraldine Brooks and Norman Rose RCA—Victor, no. L, one 12″ disc, 33⅓ RPM). Includes poems by such authors as Archibald MacLeish, Wallace Stevens, Edgar Lee Masters, Dorothy Parker, Ogden Nash, E. B. White, Hilaire Belloc, Louise Bogan, T. S. Eliot, Robinson Jeffers, Richard Eberhart, W. H. Auden, and Dylan Thomas. The poetry has been chosen for more sophisticated taste. The interpretation is excellent. Advanced students will enjoy it.

Robert Frost—Reading His Own Poems (National Council of Teachers of English Recording, RCA—Victor, six 78 RPM discs or two 10″ 33⅓ RPM discs).

Lew Sarett, Reading from his Collected Poems (By permission of Henry Holt, Clark Weaver, dist., 1426 N. E. Seventh St., Gainesville, Florida, 33⅓ RPM). Includes 14 nature poems and Indian songs.

POETRY FOR ORAL READING

AUTHOR	TITLE OF POEM	FIRST LINE OF POEM
Coffin, Robert P. Tristram	*Hound on the Church Porch*	"The farmer knew each time a friend went past"
	The Secret Heart	"Across the years he could recall"
cummings, e e	*Impression: IV*	"the hours rise up putting off stars and it is"
de la Mare, Walter	*Silver*	"Slowly, silently now the moon"
Frost, Robert	*After Apple-Picking*	"My long two-pointed ladder's sticking through a bough"
	Birches	"When I see birches bend to left and right"

AUTHOR	TITLE OF POEM	FIRST LINE OF POEM
	The Pasture	"I'm going out to clean the pasture spring"
	Stopping by Woods on a Snowy Evening	"Whose woods these are I think I know."
	Storm Fear	"When the wind blows against us in the dark,"
Hay, John	*Jim Bludso of the Prairie Bell*	"Wal, no! I can't tell whar he lives,"
Housman, A. E.	*When I was One-and-Twenty*	"When I was one-and-twenty"
Keats, John	*A Thing of Beauty Is a Joy Forever*	"A thing of beauty is a joy forever"
	On First Looking Into Chapman's Homer	"Much have I travel'd in the realms of gold"
Lowell, Amy	*Elegy In a Country Churchyard*	"The men that worked for England"
MacLeish, Archibald	*The Danger in the Air*	"On a dry day of wind"
Milton, John	*Sonnet*	"How soon hath Time the subtle thief of youth,"
	Sonnet—On His Blindness	"When I consider how my light is spent."
Noyes, Alfred	*The Highwayman*	"The wind was a torrent of darkness among the gusty trees"
Poe, Edgar Allan	*Annabel Lee*	"It was many and many a year ago"
Robinson, Edward Arlington	*Miniver Cheevy*	"Miniver Cheevy, child of scorn"
Rosetti, Christina	*Up-Hill*	"Does the road wind up-hill all the way?"
	Song	"Oh roses for the flush of youth"

Author	Title of Poem	First Line of Poem
	Song	"When I am dead, my dearest"
Sandburg, Carl	*Clark Street Bridge*	"Dust of the feet"
	Onion Days	"Mrs. Gabrielle Giovannetti comes along Peoria Street every morning at nine o'clock."
	The Sins of Kalamazoo	"The sins of Kalamazoo are neither scarlet nor crimson"
	Soup	"I saw a famous man eating soup"
	Still Life	"Cool your heels on the rail of an observation car."
Sarett, Lew	*Four Little Foxes*	"Speak gently, Spring, and make no sudden sound,"
	Thunder Drums	"Beat on the buckskin, beat on the drums."
Shakespeare, William	*Song*	"Who is Sylvia? What is she?"
	Sonnet XXIX	"When in disgrace with fortune and men's eyes."
Shaw, Frances	*Who Loves the Rain?*	"Who Loves the Rain?"
Shelley, Percy Bysshe	*When the Lamp Is Shattered*	"When the lamp is shattered"
	The World's Wanderers	"Tell me, thou Star, whose wings of light"
Suckling, John	*Song*	"Why so pale and wan, fond lover?"

AUTHOR	TITLE OF POEM	FIRST LINE OF POEM
Teasdale, Sara	*Barter*	"Life has loveliness to sell—"
Untermeyer, Louis	*Caliban in the Coal Mines*	"God, we don't like to complain"
Van Doren, Mark	*Farmers Barn Lot*	"Once there was a fence here,"
	The Incinerator	"Mornings, in a stone place"
Whitman, Walt	*I Hear America Singing*	"I hear America singing, the varied carols I hear"
	Mannahatta	"I was asking for something specific and perfect for my city—"
Wordsworth, William	*Daffodils*	"I wandered lonely as a crowd"

PROSE FOR ORAL READING

AUTHOR	SELECTION
Allen, Fred	*Treadmill to Oblivion*
Benchley, Robert	*The Benchley Round-Up*
Biblical Selection	Corinthians I, 13 The Good Samaritan, Luke 10:30-36 The Prodigal Son, Luke 15:11-32
Botkin, B. A.	*New York City Folklore* "What Brooklyn Laughs At" "What's Up" "Live and Let Live" "The Ghost of Peter Stuyvesant" "The Little Church Around the Corner" "Floorwalker"

AUTHOR	SELECTION
	"How Grover Whalen Started the Ticker Tape Welcome"
	"Street Name Crisis"
	Treasury of American Folklore
	"Roaring Ralph Stockpole"
	"Billy Earthquake"
	"The Magic Hat"
	"Miss Annie Oakley"
	"Honest Abe—The Young Store-keeper"
	"In the Land of Dixie"
	"The Adventures of Little Audrey"
	"A Snipe Hunt"
Carroll, Lewis	"On the Meaning of Words" from *Through the Looking Glass*
Cott, Ted	*A Treasury of the Spoken Word*
Day, Clarence	*Life with Father*
DeMille, Agnes	*Dance To the Piper*
Dickens, Charles	*The Cricket on the Hearth*
	Pickwick Papers
Eastman, Max	*The Enjoyment of Poetry*
Edward, Duke of Windsor	*A Few Words of My Own*
Keller, Helen	*The Story of My Life* (The section where Miss Sullivan spells out words.)
Kimbrough, Emily	*We Followed Our Hearts to Hollywood*
Lincoln, Abraham	*Letter to Mrs. Bixby*
Rogers, Will	*Autobiography*
Sandburg, Carl	*Abraham Lincoln*
	The Prairie Years
Skinner, Cornelia Otis and Emily Kimbrough	*Our Hearts Were Young and Gay*

AUTHOR	SELECTION
Stevenson, Adlai	*Call to Greatness*
Swift, Jonathan	*Gulliver's Travels*
Taylor, Deems	*Music to My Ears*
Thurber, James	*Thurber Country*
Twain, Mark	*The Adventures of Tom Sawyer* Ch. 2, "The Glorious Whitewasher"
	Life on the Mississippi Ch. 6, "A Cub Pilot's Experience" Ch. 4, "The Boy's Ambition" Ch 12, "Sounding"
	Speech on the Weather
White, E. B.	*The Second Tree from the Corner*

POETRY FOR CHORAL SPEAKING

AUTHOR	TITLE OF POEM	FIRST LINE OF POEM
Anonymous	*The Blue Bells of Scotland*	"Oh, where, tell me where, is your Highland laddie gone?"
	Hey Nonny No	"Hey Nonny no!"
	The Holly and the Ivy	"The holly and the ivy"
	James Honeyman	"James Honeyman was a child"
	London Bells	"Gay go up and gay go down"
	Lord Randal	"Oh where hae ye been, Lord Randal, my son?"
	Old Roger	"Old Roger is dead and gone to his grave"

Author	Title of Poem	First Line of Poem
	On the Banks of Sacramento	"We were the boys to make her go"
	St. Catherine	"St. Catherine, St. Catherine, o lend me thine aid."
	There Was a Frog	"There was a frog lived in a well"
	The Three Huntsmen	"There were three jovial Welshmen"
	You Tell 'Em English	"You tell 'em, mail carrier."
	Whistle, Whistle	"Whistle, whistle, auld wife and you'll get a hen."
	Who Killed Cock-Robin	"Who killed Cock-Robin?"
Beddoes, Thomas Lovell	Dream Pedlary	"If there were dreams to sell."
Blake, William	Infant Joy	"I have no name!"
Blanding, Don	Foreboding	"Zoom, zoom, zoom!
Browning, Robert	Boot and Saddle	"Boot, saddle, to horse, and away!"
	Song	"The year's at the spring"
Burns, Robert	Green Grow the Rashes	"Green grow the rashes, O;"
	Whistle an' I'll Come to Ye, My Lad	"O, Whistle an' I'll come to ye, my lad"
Calverley, C. S.	The Auld Wife	"The auld wife sat at her ivied door,"
Carroll, Lewis	Father William	" 'You are old, Father William,' the young man said"

AUTHOR	TITLE OF POEM	FIRST LINE OF POEM
Carryl, Guy Wetmore	*The Plaint of the Camel*	"Canary birds feed on sugar and seed"
Farjeon, Eleanor	*Hannibal Crossed the Alps*	"Hannibal crossed the Alps!"
Fields, James Thomas	*The Turtle and the Flamingo*	"A lively young turtle lived down by the banks"
Guiterman, Arthur	*The Wildwood Loon*	"The loon has to laugh till he dies."
Harrison, Florence	*Topply Tilts*	"Topply Tilts, he walked on stilts"
Harte, Francis Bret	*Relieving Guard*	"Came the Relief, 'What Sentry ho!' "
Kipling, Rudyard	*Boots*	"We're foot-slog-slog-slog-sloggin" over Africa!"
Lear, Edward	*The Owl and the Pussy-cat*	"The owl and the pussy cat went to sea"
Lindsay, Vachel	*An Indian Summer Day on the Prairies*	"The sun is a huntress young,"
	The Flower of Mending	"When Dragon-fly would fix his wings."
Lowell, Amy	*Nostalgia*	"Through pleasures and palaces,"
Masefield, John	*Cargoes*	"Quinquireme of Nineveh from distant Ophir,
	The Wild Duck	"Twilight, Red in the West."
Meigs, Mildred Plew	*Pirate Don Durk of Dowdee*	"Ho, for the Pirate Don Durk of Dowdee"
Nash, Ogden	*The Rhinoceros*	"The rhino is an ugly beast"

Author	Title of Poem	First Line of Poem
Sandburg, Carl	*I am the People, the Mob*	"I am the people, the mob, the crowd, the mass"
	We Must Be Polite	"We must be polite if we meet a gorilla"
Sarett, Lew	*Four Little Foxes*	"Speak gently, Spring, and make no sudden sound"
Scott, Sir Walter	*Hie Away*	"Hie away, hie away"
Teasdale, Sara	*Let It Be Forgotten*	"Let it be forgotten, as a flower is forgotten"
Towne, Charles Hanson	*The Time Clock*	"Tick-tock! Tick-tock!"
Wheelock, John Hall	*By the Gray Sea*	"Where the gray sea lay sad and vast"
Whitman, Walt	*When I Heard the Learned Astronomer*	"When I heard the learned astronomer"

EXERCISES

1. Record a student's oral reading of a short poem. In methods class show how you would use this recording to teach the student to read with more feeling.
2. Prepare an oral reading program around such a theme as "cities," "industry," "peace," "good human relationships," or "bridges."
3. Select a short poem for choral speaking. Lead a discussion with members of your methods class on its feeling and meaning. Decide on a group interpretation. Conduct the choral speaking based on the group interpretation.
4. Plan a unit on teaching the meaning of poems.
5. Find at least one selection from the following materials for oral reading: lyric poetry, narrative poetry, speeches, essays, short stories, and cuts from plays.
6. Read in the text on teaching English to high school students used in

your college's English methods course the sections on literary value. Show its application to the selection of material for oral interpretation.

7. Select a short story. Prepare it for a seven-minute reading.

8. Explain how you could use creative drama in teaching the meaning of a particular poem.

10

Storytelling

You may begin your work in storytelling by showing that story-telling is an old art, a folk art, that whenever and wherever people gather, they tell stories. In 4000 B.C. the sons of Cheops, the Egyptian King, took turns telling their father stories. Today in the city park, two four-year-olds take turns telling their mother the story of "The Three Bears." Before the birth of Christ, the Greeks and Romans invented imaginative and fascinating stories explaining the mysteries of nature. Today writers invent just as imaginative and fascinating stories explaining the mysteries of traveling in space. In the middle 1700's the lumbermen of Northern Minnesota outdid each other in telling the tall tales of Paul Bunyan. Today two men laying concrete for a super highway outdo each other in their tall tales of sportscar driving.

Such sharing through the years has given your students a wealth of material for storytelling, providing fables, parables, legends, myths, folk stories, and stories of adventure, history, and biography. By introducing your students to these stories, you make them realize that the great storytellers have also been the creators of great literature: Homer, Chaucer, Aesop, Hans Christian Andersen, Edgar Allan Poe, Jack London, and Bret Harte, among many others.

Fable

The fable is usually a story about animals who talk and act like humans which illustrates a useful truth. Since it is brief and often amusing and since it moves rapidly, it is ideal for telling in a high school class. For example, high school students enjoy the story of the hungry fox who was tempted by lovely, luscious grapes hanging just beyond his reach. He tried and tried and tried to reach them until he was limp from trying and very unhappy with himself and everyone else. He hobbled off, muttering, "Sour grapes. No gentleman would touch them."

Parable

The parable is a short narrative in the Bible to illustrate a spiritual truth. Some of your students who have attended Sunday school will recall clearly a few of the parables because of their vividness. These same students often enjoy rereading the parables or telling them to the members of the class. The Prodigal Son tells particularly well.

Myth

Myths, ancient stories associated with pagan religions, include stories about the Greek and Roman gods, about the Teutonic god Thor, and from the various tribes of American Indians. They are a rich part of our literary heritage too often neglected. High school students enjoy their imaginative, supernatural characters, and surely, storytelling hour is one place where they belong. Furthermore, the study of Greek and Roman myths often helps students of Latin, art appreciation, and English literature.

Legend

The legend, usually a tale of ideal lives in the distant past and sometimes believed to be historical, has a strong appeal for high school students. Many high school boys and girls like the romantic quality of the tales of Robin Hood, of King Arthur, of Ulysses' wanderings. Furthermore, your class in speech may be covering the English syllabus, which may require the reading of some of these legends. In such cases they serve well as material for storytelling.

Folk Story

Within this generation evidence of an upsurge in interest in folk song, dance, and story lies in the welcome television has given folk singers and folk dancers. This upsurge is fortunate, for the material usually captivates high school students; furthermore, an interest in it is of real cultural value.

In fact, you can build a unit in interpretation around American folklore. You study its historical background and investigate the careers of such characters as Paul Bunyan, Pecos Bill, Johnny Appleseed, Mike Fink, John Darling, Casey Jones, Annie Oakley, Buffalo Bill, and Daniel Boone. Your students tell tall tales or ghost stories, read poems like "Johnny Appleseed" by the Benéts or "Daniel Boone" by Arthur Guiterman, and speak together some of the old ballads. Finally the unit may provide an assembly program of folklore with singing, dancing, storytelling, and dramatization.

Sometimes students become so interested in folklore that they search their neighborhoods for it. They bring in sidewalk ditties, ghost stories, tales handed down from grandfather or grandmother to their grandchildren, and old songs. After one class had collected a variety of this material, they taped it for the use of future classes.

Stories of History and Adventure

High school boys particularly like historical and adventure stories, for these stories tell of lives and times much more exciting than their own. Heinrich Harrer's *Seven Years at Tibet* (New York, E. P. Dutton & Co., Inc., 1953) contains the tale of Harrer's escape from the British in India to Tibet during World War II. Vera M. Graham's *Treasure in the Covered Wagon* (Philadelphia, J. B. Lippincott Co., 1952) relates the story of the painful journey of early Americans across our country to Oregon. Ann Tufts' *As The Wheel Turns* describes romance in New England during the nineteenth century. Vanya Oakes' *Footprint of the Dragon* (New York, Holt, Rinehart and Winston, Inc., 1949) gives an account of the building of the Union Pacific through the High Sierra with Chinese workmen. Florence and Carl Means' *The Silver Fleece* (New York, Holt, Rinehart and Winston, Inc., 1950) depicts the struggle between the Indians and the Spanish in Mexico.

Biography

Because of their own struggles for self-realization, high school students are interested in the lives of other people. Usually they like to tell parts of the struggles of these individuals. Biographies which they particularly enjoy include:

BAKER, Rachel, *Chaim Weizmann: Builder of a Nation* (New York, Julian Messner, Inc., 1950). The biography of the first President of Israel.

CLARK, Glenwood, *Thomas Alva Edison* (New York, Aladdin, 1950).

EATON, Jeanette, *Gandhi, Fighter Without a Sword* (New York, William Morrow & Co., Inc., 1950). The story of Gandhi's peaceful resistance. Begins with his high school days.

FISHER, Clyde, *The Life of Audubon* (New York, Harper & Brothers, 1949).

GARST, Doris Shannan, *Crazy Horse: Great Warrior of the Sioux* (Boston, Houghton Mifflin Co., 1950). The story of a famous Sioux Warrior who fought for his lands against the invading whites.

GOLLOMB, JOSEPH, *Albert Schweitzer: Genius in the Jungle* (New York, Vanguard Press, 1949). The tale of Schweitzer's life as a minister, musician, and author. Tells about his spiritual leadership and his ministering to the natives of West Africa.

MEIGS, Cornelia, *Invincible Louisa* (Boston, Little, Brown & Co., 1933). Biography of Louisa May Alcott.

PEARE, Catherine Owens, *Albert Einstein* (New York, Holt, Rinehart and Winston, Inc., 1949). An account of the genius of Albert Einstein.

SHIPPEN, Katherine, *Moses* (New York, Harper & Brothers, 1949). A report of the Old Testament figure who comes alive with a sense of dedication and singleness of purpose.

YATES, Elizabeth, *Amos Fortune: Free Man* (New York, E. P. Dutton & Co., Inc., 1950). The tale of a slave who struggled all his life to buy freedom for himself and others.

Modern Short Stories

By studying and telling modern short stories, high school boys and girls sometimes come to understand themselves better. Stories like O. Henry's "The Gift of the Magi" which depicts the unselfishness of two adults, Guy de Maupassant's "The Necklace" which shows the futility of two persons' having worked to pay back for a borrowed diamond necklace which they lost, Katherine Mansfield's "The Doll's House" which tells of the longing of a poor child to see a light in a doll's house owned by a well-to-do child, stimulate discussion which frequently helps boys and girls to clarify their own problems.

Many modern books deal with similar problems. At times sections of these books can be used for storytelling, since many of these books contain incidents which are effectively narrated. Such books are:

CHURCH, Richard, *Five Boys in a Cave* (New York, John Day, 1951). The tale of boys who discover an entrance to a limestone cave, explore it, and learn the dangers of it.

GORSLINE, Douglas, *Farm Boy* (New York, The Viking Press, Inc., 1950). The narrative of a farm boy who finds himself through hard work on a farm.

MEANS, Florence Crannell, *Shuttered Windows* (Boston, Houghton Mifflin Co., 1945). The story of Harriet, a young Negro girl, who is orphaned and who leaves Minneapolis and her good friends to go to South Carolina where her great grandmother lives alone. She is discouraged by the poverty and poor education in South Carolina but she loves her grandmother. The girls who first think Harriet snobbish come to understand her.

MEANS, Florence Crannell, *House Under the Hill* (Boston, Houghton Mifflin Co., 1945). The tale of Elena, a young Mexican American, her hopes, disappointments, and struggles.

The humorous story should be included in the study of modern short stories, for high school students should become acquainted with our great American humorists like James Thurber, S. J. Perelman, Ogden Nash, Stephen Leacock, and P. G. Wodehouse. Furthermore, the stories of these humorists tell well. Two particular good anthologies of humorous stories are:

LINSCOTT, R. N., *The Best American Humorous Short Stories* (New York, Random House, 1945). Includes forty-three stories by such authors as Thurber and Perelman.

NASH, Ogden, ed., *I Couldn't Help Laughing* (Philadelphia, J. B. Lippincott Co., 1957). Contains stories particularly selected for teen-agers by such authors as Tarkington, Leacock, Thurber, Saki, and Wodehouse.

The unit, in which these stories are told, will probably be contained in a fundamentals or drama course, for seldom does storytelling comprise an entire course. It may, however, be conducted as an extracurricular activity. Some high school speech teachers provide the storytellers for the village, town, or city library. In such instances, interested students prepare stories for several grade levels, preschool, primary, and intermediate. Other high school speech teachers send their able storytellers to lower grades to tell their tales; both the children and the teacher welcome the enrichment of their day. Whether it is curricular or extracurricular, its aims are the same.

Storytelling provides for the acquisition of certain understandings, attitudes, and skills. The understandings required for effective storytelling are:

Understandings

Awareness of literary value in a story.
Elements in a short story.

Attitudes

To value a story well told.
To appreciate the literary quality of tall tales, legends, myths, and other types of stories.

Skills

To find worthwhile stories which will entertain one's listeners.
To tell a story in a way that pleases one's listeners.
To listen thoughtfully.
To listen appreciatively.
To develop creative imagination.
To organize a story for telling.
To recognize the climax and to know how to build it.

CONTENT

To achieve these aims the content may include:

Selecting the Story
  Qualities of Story
    Originality of Plot
    Naturalness in Characterization
    Clear-cut Climax
  Audience
  Ability of Story Teller
  Occasion for Telling Stories
  Types of Stories

Understanding the Meaning and Mood of the Story

Organizing for Telling a Story
  Introduction
    Elements to be Included

    Characters
    Time
    Setting
    Preliminary Action
    General Mood
  Body
    Relationship of Incidents
    Subordination of Incidents
    Building the Climax
  Conclusion

Presenting the Story
  Interpreting Meaning
    Keeping the Scenes and Their Relationship Clear
    Suggesting Characterization through Voice and Gesture
    Making the Climax Evident
  Creating Mood Through Voice
    Quality
    Pitch
    Volume
    Rate
  Maintaining a Lively Sense of Communication

PROCEDURES IN TEACHING

In selecting the story to tell to an audience, your students are putting to use many of the principles that they have learned in other units. First, they consider the age, the knowledge, and the degree of sophistication of their listeners. Second, they think of the occasion; if the story is to be told during the Christmas season, they do well to select a Christmas story. Third, they take into account their own interests and abilities. One girl was interested in Mark Twain; she, therefore, chose his "How to Tell a Story." Another girl was particularly able at imitating dialects; as a result, she found herself a Joel Chandler Harris story with a Southern dialect. A quiet scholarly boy, timid about telling a story, was enthusiastic about ghost stories; he, therefore, picked Oscar Wilde's "The Canterville Ghost." Still another girl who told stories to her Sunday school class, was desirous of improving her performance before this group. Consequently, she asked to prepare a child's story so that she could receive the criticism of the group and, as a result, do a better job with her Sunday school class.

After the students have selected their story, they prepare it for presentation. Again you make sure that they apply what they have learned in their work in oral reading. They must understand the main idea of the story and must find out something about the author, his purpose, and the times when he was writing. In addition, they must be able to comprehend the emotional impact of the story.

When they have completed their analysis of the story, they are then ready to organize it for telling. You make sure that their introduction includes who the characters are, the time, the setting, and preliminary action and that they learn to relate one incident to another, to subordinate those that are not important, and to make the climax apparent. One teacher uses her work in creative drama as a basis for teaching this organization; she reminds her students of how they broke a story into scenes, how they highlighted some and subordinated others. She suggests the same procedure for story-telling. She also recalls with them how they built climaxes in creative drama, for in a story they also build climaxes by changing tempo, by pausing, and by creating a feeling of excitement. Such preparation encourages the students not to memorize but to remember the details of important scenes and the relationship of one scene to another.

You must show your students, however, that there is a difference between dramatization and storytelling. You indicate that, in their work in creative drama, they were creating character completely while in storytelling they are only suggesting character. You point out the importance of simplicity and spontaneity in the suggestion of character.

When the students have established the meaning and mood of their story and have organized it for telling to their audience, they are ready to present it. The principles for imparting the meaning and mood of a story are the same as those for oral reading. Students must have a clear realization of the meaning as they tell the story and must re-create the thought and feeling of the story for their listeners. Their voice, articulation, and bodily movement must not detract from the telling of the story but rather be an innate, effective part of it.

EVALUATION

Most teachers hold a discussion after each performance to evaluate the storytelling. The members of the class talk about the choice of story, the reaction of the audience, and the abilities of the storyteller to portray the meaning and feeling of the story, to make clear the incidents in it and their relationship, and to build the climax.

One teacher uses the following checklist in evaluating her students' performance in storytelling.

STORYTELLING EVALUATION

GENERAL:

1. Appropriateness of the selection of the story for this group. ....
2. Evidence of understanding the meaning and mood of the story on the part of the storyteller.

   ....

   ....

3. Reaction of the audience to the telling of the story. ....

   ....

ESTABLISHING MEANING AND MOOD:

1. Making ideas clear in the story. ....

   ....

2. Showing relationship of incidents ....

   ....

3. Building the climax ....

4. Suggesting characterization ....

   ....

5. Establishing mood ....

PERFORMANCE:

1. Posture ....

2. Voice ....

3. Articulation ....

4. Use of gesture ....

5. Audience contact ....

A well-told tale delights an audience. The listeners may be campers around a fire, friends at a dinner table, or a large assemblage of persons. Or they may be the jury in a courtroom, for many lawyers tell a story to instruct or persuade as well as to entertain. Telling a story effectively is as important today as it was in the Middle Ages, when the troubadour sat at an honored spot at the king's table.

SUGGESTED READING

ARBUTHNOT, M. H., *Children and Books* (Chicago, Scott, Foresman & Company, 1947), pp. 239-248. Discusses when to read and when to tell stories. Explains how to tell stories.

SAWYER, R., *The Way of the Storyteller* (New York, The Viking Press, Inc., 1942). Gives advice on how to tell stories. Contains several unusual stories.

Storytelling (Washington, D. C., Association for Childhood Education, 1945). Tells how to tell stories to children.

FOLKLORE BIBLIOGRAPHY

BARNES, R. A., compiler, *I Hear America Singing: An Anthology of Folk Poetry* (New York, Holt, Rinehart and Winston, Inc., 1937). Contains all types and kinds of folk poetry.

BLACKINGTON, A. H., *Yankee Yarns* (New York, Dodd, Mead & Co., 1954). Includes a wealth of New England tales.

BLAIR, W., *Tall Tale America: A Legendary History of Our Humorous Heroes* (New York, Coward-McCann, Inc., 1944). Legendary histories of over twelve heroes.

BLAIR, W., and NEINE, F. J., eds., *Half Horse, Half Alligator* (Chicago, University of Chicago Press, 1956). Narrates the growth of the Mike Fink legend.

BOTKIN, B. A., ed., *The Pocket Treasury of American Folklore* (New York, Pocket Books, Inc., 1950). An abridged, paperbound edition.

———, *A Treasury of American Folklore* (New York, Crown Publishers, Inc., 1944). Includes yarns, tall tales, ballads, stories, and traditions. The miracle men are well represented.

———, *A Treasury of Mississippi River Folklore* (New York, Crown Publishers, Inc., 1951).

———, *A Treasury of New England Folklore* (New York, Crown Publishers, Inc., 1947.

———, *A Treasury of Southern Folklore* (New York, Crown Publishers, Inc., 1949).

———, *New York City Folklore* (New York, Random House, 1956). Tells of folklore, traditions, customs, stories and sayings of people of New York City.

BOWMAN, J. C., *Pecos Bill, The Greatest Cowboy of All Time* (Racine, Wisc., Whitman Publishing Co., 1937).

CARMER, C., *America Sings* (New York, Alfred A. Knopf, Inc., 1942). Contains songs, ballads, and rhymes.

———, *The Hurricane's Children: Tales from Your Neck of the Woods* (New York, Farrar and Rinehart, 1937). Includes a wealth of tall tales like "How Pecos Bill Won and Lost His Bouncing Bride," and "How Johnny Appleseed Brought Appleblossoms to the West."

CHASE, R., compiler, *American Folk Tales and Songs* (New York, New American Library of World Literature, 1956). Gives tales, songs, ballads, games, dances, sayings, and folk customs of English-American folklore.

DAUGHERTY, J. H., ed., *Their Weight in Wildcats* (Boston, Houghton Mifflin Co., 1936). Tells the tales of the Frontier.

DRUMMOND, A. M., and GARD, R. E., eds., *Lake Guns of Seneca and Cayuga* (Ithaca, N. Y., Cornell University Press, 1942). Contains plays based on the folklore of the region around Ithaca, New York.

FELTON, H. W., *Legends of Paul Bunyan* (New York, Alfred A. Knopf, Inc., 1947).

HARRIS, Joel Chandler, *The Favorite Uncle Remus* (Boston, Houghton-Mifflin Co., 1948).

HUNT, M. L., *Better Known as Johnny Appleseed* (Philadelphia, J. B. Lippincott Co., 1950).

JAGENDORF, M. A., *The Marvelous Adventures of Johnny Caesar Cicero Darling* (New York, Vanguard Press, 1949).

JAGENDORF, M. A., *Upstate Downstate: Folk Stories of the Middle Atlantic States.* (New York, Vanguard Press, 1949). Contains tales of farmers, fishermen, hunters, sailors, pirates, judges, rulers, millers, and house-wives.

———, *New England Beanpot* (New York, Vanguard Press, 1947).

Journal of American Folklore, published quarterly (American Folklore Society, Bennett Hall, University of Pennsylvania, Philadelphia, Pennsylvania).

KORSON, G. G., *Minstrels of the Mine Patch* (Philadelphia, University of Pennsylvania, 1938). Contains songs and stories of the anthracite industry.

LOWNDES, M. S., *Ghosts That Still Walk: Real Ghosts of America* (New York, Alfred A. Knopf, Inc., 1941).

McCASLIN, N., *Tall Tales and Tall Men* (Philadelphia, Macrae Smith Co., 1956). Gives twelve one-act plays based on American legends.

MARTIN, F., *Nine Tales of Coyote* (New York, Harper & Brothers, 1950). Represents Indian folklore well.

MILLER, O., *Heroes, Outlaws, and Funny Fellows of American Popular Tales* (Garden City, N. Y., Doubleday & Company, Inc., 1939).

SANDBURG, C., *The American Songbag* (New York, Harcourt, Brace & Co., 1942).

SHEPHARD, E., *Paul Bunyan* (New York, Harcourt, Brace & Co., 1941).

THOMPSON, H. W., *Body, Boots and Britches* (Philadelphia, J. B. Lippincott Co., 1940). Gives tales, legends, and ballads of New York State.

VAN WAGENEN, J., Jr., *The Golden Age of Homespun* (Ithaca, N. Y., Cornell University Press, 1953). Includes traditions, legends, and folk tales.

SUGGESTED STORIES TO TELL

AUTHOR	SELECTION
Aesop	"The Ants and the Grasshopper"
	"The Dog and His Shadow"
	"The Fox and the Raven"
	"The Lion and the Mouse" in Laura Harris, *Aesops's Fables,* (Garden City, N. Y., Doubleday & Company, Inc., 1954).
Andersen, Hans Christian	*Fairy Tales* (New York, Charles Scribner's Sons, 1950)
Andrews, Mary Shipman	"The Perfect Tribute"
Bangs, John Kendrick	"Ghosts That Have Haunted Me"
Barrie, James	"My Husband's Book"

Author	Selection
Canfield, Dorothy	"The Heyday of the Blood"
Colum, Padraic	"The Boy Who Knew What the Birds Said"
Coolidge, Olivia E.	*Greek Myths* (Boston, Houghton Mifflin, Co., 1940)
Davis, Richard Harding	"The Bar Sinister"
	"Gallegher"
de Maupassant, Guy	"The Necklace"
Freeman, Mary Wilkins	"The Revolt of Mother"
Galsworthy, John	"Quality"
Garland, Hamlin	"Under the Lion's Paw"
Grimm, Jacob and Wilhelm	*Tales* (New York, Oxford University Press, Inc., 1954)
Harte, Francis Bret	"The Luck of Roaring Camp"
Hemingway, Ernest	"The Killers"
Henry, O.	"The Last Leaf"
	"The Ransom of Red Chief"
	"The Third Ingredient"
Irving, Washington	"The Legend of Sleepy Hollow"
Kipling, Rudyard	"Rikki-tikki-tavi"
	"Toomai of the Elephants"
	"Wee Willie Winkie"
London, Jack	"Buck Wins a Wager"
	"To Build a Fire"
Mansfield, Katherine	"Miss Brill"
	"The Doll's House"
Olcott, Francis Jenkins	"Esther" in *Bible Stories to Read and Tell* (Boston, Houghton Mifflin Co.)
Paine, Ralph D.	"The Freshman Fullback"
Poe, Edgar Allan	"The Gold Bug"
	"The Pit and the Pendulum"
Poole, Ernest	"Cowboys of the Skies"
Stockton, Frank	"The Lady or the Tiger"
Tarkington, Booth	"Penrod's Busy Day"
Thurber, James	"The Catbird Seat"
	"The Secret Life of Walter Mitty"
Twain, Mark	"The Celebrated Jumping Frog"
Wharton, Edith	"The Bolted Door"
White, William Allen	"The King of Boyville"
Whitlock, Brand	"The Gold Brick"

EXERCISES

1. Plan a unit on folklore.
2. Find ten stories that high school students might be able to tell effectively.
3. Record a story told by a high school student. Use the recording as a basis for discussion of evaluation of storytelling by members of your methods class.

11

Creative Drama

THE TERM *creative drama* refers to a group activity in which boys and girls act out a meaningful experience. Both the action and the dialogue of the activity are spontaneous, although the boys and girls may have planned the general structure of "the play." The teacher does not direct the participants, but he does guide them so that the experience is worthwhile. Since the values of creative drama are for the participants rather than for their audience, the actors are selected for educational reasons rather than for their talents and abilities. The production, usually designed only for the actors and their classmates, is a simple one with little or no scenery. Throughout, the emphasis is on the development of the individual and the process and not on the entertainment of the audience or a polished performance. Other class members, however, frequently watch the performance and enjoy it. They often help in an evaluation of it. Other terms used to denote this activity are *dramatic play, educational dramatics, educational theater, creative play,* and *playmaking*.

This activity is often relegated to the elementary school, for educators think of it as meeting particularly the needs of the younger child: They talk about using it for motivating learning, for promoting better understanding of people and places, for encouraging resourceful and co-operative group participation, and for developing creative ability. Creative drama, however, for these same reasons and for the additional reason that it has a strong appeal to adolescents, should have a place in the high school speech curriculum—in the fundamentals course, in the interpretation course, and in the theater course.

ADOLESCENTS AND CREATIVE DRAMA

High school students are complex individuals—awkward, emotionally unstable, anxious for approval of their peers, longing for independence from their families, and wanting solutions to moral, philosophical, and religious problems. Much of the time they secretly play roles. They walk, talk, dress, and act like those they idolize. They identify themselves both with real people and people in books. Because of their complexity and their desire to play roles, creative drama serves a real need for them.

Adolescents, however, are shy with each other. As a result, they are loath to put themselves in a position where their classmates may criticize them. Their introduction to creative drama, therefore, is more pleasant when they work with a group and when they are sure of success. Their first introduction may well be one of group pantomime where no dialogue is necessary. When, however, they have participated in creative drama throughout the elementary school, they will gladly and easily accept a more advanced form.

PANTOMIME

You may explain pantomime through the use of pictures or cartoons. You may exhibit before your class a picture of a dejected, downhearted man who has just missed his bus. Or you may show a cartoon with a wife returning home with all sizes and shapes of bundles saying to a downhearted husband, "They practically had to shoo me out of Gimbels."[1] The students recognize the meaning of the situation and the feelings of the persons involved even without reading the caption. Members of the group then talk about the thoughts and feelings that induced the posture, actions, and expressions of the people involved. As a further step, you may show a cartoon without its caption, asking your boys and girls to supply it. You explain to them that if pantomime is done well, the viewer should be able to supply the caption.

[1] H. E. Hokinson, *The Ladies, God Bless 'Em!* (New York, E. P. Dutton & Co., Inc., 1950).

At this point, you yourself may illustrate pantomime. You may pretend to run a cleaner over a rug, to eat an apple, or to skip rope. From these illustrations, the students discuss the factors involved in expressing an idea through pantomime: use of gesture, facial expression, posture, and bodily movement.

The group may then participate in pantomimes. For example, all the members of the class may pretend to view a tennis match in which the favorite is far behind, then catches up with his opponent, and finally wins. Or they may be queued up, waiting for a bus that is twenty minutes late. Some of the group are angry; some are cheerfully gossiping; some are bored; others are just philosophically biding their time.

Your boys and girls are then ready to undertake pantomime with just two or three persons involved. Two of the group may cross an icy street, helping each other to stay erect. A father may be chiding his son for being late to dinner. An older sister may be scolding her younger sister for constantly interrupting her while she is doing her homework. A mother and daughter may be setting the table for dinner.

USES OF CREATIVE DRAMA IN THE CLASSROOM

After an introduction to creative drama through pantomime, you go on to use it in the classroom for many purposes. Creative drama should help students to: (1) understand imaginatively special fields of academic interest, (2) solve some of the problems of everyday social living, (3) understand people, their motivations, their problems, and their interrelationships, (4) appreciate characters and incidents in literature, (5) enjoy the rich experience of thinking creatively and playing an imaginative role, (6) feel free to express emotions, and (7) better adjust to the group.

Adding Meaning to Special Fields of Academic Interest

Limitless opportunities for using creative drama exist in special fields of academic interest. For example, members of a sophomore speech group dramatized episodes from Lincoln's life. One episode had to do with the arrival of Lincoln's stepmother a year after the death of Nancy Hanks Lincoln. This episode shows the stepmother's love of and compassion for children and the beginning of her good relationship with Abe.[2] A second episode had to do with the story of Lincoln's marriage to the brilliant, fashionable daughter of a Kentucky bank president. Carl Sandburg's *Abraham Lincoln: the Prairie Years* (New York, Harcourt Brace & Co., 1926) provided the source for the second dramatization.

Similarly the stories of episodes in the careers of famous musicians are dramatized by those interested in music. For example, the story of Richard Strauss' debut as a pianist and conductor is an appealing one. Richard Strauss' father, a noted musician, was always in conflict with von Bülow, a famous conductor. Consequently, the two argued furiously about Wagner's music and about Strauss' use of time and phrasing in his playing of the third bass in von Bülow's orchestra. When von Bülow heard young Strauss' *Serenade* for thirteen wind instruments, he was so impressed that he asked Strauss to compose a suite for the same instruments for his orchestra and to become its assistant conductor. As a result, Richard conducted his new compostion and also made his debut as a pianist. When Strauss' father thanked von Bülow for giving his son opportunities, von Bülow told him that what he had done was because of the son's talent and not because of him. This episode, the beginning of Richard Strauss' soar to fame, dramatizes well.[3]

For the scientists in the group, the dramatization of the work of Pierre and Marie Curie can be exciting. Their work began in an entirely unsuitable abandoned wooden shack, either too hot or too cold, drafty, and bleakly furnished with a worn kitchen table, a blackboard, which was there for no known reason, and an old cast iron stove that did not work. Here Pierre, always calm, worked on the delicate task of determining the properties of radium. Marie, the more exuberant, continued chemical experiments which would permit her to obtain salts of "pure radium." Finally came the excitement of her finding the salts. That night Pierre and Marie crept back to the shack, after putting their daughter to bed, to look once more at radium. The expression of the magic of the "evening of the glowworms" can be impressive.

[2] Bernadine Bailey, *Abe Lincoln's Other Mother* (New York, Julian Messner, Inc., 1941).

[3] K. L. Bakeless, *Story-Lives of Great Composers* (New York, Frederick Stokes, 1940).

Solving the Problems of Everyday Social Living

Creative drama is useful in teaching boys and girls to live together more gracefully. In the chapter on fundamentals, the need for students to converse effectively, to use the correct social forms, and to interview intelligently is stressed. Creative drama provides a method for teaching these three activities. The challenge to create scintillating dialogue, aimless chatter, or an expression of congratulation inspires many a worthwhile performance. In addition, an adolescent boy learns more easily how to introduce a boy to a girl, his mother to his girl friend, or his aunt to a friend of his mother's when such situations are dramatized. Lastly, a planned dramatization of an interview with a "prospective employer" may lay the basis for future successful interviews.

Understanding People, Their Problems, and Their Motivation

Adolescent boys and girls have a high interest in philosophical, ethical, and religious problems. Many of them are vitally concerned about such problems as the treatment given a less powerful person by a more powerful one. The playing of scenes of stories that involved philosophical, religious, or ethical problems helps students to discuss these problems among themselves and to think about them intelligently. For example, one group of sophomore students played "The Garden Party," by Katherine Mansfield. In this story a sixteen-year-old girl is to have a gay birthday party. When an employee of her father dies, the question arises in her mind as to whether she should have the party. Her mother rather quickly tells her to go on with the party. After the party, the mother suggests that the daughter take to the family of the employee some of the sweets. The daughter, in her party dress, goes to the employee's home. The heart-felt grief and the numbness of the family make her wonder about her choice and about her deed. The playing of the story frequently motivates children to discuss such problems as employer-employee relationships, expressions of sympathy, and attitudes of mothers toward problems of daughters.

The section of *Life With Father* that has to do with Mr. Day's being baptized plays well and serves as the basis for discussion. Mr. Day accepted religion and respected spiritual beings. He regarded them unquestioningly and yet he took a distant attitude, for although he accepted religion as a natural part of his surroundings, he would "never have invented it himself." Mrs. Day, on the other hand, was far more devout. The difference in the attitudes of Mr. and Mrs. Day challenges adolescent students to think of their own attitudes about religion.

Understanding Characters and Incidents in Literature

Many of the stories of literature become more vivid and meaningful to adolescents when they play the story. They understand the characters and their interrelationships better. Furthermore, the planning of a dramatization promotes the study of the historical and geographical background of the piece of literature.

One group of high school juniors played Stephen Vincent Benét's "The Devil and Daniel Webster." The allusions in the story motivated the boys and girls to read more about the period before the Civil War. One lad became so interested in the witchcraft mentioned in the story that he read Jonathan Edwards and Cotton Mather. Another was inspired to read some of the famous Webster debates. As the boys played the parts of Jabez Stone, the New Hampshire farmer, Daniel Webster, and Scratch, they came alive.

Expressing Strong Feelings

Adolescents express strong feeling through acting a character in a story or a character whom they have invented. Often the expression of these strong feelings provides a catharsis for the adolescent. In addition, from this expression comes a better understanding of himself and those around him. For example, one group made up a story with the father, a cruel, hard taskmaster, and with society and his family punishing him for his cruelty. Because the teacher knew one boy's family, she believed that in playing the role of the father he was expressing some of his own hostile feelings. She reported the incident to the school psychologist who was later able to give guidance to both the boy and his family.

Thinking Creatively and Playing Imaginative Roles

High school students need opportunities to think creatively and to express themselves imaginatively. Creative drama affords such opportunities. In one fundamentals class, a group depicted some of the scenes from Clarence Day's *Life With Father*. One fourteen-year-old boy, playing Mr. Day, roared, then suddenly changed to complete geniality. He had a feeling of gratification that he could "feel like, sound like, and act like" Mr. Day. Finally he and his classmates decided to put on several of the scenes for assembly, for they felt that the end product of their dramatization deserved a wider audience than their classmates. As a result, one girl gained satisfaction from collecting the necessary costumes; a boy felt a sense of accomplishment with his setting; another girl was proud of her display advertising the assembly. All of the students of the class participated in the creative endeavor.

Adjusting to the Group

Your boys and girls, like all children, have personality problems which creative drama can sometimes alleviate. The shy child may feel important in a role and through his participation lose some of his shyness. Furthermore, he may come to be an integral part of his group. On the other hand, the aggressive boy or girl may learn to share responsibility with other children; he may realize that he cannot always play the lead. From his participation, he, too, learns to be a better, more co-operative member of the group.

CHOOSING MATERIAL FOR DRAMATIC PLAY

Principles of Selection

In choosing a story, poem, or experience to play, you should make sure that the story or experience is one that in all likelihood will play successfully. Consequently, the material must have conflict. One force must be pitted against another force, or one individual, against another individual. The conflict may be a simple one; for example, a shrewd, immoral lawyer may be trying to fleece a poor widow of her last bit of property. Or the conflict may be more complex; for instance, traveling by railroad may be threatening to replace traveling by canal, or travel by air may be gradually replacing travel by train. Or the younger generation may be in discord with the older generation over the upholding of certain family traditions. The material to be played should contain conflict, simple or complex.

Second, the characters should be those whom the boys and girls can understand and, therefore, portray vividly. The characters in the

Day family are real and comprehensible. The boys and girls talk about the members of this family, deciding how they feel, how they look, how they act, how they walk, and what they say. With the exception of Mr. Day, the characters are not "different" or dramatic individuals; they are rather genuine persons. Furthermore, the characters' motivations must be authentic. For example, boys and girls perceive that the girls' feelings in "The Garden Party" are not altogether clear and they realize that they themselves would not have known how to act or think in a similar situation. Because of their discernment of her, they are able to assume her role.

Third, the situation or story must be such that it motivates dialogue. For instance, dialogue is inherent in the situation in the story of the quarrel of Strauss' father and von Bülow and von Bülow's acceptance of young Strauss as a composer and conductor. Students playing the roles are not at a loss for what to say.

Fourth, the material for high school creative drama should involve movement, for students of this age tend not to like "talky" plays. They do like to play a story that has considerable movement although it need not be a violent one. Episodes from *Life With Father* represent such material.

Lastly and perhaps most important, the material should interest the students. Because the adolescent likes to feel that he is adult, he likes to deal with adult problems. On the other hand, some of the material that carries with it a degree of fantasy appeals to the "child" in the adolescent. As mentioned earlier, interest in philosophical and ethical problems is high. Much of the material that is to be dramatized can appeal to this interest.

Sources of Material

Sources of material that contains conflict, possesses comprehensible characters, motivates dialogue, involves action, and interests high school students are many. They include ballads, folk tales, short stories, and students' original scenes based on pictures, an assortment of properties, and pairs of words.

Ballads

Boys and girls enjoy playing some of the old ballads, often adding characters and incidents. One of the ballads that almost always proves successful is "Get Up and Bar the Door." Students sometimes add

an incident to precede the refusal to bar the door. This incident can
be as mirth-provoking as the rest of the ballad. Generally, however,
in this ballad the first scene consists of the quarrel between the husband and wife and the vow of each that the first to speak should rise
to bar the door. The second scene contains the arrival of the rob-
bers, their eating of the puddings, and their threats to cut off the
goodman's beard and to kiss the wife. The climax occurs as the goodman rises in revolt. The conclusion is the satisfied remark of the
goodwife.

The ballad follows:

> It fell about the Martinmas time,
>   And a gay time it was then,
> When our goodwife got puddings to make
>   And she's boiled them in the pan.
>
> The wind sae cauld blew south and north,
>   And blew into the floor;
> Quoth our goodman to our goodwife,
>   "Get up and bar the door."
>
> "My hand is in my hussyfscap,
>   Goodman, as ye may see;
> An it should nae be barred this hundred year,
>   It'll no be barred by me."
>
> They made a paction 'tween them twa.
>   They made it firm and sure,
> That the first whaeer should speak,
>   Should rise and bar the door.
>
> Then by there came two gentlemen,
>   At twelve o'clock at night.
> And they could neither see house nor hall,
>   Nor coal nor candle-light.
>
> "Now whether is this a rich man's house,
>   Or whether is it a poor?"
> But ne'er a word wad one o' them speak,
>   For barring of the door.

And first they ate the white puddings,
  And then they ate the black;
Tho muckle thought the goodwife to hersel'.
  Yet ne'er a word she spake.

Then said the one unto the other,
  "Here, man, take ye my knife;
Do ye take off the auld man's beard,
  And I'll kiss the goodwife."

O up then started our goodman,
  An angry man was he;
"Will ye kiss my wife before my een,
  And scad me wi' puddin-bree?"

Then up and started our goodwife,
  Gied three skips on the floor;
"Goodman, you've spoken the foremost word,
  Get up and bar the door."

Other ballads that play well are "The Raggle, Taggle Gypsies," and "The Glove and the Lion."

Folklore

Second, folklore provides material for creative drama. Books such as Botkins' *Treasury of American Folklore* contain stories that have survived from generation to generation. Sometimes students in a class have access to folk tales of their grandparents that are unusual and adventurous. Legends and myths, similar in many ways to folk tales, also play well.

Stories and Plays of Today and Yesterday

Third, many of the stories and plays of today and yesterday, romantic, realistic, or adventurous, are worthwhile bases for creative drama. For instance, one of the perennial favorites is Charles Dickens' *Christmas Carol* with Scrooge as a favorite role. Another is Shakespeare's *The Taming of the Shrew.* One teacher used this play, knowing that it was to be given on television and wanting to prepare her students for watching it. After she told the students the story, she suggested that they might like to enact it. One lad played Petruchio with a kind of wild gallantry. A girl played the shrewish Kate with abandon. Another girl who portrayed Bianca dripped with sweetness. After the students had seen the play on television, they found real pleasure in comparing it with theirs. They agreed that their Baptista Minola was a more forbearing, more realistic father than the father on television. But a comparison of the other characters suggested ways in which the students could improve their performances. Other stories such as O. Henry's "The Gift of the Magi," Mark Twain's *The Prince and the Pauper,* and W. W. Jacob's "The Monkey's Paw" play beautifully. Parts of Rölvaag's *Giants of the Earth* lend themselves unusually well to dramatization.

Stories Based on Ideas and Experiences of Members of the Group

Lastly, the boys and girls invent stories to play. For instance, one teacher showed her students a picture of a very dashing pilot playing a violin. From his picture, the students built a rather sensitive story about a young man, just back from Korea, who found piloting planes lucrative. His real enjoyment, however, came from studying the violin. In the end, he partly resolved his conflict by playing second violin in the local symphony orchestra, while continuing to earn his living as a pilot. The students wound into this main theme the story of a romance with a girl who was a harpist. Another group started with the character of a silly mother who persisted in thinking that she was a young girl. The inspiration for this story came from a boy, who had spent the summer as a bellboy in a summer hotel and who had to deal with a mother who refused to act her age. Using this episode as a foundation, the members of the group made up a tale of life in a summer hotel.

In a second year high school drama class, a teacher supplied the various groups in her room with different sets of properties. For example one group received an apron, a tall silk hat, a dustpan, a mop, and a beautiful velvet cloak; a second group, a telephone, a mask of an elephant's head, a jar of maple syrup, and a pistol. The first group built its story around a foreign diplomat coming to see one of his countrymen, a poverty-stricken cleaning woman in a large business firm, to tell her that she was an heiress of a large fortune inherited from an uncle. After she received the money, she proceeded to do good to her many friends with her inheritance. The diplomat disapproved of this action. The diplomat was haughty and overbearing, whereas the cleaning woman was humble, un-selfish, and quietly sympathetic.

Another group constructs stories from pairs of words, like *docile* and *aggressive, humane* and *cruel,* and *friendly* and *unfriendly.* One group told the story of a docile mother, an aggressive father, and a completely bewildered fourteen-year-old son. The teacher and the neighbors tried to help solve the many problems of this trio. But the help was of no avail and the fourteen-year-old became more and more confused and more and more of a problem to his family, school, and community. The story ended with his being sentenced for life for murder at the age of eighteen. In these instances of play-making, you help the students to devise the character by asking questions about the feelings of the character, the reasons for his feelings, and his reactions to other characters in the story. You guide the construction of the play so that the scene is set, the action rises, conflict exists, and a definite climax occurs.

DIRECTION OF CREATIVE DRAMA

After the students have selected and have read or listened to the story, they are ready to prepare for its playing.

Planning the Dramatization

First, they discuss what the characters are like. They talk about how they act and feel, how they react to each other, how they are alike and different, what they sound like, what they look like, what they wear. In some instances they may suggest actors and actresses who could well play the parts. In this discussion, you make sure that the students start with what the character is like inside—what his drives are, what he wants. They go on to talk about the forces that make him the kind of individual he is and to find out what he was like before the play begins, as it begins, and as it progresses. These factors influence his outward appearance. This discussion prepares them to interpret the character.

In *The Devil and Daniel Webster,* the three main characters are Jabez Stone, Daniel Webster, and Scratch. The minor characters are the twelve jurors. One group of fourteen-year-olds decided that Scratch was motivated by a deep feeling of hostility to all men, that he would be wearing dark clothes with a bright red necktie, that he would slink along rather than walk, and that he would sound just a little "too smooth." One student thought quick incisive speech in keeping with his character; another imagined a sardonic drawl to be more in keeping. But one boy made the point that, to be believable to Jabez Stone, Scratch's villainy must not be too apparent. He recommended that a very New England quality, including typical New England speech, could serve to help make him comprehensible to Jabez Stone. Jabez Stone, they surmised, would think, appear, and sound like any successful man in the community. In fact, they wanted him to be the average of all successful men, for they were insistent that he not appear particularly brilliant. On the other hand, Daniel Webster was to be the dashing character with a belief in justice and a faith in mankind and with an ability to verbalize easily and to be dramatic. In addition, they insisted that he possess a spirit of kindliness obvious to all.

Second, they plan the structure by deciding on the characters to include, the number of scenes and what is to happen in each scene. Furthermore, they determine the climax or the high point of the story. Lastly, they plan on how to introduce the story and how to end it. The group just mentioned planned for two scenes in *The Devil and Daniel Webster*.

> Scene 1. A tale of the hard luck of Jabez, his pact with Scratch, and his trip to see Daniel Webster.
> Scene 2. The arrival of Daniel Webster in the kitchen of Jabez, the entrance of Scratch, and finally the trial and the rendering of the verdict of the jury. The ending was the prediction by Scratch of Daniel Webster's future.

Some of the students would have preferred to have the prediction of the future of Daniel Webster in a scene by itself. The members of the group agreed that the most exciting point of the story was the verdict of the jury.

Choosing the Cast

Some teachers allow students to volunteer for parts; other teachers ask that the group decide who should play the parts. The latter procedure seems desirable. In the discussion, you can suggest kindly that John played the lead in the last production. Or you may comment that, of course, Mary would make a delightful mother but that she has played the part of a mother recently. You may then recommend that Mary might learn more from playing a different kind of character. You make sure no child consistently plays the lead and that no child is cast just because he appears like the character.

In some instances you may do well to play one of the parts yourself. For you to play a part in the first dramatization is frequently advisable, for you can give the students a feeling of security in their first venture and can help them move the story along.

Playing the Story

After the characters have been chosen and after the content of the scenes has been agreed upon, the group enacts the first scene. The first playing may be discouraging, particularly when students are attempting creative drama for the first time. On the other hand, the first playing may be very rewarding. To partly insure making the first performance successful, you may use one of the leaders of the class to play the starring role. In addition, you encourage each student to put forth his best creative effort. As students play two or three different roles, they find that they invent dialogue easily and that each time they play they are able to tell a story more clearly and more vividly.

Evaluation

As a last step, the boys and girls evaluate their performance. In the evaluation they use the names of the characters whom they have played, not the names of the students. This procedure tends to make them more objective in their criticism. They ask themselves such questions as the following: The first three questions deal with the creation of the story by the actors. In creative drama, these are the more important. The last three deal with the less important factors related to the production.

1. *Did we make the story clear?* They find out whether or not they could have made certain incidents of the story clearer and whether they moved the story along so quickly that parts of it were not clear, or so slowly that certain points were belabored. They decide whether the climax is evident. Sometimes they suggest that more voice, a significant pause, or a slowing or quickening of the tempo would have helped to build this high point of the story.

2. *Were the characters genuine and did we stay in character?* The

students determine whether as actors they were thinking and feeling like the characters in the story—and whether they were thinking and feeling like the characters whom they wished to create. They question each other as to when they forgot and became themselves. Sometimes a more thorough analysis of the character or suggestions for voice, gesture, action, or gait help the student to make the character more real.

3. *Was the dialogue true to the characters and did it help tell the story clearly?* Here the boys and girls discuss whether the comments and the conversation really belonged to the character—or whether some of it seemed out of place. They talk about how one person's piece of dialogue can help another person. They ask each other whether they picked up their cues fast enough to really sound like two people conversing. (You will need to explain that picking up a cue quickly means that one character begins to talk just as the other character finishes his last word and that in some instances, as in moments of excitement or anger, one character will begin to speak before the other character actually finishes.)

4. *Was our movement widespread enough and did it help us tell the story?* Here the boys and girls talk about using all of the stage and having the movement fit the dialogue and the characters.

5. *Did we time our story well?* Here the students talk about where they could have speeded up and where they could have slowed down. Sometimes the timing seems just right for the play. They recognize that the speed or slowness with which they pick up their cues affects the timing of the play.

6. *Were our voices appropriate and our diction clear?* They ask themselves whether or not the quality of their voices fitted the characters and whether they expressed the desired feeling through the use of their voices. They decide whether they should speak more softly or more loudly, at a different rate, or on a different pitch level. They point out the parts where their diction was particularly effective and where it did not sound clear. They indicate the mispronunciations of words by any of the characters.

Throughout they try to keep their comments positive rather than negative. Telling first what was done effectively can become a habit of the members of the class.

This chapter has dealt with creative drama in which boys and girls play experiences, poems, or stories. There is no set dialogue. The scenery, costuming, lighting, and properties are minimal although the participants may make use of some or all of them to help tell the story. The director in creative drama helps the boys and girls to create consistent, imaginative characters, to tell the story clearly, and to keep it moving.

The next chapter will deal largely with play production. In play production the boys and girls act in a play selected for its theme and plot and because its requirements in terms of staging, actors, and audience suit your particular group. When given in an auditorium, the performance needs lighting and makeup to project the action and characters to the back of the auditorium. Frequently it requires carefully designed scenery and costuming. The director in collaboration with his actors and actresses plans the movement, the interpretation, and the action of the play. He helps his students to understand the play's lines, its characters, and its meaning. Play production is more formal and its emphasis is on artistic achievement, whereas creative drama is more informal and its major emphasis is on creative and emotional development of the individual.

SUGGESTED READING

AXLINE, V., *Play Therapy* (Boston, Houghton Mifflin Co., 1943). Discusses the therapeutic value of dramatic play.

BURGER, I. B., *Creative Play Acting* (New York, A. S. Barnes & Co., 1950).

LEASE, R., and SIKS, G. B., *Creative Dramatics in Home, School and Community* (New York, Harper & Brothers, 1952). Contains a chapter on creative dramatics for the junior high school student.

PARDOE, T. D., *Pantomime for Stage and Study* (New York, D. Appleton-Century Company, Inc., 1931).

POMERANZ, R. C., "A Creative Drama Club," *English Journal*, XXXXI (June, 1952), 303-306. Tells how junior high school students wrote and produced their own play. Indicates the emotional values derived from character analysis.

WARD, W., *Creative Dramatics for the Upper Grades and Junior High School* (New York, D. Appleton-Century Company, Inc., 1930).

————, *Playmaking with Children*, 2nd ed. (New York, Appleton-Century-Crofts, Inc., 1957).

————, *Stories to Dramatize* (Kentucky, Anchorage Press, 1954).

SUGGESTED STORIES FOR CREATIVE DRAMATICS

AUTHOR	SELECTION
Folk Ballads	
Friedman, A. B., ed.	*Viking Book of Folk Ballads of the English Speaking World* (New York, The Viking Press, Inc., 1956).
Stories	
de Maupassant, Guy	"The Necklace"
Johnson, Harold	"Baby Sitter" from R. Strang and T. Roberts, eds., *Teen Age Tales* (Boston, D. C. Heath & Company, 1954).
London, Jack	"Buck Wins a Wager"
Mansfield, Katherine	"The Garden Party"
O. Henry	"The Cop and the Anthem"
	"The Gift of the Magi"
Thurber, James	"The Catbird Seat" from Milton Crane, ed., *Fifty Great Short Stories,* (New York, Bantam Books, Inc., 1952).
Wharton, Edith	"The Bolted Door"
White, William Allen	"The King of Boyville"

EXERCISES

1. List three stories and two ballads that could be used as a basis for creative drama. Find two pictures that could serve the same purpose.
2. Visit a social studies class. Write a short report indicating whether creative drama could have been used in the class and if it could, how. If it could not, explain why not.
3. Explain how creative drama can be used in two different units in a fundamentals course.
4. Plan an assembly program based on creative drama.

12

Theater
in the High School

"WHAT SHOULD OUR COURSE in theater include?" was the topic of discussion in a class in which the teacher was planning the course with his students. As a first step in the discussion, the teacher suggested that they define *theater*. He advised them to list performances that could be included under *theater* and then to analyze these performances for their common elements.

The responses of his students were varied and all-inclusive. At first, the students replied in a conventional way, naming certain dramas, musicals, and revues. One student, however, mentioned opera. The students then designated forms of dramatic entertainment seen on movie and television screens, such plays as *Richard II, Macbeth, No Time for Comedy,* and *Winterset.* At this point, one fifteen-year-old girl referred to the Royal Ballet; another sixteen-year-old, to a monologue seen on a television show portraying a flighty housewife; still another, to a pantomime artist whom he, too, had seen on television.

The boys and girls then analyzed these performances for their common elements. They decided that in each instance at least one performer was involved. The performers were actors and actresses, pantomime artists, dancers, and singers. Secondly, they showed that the performers told, danced, sang, or enacted a story. They specified briefly the themes of some of the stories which the performers created. Thirdly, they noted that an audience reacted to the performance. Fourthly, they talked about the backgrounds and settings against which the stories were played and the kinds of stages on which the performers executed their roles. Lastly, they pointed out the graceful movements of the performers and the meaningful reading of lines both of which might have resulted from special skills of the performers or from able direction.

As a result of this analysis, the students arrived at this definition: Theater is creating or recreating a story or an idea on a stage by performers for the pleasure of an audience.

The study of theater in high schools generally serves five purposes: (1) It helps the high school student to appreciate dramatic productions and to recognize their influence on our culture. (2) It aids the students in understanding other human beings, their problems in living in today's world, their solutions to these problems, and the forces of environment and character which induced the problems in the first place. (3) It gives the student a body of knowledge concerning periods in our history of the theater, great plays of all times, and the more important theatrical figures. (4) It encourages the student to strive for artistic achievement by using his imaginative powers in his work in the theater. (5) It motivates the student to improve his voice and articulation.

PURPOSES OF PLAY PRODUCTION

Developing Appreciation of Dramatic Productions

Today theater is all around your students. They serve as an audience for plays on television and on the moving-picture screen and given by countless churches, charitable organizations, and little theater groups in the community. You have the responsibility to train your students to serve as a discriminating audience for these performances. As your students learn more about the theater, as they view superior productions, as they participate in the giving of plays, they become more discriminating. For example, recently all the members of a high school drama class listened to *Green Pastures* on television. They were, on the whole, enthusiastic about the play and the production. As they discussed the characterization, however, one lad indicated that he thought that William Warfield as de Lawd had "hammed it up." He referred specifically to a place in the play where de Lawd had stood by a window saying, "I won't come down. I won't come down." Another member of the group said that she believed that de Lawd was a simple presentation of a simple people who had a gentle superiority and that William Warfield had the kind of authority that the Lord would have. They concluded that their feelings about the characterization depended somewhat on the different pictures of de Lawd which they had in their own minds.[1] Such a discussion helps students to look critically at actors' interpretations of roles.

Understanding the Problems of Living in Today's World

As the section on creative drama mentioned, adolescents like to think and talk about the ethical and moral issues which they face. Through analyzing characters, boys and girls develop sympathy for and understanding of problems of different individuals. In addition, when they see these problems portrayed on the stage, they often comprehend better why the characters act and react as they do. For example, the members of one drama class talked about the character of Miss Dyer in *Joint Owners In Spain*. Miss Dyer is a complaining, whining individual who at any moment may "dribble into silent tears." Her air of being sorely tried, her exacting nature, and her will to dominate make her difficult to live with. One teenager, who participated in this discussion in preparation for playing the role, indicated that observing one of her neighbors helped her to interpret Miss Dyer. Furthermore, she later remarked, "Somehow after playing Miss Dyer, I know Aunt Jenny (the neighbor) better. She no longer irritates me. I think I now know why she acts the way she does."

Similarly an analysis of Mrs. Craig in *Craig's Wife* by George Kelly helps students to be more discerning of the woman who dominates her husband and her relatives. Mrs. Craig wants to be secure, to be sure of her husband's love and loyalty. By excluding her friends who might weaken her hold, by subtly dominating, and by curtailing individual freedom, she reigns supreme for a number of years. One by one, however, the members of her household, on discovering her practices, leave. In the end, she is alone and friendless with only material possessions to console her. Comprehending

---

[1] Drama class, Martin Van Buren High School, New York City, Teacher: Mary Desser, Chairman Department of Speech.

the motivation of Mrs. Craig and the effects of her domination helps high school boys and girls to understand similar household problems.

Gaining Knowledge of the Theater, Past and Present

You hope that your students, as they become educated men and women, have as one of their interests, the theater. When the student knows about the structure of plays, the types of drama, the chief periods of our theatrical history, and the outstanding contributors to theatrical productions, he gains insight into the theater as a significant part of our cultural heritage. This body of knowledge includes the use of masks in early drama; the unities of time, place, and action in Greek drama; the miracle, mystery, and morality play of the Middle Ages; the Elizabethan drama; the influence of Shakespeare; acquaintance with such names as Euripides, Sophocles, Plautus, Molière, Sheridan, Goethe, Ibsen, George Bernard Shaw, Eugene O'Neill, David Garrick, Sarah Bernhardt, the Lunts, Helen Hayes, Arthur Miller, and Elia Kazan.

Encouraging the Student to Use His Imaginative Powers

The actor, costumer, and scene designer are artists who take pride in creating an illusion for their audience. These artistic participants of a theatrical production experience the excitement of being an integral part of an imaginative, finished production. As a teacher, you encourage the student, be he actor or designer, to use all of his talent and to develop his imaginative power fully. The actor should give to his audience, no matter how small, his best performance. As his teacher, you try to keep this actor a sincere, interested, honest, creative performer with little or no artificiality or conceit.

Motivating Effective Voice and Articulation

In the *Quarterly Journal of Speech* Bavely[2] reports the results of a study to determine the reasons of 883 high school students for electing a theater course: 508 chose as their first reason, "To acquire better command of language, better physical and emotional control, and to improve personality." This bit of evidence seems to indicate

---

[2] Ernest Bavely, "High School Students Rate Dramatic Arts," *Quarterly Journal of Speech*, XXXV (October, 1949), 334-337.

that you have a direct responsibility to your students to encourage them to improve their voice, diction, and bodily movements—all elements of their personality—in a drama class.

CONTENT OF THEATER COURSE OR UNIT

The amount and kind of dramatic material that you plan for your students depend on their school level, their needs, their general intellectual level, and the length of the course.

An elective full-year course designed for superior students in the eleventh or twelfth year may well contain the following units: introduction to theater, the structure and types of the play, acting, directing, production techniques including scenery, lighting, stagecraft, costuming, makeup, organization for production, and history of the theater. In a one semester course you can cover only half this amount of work. For a unit in a fundamentals course you select that material which meets the needs of your particular students. In some instances you may use only the work on creative drama described in the first half of this chapter. In others, you may choose to have the students read or act a dramatic dialogue.

METHODS OF TEACHING THEATER

Introducing the Course

In this section you motivate your students to work in the theater and to investigate its broad field, usually by making use of the dramatic activities available in the community. For example, you may start by having the entire group attend a college performance, listen to a play on television, attend a movie, discuss moving picture awards, or survey the dramatic criticism of present Broadway plays. With this common experience or background, you and the group decide what theater is, how important the play, the actors, the stage, and the audience are, and what place each holds in the production.

The Play

After you have introduced your students to theater, they usually study the play—its type and structure. One teacher begins her work with the play with the explanation that in every play there is a kind of conflict which may be between such opposing forces as persons, groups, ideas, or eras. She goes on to explain that the play catches this conflict at its very exciting crisis and follows it through. After the general explanation, she makes clear the types of plays: comedy, tragedy, melodrama, farce, and fantasy.

This clarification takes place through the invention of different types of stories by her students. She submits the idea that the conflict may well be of a man who marries a stupid wife. She asks how this problem can be solved happily and satisfactorily. One boy may suggest that whereas the wife is stupid, she is also kind and good-natured. When the husband finally realizes the value of these positive attributes, they live a happy life. The teacher indicates that this play represents *comedy*. She then asks the members of her group to construct a plot in which both the husband and wife are defeated. One girl may say that the husband and wife divorce each other with the wife finishing her days unhappily bemoaning her fate. The husband, on the other hand, feeling guilty that he left his first wife and always in financial straits, is not content with his second wife, who is as clever as the first wife was stupid. This play the teacher explains is *tragedy*. She then asks that they make their story unbelievably tragic with a happy ending. One group may compose a story in which the husband and wife are both unhappy, for the children are stupid, a flood destroys their home, and, as a final straw, the husband loses his month's wages. But a rich uncle leaves them a fortune so that all is finally well. She tells them that they have just created a *melodrama*. She then asks them to fashion a story that is very funny, even to the point of being silly. A kind of Gracie Allen-George Burns story may ensue. At this point she gives them the word, *farce,* which denotes this kind of a play. Finally she recommends that they bring to the story a fantastic, unbelievable quality. Someone may suggest that two genies come to direct the husband and wife so that their household runs smoothly. The teacher makes clear that this type of play is called a *fantasy*.

Her assignment is that members of the class read several plays, indicate the plots briefly, and select a short representative scene of two or three pages to read to the group. The group then decides on the type of play represented. She assigns such plays as *She Stoops* to Conquer, All My Sons, The Drunkard, The Imaginary Invalid, Blithe Spirit, Candida, The Trial of Mary Dugan, The Importance of Being Earnest, Charley's Aunt, and Our Town. To include a play such as Our Town is important for it shows that many plays are blends of the various forms.

Understanding the Structure of the Play

Finding the Theme

Each of these plays has a theme. You teach your students to express it, just as you asked them to express the main idea of a selection to be read aloud or of a talk to be given. In each instance the main idea is stated in a single sentence.

Students should recognize that finding the theme of a play is very like finding the theme of a poem. The title may help. For example, the titles of the plays Beyond the Horizon and You Can't Take It With You give strong hints. Students look for other clues. Some playwrights may write an introduction to their play. Others have one of their main characters state the theme explicitly. In some plays, as in some poems, the theme may be implicit; and, consequently, it is from the study of the speeches of the players that the student arrives at the theme.

The level of your group dictates how you go about teaching the expression of the theme. In some instances, you talk about the play and, as a result of this talk, the students state the theme in one sentence. After they have stated it accurately, they discuss its universality and evidence of it within the play. In other instances, you ask your students to write the theme in a single sentence and to explain how the characters in the play make it clear. If your students are intelligent and mature and if they have had considerable work with literary appreciation in English classes, they can express the theme with little assistance from you.

In both a speech and a reading not only must the speaker or reader be able to express the central thought of the author but he must also impart it to his audience. So, too, in a play, the actors make clear the play's central idea to the audience. In speaking and reading, the central idea dictates what words are spoken and how they are spoken. Similarly in a production of a play, the actor must give the impression which the theme requires. The actor becomes, as did the reader, an interpreter and a creator whose interpretation and creation are consistent with the playwright's central idea.

One teacher's group of drama students had all read *Macbeth*. Most of the students expressed the central idea as "Crime doesn't pay;" others, however, expressed it as, "Too much ambition leads to downfall," or "Too much guidance by supernatural forces causes disaster." The boys and girls discussed how these variously expressed themes, all consistent with the playwright's intent, would affect such aspects of the production as the interpretation of characters and the designing of the scenery and costumes.

Besides finding the theme of a play, students must determine its setting, atmosphere, purposes and motives of the characters, and plot.

Setting

Students, to understand a play, must know where and when the action is taking place, who is engaging in the action and in what situation the characters are acting. Some teachers call these the where, when, why, and what of the beginning of the play. Boys and girls look at programs, listen to and read plays to discover the where, when, why, and what of the plays.

Atmosphere

Students must recognize that the atmosphere of the play depends on the play's setting and its main idea. They study how the scenery, the lighting, the tempo and the actions and speech of the actors indicate the play's mood. In studying the atmosphere, one teacher suggests that the boys and girl recommend a color for a particular play and explain why they have chosen the color.

Characters

Your pupils study the characters in the play in relationship to their interpretation of theme. As a result of different views of the theme, interpretations of characters can be almost diametrically opposed. One fifteen-year-old's major impression of the mother in *The Glass Menagerie* was that of a comic creature who lived in a dream of an imagined Southern past. Another's major impression was that she was a tragic figure with a crippled daughter, a husband who deserted her, and very little to hope for in the future. Their view of the theme of the play guided the direction of their analyses of the mother.

As an assignment one drama teacher asks his students to examine carefully one of the characters in the play that they are reading. The students indicate on which side of the conflict the character is, why he was introduced into the story, how he thinks, and why he thinks as he does. In earlier assignments the students have given the theme of the play, its mood, and its basic conflict.

Plot

In addition to finding the theme, mood, and analyzing the characters, students must understand that each play has an exposition, a rising action, a climax, a falling action, and an outcome. When students have worked with creative drama activities, they have used these logical divisions. You can show that the same structure exists in a story played creatively and in a play. For example, one teacher brought to the class a picture of a father's watching with anger his eighteen-year-old daughter's playing the violin. When the teacher asked what the picture represented, one student replied that the father was forcing his daughter, a violin prodigy, to play *his* interpretation of a particular bit of music. The daughter was beginning to revolt, to want to interpret music in her own way. The teacher explained that this situation might be the exposition, that as the father and daughter began to do something about the situation, rising action would commence, and that the conflicting forces would work on each other until they arrived at a high point of intensity, the climax. In telling the story of the violinist the students started with a scene depicting the daughter's preparation for a concert and a minor argument with her father. The most intense conflict arose when the girl, having fallen in love with a pianist who encouraged her to interpret music her own way, did so in a concert in the town's leading hall. That this intense conflict was the climax was obvious. The students then provided the falling action, untangling the situation by the father's going to live as a recluse and by the daughter's achieving artistic success. The outcome was the marriage of the daughter to the pianist and the start of a brilliant concert career for her. Members of the group then indicated how other stories which they had enacted provided the structure of a play. As an assignment, the teacher asked that each student read one one-act play and write brief notations on its exposition, rising action, climax, falling action, and final outcome.

Acting

Almost every theater course contains a unit on acting. Most teachers feel that this unit is a significant part of the course, for from it the students develop an appreciation of fine acting. Furthermore, by analysis of a character's ideas, emotions, purposes of being, and relationship to others, the students better understand human beings. In addition, they often become aware of the need for a poised, well-co-ordinated body, for a clear, expressive voice, and for distinct articulation.

Some teachers stress improvisation in this unit with emphasis on sense memory, emotion memory, power of concentration, and imagination. Others stress the fundamental techniques of acting—the use of the body and the control of voice and diction. Most teachers are now using the first approach, starting with simple improvisations and the enactment of uncomplicated scenes.

For example, one high school drama teacher[3] begins her unit on acting by encouraging her students to use all of their senses and by creating in them a desire to observe keenly what is going on around them. Frequently she starts this unit in October when the leaves are turning color, when some of the days are brisk ones, good for riding horseback, while others are sultry ones, good for lying lazily in a hammock. She describes for her students activities and moods prevalent in the fall:

1. Lying in a hammock passively and peacefully, looking up at the bright clear blue sky, watching a younger brother raking up leaves, smelling the burning of the leaves.

2. With soft breezes blowing, walking leisurely, kicking the leaves quietly, admiring their gay reds and oranges.

3. Riding through the woods on horseback, hearing the crackling sound of the leaves under the horses' feet.

4. Sitting in a classroom, thinking, "What am I doing in this musty school when the day is such a lovely one?"

5. Eating fresh, crunchy, delicious apples just picked from a tree.

[3] Mary Desser, Chairman of Speech Department, Martin Van Buren High School, New York City.

The students talk about the senses that are being aroused. They then think about ways of creating the scenes. The teacher explains that the stimuli she has given them are not real but imaginative and that their reactions are coming about without real stimuli. She further indicates that an awareness of their own reactions, as their senses are aroused, helps them to portray feelings accurately and genuinely.

After this exercise, she marches to the door slamming it angrily. The students make such comments as: "I was startled," "The sound disturbed me," "I was amazed," and "I felt annoyed." Next she walks to the door quietly, slowly, nonchalantly; but she again slams it. This time their observations include: "I expected you to close it quietly," "I didn't think anything much would happen," "I looked at your eyes. I knew what you were up to." The third time she walks to the door, she leaves it open. This time the students remark, "I felt a certain amount of tension," "I thought that you were going to fool us again." Then she asks them to close their eyes, to think about the time that she slammed the door after walking slowly toward it. Their remarks vary: "I saw you open the door, heard it slam," "It was like a silent moving picture with a commentary," "It was like a villain creeping along," "I felt tense. I heard the slam," "I had a chill-like feeling." They talk about how, when the door was slammed, their reactions to the stimuli were quite alike, but how, as they recalled the instance later, their reactions differed.

On one particular day after such an introduction, she proposed the following dialogue for a boy and a girl:

Boy. You will never see me again.
Girl. You hope.
Boy. I'm sorry.
Girl. Let's try again.
(Boy turns, goes to the door, slams it, and leaves.)

She asked them first to make up the story behind the dialogue and then to enact it. The first couple made up a story in which false pride was influencing the boy. The dialogue came as the result of a bitter quarrel between the boy and girl, with the boy unwilling to admit his mistake. After they acted the small scene, members of the group talked about whether the motivations were made clear and what helped make them clear.

At times, this teacher uses other scenes. Two that she often uses are: (1) Coming home, opening the closet door to the smell of moth balls. (2) Coming home very hungry, finding food on the stove, poking one's finger in the pot, and getting burned. She points out that in both instances the audience must know what the actors are doing and why they are acting as they are. The students evaluate the performances giving comments like "John didn't give the impression that he felt pain," "He jumped back too quickly," "His 'Oh' didn't sound as if he were hurt," and "He sounded a little meek."

Using Pantomime

Another drama teacher, who emphasizes techniques, begins her unit on acting with work on pantomime. She devises several situations: (1) A courtroom scene with the lawyer pleading for his client, an old man who has run down a young man at a busy intersection. The scene includes twelve jurors who are each assigned a definite character like a silly vain woman, a pompous, smug retired army man, an overly sweet grandmother. (2) An orchestra rehearsal with a new director whom the orchestra members resent. The director is a patient, respected musician who is striving for good musicianship. (3) A backyard scene with two grandfathers gossiping about their grandchildren. After the students have performed, the teacher emphasizes the need for understanding the character and his motivation thoroughly. During this study of pantomime she helps her students to attack their actions slowly when necessary, to respond first with the eye, then with the face, and then with the whole body. When they have succeeded in acquiring these techniques, she explains to them the necessity for a balanced stage picture, a center of interest, and action planned to help tell the story, visible to all members of the audience.

Creating a Role

After students recognize the need for using all their senses and for understanding motivation in character, they go on to study a specific character. As background material, they have studied the play itself, its theme, its period, its conflicting forces, and its structure. They are then ready to analyze the characters whom they are to create. As in creative drama, they must find out how the character feels and thinks, what his motivations are, how he looks, how he sounds, how he acts, and how he stands and walks. For this purpose, sometimes you ask students to write a biography of the character up to the time he appears in the play. Other times you suggest to your students that they find photographs from magazines that may well have represented the character at different ages. Or you advise them to observe people who, in some way or other, are like the characters and report on these observations. The students always study the lines of the play carefully to find clues to the character. They examine what the character himself says and what others have said about him in the play. Finally, they study the character's relationship to the play as a whole, the reasons for his being in the play, and his reactions to other characters.

The students' analyses help them to understand their roles and to give direction to their interpretations. Now that they have built intellectual concepts of the roles and the play, they must by their imaginations adapt themselves to these concepts. They must make clear by the use of their bodies and their voices the meanings and feelings of the characters. Furthermore, they must recognize that these meanings and feelings must be projected to an audience.

Projecting the Character

At this point, you guide your actors toward an economy of action to avoid the unnecessary and the awkward, to give freedom for expression of emotion, and to make possible changes of tempo. For example, as required, you ask actors to move in straight lines, to go directly to where they wish to move, or to start with the foot that is nearest to the place that they intend to go. You also suggest to actors to play important scenes downstage, to make important crosses downstage, or less important ones upstage.

As part of projecting the character, one teacher assigns the following scene:

A. Hi. (Enters from left.)
B. Hi. (Enters from right.)
A. What's new?
B. Jane's getting married.
A. Oh no! . . . . I can't believe it.
B. The date's set—June eighteenth.
A. I can't believe it. I just can't believe it.

She asks that the students play the scene in three ways:

1. Play it straight as if Jane's getting married *is* news, for Jane never could make up her mind whom to marry. Now she has.
2. Play it as if *A* is badly hurt. He himself had intended to marry Jane. The announcement is a real blow to him.
3. Play it as if Jane's getting married is a joke. Since getting married has been her constantly expressed wish, her friends are entertained at the realization of her goal.

Her next assignment is to enact scenes from plays. In each instance, the students have read the plays first, examined their structure, determined their themes, and analyzed the characters whom they are to play. As the students enact the scenes, the teacher helps them to select the details of characterization that make for genuine playing of the characters, to move on the stage economically, and to respond appropriately to other characters. She also shows them how to be effective members of a group on a stage.

Some aspects of projecting a role are decidedly your responsibility. For instance, in order that the audience understands the plot of the play, you must make sure that your actors emphasize business essential to the plot. If a diamond is to be an important property, you make certain that the audience sees it and the actor's handling of it. Likewise, you encourage the characters to emphasize those lines necessary to an understanding of the plot: the lines, for example, which explain motivation, give necessary background material, or show relationships. In these instances, you make clear that the audience must see and hear the actors. You do not allow them to hide behind furniture, to bury gestures behind other actors' backs, or to cover their gestures with their own bodies.

Beyond stimulating the students to make the characters and the story clear to the audience, you motivate them to keep the characters alive and interesting. Furthermore, you must see that the play moves at the right speed, that the actors do not imitate each other in action or in voice, and that they do build the necessary climaxes in the play.

Place of Voice and Diction in the Theater Class

Throughout you must encourage your actors to speak with clear voice and articulation. Poor voice quality and inaccurate careless articulation interfere with the actor's interpretation of character and detract from the response of the audience. You are fortunate when your students have already learned to use acceptable diction and effective voice. To place a student in a drama class for the purpose of improving his speech does a disservice both to the student and to the speech program. Students in a drama class should possess normally good voices, clear, resonant, flexible, and responsive to the meaning and feeling of the lines to be read.

Using Effective Voice

You must help your students to avoid the common vocal faults of amateur actors. First, they frequently read lines too quickly, regardless of the tempo that the meaning of the lines dictates. Recordings help young players to recognize the errors of their speedy attacks. Second, they often read the first part of a line clearly and then fade away in the last part. It is important that they recognize that centers exist in the final phrases as well as in the beginning phrases and that much of the meaning may occur at the end of the line. Third, some students tend to read with a recurrent melody pattern. This fault distracts from and distorts the intended meaning. Fourth, still others tend to read on one pitch level. The resulting monotony interferes with communication. Fifth, to be heard, amateurs often increase their volume unnecessarily. They must understand that clear articulation, reading of lines with meaning and with the resulting correct centering and phrasing, and reading at an appropriate rate are important in being heard. In other words, they must apply the principles of effective voice and articulation and of oral reading given in Chapters IV and IX to their reading of lines in a play.

Some teachers use a variety of exercises to show the importance of voice quality, intonation, stress, and rate in reading lines effectively. They indicate how these aspects can point up quite different feelings and meanings. One teacher asks her students to suggest various kinds of stories while saying the letters of the alphabet. One student will tell a sad story; another, a juicy bit of gossip; another, a fairy tale; another, a tale of sincere admiration for a great man; and still another, a tale of woe and anguish. She also asks her students to think of a motivation for "I've said no a thousand times. I will not change my mind." The students then read the lines as the motivation dictates. For example, one student reads the line in anger, playing the part of a father refusing his son a car; his son had been arrested five times for drunken driving. Another reads it with an undercurrent of sadness; he would have liked to give the hand of his daughter to John, but John is the son of his bitterest business enemy. The students then discuss the part that voice quality, intonation, rate, and stress have played in giving meaning and feeling to the lines.

Using Clear Articulation and Appropriate Pronunciation

The articulation of the young actor should be clear and accurate and should not draw attention to itself. As he plays the part of an educated person, he should overcome excessive substandard assimilations, and should correct his vulgate speech errors such as omissions, additions, insertions, and distortions. On the other hand, overprecise and affected speech is just as offensive as substandard speech. Generally, in amateur theater, students do well to speak the speech of the educated men and women in their community, for as indicated in the chapter on voice and articulation, no single standard of pronunciation exists in the United States.

Usually the student actors' speech should follow the same standard. To have the mother say *path* with a broad *a* and the daughter to say the word with a narrow *a* is obviously inconsistent and incongruous. In circumstances, however, where the play calls for a particular speech pattern, you usually suggest a minimal number of sounds to give the flavor of the dialect. To train a high school student to use a consistent dialect is difficult and time-consuming.

Evaluating Acting

The student should learn to evaluate his own acting and that of his fellow students. Such questions as the following help students to judge their acting.

1. Is this the kind of character that the playwright wishes to portray?
2. Does the actor understand the character and his ideas?
3. Does the actor understand the character's relationship to the play and to the other characters?
4. Does the actor understand the character and his emotions, his motivations?
5. Does he read the lines with meaning and feeling?
6. Are the volume, pitch, and rate of the voice of the character appropriate?

7. Is the bodily movement of the character appropriate?
8. Is the stage business of the character appropriate?
9. Does the character contribute to the telling of the story?
10. Do you see and hear the actor adequately?
11. Does the character stay with his characterization consistently?
12. Does the character become an integral part of the play?
13. Was the character emotionally moving?
14. Did you laugh with the actor?

Historical Background

Teachers vary in their attitudes toward including a history of the theater in their drama course. Some claim that a student cannot understand a play when it is not related to the development of the theater, and they feel that theater is an integral part of a nation's culture. They point to the influence of the theater from the Greeks to the present day, its social significance, and its contribution to all cultures. Other teachers indicate that most students elect the theater course to perform and to learn the technical aspects of theater. These teachers do not believe that a knowledge of the historical background of the theater is necessary to understand today's theater. One teacher may include none of the history of the theater; another may spend four fifths of the semester on it. Some include the Greek period, the Roman period, the Renaissance and the Elizabethan era, the Neoclassic period, the eighteenth century, the nineteenth century, and contemporary theater. Others include in addition such items as the Oriental theater, the medieval church and marketplace theater, the folk theaters of Italy, Spain, Germany, and France.

Assignments also differ. Some teachers assign plays of each period to be read and reported on and representative scenes to be played. Others give emphasis to a general study of the culture and events of the time in order for students to gain the necessary perspective. Still other teachers stress the production, its place and its type, and the contributions of the actors and actresses. These teachers ask students interested in costuming, lighting, or makeup to trace the theory of these techniques throughout the ages. They ask other students to study the kinds of audiences who appeared in the different eras. Still other teachers relate the play as written to the physical aspects of the playhouse in which it was performed. Many teachers regard this aspect the most important in teaching theater history. You do teach theater history from a definite viewpoint.

Directing

Not all instructors of theater include directing in their course of study. But for advanced, mature, intellectually able students, this unit is valuable. The student director selects the play, casts it, guides its interpretation and its style of production, and co-ordinates the final performance.

The student director must depend to a large extent in his direction on your advice since your training and experience are so much wider than his. As the student director talks over with his cast the purpose of the playwright and the theme of the play, he may need your assistance. Surely he must have your counsel in making a promptbook. The student has had little experience with the blocking of movement. You must, therefore, give him help in moving his characters meaningfully. You will check the promptbook carefully before rehearsal begins. The student director is likely to do better in establishing the meaning and feeling of the lines, in guiding character portrayal, in providing motivations, and in making the story clear, for he has in all likelihood worked on a part himself and has had experience in these aspects of play direction. Again he may find difficulty in co-ordinating all phases of the production, for experience as an actor or as a manager of one phase of production is too narrow. Here too you advise the student.

One teacher asked her students to get ready to direct two or three scenes from a specific play, to direct them, and finally to evaluate the direction. She prepared them for this assignment by demonstrating the steps involved. First she set up with them criteria for selecting a play for class production. Keeping these criteria in mind, the students read a number of plays from which they chose to produce Barrie's *Quality Street*. Second, after the students and the teacher determined the play's theme and structure and discussed the conflicts and the characters in the play, the group prepared several scenes for direction. This preparation involved the making of the pages of a promptbook to include the movements and business of the characters and the necessary staging and producing directions. Third, after the teacher herself cast the students in the parts, she began to rehearse the scenes: the teaparty of the old ladies in the first act and the return of the soldier in the last act. In the first rehearsals, she pointed out how the actors carried out her plans for groupings and movements, how they responded to her suggestions in interpreting meaning and feeling and in building characterizations, and how they projected their portrayal to the audience. In the subsequent rehearsals, she showed how to add details in business and movement, how to correct dull or false movements and ineffective interpretation, how to set the pace of the play, and how to give a final polish for a smooth performance.

As an assignment, she asked her students to lay similar groundwork for directing other short scenes of *Quality Street* and to be ready to direct them in class. After the direction, she and the members of the class evaluated both the students' preparation and their direction.

Other assignments may include the study of the methods of well-known directors, visits to directors at work, analyses of the probable direction of a television production, and working out of promptbooks. More theoretical assignments are papers on such subjects as the rise of the director or methods of tryouts.

Production

How much study of technical production is to be included in a course in theater depends on the aims of you and the students, the ability of the students, the length of the course, and the availability of facilities. In some instances you may wish to develop student directors to handle minor school productions completely. In other instances you may feel that students must themselves work with the technical aspects of production to be able to appreciate this phase of drama in today's theater. The technical aspects are scenic design and stagecraft, lighting, costuming, makeup, and the designing and construction of properties and sound effects.

Scenic Design and Stagecraft

Your pupils may study the basic requirements of an effectively designed setting, be able to interpret a play's mood through scenic design, and know how to adapt their scenic design to their school stage. In some cases you may feel that your students should recognize such styles of scenic design as realism, expressionism, constructivism, stylism, and formalism.

Where scenic design and stagecraft are to be taught, the following may well comprise the unit: the principles of scenic design including the use of line, color, and mass, the purpose of the setting, the kinds and types of settings, the making of floor plans and models, the constructing of at least two kinds of flats and the covering and the painting of them, and the assembling of scenery. Constructing and assembling scenery, however, is feasible only when time, money, and space are readily available. Such work requires weeks of students' time, money to pay for the lumber, canvas, and paint, and space for an adequate workshop. Without such resources, the unit is decidedly limited in value.

A particular teacher used as a basis for her assignment in teaching stage design *The Male Animal,* which the students were to produce later in the year. They talked about the colors and the lines that would best interpret the theme of this play. After they had decided on the colors, yellow, orange, and brown, and on the lines, largely long curves, they made their floor plan to scale and then their model. The members of this theater class designed and executed the entire setting. They built the flats, painted them, assembled them, and took them down. As a result of their work and the guidance of the teacher, the set was tasteful, good-looking, and functional. This group, however, had ample time, money, and facilities for the undertaking.

Members of another class worked in a more theoretical way. Each of this group made a scaled floor plan and a model set for a play. After they had made these, they broke into three groups each of which built a flat, covered it, and painted it. Each group worked on a different type of flat: a plain unit, a unit with a fireplace, and one with a window; each group painted its flat in a different way. As a final activity, all the members of the class watched the school stage crew assemble and shift scenery.

Other assignments may include reports on designs by such designers as Robert Edmond Jones, Gordon Craig, David Belasco, Jo Mielziner, making different designs for the same play, and preparing a bulletin board showing designs of current Broadway productions or one showing the types of design.

Lighting

As in stage design, your students learn how lighting helps to tell the story of the play, emphasizes its important elements, and suggests its atmosphere. In addition, they learn how it serves its most simple function, making the actors and their actions visible to the audience. Through a study of lighting and through practice with lighting equipment, your students learn to appreciate the part that lighting plays in the production of a particular play and to use their lighting equipment effectively.

Assignments in lighting vary. Most teachers require their students to know the purposes of lighting and ask them to make a light plot and to work out a light cue sheet. Frequently students experiment with the school lighting equipment to determine what effects they can get. In one class one group lit a moonlight scene; another, a daytime outdoor scene; and a third, a scene in which a murder was about to be committed with a stiletto. Each group demonstrated how it achieved its particular effects. These groups learned the functions of different kinds of lighting equipment and the effects created by different colored gelatins.

Costuming

Your students appreciate the contribution of costuming to a production and find out how to clothe their actors when they study costuming as they have studied stage design and lighting. They consider how costumes add to the play as a whole, how they help delineate character in terms of class, regional influences, and occupation, and how they show relationships among the characters. Often the students help execute the costumes which they have designed. Members of one theater class costumed completely Gilbert and Sullivan's *Trial by Jury,* put on by the school's music department. Another group designed and made the costumes for an assembly, *Christmas in Many Lands.* First they made the costume plates. Then they purchased the material with careful consideration for the texture, cut it, dyed it, and sewed it. For example, in dressing a chorus of Polish lasses, they learned how to make belts from black oil cloth and how to stencil a plain cambric-like material with a colorful border.

Although assignments may include the making of costume plates and the actual execution of certain costumes, students may attack the problem in a more theoretical way. One teacher based her assignment to her theater class on the costumes in a forthcoming television production of *The Taming of the Shrew*. She prepared them for this assignment by explaining the use of color and line in costume, by showing them pictures of Elizabethan costumes, and by giving them dittoed copies of typical Elizabethan costumes for a man and a woman. She asked them to watch *The Taming of the Shrew* and to decide what colors would be appropriate for the costumes for Petruchio, Kate, and her sister and to note how these costumes were or were not typically Elizabethan. The resulting class discussion was a fruitful one.

Makeup

Another aspect of technical production is makeup. It is included in a course to help the student to appreciate the makeup that he sees in the theater and to teach students to put on makeup for a production. For this second purpose, students must learn the theory and the techniques of the application of makeup. You may well demonstrate to the members of your class at least the three basic types of makeup (juvenile, middle age, and old age). Your students, working in pairs, then make up each other. After the basic instruction they may make up the cast of a school production.

Other assignments are more theoretical. One teacher encourages some of her students to prepare a bulletin board with pictures, showing the various kinds of stage makeup prevalent on the Broadway stage. Members of another group described how the genie in the television production of *Aladdin* was made up.

Properties and Sound Effects

Like the other aspects of technical production, properties and sound effects help to interpret the play, to project its mood, and to tell its story. After students understand these functions, they should be able to make properties for a production or procure them in some other way. Because many properties are borrowed, they should learn to keep a systematized list and to be careful of properties. They should also be taught to take precautions in handling and storing them.

EXTRACURRICULAR ACTIVITIES OF THE HIGH SCHOOL THEATER

Objectives

A school theater should exist for definitely stated purposes and should take advantage of the values inherent in dramatic activities. The organization should offer opportunities for members to develop poise, to express themselves with creativity and imagination, and to develop an appreciation of good theater. It should give its members a chance to participate in all phases of theater: acting, designing and constructing scenery and costumes, working out lighting effects, making up characters, and developing business acumen in theater management. To achieve these purposes, clubs participate in various kinds of activities such as putting on shows, purchasing theatrical equipment, participating in dramatic festivals, attending dramatic performances, inviting authorities to talk about various phases of the theater, and experimenting with producing and acting techniques.

Organization

Most dramatic clubs are organized with a president, vice-president, treasurer, and secretary. In addition, many have an executive board made up of the stage manager, the property manager, costume manager, business manager, lighting manager, and makeup manager. Frequently these managers are under the direction of a production manager. You serve as sponsor and advisor to the group.

You help these students to plan for and carry out their duties in a variety of ways: For instance, you set up a bookkeeping system with the treasurer so that his account of all moneys taken in and paid out is accurate. You make sure that the property manager keeps a record of all borrowed properties and that he returns them in good condition after a production. You teach the lighting manager how to make a cue sheet, the costume manager how to stencil, or the makeup manager to put on a beard. You make certain that the managers have assigned crew members to specific duties well ahead of the beginning date of rehearsals. In each case, you decide for yourself how much and what kind of guidance the students need.

Some students will need considerable advice and instruction; others, very little.

Choosing the Play

One of the first tasks you and your organization face is to select a play. You plan beforehand the method and criteria of selection.

Method of Selection

Many high school organizations have play-selecting committees sometimes headed by the vice-president of the club. To prevent, however, a selection by students of a play impossible to produce effectively, you should limit the selection of plays to those which you suggest. You may give your students six plays to choose from, stressing the importance of a varied program. You may recommend that over a period of years the club should produce a melodrama, a tragedy, a comedy, a fantasy, and a farce and that the themes should be quite different. For example, in the fall you may present a comedy dealing with a problem of youth; and in the spring, a tragedy dealing with a serious contemporary problem.

Since you are to suggest plays, it is important that you read many plays and have in mind many choices for possible production. One high school teacher spends three days in a New York City drama bookshop each year reading and rereading plays that he has listed during the year. He compiles this list from many sources. At speech conventions when he talks with play-producing colleagues, he notes the plays which they have produced successfully. He adds to his list those which *The Speech Teacher, The Quarterly Journal of Speech,* and *The New York State Reports* indicate are being produced. Consequently, he is never without a play to produce.

In selecting the plays appropriate for high school production, you take into account your actors, your audience, your staging facilities, literary value of plays, the amount of money you can spend for production, and any problems peculiar to your school or community.

Criteria for Choosing the Play

Actors. An important consideration in choosing a play is your actors. You must think of their number, their abilities, their experience, and their maturity. Sometimes a play demands a particular ability of an actor or actress. For example, one high school director had a particularly able young man who played older parts well. Without him, *The Man Who Came to Dinner* would have been a formidable undertaking. If you have few experienced, mature actors available, you choose a play that is not difficult. With inexperienced, immature actors, you will be successful if you exceed their intellectual grasp but not their emotional grasp. As you choose your play, you must keep in mind the actors that you can cast.

Audience. Second, the nature of your audience is important. Are its members more sophisticated than naive? Have they had considerable theater-going opportunities? Are they young or old? As an inexperienced teacher, you may feel that your first attempt should be a well-known, recognized, somewhat difficult play. But you must take your audience, as well as your students, as they are and educate them. An inexperienced audience will be mystified and even offended by a play that is far too difficult for them, but as the experience of the actors and the audience becomes wider, they will be willing and glad to accept plays which require serious concentration. The author was interested in the history of the selection of plays and their production in a New York State regional festival. The first year a large number of the plays were poorly selected and poorly produced. In subsequent years, the quality of the choice of play, of production, and of interpretation greatly improved.

Staging and Production. Third, your staging and producing facilities are an important factor in your choice. If this is your first year of production, if your stage has little equipment, if you must build your own sets, if you have few stage carpenters available, you will do well to do a production like *Our Town* which needs little scenery or to do one like *Quality Street* which calls for one set. Your costuming crew's abilities also influence the choice of a play. In some instances, as in *The Midsummer Night's Dream,* the need for elaborate costuming rules out a play. In others, the same need challenges the efforts and imagination of a competent costuming staff. You must further consider the expertness and equipment of the lighting and makeup crews, because some plays require elaborate lighting and makeup. You must, therefore, take into account production requirements in choosing a play. A simple production effectively executed gives the workers inspiration and experience to attempt a more elaborate production. The production, however, should inspire the creative, artistic abilities of your production staff.

Literary Value. Fourth, the play should have literary value. Its theme, sincere and universal, should be expressed in clear dramatic structure and in a style that adds to theatrical portrayal. The play should kindle the imagination of the actors and the technicians to interpret its meaning and feeling effectively. Actors and directors tire of plays in which the lines are dull and the characters stereotypes. On the other hand, a great play remains fresh and interesting, for it motivates the actors to be constantly alert for new meanings in the lines and additional motivations for the characters. That many high schools produce plays of little literary value is obvious. Throughout the country the standards of high school play selection are too low. Ronald Gee and John Dietrich[4] in a survey of 367 plays produced in 211 Wisconsin high schools found that 80 per cent of the plays were of extremely doubtful merit.

Royalty. Lastly, how much royalty can you afford? For the performance of modern plays, almost all play-publishing firms require a certain fee. Except for the classics, most royalty-free plays are not worthy of production. Many directors, however, neglect the royalty-free classics. The author has seen the following classics produced effectively by high school groups: Moliere's *The Imaginary Invalid,* Shakespeare's *Midsummer Night's Dream* and *The Taming of the Shrew,* Goldsmith's *She Stoops to Conquer,* Wilde's *The Importance of Being Earnest,* and Sheridan's *The School for Scandal.* If you feel that you cannot afford a particular royalty, write to the play-publishing house and tell them your circumstances. In many instances the house will reduce the royalty.

Special Problems in Selecting a High School Play

Besides these four factors which are always important in selecting a play, your community may present special problems. Many communities are loath to accept high school plays which involve profanity, emphasis on sex or on drinking.

The profanity in many modern plays may present a problem. Members of a high school audience often react unfavorably to one of their neighbor's children swearing in a part in a play whereas they listen with equanimity to professional, college, or community actors

---

[4] R. C. Gee and J. E. Dietrich, "A Survey of Dramatic Activity in Wisconsin High Schools, 1947-1948," *Quarterly Journal of Speech,* XXXVI (February, 1950), 65-70.

playing the same parts using the same words. Since profane words usually are not necessary to the plot, you can omit them with impunity. Your students, however, should understand your reasons for the cut from the beginning so that they will not insert the swearing the evening of the performance.

Your second problem is that many plays treat the sex theme openly and frankly. In some instances, sex is the subject matter of the play, and thus you cannot eradicate references to it without destroying the theme of the play. In such cases choose another play where sex is treated in what is considered a wholesome way.

Your third problem is the amount of drinking in a play. Drinking, like swearing, can usually be eliminated without harming the play. In some plays, however, like *The Male Animal,* a character's getting drunk is an integral part of the plot. Where it is an integral part and where the attitudes of the community are such as to condemn a high school student's playing a drunk, you will do well to choose a play with no drinking character.

These three problems are the most frequent. Others include emphasis on crime, religion, intolerance, or bigotry. Plays which stress these topics are often unacceptable to community audiences.

Preparing for the Production

The Promptbook

You prepare for the production of a play by making a promptbook which contains such material as clues to interpretation and movements, floor plans, scene plots, details on setting and costuming, property lists, and a lighting plot. This preparation is essential for an artistic, successful performance. For example, you furnish the basis for dramatic balance and variety by indicating the movements of your actors and the stage areas where you wish them to be. You provide a foundation for lighting scenes effectively. You lay the groundwork for the kind of costuming that helps to interpret character. The play production texts listed in the bibliography contain advice on preparing a promptbook.

Tryouts for the Play

After you have prepared for the production, you are ready to cast the play. For a public performance you want to find the best equipped actors for particular parts and the kind who will co-operate with the other students and with you to make the performance profitable to the actors and enjoyable to the audience. Tryouts are usually a partial answer to this problem. Admittedly, in tryouts you may miss a talented person who, nervous because of the competition, may not do his best; and you may occasionally cast an overly self-possessed person who reads easily and moves gracefully but whose accomplishments are superficial. Nevertheless, tryouts still are the most efficient and democratic way of casting a school play.

In most instances you ask the potential actor to fill out a card giving his name, address, telephone number, age, weight, height, color of eyes and hair, acting experience, and special talents. You may also have him include his home-room number and his other school activities. Lastly, you request him to indicate the days and the hours when he will be free for rehearsals and to indicate any previous commitments that may interfere with a rehearsal schedule.

Your tryouts cover several days and include two periods: in the first one you hear many potential actors and in the second you decide on your cast. In the first period the potential actors read the parts of their choice with other actors and frequently read other parts for which you feel that they may be fitted. You evaluate their performance on their ability to move on the stage, to read lines, to use voice fitting to the characters, to react to other actors, and most importantly to display an imaginative grasp of the character. You then call a second tryout period after selecting several likely actors and actresses for each of the parts. You want to see them working together. Finally you announce the results on a bulletin board at a definite time. Some directors make this casting tentative until they are sure that they have chosen their actors well. When you follow this procedure, you indicate that the cast is tentative for a period of four or five rehearsals.

Some directors prefer a double cast. The advantages are that two students instead of one get the experience of a public performance and that there is always an understudy if anything happens to an actor. On the other hand, the director must spend more time rehearsing, and, in spite of the director's effort, an undesirable spirit of competition may arise between the two actors.

Getting Ready for Rehearsals

With your cast chosen, you are ready to plan for rehearsals. You must work out the rehearsal schedule before the play begins, taking into account dates for examinations and other important school events. In the schedule leave more time for rehearsing segments of the play in the earlier rehearsals than the later ones, because deciding on action and setting the basic characterizations are slow and time-consuming. The schedule should include day, date, time, and act or scene to be rehearsed.

After making the schedule, you should announce it and adhere to it strictly. Your actors should be expected to arrive promptly. Permitting students to be late or to miss a rehearsal is bad for the morale of the whole group. Furthermore, parents appreciate knowing the rehearsal schedule. If students know that their parents have the schedule, they will not use play rehearsals as an excuse for being out late. When the schedules are regularly sent to parents, students accept the procedure as routine.

One director sends dittoed letters to parents of the boys and girls in her group. Such a letter follows:

Dear Mrs. Jones:

Your son has been chosen to play one of the parts in our forthcoming production, *The Importance of Being Earnest.* He was selected because he read the lines well and showed an imaginative understanding of the character he is to play. Furthermore, since he appears to be responsible and co-operative, he will work to make the production a success.

Participation in this activity is admittedly time-consuming. It does, however, bring to the student certain rewards. Performance before the public will add to your son's poise. His study of character will challenge his imagination. He will gain from working in a co-operative endeavor with others on an important school project.

I am enclosing a schedule of rehearsals so that you will know what is expected of him.

If you like, I shall be glad to talk over with you his participation in this activity.

Sincerely yours,
Mary Fish
Theater Director

Another director has her students sign a contract. The contract indicates that the actor promises to be at all rehearsals promptly, to learn his lines by the dates agreed upon, and to work well with others. The contract includes a list of rehearsal periods. The director and the student sign three copies of which one is sent to the parents, one is retained by the student, and one is filed in the dramatics office.

Rehearsing

Writing for the *Dramatics Director's Handbook,* David Sievers establishes these general principles for rehearsals:[5]

1. Study new material in small units, with frequent repetitions.
2. Never drop a scene for more than three days without a review.
3. Rehearse the acts separately at first, and the whole play as a unit the last two weeks before performance.
4. Allow "warm up" after rest periods.
5. Be sure the actors understand the character's motivation for every line and movement.
6. Announce your rehearsal schedule, including date of performance and stick to it. Set a deadline for the learning of lines, and adhere to it.

If possible, during the first five weeks rehearsals are best held after school. This scheme leaves evenings free for homework. One high school teacher rehearses her group from 3:30 until 5:30 each day and from 10:00 until 1:00 on Saturdays. Some schools provide time during the school day for such activities as rehearsals.

Program

For each public performance, a program should be provided. The program serves as a memento of the performance and gives the audience essential information about the play. It may also tell the audience about the history and the plans of the dramatic club.

Some programs have covers, others do not. One high school group always uses a picture of their particular stage on its program cover. Another high school group designs covers, quite different, for each performance. For example, for *Our Hearts Were Young and Gay,* students composed a cover on which two young women, draped

[5] David W. Sievers, "The Play Rehearsal Schedule," in *Dramatic Director's Handbook,* Ernest Bavely ed. (Cincinnati, Ohio, The National Thespian Society, 1949), p. 47.

in the clothes of the twenties and hung with long chains of beads, were obviously dramatizing themselves. This cartoon-like drawing suggested the mood of the play.

The title page usually has the name of the producing organization, the name of the play and author, the date and time of performance, and the place of the performance.

The body of the program includes the cast in the order of the players' appearance, with the extra players and the groups appearing last. After this a synopsis of the scenes occurs. Next on the program are the names of the production staff. One program used at Bryant High School, New York City, listed faculty committees (dramatic, direction, production, stage manager, scenery, business manager, costumes, makeup, music, program, sound and light technicians, publicity, usher, and auditorium) and the student committees (assistant directors, assistant stage managers, technical directors, curtain crew, costume crew, light crew, makeup crew, photography crew, property crew, publicity crew, scenery crew, property, and transportation.)

The program may also contain other information: a brief synopsis of the play, a short statement concerning the author of the play, a *Who's Who* of the leading actors and actresses in the cast and of managers of the production staff, and publicity concerning forthcoming productions.

Frequently students sell advertising space in their programs. The advertisements help to bring in needed income. For example, one program included advertisements from record shops, beauty salons, a dress shop, cleaners, bakeries and from some of the speech and English classes of the school. The speech classes listed their officers and sometimes attached a poem. For example, one speech class used this jingle:[6]

> Hear ye, hear ye, one and all
> Speech 608 is on the ball.
> If you have a Southern drawl,
> Don't worry, we'll cure "you all."

The Theater Director's Use of the Auditorium

The theater director must co-operate with other faculty members who are going to use the same facilities as he. To make this co-

[6] Program for *Our Hearts Were Young and Gay*, Bryant High School, Long Island City, 1958.

operation easier, he must organize and plan well. He must be able to announce when he will be rehearsing in the auditorium and when the play is to be produced. On the other hand, the music director, the person who most often uses the same facilities, must know when he will be rehearsing in the auditorium, and when his concert is to be given. If both plan ahead and stick to their plans, neither rehearsals nor performance need conflict.

BIBLIOGRAPHY AND SUGGESTED READING

Acting

ALBRIGHT, H. D., *Working Up a Part: A Manual for the Beginning Actor* (Boston, Houghton Mifflin Co., 1947). Shows how to analyze, rehearse, and play a part. Excellent suggestions for exercises.

DOLMAN, J., Jr., *The Art of Acting* (New York, Harper & Brothers, 1949). Lays down principles in the first part of the book which are applied in later chapters. Chapters are devoted to comedy, tragedy, reaction and by-play, voice, diction, bodily action, and performance.

FRANKLIN, M., *Rehearsal: The Principles and Practices of Acting For the Stage*, 3rd ed. (Englewood Cliffs, N. J., Prentice-Hall, Inc., 1950). Gives theory of acting and exercises on it. Many of the exercises can be used by high school students.

McGAW, C., *Acting Is Believing* (New York, Rinehart & Company, 1955). Gives sound advice on teaching acting.

STRICKLAND, F. C., *The Technique of Acting* (New York, McGraw-Hill Book Co., 1956). Breaks acting into categories such as entering, phrasing, actions in relation to thoughts, building a climax, timing, and explains the techniques inherent in each. Contains numerous exercises for developing techniques of acting many of which are adaptable for high school students.

TEPPER, Maxine E., "A Method of Teaching Acting," *The Speech Teacher*, V (March, 1956), 121-124. Explains that improvisation is the most useful tool in teaching acting. Shows how each student is asked to choose a scene for one to three actors without naming the characters or the play. Then without reading the play, the students improvise the scene.

Collection of Plays and Scenes

"Bibliography of One Act Plays," *Dramatics*, XX (November, 1951), 34-35. Lists one-act plays by recognized authors. Annotated.

COSGROVE, F., *Scenes for Student Actors,* 5 vols. (New York, Samuel French, Inc., 1936-1947). Includes scenes for individuals and for several men and women.

FRIEDERICH, W. J., *Directory of Three-Act Plays for High School* (Cincinnati, Ohio, The National Thespian Society).

GASSNER, J., ed., *Best American Plays: Third Series—1945-1951.* (New York, Crown Publishers, Inc., 1952). Includes seventeen plays by such authors as Tennessee Williams, Arthur Miller, Sidney Kingsley, Maxwell Anderson, Eugene O'Neill, John van Druten, Lillian Hellman.

KESTER, K., *Problem Projects in Acting* (New York, Samuel French, Inc., 1937). Gives thirty scenes for rehearsal.

MACALVANY, N., and COMER, V. L., *First Performance: Plays for the Junior High School Age* (New York, Harcourt, Brace & Co., 1952). Contains plays of different types that will appeal alike to high school students and their audiences.

MERSAND, J., Chairman of Committee on Play List of the National Council of Teachers of English, *Guide to Play Production,* 2nd ed. (New York, Appleton-Century-Crofts, Inc., 1958). Lists full-length plays, one-act plays, television plays, guidance and mental health plays, and 536 anthologies of long and short plays.

MILLER, H. L., *Holiday Plays for Teen-Agers: A Collection of One-Act Royalty-Free Plays for Important Occasions* (Boston, Plays, Inc., 1952) .

NAGELBERG, M. M., ed., *Drama in Our Time* (New York, Harcourt Brace & Co., 1948). Offers high school juniors and seniors a broad selective sampling of contemporary drama. Includes *Watch on the Rhine, Our Town, R.U.R., Abe Lincoln in Illinois, Yellow Jack,* and *One-Third of a Nation.*

Play Index, 1949-1952 (New York, the H. W. Wilson Co., 1953). An index to 2616 plays with a listing of author, subject, and title. Cast analysis.

PEARSON, T., *Director of Three Act Plays for High School* (Cincinnati, Ohio. The National Thespian Society, no date) .

SPER, F., ed., *Modern Short Plays* (New York, Globe Book Co., 1952). Contains fourteen carefully selected one-act plays of different types. Includes plays by Molnar, Wilde, Conkle, O'Neill, and Florence Ryerson and Colin Clements.

THOMAS, R. G., *Index to Full Length Plays,* 1895 to 1925 (Boston, F. W. Faxon Co., Inc., 1956). Catalogues 562 full-length plays. Entries include author, number of acts, characters, set, subject matter, and period. Non-royalty plays are indicated. The letter *A* warns that the play is for advanced groups.

Courses of Study and Philosophy of Teaching Dramatics

A Suggested Outline for a Course of Study in Dramatic Arts in the Secondary School (Stanford, California, American Educational Theater Association, Stanford University, 1950). Contains aims, philosophy for teaching dramatic arts, and units on dramatics. The suggested activities are carefully chosen and well-fitted to high school students.

A Selected Bibliography and Critical Comment on the Art, Theory, and Technique of Acting (Minneapolis, Minnesota, American Educational Theater Association, 306 Nicholson Hall, University of Minnesota).

BALL, E., "Drama and the Community," *Dramatics,* XXIV (May, 1953), 12-13. Emphasizes the values of drama festivals and interchange of plays. Based on projects of one large city system.

BOUEE, M. E., "Allied Activities and Dramatics," *Dramatics,* XXIV (October, 1952), 6-17. Tells how dramatic teachers can co-operate with teachers in other departments and with the whole school program. Discusses assembly programs.

Dramatics in the Secondary School, Bulletin of the National Association of Secondary School Principals (Washington, D. C., 1201 Sixteenth Street, N. W., December, 1949). Includes articles written by drama teachers. Widespread coverage.

ELLEFSON, M. M., *Dramatic Arts in the Secondary School: A Teacher's Guide* (Eugene, Oregon, University of Oregon, 1953).

ELKIND, S., "Principles of Learning: Their Application to Rehearsal," *The Speech Teacher,* V (January, 1956), 51-59. Indicates the need for a stimulating atmosphere and a motivation for learning and for sound teaching techniques in play production.

FRIEDERICH, W. J., *The High School Drama Course* (Cincinnati, Ohio, The National Thespian Society, 1955). Gives the units for a high school drama course. Includes a large number of well-chosen and practical assignments and projects.

FRIEDERICH, W. J., and WILCOX, R., *Teaching Speech in High Schools* (New York, The Macmillan Co., 1953), pp. 273-364. Lists goals of teaching dramatics and suggests content of units in this area. Contains many teaching suggestions.

KONIGSBERG, E., "An Outline Course of Study in Dramatics," *The Speech Teacher,* IV (January, 1955), 27-31. Outlines a course in dramatics. Units included are: exploring the field, the play, preparing the student actor, preparing the student director, training the stage technicians, costuming the play, training the audience, the performance, and the history of the theater.

McNESS, W., "An Orientation Course in Creative Skills for First Year

Junior High School Students," *The Speech Teacher,* I (November, 1952), 279-287. Contains a unit on bodily action that could be used in a dramatics class.

MILLER, L. C., "The Dramatic Arts," *The Bulletin of Secondary Principals,* XXXVI (February, 1952), 74-80. Contains practical information for the dramatics teacher on finding a good play and bibliographical information on magazines and books dealing with dramatics. Shows the place of dramatic arts in the curriculum.

REID, L., *Teaching Speech,* 2nd ed. (Columbia, Missouri, Artcraft Press, 1956), pp. 206-228, 336-349. Gives advice on directing a play. Contains a list of suggested one-act and three-act plays for high school students with number of sets and number of characters and royalty.

High School Texts on Dramatics

BARNES, G., and SUTCLIFFE, M. J., *On Stage, Everyone* (New York, The Macmillan Co., 1954).

OMMANNEY, K., and OMMANNEY, P., *The Stage and the School,* 2nd ed. (New York, McGraw-Hill Book Co., 1950) .

SMITH, MILTON, *Play Production,* student's ed. (New York, Appleton-Century-Crofts, Inc., 1947) . A college text but some high school teachers use it.

History of Theater

CHENEY, S., *Three Thousand Years of the Drama,* rev. ed. (New York, Longmans, & Co., Inc., 1952).

GASSNER, J., *Masters of the Drama,* 3rd ed. (New York, Dover Publications, Inc., 1954) . Gives a complete history of world theater and drama. Uniquely encyclopedic. Written with charm.

————, *The Theatre in Our Time* (New York, Crown Publishers, Inc., 1954). Contains eighty separate though interrelated historical, critical, and theoretical discussions of modern drama and theater.

MacGOWAN, K., and W. MELNITZ, *The Living Stage: A History of the World Theater* (Englewood Cliffs, N. J., Prentice-Hall, Inc., 1955). Surveys theater and drama, performers and managers of the world theater.

NICOLL, A., *The Development of the Theatre,* rev. ed. (New York, Harcourt, Brace & Co., 1948) . Traces the development of the physical theater.

Periodicals

Dramatics (National Thespian Society, College Hill Station, Cincinnati 24, Ohio. Monthly). Contains many articles on high school production. Well illustrated.

The Educational Theatre Journal (American Educational Theatre Association, University of Minnesota, 306 Nicholson Hall, Minneapolis 14,

Minn. Quarterly). Includes articles on productions, acting, and business management of plays.

Lagniappe (Row Peterson Co., 1911 Ridge Avenue, Evanston, Ill. Quarterly, free). Tells how to put on school plays. Well illustrated.

Plays, The Drama Magazine for Young People (Plays, Inc., 8 Arlington Street, Boston 16, Mass. 8 issues). Contains play scripts for various school levels and suggestions for other dramatic programs.

Players Magazine (National Collegiate Players, Box 339, Gainesville, Fla. Monthly). Consists of material on acting in and producing plays.

Theatre Arts (1545 Broadway, New York 36, N. Y. Monthly). Reviews Broadway and educational theatre productions. Gives information about films, music, television, books, and records.

Production

ALBRIGHT, H. D. HALSTEAD, W. P., and MITCHELL, L., *Principles of Theatre Art* (Boston, Houghton Mifflin Co., 1955). Covers every facet of theatre. Amply illustrated.

BAIRD, J. F., *Makeup*, rev. ed. (New York, Samuel French, Inc., 1942). Explains the process of makeup. Simple and complete.

BARTON, L., *Historic Costume for the Stage* (Boston, Walter H. Baker Co., 1938). Complete.

BAVELY, E., *Dramatics Directors Handbook*, rev. ed. (Cincinnati, Ohio, National Thespian Society, 1949). Tells how to teach dramatics, how to organize a dramatics club, and how to prepare and put on plays for the public. Includes a section on getting along with the faculty.

BOWMAN, W., *Modern Theatre Lighting* (New York, Harper & Brothers, 1957). Tells how to light a theater. Explained clearly and in detail.

BRADWELL, E., *Play Production for Amateurs* (New York, The Macmillan Co., 1953). Contains good, basic information.

CORSON, R., *Stage Makeup*, 3rd ed. (New York, Appleton-Century-Crofts, Inc., 1960). Explains well and clearly the process of makeup.

CORTRIGHT, E. S., "Selecting, Casting and Rehearsing the High School Play," *Quarterly Journal of Speech*, XXIX (December, 1943), 443-451. Has an excellent list of suggested plays. Gives the factors to consider in casting a play, aims in direction, and possible errors in rehearsing.

CURRIE, F. G., "Arena Staging on a Shoe String," *The Speech Teacher*, V (November, 1956), 290-295. Discusses problems of arena staging including technical problems and the selection and adaptation of a play.

DEAN, A., *Fundamentals of Directing* (New York, Farrar and Rinehart & Company, 1941). Includes material on composition, picturization, movement, rhythm, and pantomime.

DIETRICH, J. E., *Play Direction* (Englewood Cliffs, N. J., Prentice-Hall, Inc., 1953). Gives basic principles of play direction.

DOLMAN, J., Jr., *The Art of Play Production*, rev. ed. (New York, Harper & Brothers, 1946). Possesses complete directions on producing a play.

ENSLEY, R. W., *High School Theatre* (Cincinnati, Ohio, National Thespian Society). Pamphlet on play production in the high school.

FUCHS, T., *Home-Built Lighting Equipment for the Small Stage* (New York, Samuel French, Inc., 1939).

GEE, R. C., and DIETRICH, J. E., "A Survey of Dramatic Activity in Wisconsin High Schools, 1947-48," *Quarterly Journal of Speech*, XXXVI (February, 1950), 65-70.

GILLETTE, A. S., *Planning and Equipping the Educational Theatre* (Cincinnati, Ohio, The National Thespian Society, 1945). Contains material on equipping a stage.

GROSS, E. A., and GROSS, N. A., *Teen Theatre: A Guide to Play Production* (New York, McGraw-Hill Book Co., 1953). Lists duties and analyzes and solves problem of the amateur director. For beginners.

HEFFNER, H. C., SELDEN, S., and SELLMAN, H. D., *Modern Theatre Practice*, 3rd ed. (New York, Appleton-Century-Crofts, Inc., 1947). Includes material on scenery, lighting, makeup, and costuming.

HETLER, L., "But Can He Act," *Players Magazine*, XXXIII (December, 1956), 52-54. Presents a way of testing rhythm-sense, timing, physical control, and creative imagination.

HEWITT, B., FOSTER, J. F., and WOLLE, M. S., *Play Production Theory and Practice* (Chicago, J. B. Lippincott Co., 1952). Provides a thorough background in the theory and practice of producing plays, fundamentals of the play and its communication to the audience, problems of the actor, of costuming, and of scenery. Simply presented.

McCANDLESS, S., *A Method of Lighting the Stage*, 3rd ed. (New York, Theatre Art Books, 1953). Explains clearly how to light a stage.

NELMS, H., *Play Production* (New York, Barnes & Noble, Inc., 1950). Gives basic information on how to produce a play. Sometimes used as a high school text.

PHILLIPI, H., *Stagecraft and Scene Design* (Boston, Houghton Mifflin Co., 1953). Contains material on design, building sets, and stage properties. Complete instructions on painting the set.

PLETTE, W. F., *Directory of Stage Equipment and Supply Houses,* rev. ed. (Cincinnati, Ohio, The National Thespian Society, 1950).

PORTIER, D. G., "Selecting the High School Play," *The Speech Teacher*, II (March, 1953), 109-113. Indicates ideal standards for choosing a play and discusses the problems of selecting a play for high school students.

SAUNDERS, D., *Costuming the Amateur Show* (New York, Samuel French, Inc., 1957).

SELDEN, S., and SELLMAN, H. D., *Stage Scenery and Lighting*, 3rd ed. (New York, Appleton-Century-Crofts, Inc., 1958). Explains clearly and well how to construct scenery and how to light a stage.

AUDIO-VISUAL AIDS

Acting Problems (International Film Bureau, 16 mm., black and white, 11 minutes). Shows how to develop character and how to arrive at the right tempo and rhythm.

Building a Set (International Film Bureau, 16 mm., black and white, 11 minutes). Tells how to construct a flat. Uses as a basis *Tom Sawyer*.

Designing a Set (International Film Bureau, 16 mm., color, 10 minutes). Uses *Tom Sawyer* as illustration.

Directing a Play (International Film Bureau, 16 mm., black and white, 10 minutes).

"Film Strips, Film Slides for Use in Teaching Theatre," *Educational Theatre Journal* (October, 1947).

"16 mm. Films for Use in Teaching Theatre," *Educational Theatre Journal* (December, 1950).

Four Ways to Drama (California University, 16 mm., black and white, 33 minutes). Presents a short dramatic episode in versions for stage, radio, television, and motion pictures.

Julius Caesar (Brandon Films, 1951, 16 mm., black and white, 90 minutes). Excellent film. Good photography. Can be used for play-production classes.

Literature Appreciation: How to Read Plays (Coronet Instructional Films, 16 mm., black and white, 11 minutes). Tells how to construct the scene imaginatively and how to build a character.

Makeup Straight and Old Age (Bureau of Audio-Visual Instruction, University of Wisconsin Extension Division, 16 mm., 16 minutes). Demonstrates the effect of stage lighting on makeup and tells how to effect an old age makeup.

Macbeth (British Information Service, 16 mm., black and white, 15 minutes). Includes the murder and sleepwalking scenes.

Make-Up Film Strip in Color (Paramount, 70 frames, 35 minutes).

Make-Up for the Theatre (California University, 16 mm., color, 15 minutes). Shows steps of makeup.

One Way to Build a Flat (California University, 16 mm., black and white, 15 minutes). Shows how to build a flat.

Romeo and Juliet (Teaching Films Custodians Inc., 16 mm., black and white, 40 minutes). Includes excerpts dealing with the love story of Romeo and Juliet.

Shakespeare's Theatre (International Film Bureau, 16 mm., color, 19 minutes). Illustrates theater in Shakespeare's time.

ADDRESSES OF PLAY PUBLISHERS

Walter H. Baker Co., 100 Summer Street, Boston 10, Mass.

Banner Play Bureau, Inc., 619 Post Street, San Francisco 9, Calif.

Dramatic Publishing Co., 179 North Michigan Avenue, Chicago 1, Ill.

*Dramatists Play Service, Inc., 14 East 38th Street, New York 16, N. Y.

Eldridge Publishing Company, Franklin, Ohio.

*Samuel French, Inc., 25 West 45th Street, New York 36, N. Y.; 7623 Sunset Boulevard, Hollywood 46, Calif.

Harcourt, Brace & Co., 383 Madison Avenue, New York 17, N. Y.

Heuer Publishing Co., Box 551, Cedar Rapids, Iowa.

Longmans, Green & Co., Inc., 119 West 40th Street, New York 18, N. Y.

Northwestern Press, 321 Fifth Avenue South, Minneapolis 15, Minn.

Plays, Inc., 8 Arlington Street, Boston 16, Mass.

Row, Peterson & Company, 2500 Crawford Avenue, Evanston, Ill.

Wetmore Declamation Bureau, 1631 South Paxton Street, Sioux City 6, Iowa.

ADDRESSES OF FIRMS SUPPLYING PRODUCTION MATERIALS

The following list is suggestive. By looking in the classified section of the telephone book, you will find many more.

Brooks Costume Co., Inc., 3 West 61st Street, New York 23, N. Y.

Capitol Records, Inc., 1730 Broadway, New York 19, N. Y. (Sound effects)

J. R. Clancy, 1000-1020 West Belden Ave., Syracuse 4, N. Y. (Stage hardware and equipment)

Colorado Costume Company, Denver, Col.

Dazian's, Inc., 142 West 44th Street, New York 18, N. Y.; 125 No. Wabash Ave., Chicago 2, Ill.; 726 So. Flower St., Los Angeles 17, Calif. (Materials for costumes)

Eaves Costume Co., Inc., 151 West 46th Street, New York 19, N. Y.

* These two publishers supply most of the plays.

Max Factor, Max Factor Studios, Hollywood, Calif. (Makeup)

Gothic Color Co., 90 Ninth Ave., New York 11, N. Y. (Scenic artists' supplies)

Grand Stage Lighting Company, 23½ West Hubbard Street, Chicago 10, Ill.

Kliegl Bros. Universal Electric Stage Lighting Co., Inc., 321 West 50th Street, New York 19, N. Y. (Lighting)

Linguaphone Institute, 30 Rockefeller Plaza, New York 20, N. Y. (Sound effects)

Major Stage Lighting Company, Chicago, Ill.

Manhattan Costume Company, Inc., 549 West 52nd Street, New York 19, N. Y.

Midwest Stage Lighting Co., 55 West Walker Drive, Chicago 1, Ill.

Miner, Inc., 36 East 12th Street, New York 3, N. Y. (Makeup)

Northwestern Theatre Associates, 1000 Foster Street, Evanston, Ill. (Lighting, hardware, paint, makeup, canvas)

Paramount Cosmetics and Theatrical Makeup Co., 242 West 27th Street, New York 1, N. Y. (Records and makeup)

Rosco Laboratories, 29 Moore Street, Brooklyn 6, N. Y. (Gelatins)

Stein Cosmetic Company, 430 Broome Street, New York 12, N. Y.

Theatre Production Service, 52 West 46th Street, New York 36, N. Y. (Curtains, scenery, lighting, hardware, paints)

Thomas J. Valentino Company, 150 West 46th Street, New York 19, N. Y. (Sound effects)

Van Horn and Son, 232 North 11th Street, Philadelphia, Pa. (Costumes)

Western Costume Co., 5335 Melrose Avenue, Hollywood 38, Calif.

EXERCISES

1. Read the McGaw book and extract from it five exercises that could be used in a high school theater class.
2. View one of the suggested films. Explain how it could be used in teaching a lesson in a high school theater course.
3. Prepare a promptbook for a one-act play suitable for high school presentation in assembly.
4. Make a list of ten one-act and three long plays suitable for production by a particular high school. Include number of men and women, setting, type of play, theme of the play, royalty, publisher, and any predictable production difficulties.
5. Make a list of minimum essential equipment for lighting a small high school stage.
6. Prepare a bulletin board on the history of the theater.

7. Cast and direct a scene from a well-known play in your methods class. Discuss with the group ways of improving the acting of the players.
8. Guide the discussion of a theme of a play which all members of the methods class have read.
9. Explain how you would demonstrate makeup to a group of high school theater students.

V

TEACHING
RADIO AND TELEVISION

13

Television and Radio

in the High School

ALTHOUGH ALMOST ALL speech courses and many English and journalism courses in high schools contain speaking activities based on television and radio, courses in these two media in our secondary schools are few in number and differ widely. The first basic difference in the courses is in the amount of technical knowledge taught, often conditioned by the presence or lack of equipment. In some instances, where the television and radio course replaces the fundamentals course, television and radio work is used largely to motivate the acquisition of basic skills of oral communication. In such high schools the television and radio equipment may be minimal—perhaps no more than a public-address system and a tape recorder. In other instances, the high school television and radio course follows a required speech course and includes a study of the influence of television and radio in our society, an analysis of present-day programs, an examination of equipment and techniques of television and radio, and the production of programs which are sometimes broadcast to the community from a local station. In such a course the equipment, involving some method of transmission, is quite complex. Students, however, are trained to handle such equipment; in fact, experience has shown that students can operate the equipment of a closed-circuit television competently. But the teacher himself must have the necessary background and training to teach his students the operation. A second basic difference is in the major emphasis of the course. Is it on the student as a consumer of television and radio, as a performer, or equally as a consumer and a performer? The type of course then depends upon the students' needs, interests, and abilities, upon the teacher's background, and upon the school's equipment.

AIMS

The basic purpose of the television and radio course, therefore, affects its aims. One set of aims will emphasize the acquisition of basic speech skills whereas another will emphasize the acquisition of knowledge and skills necessary for the understanding and production of television and radio programs. The following set of aims is for the second or more-specialized course:

Understandings:

To be aware of the influence of television and radio on our culture.

To become acquainted with the various types of television and radio programs.

To set up criteria for discriminating listening and viewing.

To find out about critics of television and radio.

To learn about awards made for television and radio productions.

To understand television and radio equipment and its operation.

To be informed about broadcasting techniques of production and performance.

To know the fundamentals of speaking, reading, and acting over television and radio.

To be aware of the requirements for writing different kinds of television and radio scripts.

Skills:

To listen to and view programs with discrimination.

To use a professional standard of voice, articulation, and pronunciation.

To read, speak, and act over television and radio effectively.

To develop some skill in broadcasting techniques and in the production of programs.

To produce and direct a television or radio show.

To write adequate scripts for various types of programs.

To evaluate the television and radio programs produced by the group.

Attitudes:

> To support current programs of real worth.
> To be alert to the function of television and radio in a democracy.
> To be objective in listening to content programs such as documentaries, newscasts, and discussion programs.

Obviously to accomplish all that this particular set of aims implies is difficult in one semester. Since the set of aims is comprehensive, it is assumed that you will select those that seem appropriate for your particular group. The aims which you choose to achieve will influence the content of your course.

CONTENT

The content of a television and radio course may contain such units as the following:

Influence of Television and Radio
    On Individuals
    On the Community

Kinds of Programs
    Newscasts
    Drama
    Music
    Sport
    Variety
    Audience Participation Shows
    Panel Shows

Advertising
    Kinds of Appeals
    Functions of the Agency

Criticism of Present-Day Shows
    Building Criteria for Evaluation
    Criticism in Newspapers and Magazines
    Role of Audience-Research Organizations

Fundamentals of Broadcasting
    History of Broadcasting
    American Broadcasting
        Kinds and Organizations of Stations
        Need for Governmental Controls

Regulations for Television and Radio
International Broadcasting
Production Equipment and Techniques

Production of Shows
Writing Scripts for Various Kinds of Programs
Reading and Speaking to Meet the Demands of the Media
Enacting Parts to Meet the Demands of the Media
Staging the Show
Using Broadcasting Equipment
Producing and Directing the Show

The activities involved in teaching such units include both work in the classroom and laboratory experiences. Examples of work in the classroom are learning the vocabulary used in television and radio, a study of sound effects and of musical effects, an analysis of program planning, reports on such material as advertising, audience measurement, public-service responsibilities, camera techniques, microphone techniques, organization of the large networks, outstanding programs of the networks, discussion of such topics as FCC, NAB, educational broadcasting, censorship, quality of children's programs, importance of broadcasting in politics, and script-writing. Laboratory activities are practicing hand signals, recording and playing back short talks, playing transcriptions and records, handling musical and sound effects, learning steps involved in transmitting voice from the station to the home receiver, making use of various devices in dramatic programs, viewing kinescopes and video tapes, and putting on programs of various types.

When planning your course of study for television and radio, you do well to examine other such courses of study. The National Association of Educational Broadcasters in the February, March, April, and May, 1958, issues of the *National Association of Educational Broadcasters' Journal* has included a complete course of study in radio and television speech for high schools. It contains a comprehensive set of aims, suggested units, activities, and equipment. You select from this course that which is applicable to your situation.

A representative course of study for television and radio planned by the speech staff of Jamaica High School[1] follows. Eleventh and

[1] Rose Kirchman, Chairman Speech Department, Jamaica High School, Jamaica, New York.

twelfth grade students elect this course because of a special interest in the area.

JAMAICA HIGH SCHOOL

Speech Department

SUGGESTED SYLLABUS FOR RADIO-TELEVISION COURSE

Length of course: One semester   Credit: ½ cr.

FIRST SIX WEEKS
1. Place of Mass Media in Our Culture.
2. Voice and Diction; Diagnostic Survey.
   Ear-Training.
   Standards of Pronunciation.
   Requirements of Radio Diction.
   Vocal Mechanism—Volume, Pitch, Resonance, Quality.
   Use of Voice in Oral Reading—Phrasing, Pausing, Emphasis, Inflection.
3. Fundamentals of Broadcasting.
   Use of Broadcasting Facilities.
   History of Broadcasting.
   FCC Regulations.
4. Written Book Report.
   Book in the Field of Radio or Television.
5. Composition—Critical Review of Television Play.
6. News Programs.
   Content and Organization; Style and Delivery.
   Oral Performance of Newscast or Commentary.
7. The Radio or Television Interview.
   Analysis of Examples.
   Oral Performance—Two students Collaborate on a Five-Minute Interview.

SECOND SIX WEEKS
1. Study of Commercials; Styles and Delivery.
2. Study of Music Programs.
3. Study of Poetry Programs with Musical Background.
   Two students may collaborate on interview or discussion program centering on poetry of one author. Students will read poetry and the group will evaluate the reading.
4. Acting on Radio and Television.
   Duties and Qualifications of Director and Producer.

Terminology and Signals.
Sound Effects.
5. Continuation of Voice and Articulation Training.
Lists of Frequently Mispronounced Words.
6. Oral Examination—Report on Novel for Television Program (3 minutes).

THIRD SIX WEEKS

1. The Radio or Television Play.
Teacher will assign student directors and actors.
2. The Forum and Discussion Program.
Written Report on an Outstanding Discussion Program.
Programs in Class by a Moderator and Three or Four Panelists.
3. Written Report on Radio or Television Drama.
4. Performances of Radio or Television Drama Programs by Groups.
5. Study of Quiz Programs and Children's Programs (Optional).

BIBLIOGRAPHY FOR THE COURSE

ABBOTT, W., and RIDER, R. L., *Handbook of Broadcasting* (New York, Mc-Graw-Hill Book Co., 1957).

ANNER, G., *Elements of Television Systems* (Englewood Cliffs, N. J., Prentice-Hall, Inc., 1951).

BARNOUW, E., *Handbook of Radio Writing* (Boston, Little, Brown & Co., 1947).

BEGLEY, M., and MACCRAE, D., *Auditioning for TV* (New York, Hastings House, Publishers, Inc., 1955).

BREAN, H., *The Mystery Writer's Handbook* (New York, Harper & Brothers, 1946).

CROSBY, J., *Out of the Blue* (New York, Simon and Schuster, Inc., 1946).

FLOHERTY, J., *Behind the Microphone* (New York, J. B. Lippincott Co., 1944).

HUTCHINSON, T., *Here Is Television* (New York, Hastings House, Publishers, Inc., 1946).

JOELS, M. E., *Acting Is a Business* (New York, Hastings House, Publishers, Inc., 1955).

KINGSON, W. K., and COWGILL, R., *Radio Drama, Acting and Production: A Handbook* (New York, Holt, Rinehart and Winston, Inc., 1957).

MARCUS, A. *Elements of Radio* (Englewood Cliffs, N. J., Prentice-Hall, Inc., 1943).

MEAD, S., *How to Get Rich in TV—Without Really Trying* (New York, Simon and Schuster, Inc., 1956).

SELDES, G., *The Public Arts* (New York, Simon and Schuster, Inc., 1956).

WADE, R., *Staging TV Programs and Commercials* (New York, Hastings House, Publishers, Inc., 1954).

Radio and Television Plays

BARNOUW, E., *Radio Drama in Action* (New York, Rinehart and Co., 1945).

BITTON, F., Ed., *Best Television Plays of 1957* (New York, Ballantine Books, Inc., 1957).

CHAYEFSKY, P., *Television Plays* (New York, Simon and Schuster, Inc., 1954).

CORWIN, M., *Thirteen by Corwin* (New York, Perry Dolt and Co., 1942).

KAUFMAN, W. I., *The Best Television Plays of 1950-51* (New York, Merlin Press, 1952).

MOSEL, R., *Other People's Houses* (New York, Simon and Schuster, Inc., 1956).

PARKER, K., *Parker's Television Plays* (Minneapolis, Minn., Northwestern Press, 1954).

ROSE, R., *Six Television Plays* (New York, Simon and Schuster, Inc., 1956).

VIDAL, G., *Best Television Plays* (New York, Ballantine Books, Inc., 1956).

Writers Guild of America, *The Prize Plays of Radio and Television 1956* (New York, Random House, 1957).

METHODOLOGY

Introduction to Television and Radio

Some teachers begin their course with a discussion of the influence of television and radio on present-day culture. Frequently they start with the specific discussion of how much their students listen to television and radio and what programs they like best. The students then compare their favorite programs with those on a published list such as the list of high school students' favorite programs reported annually by Paul Witty in *Elementary English*. After this survey has been completed, the students analyze what they are listening to and viewing and decide on how they can be more intelligent consumers of television and radio.

Other teachers take their students on a trip to a television or radio station, preparing them for the trip by describing to them what they will see and by pointing out what to observe. Others examine with their students the sociological implications of television and radio. Others ask their students to compare radio with television.

One teacher asked the students to prepare an assignment in which they contrasted the evening programs on radio with those on television.

After one such assignment students began the lesson by pointing out that sound effects are exaggerated in radio but that they are blended with the visual effects in television. They also showed that in radio, the narrator, the voices of characters, music and sound effects, and the script set the mood of the production, whereas in television the appearance and movement of the characters, the costumes, and the staging are as important in setting the mood. They emphasized that radio has only a listening appeal, whereas television has a viewing appeal as well. They further noted that since radio has only an aural appeal, its writers and producers must be inventive in their use of verbal clues to incite the imagination of the listener and in turn the listener must be creative in his listening.

Still other teachers compare the covering of two similar events in the same medium but by two different networks. U. N. meetings, political conventions, discussions of trips by heads of state, crises in domestic or foreign affairs, juvenile delinquency, traffic congestion, and conditions in a foreign land are frequently covered by two different networks. By mentioning specific details to look for, the teacher guides the comparison.

Analysis of Different Types of Programs

In analyzing programs, teachers emphasize the techniques of speaking and reading aloud well, of acting a part convincingly, and of participating effectively in a group discussion or debate. They point out that persuading an audience to a particular point of view, reading a poem with meaning and feeling, taking part in a discussion or a debate requires the same skill and knowledge on and off television. They make clear also that good acting is good acting on or off television. But, in addition, they explain the special requirements of television and the technical problems of broadcasting.

For instance, when teachers analyze a television or radio play, they talk about many of the same things that they would talk about in a drama class. One teacher[2] assigned *A Matter of Pride* from the pocketbook edition of *Best Television Plays of 1956* (Florence

[2] Mary Desser, Chairman Speech Department, Martin Van Buren High School, Queens County, New York City.

Britton, ed., Ballantine Books, Inc., New York). She asked that the students answer questions which are similar to those that might be asked in a drama class:

1. Why do "people want to conform"?
2. Explain the speech on page 25 that begins, "I'm sixteen years old not fifteen."
3. Tell us why there is or is not a chance of Jeff's changing.
4. Describe Grandpa. Do you think you could have done what Neil did for Grandpa's sake? Explain.
5. Does the principal have the right to dictate the kind of wearing apparel for graduation? Why or why not?
6. What is the significance of the title?

However, in discussing the play this teacher emphasized some points that particularly pertain to television: On another day she asked her students to consider answers to the following questions on the same play:

1. What unusual camera angles would you strive for to make the graduation scene more meaningful to the audience?
2. What audio techniques would you use in various parts of the play? Why?
3. Would you incorporate music in this play? If so, why and what kind?
4. In casting for this play what kind of personality and voice would you prefer for Jeff, Neil, Grandpa, and the Narrator?
5. Would this play be a difficult or simple production to present on television? Why or why not?

These questions emphasize some of the technical problems of production.

Criticism

After an analysis of the kinds of programs on the air and their effectiveness, your students are then ready to read reports of the critics. With this study criticism becomes meaningful. Some teachers ask students to write criticisms of a particular show; for this purpose they may supply such a form as given on page 207 of *Speak Up*.[3] The students then bring their criticisms to class and compare them with those given by well-known television and radio critics. This

[3] H. M. Adams and T. C. Pollock, *Speak Up* (New York, The Macmillan Co., 1956).

study leads naturally to reports on audience reaction agencies and finally into building students' own standards for selection and evaluation of programs.

Fundamentals of Broadcasting

How much technical material is covered in this unit depends on the teacher. Some teachers omit the unit altogether. Others cover the history of broadcasting but give little attention to technical aspects of television and radio. Still others cover technical aspects with considerable detail. For instance, the members of one class[4] made clear through student reports the differences in microphones used for television and for radio and the importance of the placement of microphones in both media. In addition, students explained the various camera shots. As a review of the material on camera shots, Mrs. Desser asked these questions:

1. What is the name of the shot that takes in an entire room? (*Answer*—Orientation long shot.)
2. If a director wants to show a big city and then various elements in it such as a skyscraper, people, or a street, what process is used? (*Answer*—Series of related pictures which gives you a montage effect.)
3. What is a long shot?
   (*Answers:* *a.* The viewer is not at the scene. He is looking at it from a distance.
   b. You may be watching Westerners walking down the street from a long way off.)
4. What shot in television shows the picture of a face?
   (*Answers:* *a.* An example is the "halo girl."
   b. Tight close-up.)
5. What is the name of the shot going from picture to black? (*Answer*—Fadeout.)
6. What is it called when you go directly from one camera shot to another? (*Answer*—A cut.)
7. After a person has been knocked out, the next scene may begin in a blur. This blur helps the audience to empathize with the actor. What is the process by which this blurring is achieved? (*Answer*—Defocus.)
10. What type shot is good for conversation? (*Answer*—Reverse angle.)
11. What is the blending of two shots called?

[4] Mary Desser, *Television and Radio Class*, Martin Van Buren High School, Queens County, New York.

(*Answers—a.* Superimposition.

        b. If you are a camera fan, you know that this blending is pretty difficult.)

12. What are the television screens in the studio called? (*Answer—* Monitors.)

13. How do you show the blown up pictures behind the newscasters? (*Answer—*Rear-view projection.)

Production of Shows

Teachers of television and radio produce both simple and complex shows. In some instances, the shows are in reality classroom speaking activities with little attention given to organization for television and radio production. In other instances, the shows are produced for specific audiences and are organized with a general manager, program manager, continuity writer, advertising staff, engineers, camera operators, sound-effect crews, actors, musicians, business officers, scene designers, costumers, and a makeup crew. In some cases students read news bulletins or interview a school sports figure. In other cases, students prepare to discuss an important question or to present a dramatic show that will be transmitted to the community over a local station. Sometimes the material is broadcast to just the class; sometimes, to the entire school and sometimes to the community over a local station. The complexity of the production in your class depends upon its members, their abilities and talents, the time that you and the students have for production, the amount of television and radio equipment available, the budget, the school's program, and your own training.

Evaluation

Students should be equipped to evaluate their own productions, for they have made a study of television and radio criticism and have worked out their own standards for evaluation. They study each aspect, show where it could be improved, and decide what changes they would make another time. When the teacher can play back a tape made of a radio program or show the videotape or film of a television production, students are able to analyze more thoughtfully and objectively. In a study of radio, they may retape the entire show, having learned from their previous mistakes.

The teacher is responsible for the evaluation of the knowledge acquired by the students and, to a certain extent, their attitudes toward television and radio. She evaluates the knowledge largely through written tests—both short-answer and essay—and compositions which have been prepared on various aspects of television and radio. The attitudes can be measured through a careful reading of students' criticisms of television shows and of their viewing diaries which many teachers require and through a study of students' remarks in class.

EXTRACURRICULAR ACTIVITIES

A large number of high schools have radio workshops. Their activities include visits to television and radio stations, studies of particular phases of television and radio, and speeches by invited guests on some areas of the two media. In addition, the members of the workshop may produce shows. One radio workshop, for example, takes charge of the opening exercises of the school. Its members broadcast a review of the day's news, announcements of school events, and some other feature. The feature may be an interview with a new teacher, with the football captain, or with the Westinghouse Scholarship winner, a skit asking students to support the Red Cross campaign, an explanation of the assembly calendar for the year, a panel discussion centering around books, or choral speaking by one of the classes. Frequently the workshop keeps a supply of audio tapes on hand, some of which are made in classes and some of which are prepared by members of the workshop. These tapes are appropriate for certain days of the year.

You will find that the study of radio and television is valuable in itself and in speech classes. The number of hours students devote to radio listening and to television viewing show the importance of the media as learning and recreational activities. You, therefore should help your students to be intelligent consumers of these media. In addition, since students know and are impressed by today's radio and television personalities and by many of the current shows, you can use these experiences to motivate good classroom speaking. Radio and television speaking activities, used as a means and not as an end, promote effective forensic and interpretative speaking.

SUGGESTED READING

ABBOT, W., and RIDER, R. L., *Handbook of Broadcasting*, 4th ed. (New York, McGraw-Hill Book Co., 1957). Gives the basic material of broadcasting.

BARNOUW, E., *Mass Communication: Television, Radio, Film, Press* (New York, Rinehart and Company, 1956). Presents the essential characteristics of the four media of communication.

BECKER, S. L., and HARSHBERGER, H. C., *Television: Techniques for Planning and Performance* (New York, Henry Holt & Company, Inc., 1958). Concentrates on the development of effective speech for television. Contains a series of projects which could be used effectively in high school classes.

BERMAN, B., "By Their Speech You Shall Know Them," *The Speech Teacher*, II (March, 1953), 129-133. Contains a radio script which shows the need for good voice and diction.

BETTINGER, H., *Television Techniques*, rev. by S. Cornberg (New York, Harper & Brothers, 1955). Has to do with production techniques such as video and audio techniques, television writing, directing, and producing.

CHESTER, G., and GARRISON, G. R., *Television and Radio: An Introduction*, 2nd ed. (New York, Appleton-Century-Crofts, Inc., 1956). Contains two sections: I. Television and Radio in Society and II. Television and Radio in the Studio. A good basic text for the teacher.

Classroom Radio Receivers (Washington, D. C., Radio Section, U. S. Department of Education, Department of Health, Education and Welfare). Gives specifications for school audio equipment.

COBIN, M., "Utilizing Television in the Interpretation Program," *The Speech Teacher*, VIII (January, 1959), 31-36. Describes an experiment at University of Illinois utilizing television in curricular and extracurricular programs in oral interpretation.

Columbia Broadcasting Company Program Guides (New York, Information Office, CBS Reference Department, Columbia Broadcasting System, free). Contains annotated classified lists of programs.

Columbia Broadcasting System News Staff, *Television News Reporting* (New York, McGraw-Hill Book Co., 1958). Tells about the selection and preparation of television news.

DEMARCO, N., ed., *Radio Program Suggestions* (Cincinnati, Ohio, National Thespian Society, 1951). Contains descriptions of 55 radio programs presented throughout the country. Suggests sources for radio scripts.

FIELD, S., *Television and Radio Writing* (Boston, Houghton Mifflin Co., 1958). Gives an idealistic and practical approach to television writing.

KAUFMAN, W. I., ed., *How to Direct for Television* (New York, Hastings House, 1955). Contains nine articles by directors of such programs as *Omnibus, Producer's Showcase, Lux Video Theater,* and *Kraft Television Theater.*

————, *How to Write for Television* (New York, Hastings House, 1955). Includes many aspects of television writing, among them dialogue, characterization, story-line, creating conflict, and educational programs.

National Broadcasting Company Program Information. Tells about NBC radio and television programs. Published periodically.

ROBERTS, E. B., *Television Writing and Selling,* 2nd ed. (Boston, The Writer, Inc., 1957). Tells how to prepare dramatic writing for television.

SELDES, G., *The Public Arts* (New York, Simon and Schuster, Inc., 1956). Explains the influence of television on our culture.

SIEPMANN, C., *Television and Our School Crisis* (New York, Dodd, Mead, & Co., 1958). Describes the importance of television for our educational institutions.

Standards of Good Practice for Radio Broadcasters in the United States, rev. ed. (New York, National Association of Broadcasters, 1958). Gives creed for radio broadcasters and standards for various types of programs.

STASHEFF, E., and MILLER, N. E., "Televising a Debate in a Courtroom Setting," *The Speech Teacher,* III (September, 1954), 215-219. Tells how presenting a debate in the form of a trial retains the merits of forensics and adds additional elements of showmanship.

Television in Our Schools (Bulletin #16. U. S. Office of Education). Tells about the use of television in the classroom.

WISEMAN, J. D., JR., "A Radio Project for a Speech Class," *School Activities,* XXVI (March, 1955), 285-287. Describes high school speech class' project of operating a radio station for an entire day.

AUDIO-VISUAL MATERIALS

Radio and Television (Vocational Guidance Films, black and white, 11 minutes). Gives the basic skills needed for broadcasting.

Sightseeing at Home (General Electric Company, black and white, 25 minutes). Tells how programs are produced. Takes students on a visit to a television studio.

Stepping Along with Television (Bell Telephone Company, 11 minutes). Explains the technical processes of television.

Television: How it Works (Coronet Films, black and white, color, 10 minutes). Shows how the electron beams bring an image to the television set.

Television in Your Community (Coronet Films, black and white, color, 11 minutes). Shows the personnel, equipment, and organization of a simple television station which is necessary to provide service to the community.

EXERCISES

1. Select four radio or television programs that could be studied for four different specific purposes in a fundamentals course. Explain how each program achieves its purpose.
2. Tell how a specific television program could be used in the acting unit of a theater course.
3. Select evening television programs during one week, which you believe your students might well watch. Give reasons for your selection.
4. Find out the ten favorite programs of the members of a high school class. Watch these programs and evaluate their worth. If you do not have a class, watch those programs which Witty lists in *Elementary English* as being the favorite of high school students.
5. Plan a half-hour program that a high school radio workshop might broadcast over the local radio station.

VI

EVALUATION

14

Testing in the
Speech Program

AT THE BEGINNING of each unit you measure what understandings and what skills and attitudes your students need to develop. As a result of this diagnosis, you guide them in gaining certain understandings, skills, and attitudes. After you have provided the guidance, you measure the understandings, skills, and attitudes possessed by the students. Such measurement, which helps you to appraise both the students' growth and your own teaching, involves administration of standardized tests, giving of short-answer and essay tests which you construct, and your own observation and analysis of speakng performances.

STANDARDIZED HIGH SCHOOL TESTS

Attitude Scale, Speech Experience Inventory, Listening Tests

Few standardized high school tests of speaking and listening are available. Research and experimentation in these two areas have been limited, particularly as compared to the research on silent reading. C. H. Stoelting Company publishes two scales of speech: *Speech Attitude Scale* and *Speech Experience Scale*. *The Speech Attitude Scale* finds out and diagnoses an individual's attitudes toward speech. *The Speech Experience Inventory* discovers the range and kind of speaking experiences in which an individual engages. Two listening tests are designed for high school students: *Brown-Carlsen Listening Comprehension Test* and *The Listening Comprehension Test*. The *Brown-Carlsen Listening Comprehension Test* (World Book Company) measures the ability of students to understand what they hear. The test consists of 76 questions organized into five parts to appraise: (1) immediate recall, (2) following directions, (3) recognizing transitions, (4) recognizing meanings, and (5) comprehending a lecture. *The Listening Comprehension Test* (The Educational Testing Service) rates the student's comprehension, interpretation, and evaluation of what he hears.

Tests in Related Areas

A high school test in a field related to public address is the *Watson-Glaser Test of Critical Thinking* (World Book Company, grades 10-16). This test measures the ability of the student to think critically. It appraises the student's handling of generalizations, inferences, recognition of assumptions, and certain types of attitudes and opinions. A similar test is the *Logical Reasoning Test* (Educational Testing Service) which was one of the evaluation instruments in the Eight Year Study of the Progressive Education Association.

In oral interpretation teachers stress finding the meaning and mood of selections. Several tests estimate abilities of students to do these two things. Such tests include the *Iowa Test of Educational Development: Test 7, Interpretation of Literary Materials* (Science Research Associates, grades 9-12) which assess a student's ability to find the purpose and mood of a passage and *The Co-operative Literary Comprehension and Appreciation Test* (Educational Testing Service, grades 10-16) which computes the student's ability to perceive the author's viewpoint, to recognize literary devices, and to appreciate style and rhythm.

TESTING FOR KNOWLEDGE

You construct written tests of the understanding of the principles and concepts of speech. The requirements of such a test are:

1. It is valid. (It measures what it purports to measure.)
2. It is reliable. (It is consistent in its measurement.)
3. It has a clear design to test achievement.
4. It presents students in a rank order.

5. It gives emphasis to what was stressed in teaching.

6. It uses items of several types to extend the scope of measurement.

7. It is easily administered.

Essay Questions

Tests fall generally into two categories: essay and short-answer. The essay question has advantages. Properly constructed an essay test stimulates a student's thinking. He must compare, interpret facts, criticize, or defend his opinion. In other words, the essay question can test the student's ability to use his knowledge. Nevertheless, it has its disadvantages. Some authorities claim that it calls forth less than half the knowledge that the average student possesses on a subject as compared with the results of a short-answer test and that it takes twice the time to write. They also note that it places stress on knowing how to write rather than on what to write. Lastly they indicate that the grading of it tends to be subjective.

The *c* section of the following question[1] does motivate students to apply what they know about antecedent action and to be original in their thinking. It is a good example of an essay type question.

V. CRITICAL READING.   (20)

After reading the following lines from *Mansions* by Hildegarde Flanner, answer the following:

   a. How old do you think Harriet and Lydia are?

   b. Apply *two* descriptive adjectives to each.

   c. What antecedent action could possibly explain these character traits?

HARRIET: Lydia! What are you doing, Lydia?

LYDIA: I have been trimming the rose hedge along the south garden, Aunt Harriet.

HARRIET: But surely you can find something better to do than that, my dear. Some one might see in if you trim it too much. We want a bit of privacy in these inquisitive times.

LYDIA: The young plants on the edge of the walk needed sun.

HARRIET: Move the young plants. Don't sacrifice the rose hedge. It seems to me that the furniture has been disarranged.

LYDIA: I was changing it a little this morning.

HARRIET: May I ask why?

LYDIA: Oh just—just to be changing. Don't you think it is an improvement?

HARRIET: It does very well. But I prefer it as it was. You know yourself

---

[1] Prepared by Eleanor Campbell and Rose Kirchman, Chairman of the Speech Department, Jamaica High School, for a drama class in the spring of 1958.

that this room has never been changed since your grandfather died. And as long as I am mistress in this house, it shall remain exactly as he liked it. The courthouse will be done before your brother is well enough to come downstairs, Lydia. How astonished he will be to see it completed.

LYDIA: Yes. But he would much rather watch while it is being done.

HARRIET: Well naturally. But from upstairs you can't see through the leaves of the maple tree. Why, Lydia, there isn't another tree for miles around with such marvelous foliage. Great grandfather Wilde did not know, when he set out a sapling, that the county courthouse was to be built—almost in its very shadow.

LYDIA: You always did admire any kind of a family tree.

HARRIET: If great grandfather Wilde heard you say that—

LYDIA: If great grandfather Wilde heard me say that. It may be he would have the excellent sense to come back and chop off a limb or two so that Joe could have sunlight in that little dark room up there, and see out.

HARRIET: Lydia, my dear child, I am not responsible for your disposition this lovely morning. Moreover, this is a fruitless—

LYDIA: Fruitless, fruitless! *Why* couldn't he have planted an apple tree? With blossoms in the spring and fruit in the summer—

HARRIET: I beg your pardon?

LYDIA: With blossoms in the spring and fruit in the summer. Sounds rather pretty, doesn't it?

HARRIET: I do not understand what you are talking about.

In constructing essay questions, Grambs suggests that you increase the number of questions, restrict the length of responses and indicate specific areas to be discussed.[2] The following questions from test mentioned previously meet these criteria:

II. STRUCTURE AND STYLE: (15)

Write *one* well-constructed sentence about each of the following topics:

a. Theme vs. plot.
b. The dangers and advantages of "vicarious living" as applied to the theater. (One sentence for each)
c. The difference between "learning a part" and "learning lines" in acting.
d. "No movement without meaning."
e. The difference between realism and romanticism.

III. TERMINOLOGY: (10)

Define each of the following with reference to the stage or to acting.

[2] J. D. Grambs, W. J. Iverson, and F. K. Patterson, *Modern Methods in Secondary Education* (New York, Henry Holt & Co., Inc., 1958), p. 469.

a. To give on a cross.

b. To point a line.

c. Stealing a scene.

d. Cyclorama.

e. Stage balance.

f. Wings

g. Top a cut cue.

h. Proscenium arch.

i. Strike a set.

j. Apron.

Grambs advises that in scoring you prepare a response to each question in advance with each point being given weight for scoring, that you read the papers once for organization and a second time for detail, and that you note each error or point omitted and write down the amount deducted. In addition, he recommends that you read the answers in all the papers to one question at a time.[3]

On the other hand, Sims recommends quite a different technique which involves sorting the students' papers into five groups: very superior, superior, average, inferior, and very inferior on the basis of a first quick reading. A second more careful reading follows to correct mistakes of the first evaluation. She believes that approximately 10 per cent will be very superior; 10 per cent, very inferior; 20 per cent, superior; 20 per cent, inferior; and 40 per cent, average.[4]

Short-Answer Examinations

As opposed to essay questions, short-answer questions do have certain definite advantages. The students can answer many more questions in the same amount of time and the scoring is reliable and easy. The limitations are that students do guess and that the test is difficult to construct if its aim is to appraise more than to recall. The forms of short answers are completion, matching, multiple choice, and alternate response.

Completion Questions

Completion items consist of a series of sentences in which blanks are left for certain important words or phrases. This test tends to measure only rote memory. In its construction you should make sure that it calls for a simple, specific response and that you do not take the statement directly from the text. The following is an example of a good completion question:

[3] *Ibid.,* p. 469.

[4] V. M. Sims, "The Objectivity, Reliability and Validity of an Essay Examination Graded by Rating," *Journal of Educational Research,* XXIV (October, 1931), 216-223.

The sounds *s* and *z* are produced alike except that *s* is a sound which

is . . . . whereas *z* is a sound which is . . . .

Matching Questions

A matching question involves the association of two things in the mind of the learner by requiring him to pair two items. They are likely to be highly factual in nature and to make use of the who, what, when, and where type of relationship or of naming abilities. The following is an example of a matching test, also taken from the test mentioned on page 349.

I. BACKGROUND: (15)

Write the numbers in column 1 on your answer paper and place the correct letter of column 2 beside it.

Column 1	*Column 2*
1. Walter Kerr	*a.* A great contemporary actress
2. George Bernard Shaw	*b.* A symbolic play
3. Elia Kazan	*c.* *New Yorker* theatrical critic
4. Konstantin Stanislavsky	*d.* English Shakespearean actor
5. *The Blue Bird*	*e.* Director of Metropolitan Opera
6. Helen Hayes	*f.* Medieval allegory
7. *Oedipus Rex*	*g.* Realistic play on Broadway
8. Brooks Atkinson	*h.* Irish playwright and social critic
9. Wolcott Gibbs	*i.* Folk play
10. John Gielgud	*j.* *Herald Tribune* theatrical critic
11. *Look Back in Anger*	*k.* Director of Moscow Art Theatre
12. Rudolph Bing	*l.* Classic Greek Tragedy
13. Jo Mielziner	*m.* *New York Times* theatrical critic
14. *Everyman*	*n.* Modern American director
15. *Green Pastures*	*o.* Modern American scenic designer

Multiple Choice Questions

Multiple choice are the most popular form of short-answer questions. It is a recognition item type consisting of a question followed by several responses that answer the question with varying degrees of accuracy. The student is expected to choose the correct answer or the most accurate answer. It is used to measure such abilities as ability to define, and to identify purposes, causes, similarities and differ-ences. The following is an example:

The main idea, "Our school should pay tribute to its honor students," has which of the following purposes?
   a. to inform.
   b. to persuade
   c. to impress.
   d. to entertain.

Alternative Response Question

An alternative response question is one which has only two possi-ble responses. The most familiar form is the true-false. These are difficult to construct; you must avoid words like *always,* and *none,* trick statements, statements partly true and partly false, and long complex sentences. A typical alternative response item is:

True or false: *s* is the unvoiced counterpart of *z.*

OBSERVATIONAL EVALUATION

The written test, however, is obviously inadequate in measuring speaking skills. The only solution at present is an evaluation by you, a trained observer. This observational evaluation is admittedly in-fluenced by your ability to know what you are looking for, to listen accurately and critically, and to remain attentive. Knower indicates that there are three ways of rendering observational evaluation: intuitive, analytically systematic, and instrumental. He notes that "although the intuitive method is often hasty, biased, and whimsi-cal, it may be as accurate for general evaluation if carried out by socially and intellectually sensitive persons as the more analytical type."[5]

The analytically systematic evaluation depends on the use of a rating scale or a checklist. Such scales and checks guide you in know-ing what to look for and serve as a permanent record of the evalua-tion. Such a scale should not contain too many items and should not attempt to discriminate too finely. Probably a five-point scale is the most desirable. The following is an example of such a checklist:

[5] F. K. Knower, "What Is a Speech Test," *Quarterly Journal of Speech,* XXX (December, 1944), 490.

INFORMATIVE SPEECH

NAME .... REG. CLASS .... SPEECH CLASS ....

DATE .... TEACHER ....•

Elements of Assignment	Comments	Rating
CHOICE OF TOPIC		
DEVELOPMENT OF IDEAS		
ORGANIZATION OF IDEAS		
WAYS OF HOLDING INTEREST		
DELIVERY		
TOTAL IMPRESSION		
GRADE		

Rating scale: 1, decidedly superior; 2, superior; 3, average; 4, inferior; 5, decidedly inferior.

Such a checklist serves as a guidepost in evaluating, emphasizing items to consider. As was pointed out in the evaluation section of the chapter on public speaking, you are making value judgments on a number of abilities. The abilities you are looking for guide your listening. For example, a girl's sincerity and fluent, forceful delivery may make an excellent impression. When, however, you consider her ability to organize, you may find it inadequate. On the other hand, you must not pay so much attention to each item on the check-list that you are not aware of the total impression.

A second value of the checklist is that it serves as a record for the students of what they have done well and what they need to improve. Boys and girls like to know specifically what they have done well and need to have concrete information on how to improve. Comments like "excellent organization" mean little; you do well to indicate the reason for the excellence: "Your use of problem-solving good for the development of this topic." In fact, all comments should usually be specific such as: "You gave only one advantage of your particular solution. Others exist. What are they?" "Is John Black's testimony significant?" "Good use of authority in the quotation by the Secretary of Labor." "You said *jist* for *just* six times and *git* for *get* four times." "You did not make a single error on the *ng* sound." "You established well the motivation of greed in your characterization." "You did not indicate parallel attention in reading your poem."

Such comments motivate students to keep improving and to hold on to gains already made. To insure improvement, however, you must make sure that the students understand the items on a checklist if you use one, your comments concerning the items, and your standards for each performance. Frequently you need to follow the written comments with individual conferences.

The standard for achievement may be: (1) one set by you which you expect all students to achieve, (2) one based on the average achievement of your particular group, or (3) one based on the amount of improvement of each individual student. First, you will find it possible either by yourself or with other teachers to set up standards in regard to understandings but you will find it more difficult to set them up for listening and speaking skills and attitudes. You can, however, achieve some objectivity in measuring skills by listening with other teachers to recordings of students' speaking and reading performances and by analyzing them together with care. The second standard, derived from ranking members of your group, is quite easily arrived at and readily comprehended by students and their parents. The disadvantage, however, of comparing a less gifted student with a more gifted one is obvious. The third standard, dependent on improvement, is advantageous in that you take the student where he is and guide him to his greatest potential growth. But here you may find difficulty in evaluating the amount of *potential* growth. You will probably use a combination of these three standards in your evaluation procedures.

In measuring your students' acquisition of understandings, skills, and attitudes, you will use many methods and procedures which you will try to make valid and reliable. You recognize that good tests and checklists do not just happen but that they need thoughtful and careful planning. That you develop proficiency in your techniques for testing knowledge, for measuring the skill of speaking, reading, and listening of your students, and for determining attitudes is highly important.

SUGGESTED READING

BECKER, S. L., "Rating Discussants," *The Speech Teacher*, V (January, 1956), 60-65. Includes a table giving criteria for rating discussants.

DAVIS, F. B., "Speech and Grades: A Request for Further Research," *The Speech Teacher*, III (November, 1954), 255-258. Poses questions about college grading of speech. Much of the material is applicable to the evaluation of high school speech.

DOUGLAS, J., "The Measurement of Speech in the Classroom," *The Speech Teacher*, VII (November, 1958), 309-319. Explains clearly the problems of evaluating speech performances. Talks about the nature and the functions of measurement. An unusually sound and clear exposition of measurement.

FRIEDERICH, W. J., and WILCOX, R. A., *Teaching Speech in High School* (New York, The Macmillan Co., 1953), Ch. 18. Explains instrumental, written, and performance measurements. Contains a large variety of checklists.

KNOWER, F. K., "What Is a Speech Test," *Quarterly Journal of Speech,* XXX (December, 1944), 492-493. Discusses test values, fundamental problems, test criteria, observational tests, objective testing, pragmatic tests, and evaluational techniques. One of the best articles on speaking evaluation.

Montgomery, K. E., "How to Criticize Student Speeches," *The Speech Teacher*, VI (September, 1957), 200-204. Gives a method, cumulative and repetitive, of evaluating public speaking.

Reid, L., *Teaching Speech* (Columbia, Mo., Artcraft Press, 1956), Ch. 15. Gives good advice on how to criticize speeches.

Robinson, K. F., *Teaching Speech in the Secondary School*, (New York, Longmans, Green & Co., Inc., 1954), Ch. 10. Gives a complete and thorough treatment of diagnosis, evaluation, testing, and criticism.

Utterback, W. E., "Evaluation of Performance in the Discussion Course at Ohio State University," *The Speech Teacher*, VII (September, 1958), 209-215. Gives one method of evaluating performance of discussants.

Weaver, A. T., Borchers, G. L., and Smith, D. K., *The Teaching of Speech* (Englewood Cliffs, N. J., Prentice-Hall, Inc., 1952), pp. 491-550. Explains clearly ways of criticizing classroom speaking and measuring the results of instruction.

EXERCISES

1. Critize the following short answer questions:

Completion:

   a. Three kinds of sounds used in English are ...., ...

     and ....

   b. List five different spellings for the sound *a* as in *made:* ....,

     ...., ..., ..., ...

   c. Name three personalities of television who represent effective oral

     interpretation: ...., ..., and

     ....

   d. M, n, and *ng* are all..........sounds.

Multiple Choice:

   a. The television critic for the *New York World-Telegram and Sun* is:

     Jack Gould

     Walter Kerr

     Harriet Van Horne

     Abraham Laub

   b. The apron is:

     (1) Extension placed in front of the stage.

     (2) Drop used to decrease the heighth of the stage.

(3) Flat used to decrease the width of the stage.

(4) Playing area down stage.

True or False:

a. Educated Americans speak alike.

b. A speaker's voice quality has more effect on his listeners than what he says.

c. The last word of all questions should have a rising inflection.

2. Criticize the following essay questions:

a. Give four rules you should keep in mind when being interviewed.

b. After listening to a recording of a well-organized, effectively-composed, and well-delivered speech, students are to answer:

(1) What is the main idea of the speech?

(2) Give three kinds of support used. Mention specific instance of each use.

(3) How was the introduction of the speech made effective or ineffective?

c. Discuss briefly two personal qualities that you have developed through your study of acting.

d. Plays give us insight into human behavior. Indicate one character in a play whom you know intimately and give us your insight into his behavior.

3. Criticize the following form for evaluating the performance of an actor:

Understanding of Scene:

Development of Character:

    Bodily Movement:

    Voice:

    Articulation:

    Emphasis and Pausing:

    Phrasing:

    Use of Pitch:

Understanding of Character:

    Motivation:

Knowledge of Stage Techniques:

    Stage Movement:

    Audience Contact:

    Projection of Character:

Relationship to Other Actors:

    Scene Stealing:

    Picking up Cues:

    Entrances:

    Exits:

4. Play the role of a speech teacher and a student complaining about his grade. The members of the methods class will evaluate the teacher's handling of the situation.

5. Prepare a ten-minute short-answer test. Administer it to your methods class. Grade the papers. Report the results.

6. Construct a test on a particular unit in speech which includes four different types of short-answer questions and one essay question.

7. Listen to a group of student speeches. Prepare critical comments on each presentation.

VII

TANGENTIAL SERVICES

15

Assemblies

ALMOST ALL high schools present assembly programs and speech teachers are usually intimately involved in them. If you are the only speech teacher in your school, you will in all likelihood be asked to take charge of the assemblies. If you are one of several, you will probably serve sooner or later on the assembly committee.

An assembly program is a show case for the work of the school; in fact, it presents dramatically the educational philosophy and practices of the entire school. Since it is an important showcase, you must examine carefully its aims, its content, and its organization.

AIMS OF ASSEMBLY PROGRAMS

1. *To acquaint the public with the school's curriculum and its policies.* Today when some of the public is criticizing education, the assembly provides a showcase for answering some of the criticism honestly, persuasively, and attractively. For example, one group may claim that the school is ignoring mental disciplines like science and mathematics while another may declare that the school is losing sight of artistic achievement because of "crash" programs in science and mathematics. Since your school probably provides a balance of the two activities, your showcase must at one time include the best of its academic disciplines and at another time the best of its artistic accomplishments. The series of assembly programs should represent clearly and effectively the educational philosophy of the school.

2. *To motivate students' interest in intellectual activities.* Not only must the assembly make the public aware of the students' intellectual attainments, but it must also motivate the high school student to broaden his intellectual horizons. A student may major in music in high school and not know about important new discoveries in chemistry. Thus, an assembly on chemistry's function in providing materials for daily living can open new vistas to the music major. Or a panel discussion on "Who will be our next President?" can stimulate the chemistry major to take an interest in the campaign, to be cognizant of the issues involved, and to read the speeches of the campaigners more critically.

3. *To motivate interest in creative, artistic activities.* On the other hand, a performance of the school orchestra may awaken in the young scientist an interest in music. Or the assembly which presents and explains the original compositions of music majors may encourage him to study harmony. Or an able presentation of a play may stir in him a lifelong interest in the theater. Or the reading of original poetry may inspire him to try his own hand at creative writing. One purpose of assemblies is to encourage appreciation of aesthetic values.

4. *To learn to be a good listener as a member of a large audience.* Almost nowhere else in the school is the opportunity to learn how to listen as a member of a large audience present. Planning how to achieve this purpose is important. For instance, homeroom teachers can advise their students on what to listen for when they are provided with advance reports of the assembly. In addition, teachers can motivate students to listen by evaluating with them the assembly performances. Lastly they may suggest that students talk about their own participation as an audience.

5. *To learn how to evaluate public performances.* As just indicated, members of a homeroom group may discuss the performance. After the discussion, they often write to the assembly committee to suggest ways of improving assemblies. Other opportunities for evaluation should be present: Students may answer questionnaires as recommended later in the chapter. School newspaper reporters may write critical reviews for their papers, establishing standards and then judging performances against them. Members of particular classes may talk about the good and bad features of a

particular assembly; for example, the drama class may well analyze the production of a play given in assembly.

6. *To give some students opportunities to develop abilities in leadership and management.* In addition to participating in the evaluation of assemblies, many students have an opportunity to lead others in the production of assembly programs. Most high schools have an assembly committee of students and teachers who superintend the assembly programs with the advice and guidance of the assembly co-ordinator. Furthermore, a large number of students will be assigned responsibilities for conducting and performing in specific assemblies throughout the year. Thus, the assembly gives many students chances to develop abilities in leadership.

7. *To promote a healthy school morale.* Although no studies have been conducted to show the part the assembly plays in building school morale, many educators believe that the assembly is an important factor. In their writings they note that because the assembly begins or carries on tradition in the school and because it fosters a feeling of belongingness, it promotes unity in a student body. Traditions in assemblies are important to students. For example, the parade of color bearers in assemblies is a ritual which students long remember as meaningful tradition in their school. Even the principal's opening of the assembly by reading from the Bible may be significant to students. For instance, one former student said, "I remember with pleasure Mr. Wilton's participation in our assemblies—his white hair, his scholarly demeanor, his courtliness, and his superb reading of the Bible." The feeling of unity comes about in part from the enacting of traditions and in part from seeing all the members of the school—students and faculty—reacting together to the same program.

A study by the National Association of Secondary School Principals of 336 secondary schools throughout the United States notes that 93 per cent of the schools answering the questionnaire believe that developing school spirit should be a purpose of the assembly. In fact, this purpose received the highest percentage of any objective. In addition, the study indicates the programs which schools believe helpful in promoting unity; the percentages of schools reporting a particular kind of assembly as important to unity follow:[1]

---

[1] "The Assembly Program in the Secondary School," *Bulletin of the National Association of Secondary School Principals,* XXX (November, 1946), 2-10.

Programs with themes of interest to all students..............100%
Patriotic programs.. 93%
Student council activities................................... 78%
Rally, booster, and pep programs............................ 61%
Open discussion of school problems.......................... 44%
School sings.. 10%
Demonstrations of class work................................ 4%
Talks by outsiders.. 3%
Honor assemblies.. 3%
Student talent programs..................................... 3%
Programs to promote interracial understanding............... 2%
Publicity for school achievements........................... 2%

8. *To recognize worthy achievement.* Closely allied to the development of school morale is the recognition of successful performances of students. Rewards for successful performances are important to high school students. The bright freshman hopes for the day when he will become a member of Arista, a school honor society in which character, service, and scholarship are stressed. He works hard to achieve this distinction. When it is conferred, he is proud; furthermore, the members of the school are glad to pay tribute to him at the induction ceremony. The freshman basketball player longs for the time when he will walk onto the high school stage to get his varsity letter. The freshman actress sees herself in her senior year receiving the award for outstanding service in the school theater. The aspiring editor looks forward to the moment when he may accept the editor's key from the retiring editor and announce his staff for the following year. To use the assembly to give recognition to those in the school who have achieved outstanding success in various fields is common. The programs can leave lasting impressions on all who attend.

Not all assembly committees will agree with these eight aims. Some committees will want to delete; others to add. Statistics from the study just mentioned point to agreement and disagreement as to aims: 93 per cent of the schools investigated reported the purpose of developing school spirit; 92 per cent, of furthering education or culture of school members; 79 per cent, of providing guidance; 78 per cent, of furnishing recreational opportunities; 57 per cent, of demonstrating the work of classes; 54 per cent, of supplementing it; and 48 per cent, of motivating it.[2]

[2] *Ibid.,* pp. 2-10.

ADMINISTERING THE ASSEMBLY PROGRAM

The Assembly Committee

A series of assembly programs to fulfill these purposes are planned and directed by a committee of faculty and students under the guidance of a faculty assembly co-ordinator and a student chairman. The teachers on the committee frequently are delegates from those departments most vitally concerned with the production of assemblies: speech, music, and art. The students are representatives of various homerooms, classes, or organizations or are a group appointed by the governing body of the school. The co-ordinator is a teacher, often a speech teacher, almost always selected by the administration of the school. This committee meets regularly throughout the year to plan, conduct, and evaluate the program of assemblies.

After the committee has discussed and come to an understanding concerning the aims of assemblies, one of its first tasks is to decide on a schedule for their assemblies.

Scheduling

Kinds of Schedules

School authorities schedule assemblies regularly or when the need for them arises. When assemblies are scheduled regularly, the calendar of assemblies is prepared as much as a semester in advance. Each sponsoring group knows when it is to perform and the type of performance expected from it. This system has several advantages: (1) The assembly is presented regularly. (2) Time is given for careful preparation. (3) The committee can plan a balanced program.

On the other hand, assemblies may be scheduled as the need arises. When a high school class wishes to share the results of its work with the rest of the school, it asks for an assembly date. When a well-known alumnus appears in town, the assembly co-ordinator asks him to speak. With this kind of schedule, however, certain assemblies such as those intended to celebrate holidays like Christmas or Thanksgiving are planned well ahead. The advantages of this type of scheduling are that it capitalizes on special events and that it provides an opportunity for members of a class to share exciting learning just as it has taken place. The disadvantage is that there may be a dearth of assemblies one month and an excess the next.

Time

Some school administrators provide a definite time in their schedule for assemblies. They plan them weekly or biweekly on a particular day at a particular hour. Often the administrator places them at the first period in the morning or, where all students have the same lunch hour, the first period after lunch. These times are advantageous, for students participating in a program can arrive early or use their lunch hour for preparing the assembly. According to a report of the National Association of Secondary School Principals, 31 per cent prefer Friday and 30 per cent Wednesday.[3] Other administrators, however, do not want a regularly scheduled time for assemblies; rather they shorten all periods on the day the assembly is to be held.

Mechanics of the Assembly Program

Preparing the Calendar

After the students have worked out their principles for providing assemblies and have received suggestions for them from other students and the faculty, they prepare the assembly calendar. They know that it will contain programs at certain times of the year such as Thanksgiving, Christmas, and May Day. It may also traditionally include a get-acquainted day, a senior day, a junior day, a football rally, and an awards day. A typical program follows:

Thursday, September 11	Get Acquainted Day
September 25	Organization Day
October 10	Football Rally
October 24	Radio Workshop
November 6	Music Department
November 20	Thanksgiving Day Program
December 4	Physical Education Department
December 18	Christmas Program
January 9	Science Department

[3] *Ibid.,* p. 12.

February 12	English Department
February 26	Social Studies Department
March 6	Play Advertisement
March 20	Language Department
April 17	Student Government Campaign Day
April 24	Drama Workshop
May 1	May Day Program
May 15	Awards Day
June 5	Moving-Up Day

In this program the student organization is responsible for the Get Acquainted Day, Organization Day, Student Government Campaign Day, Moving-Up Day, and Awards Day. The Assembly Committee concerns itself with the Thanksgiving, Christmas, and May Day performances. The Speech Department takes charge of the Radio Workshop, Drama Workshop, and play advertisement programs. The other departments such as English, science, physical education, and language oversee their programs.

Keeping Records on Individual Programs

For each program the sponsoring agent may well supply information such as the following:

CENTRAL HIGH SCHOOL
PLAN FOR ASSEMBLY PROGRAM

Title .... Faculty Advisor ....

Sponsor .... Date ....

Announcer ....

Type: ....

Purpose: ....

....

....

Stage setting* ....

Lighting Effects* ....

Participants: ....

....

....

Program* ....

....

....

....

....

....

....

....

....

* If you wish the committee to take care of stage setting, lighting effects, or mimeographing the program, please notify the committee two weeks in advance. Include diagram of setting, description of lighting effects, and copy for program.

For each program, the co-ordinator may well keep such a record as the following:

ASSEMBLY PROGRAM CHECKLIST

PROGRAM .... DATE ....

Duty	Name of Person to Carry out Duty	When Notified	When Carried Out
OUTSIDE SPEAKER			
Who is to meet him?			
Who is to introduce him?			
What faculty member is to approve student's introduction?			
Who is to take charge of speaker after assembly?			
STUDENT AND FACULTY PROGRAMS			
Who is to invite sponsor to give program?			
Who is to observe the rehearsal?			
Who is to be master of ceremonies?			
Who is to rehearse the master of ceremonies?			
PUBLICITY			
Who is to assemble information?			
Who is to send information to the school newspaper?			
Who is to see that posters are made?			
Who is to make announcements over P.A. system?			
Who is to see that dittoed sheets are sent to homeroom teachers?			
MUSIC			
Who is to invite the Music Department to perform?			
What Music Department faculty member is in charge?			

BIBLICAL READING			
Who is to choose the selection?			
Selection chosen:			
Who is to read the selection?			
What faculty is to approve the reading?			
PROGRAMS			
Who is to secure the material?			
Who is to see that the material is dittoed?			
STAGING			
Who is to clear the stage?			
Who is to put up the apron (if required)?			
Who is to set up the risers (if required)?			
Who is to see that a lectern or music stands are provided?			
Who is to provide water?			
Who is to check the lights?			
Who is to check the P.A. system?			
Who is to check the chairs?			
Who is to check the piano?			
Who is to make sure that the ventilation is adequate?			
SPECIAL EQUIPMENT List below:			

Form of Assembly

The committee recommends a form, for usually all assemblies in a particular school do follow a prescribed form. Tradition in assemblies is apparent. In the early days of our country, most colleges required attendance at morning chapel with reading from the Bible and prayer. Our early secondary schools, the academies, adopted this tradition. Today many of our schools still preserve this form; a student or faculty member reads from the Bible and leads the student body in the Lord's prayer.

The reading from the Bible should bear some relationship to the program. For instance, on the day of the United Nations program a choral reading group might well be:

1. God be merciful unto us, and bless us; and cause his face to shine upon us.
2. That thy way may be known upon earth, thy saving health among all nations.
3. Let the people praise thee, O God; let all the people praise thee.
4. O, let the nations be glad, and sing for joy; for thou shalt judge the people righteously, and govern the nations upon earth.
5. Let the people praise thee, O God; let all the people praise thee.
6. Then shall the earth yield her increase; and God, even our God, shall bless us.
7. God shall bless us; and all the ends of the earth shall fear him.

Psalm 67:1-7

To the reading of the Bible, the salute to the flag, the singing of "The Star Spangled Banner" or "My Country 'Tis of Thee" are usually added. A musical processional and recessional are also sometimes included. The establishment of such form helps to keep the meeting orderly.

Advertising the Assembly

Besides selecting the assemblies, scheduling them, and establishing the form, the committee takes charge of publicizing them in various ways. Its members send mimeographed notices to homeroom teachers to read to their students. For instance, if the assembly is a play, the committee includes its type, its theme, and a little of the background of the playwright. The committee may also describe the experience of some of the actors and actresses. Second, the committee may announce the forthcoming attraction over the public-address system. Third, it usually gives to the school newspaper reporter a brief resumé of what the assembly is to contain and other information which will help the audience to understand and appreciate the production. Lastly, it prepares posters advertising the performance. Since attendance at assemblies is almost always compulsory, the committee has a captive audience. It should, however, still make attendance seem desirable and attractive.

Organizing for the Performance

The last duty of the committee involves several responsibilities for the performance. First, it should see that the flag, Bible, scenery, and properties are readily available and that the microphone and lighting equipment are in proper order. Second, it plans the seating arrangements for the audience. Many committees assign a seat to each student before the first assembly. The homeroom teachers have charts and take charge of the seating of their groups. A visitors' section is included. Third, the committee makes the decisions on the presiding officers for assemblies. The study mentioned earlier shows that 30 per cent have student leaders presiding, 26 per cent the president of the student body, 21 per cent different persons for each performance, 11 per cent the principal, 4 per cent the faculty member sponsoring the group, 3 per cent the chairman of the assembly committee, and 3 per cent someone assigned by the principal.[4] Most speech teachers believe that students should be the presiding officers, since presiding offers excellent training in speech for high school boys and girls.

SOURCES OF PROGRAMS

The committee has many sources for programs. They include the school's departmental curricular and extracurricular groups, the student governing body, several departments working co-operatively, faculty, and performers chosen from outside the school.

4 *Ibid.*, page 21.

Within the School

Departmental

Various departments present programs. An English department may give several types of which three are suggested here. First, it may offer creative dramatizations of incidents from books. In this case, the art department may co-operate by making large covers to introduce each scene. Second, students in English writing classes may contribute samples of creative writing. Here the speech department may work with the English department in presenting some of the material in choral speaking. Or the music department may set some of the poetry to music. Third, a panel from an English class may evaluate the leading newspapers of the state.

Other departments present appropriate programs. Students from an art department may throw on a screen advertisements representative of good design and then explain the principles involved. Or members from an art department may display household articles borrowed from the local ten-cent store and then make clear how they exemplify the principles of good design. Or they may explain the art of the Elizabethan era.

Many interesting programs emanate from language departments. A Latin department may tell the Greek and Roman myths. Students of a modern language department may explain a series of situations and then participate in them in French, German, Spanish, or Russian. Or they may dramatize holidays celebrated in foreign countries.

Still other departments present stimulating programs. A mathematics department may run a contest of the advanced mathematics students to see who is the most rapid calculator of mathematical problems. A panel from the social studies department may discuss "How can we control inflation in our country?" A biology department may show slides of the birds, trees, or wild flowers of the region—explaining where they can be found. A speech department can give a demonstration of parliamentary procedure or makeup, a discussion of the outstanding plays or speeches of the year, or a debate on a timely topic. A physical education department can present folk dances. A guidance department can invite several alumni now teaching to talk about "Why I Like Teaching." This program is particularly appropriate on Teacher Recognition Day.

All-School Programs

The assembly committee will sponsor certain all-school programs. For example, the Christmas program may be a co-operative endeavor of the speech, art, and music departments; plays like *Why the Chimes Rang* or *The Boy on the Meadow* need the work of all three departments. Or when the scriptures telling the Christmas story are to be read and interpreted, the committee often asks the art department to provide settings; the speech department, the choral speaking and pantomime; and the music department, the choral singing. Similarly a May Day pageant or a gay nineties revue draws on the talents and services of these three departments and often on those of the physical education department. Other programs like a representation of the holidays of the year, a dramatization of the meaning of Thanksgiving, or a living newspaper also require co-operative endeavor.

Student Organization

The student organization arranges for such assemblies as Awards Day, Moving-Up Day, and football rallies all of which need faculty supervision. Frequently the assembly co-ordinator furnishes the guidance. For instance, he may help plan an impressive program for giving out awards. This assembly should be simple, formal, and moving. A candlelighting service, the provision of carnations for the honored boys and girls, the addition of music, and an inspiring address by a faculty member can make this event memorable and stirring.

Faculty

The special talents and interests of the faculty can be utilized. For example, in one assembly four faculty members demonstrated their hobbies. One recounted his tales of hunting for antique spelling books; he showed his finds. Another told about taking photographs; he illustrated the results of his hobby by throwing them on a screen. Still another described his interest in oil painting; his paintings hung in the lobby. Still another told of playing the oboe in high school, in college, and now in the local symphony orchestra; he demonstrated with his oboe. The presentation showed some of the nonprofessional interests of a group of educated men and women.

Outside Agencies

Outside agencies can also supply material for assemblies. For instance, the General Electric assembly is always a favorite with students. The special knowledge and abilities of local lawyers, historians, designers, or public officials serve the purposes of assemblies well. Most teachers believe, however, that assemblies should be student-centered and that the use of outside talent should be minimal.

EVALUATION

Most assembly committees think that their own evaluation and the evaluation of the students and faculty are important in determining the worth of individual programs and of the year's total programs. Questionnaires such as the following may be filled out by a sampling of students from all classes or by members of two or three homerooms to determine the worth of individual programs. The committee then analyzes the replies.

CENTRAL HIGH SCHOOL
ASSEMBLY QUESTIONNAIRE

Your committee provides assemblies to further your education. Its members want to know whether we are bringing you worthwhile material. Would you, therefore, answer the following questions carefully and return the questionnaire to the assembly box in the Administration Office?

Title of Assembly: .... Date ....

General Impression of the Assembly. ......1, ...2, ...3, ...4,
......5.

(Rate from 1 to 5. 1. Very poor. 2. Poor. 3. Average. 4. Good. 5. Superior.)
Answer the following as completely as you can:

Main idea:

Reaction of Audience:

Use of Material:

Strong Points of Program:

Weak Points of Program:

Thank you for your help. We appreciate your taking time to fill out this questionnaire.

The Assembly Committee.

The following is another questionnaire which might be used alternately with the preceding one:

CENTRAL HIGH SCHOOL
ASSEMBLY QUESTIONNAIRE

Title .... Date ....

Why did we present this assembly?

Did it hold your interest?

Did you profit from the information? Not at all......A little......About

as usual......Very much......

(The above question depends upon the type of assembly. You may ask: Did you enjoy the entertainment? Were you persuaded by the program? Were you inspired by the program?)

Would you recommend a similar program for next year? Yes......No......

Did the program appear well organized? Yes......No......

Could you see easily? Yes......No......

Could you hear easily? Yes......No......

The following questionnaire may be distributed to a representative group at the end of the year:

CENTRAL HIGH SCHOOL
END OF TERM QUESTIONNAIRE ON ASSEMBLIES

What assembly did you consider most worthwhile? ....

....

Why? ....

....

....

What assembly did you consider least worthwhile? ....

....

Why? ....

....

....

From a study and analysis of these evaluation sheets, the committee can measure to some extent the success of its program. It uses the evaluation in planning the next year's series.

Since evaluation is so important, and since much learning takes place during the committee meetings, it is desirable to have committee members serve on the assembly committee for two or more years. This plan gives continuity to the committee. Both students and faculty learn from being associated with the series of programs.

As a speech teacher, you do your part to make the assembly an attractive, educationally sound, and honest showcase of the philosophy and work of the school. You make sure that each program fulfills sound aims, is planned carefully and intelligently, and represents the best work of the school. You help to see that the series meets the needs of the students in the school. When no evaluative procedure is used, you suggest one. Sound evaluation will lead to good assemblies.

SUGGESTED READING

ABELL, A., and ANDERSON, A. J., *Programs for High School Assemblies* (Minneapolis, Minn., Northwestern Press, 1942). Contains suggestions for high school assemblies.

Assembly Guide (Curriculum Bulletin Number 11, Board of Education, City of New York, 110 Livingston Street, Brooklyn, N. Y., 1956).

"The Assembly Program in the Secondary School," *The Bulletin of the National Association of Secondary School Principals*, XXX (November, 1946). Includes material on purposes, evaluation of effectiveness, and examples of various types of assembly programs.

BRAUN, C. E., "The School Assembly," *School Activities*, XXIII (February, 1952), 181-183. Explains the purposes of school assemblies. Recommends types of assemblies.

DeMARCO, N., ed., *Assembly Program Suggestions* (College Hill Station, Cincinnati 24, Ohio, National Thespian Society, 1951).

DUBAR, R. R., "Road Show Assemblies: Four Schools Exchange Programs," *Clearing House*, XXV (October, 1950), 74. Explains how four Massachusetts schools exchange high school programs.

FRIEDERICH, W. J., and WILCOX, R. A., *Teaching Speech in High Schools* (New York, The Macmillan Co., 1953), pp. 410-419. Gives the principles for the planning and preparation of high school assemblies. Discusses programming.

GRUBER, F. C., and BEATTY, T. B., *Secondary School Activities* (New York, McGraw-Hill Book Co., 1954), pp. 169-182. Gives principles of organizing, scheduling, and providing assemblies. Excellent list of suggested assemblies growing out of departmental activities.

JOHNSTON, E. G., and FAUNCE, R. C., *Student Activities in Secondary Schools* (New York, The Ronald Press Company, 1952), pp. 89-109. Explains objectives of assemblies. Tells how to plan and evaluate them. Describes an unusual Thanksgiving program and an impressive installation of officers of student government.

KILZER, L. R., STEPHENSON, H. H., and NORDBERG, H. O., *Allied Activities in the Secondary School* (New York, Harper & Brothers, 1956). Gives aims and definitions of assemblies. Tells how to organize, find sources, and evaluate. Excellent advice on evaluation.

THOMPSON, N. Z., *Vitalizing Assemblies* (New York, E. P. Dutton & Co., Inc., 1952). Contains practical suggestions for improving assembly programs.

EXERCISES

1. Assume roles of three high school students, a music director, and a speech teacher. With the speech teacher as chairman, hold a first meeting to discuss the type of Christmas program that should be given this year.
2. Plan one of the following assemblies:
   a. One based on choral speaking and modern dance.
   b. One based on the scientific achievements of the year.
   c. One celebrating Education Week.
   d. One celebrating Book Week.
3. Interview a student who is majoring in an area other than speech but who is planning to teach. Talk with him about a possible joint departmental assembly.

16

Offering Services in Speech Correction to the High School Student

MORE AND MORE schools employ one person to teach courses such as fundamentals, theater, and public speaking and a second person to do speech therapy. In many schools, however, the same person may devote part of his time to teaching classes of speech and the rest of it to speech therapy. You should not accept such a position with dual proficiencies and dual responsibilities unless you are qualified; you should have the necessary training both in speech arts (dramatics, oral reading, public speaking, debate and discussion) and in speech science (phonetics, anatomy of the speech mechanism, speech correction for both functional and organic difficulties, practicum in speech correction and audiology.)

TEACHER'S SCHEDULE OF CLASSES IN SPEECH THERAPY

Where you are expected to teach speech courses and to do speech therapy, the planning of the therapy program frequently falls within your jurisdiction. You will likely find that your administrator has scheduled your courses in speech but that he expects you to schedule the sessions for speech therapy. You may work out such a plan as the following:

TEACHER'S SCHEDULE

NAME. . . . . .AREA: Speech

	Monday	Tuesday	Wednesday	Thursday	Friday
9:00	Funds.	Funds.	Funds.	Funds.	Funds.
9:45	Free	Free	Free	Free	Free
10:30	Therapy	Therapy	Therapy	Therapy	Therapy
11:15	Therapy	Therapy	Therapy	Therapy	Therapy
12:00	LUNCH HOUR				
1:00	Funds.	Funds.	Funds.	Funds.	Funds.
1:45	Theater	Theater	Theater	Theater	Theater
2:30	Therapy	Therapy	Therapy	Therapy	Therapy
3:15	ACTIVITIES HOUR				

Here you devote fifteen periods to teaching fundamentals and theater courses and fifteen periods to doing speech therapy work. Your fifteen periods labeled "therapy" include twelve periods devoted to corrective work and three periods to conferring with speech-handicapped individuals or their parents or writing the necessary reports.

In such a schedule, you may see your speech-handicapped students from once to five times a week, from fifteen minutes to an hour, and as individuals or in groups. These decisions depend on you, the needs of your students, and the wishes of your administrator. In planning time for therapy, you may assume that an ideal arrangement is one where you see each handicapped student twice a week for a half period. Whether you meet him as an individual or in a group depends on the degree and nature of his handicap. If the student has a severe cleft palate, you may wish to work with him alone. But if he is a severely handicapped stutterer, you may wish to work with him in a group. If his difficulty is a minor articulatory one, you may wish to have him come with as many as eight others. You are not, however, always free to plan this work exactly as you wish. Some school authorities, for instance, are insistent that you keep students the full period, for they are apprehensive about students' leaving study halls for part of a period. You adjust to the situation by meeting the students only once a week. Still other administrators ask that you meet the same group five times a week in order not to disrupt programs. You adjust to this situation by having large groups of speech-handicapped students meet with you daily. You make the best schedule possible, keeping in mind the needs of the students and, at the same time, meeting the demands of your administration.

FINDING A PLACE TO WORK

Not only do you plan for the times when you can see your speech handicapped students, but you also plan for a place to work with them. The school administrator may have already arranged for this room. When he has not, you recommend that it be a well-lighted, well-ventilated, quiet spot easily accessible to the students. You ask that it be equipped with chairs, a table, three or four medium-sized mirrors, a letter-size file with a lock, a cupboard with a lock to keep books and materials, a blackboard, a tape recorder, and an audiometer if you are to give the hearing tests. You, however, may have to accept less desirable facilities with good grace. A suitable room with equipment that meets the therapeutic needs of your students is eminently desirable for the success of the program.

FINDING THE SPEECH HANDICAPPED

After you have worked out the hours to do your therapy and found a place to do it, you must locate the speech handicapped students. When the speech therapy program has been in effect previously, records will indicate what work has been done with what students, what students need more work, how much more, and what kind. In this case you survey only the new students. You can then proceed to schedule those whom you discover and those whom the records show need speech work.

Referral

In other cases, as when you are first therapist in a school, you must find all the handicapped students either through referral or through a survey. Frequently high school teachers, other than speech teachers, refer those students needing speech work. But unless you train these teachers carefully, explaining and illustrating the kinds of speech problems which they are likely to find, you miss some students with glaring speech handicaps and include others with very minor difficulties. Diehl and Stinnett[1] conclude that teachers with no orientation to speech therapy can be expected to miss two of every five children classified as defective. When you use many teachers, the school psychologist, and the school nurse and give them explicit instruction in detecting speech difficulties, you may be successful in finding the students handicapped in speech through referral. In this instance, however, many will be referred to you who do not need help.

Screening the Student Body

A more accurate way of locating the speech handicapped students is for you to screen the entire school population. You should be able to screen from fifteen to twenty students per hour, engaging them in conversation and having them read loaded material. Admittedly the method presents problems. For instance, if you are teaching regularly scheduled classes, you may find difficulty in reaching all the students. Since, however, high school students usually take four subjects and since their schedules tend to fall into similar patterns, the timing of your survey is somewhat flexible.

You undertake this survey in an orderly and efficient fashion. You first explain to all the teachers the need for the survey so that they understand what you are trying to accomplish. You also are careful to notify them of the time of the survey well ahead so that they know that they will lose a particular teaching hour. You come to the classrooms prepared with a sheet for each student on which he will write his own name and address, the name, address and telephone number of his guardian, his homeroom number, his English

[1] C. F. Diehl and C. D. Stinnett, "Efficiency of Teacher Referrals in a School Speech Testing Program," *Journal of Speech and Hearing Disorders*, XXIV (February, 1959), 34-36.

section, and his free periods. As you test, you indicate on this sheet his speech difficulty or the absence of one.

SCHEDULING THE SPEECH HANDICAPPED

Now that you have found your speech handicapped students, you are ready to fit them into your schedule. To your dismay, you may discover that although your half-time therapy schedule can take care of only fifty, you have 152. The fifty is based on a recommended case load of about a hundred for a full-time speech therapist. Your situation leaves you with three alternatives:

1. You can give a little help in large groups to all 152.
2. You can train the English teachers to take care of the less severely handicapped.
3. You can give adequate training to fifty.

Selecting Handicapped Students for Therapy

Neither the first nor the second choice is feasible. The first one, of giving a little help to all the handicapped, is not, since a small amount of training usually results in a small amount of improvement which will consequently detract from the entire speech program. Success is based on effectively treated students. The second choice, of using the English teachers, is also not feasible, for neither you nor the English teachers have time for this procedure. Many high school English teachers justifiably believe that their emphasis must be on preparing students for college.

The third alternative, that of giving training to only fifty students, seems, therefore, the wisest choice; but you must make the selection of the fifty according to valid principles. Disgruntled parents whose children have been deprived of speech therapy or those whose children have been asked to take it will arrive at your office for an explanation. You need, therefore, to have sound reasons for your selection and to be able to defend your position.

The selection of these fifty students may be based on grade placement, on the severity of the handicap, on their ability to benefit from training, or on a combination of the three. You may believe that seniors should receive the training since they are graduating. But some of them may be quite apathetic about receiving help. You may think that the most severely handicapped should receive it, since their communication is most seriously affected. Yet the boy with a severe lisp caused by malocclusion really needs orthodontic work before speech work can be truly effective. You may hold that students of low intelligence benefit less from the work than the more able. Administrators, however, generally do not approve of this attitude. Consequently you may well base your selection not on any one of these factors but on the combined effect of all of them.

Placing Students in Speech Therapy Sessions

After selecting those who will receive help, you prepare a schedule for them. You must consider the times that both you and the students are free. In addition, you may want to group your students homogeneously. For example, you may place the stutterers or lispers together or you may place those of the same grade together. You cannot introduce too many factors in your grouping; for example, you may well have to put stutterers of different age levels in the same group; or in some instances you many find it necessary to group together such difficulties as lalling and lisping. You work out the groupings which will best serve the therapeutic needs of your students.

When the correction program is new to the school or town, you notify the parents of the students who are to come for speech help. With the advice and consent of your supervisor, or principal, you write such a letter as the following:

Dear Mrs. ———:

A recent test shows that your son can profit from some work in speech. I have, therefore, scheduled him to work with me twice a week during which time I shall try to teach him to speak more clearly.

I shall be glad to have your help. You can, I am sure, give me information and advice which will make my work with your son more effective. Won't you come to see me next week when I have planned conferences with parents? Would Tuesday at 3:00 be a possible time? If it is not, please call me between three and five on Friday at Forest 6-7000, extension 7, and I shall try to arrange another time.

Sincerely yours,

You will find other sample letters in Houchin's article, "Notes on Organizing a Speech Correction Program in the Public Schools," listed in the bibliography at the end of the chapter.

GETTING TO KNOW YOUR HANDICAPPED STUDENTS

The next step is to get to know your handicapped students. Obviously you cannot use the method for compiling case histories you have been accustomed to in your college or university clinic. You have other ways, however, of finding out about your students.

Information in School Records

One way is through an examination of the cumulative records of individuals kept in the school. You may well have available the scholastic, personality, and health record of a youngster for his entire school career. From one such report on a fourteen-year-old, a therapist compiled the following information:

SPEAKING: Difficult to understand. Has always liked to speak and speaks often even with his difficulty.

PERSONALITY: Pleasant personality. Dependable, co-operative, well-adjusted. Well-liked by his peers and teachers.

SCHOLARSHIP: I.Q. of 128 with a nonlanguage test; I.Q. of 113 on the Terman Revision of the Binet Simon Test. On the whole a poor student. Best work in science and social studies; poorest in languages and English. Does not do as well as he can (indicated by half his teachers).

VOCATIONAL PLANS: Wants to be a carpenter. Aptitude tests show that his score is high in mechanical areas like carpentry.

HEALTH: No unusual illnesses. Has lost little or no time from school because of illness.

HOME BACKGROUND: Rather low socioeconomic status with co-operative hard-working parents. Mother high strung; father easy-going. Both completed eighth grade but left high school in their sophomore years. Both enjoy their child and are understanding of his problems.

Information, such as that given above, is helpful to you in working with your speech handicapped children.

Not all schools keep such complete records. But even from a study of a scholastic record alone, you can learn whether a child repeated grades or courses, what courses he does well in, whether he maintains consistently superior marks, and what courses he has had difficulty with. Usually you can learn his I. Q.

Information from Teachers, Guidance Counselors, and Autobiographies

You have other methods of learning about your handicapped students. First, homeroom teachers can give you much information. Comments from them like "He's a leader," "He's almost too quiet," "He's always in trouble" tell you much about the boy. Second, the guidance counselor can frequently supply you with needed facts.

Third, autobiographies of high school students are a source of information. For instance, you may ask your students to write about their life indicating the influences of their parents, teachers, and friends. Furthermore, you may ask them to react to their class work, the punishments given at home, and the discipline given at school and to relate to you their fears, desires, and wishes. In addition, you may suggest that they include their special talents, abilities, and interests. If they have not already written such an autobiography, they will enjoy writing it. If they have been asked to write similar material, they resent the assignment. One high school girl of fifteen said, "I've written my autobiography for two English teachers, for my citizenship teacher, and now my speech teacher wants it!" In such cases you may ask them to write a speaking biography, indicating influences that have made their speech what it is.

Interviews with Students and their Parents

When you do not get the information you want from these sources, you interview the child or the child's parent. Often you can learn much from and about the child by letting him talk and by not structuring the interview. You, however, are warm, friendly, and show no displeasure or excitement about any of the information which he offers. In such instances, of course, you do not seem to approve antisocial behavior. Or you may interview the parent. Since almost all parents want the best for their children, they are usually glad to come to school to visit. But if you are a young teacher, they may be amused at the idea of your being in charge of a correction program in the high school. Subtly you identify yourself with your profession, showing unobtrusively that you have been well-trained and that you have handled similar cases. Your professional manner and your sincere, genuine interest in the child bring about a co-operative attitude on the part of the parents.

Role Playing

You may use still other techniques to learn more about your students with speech difficulties. Playing with puppets often unmasks fears, hostilities, and insecurities. The boy who consistently killed or maimed a brother while playing roles was referred to a school psychologist who found an unusually high degree of sibling rivalry. Role-playing where you define a usual problem, state the situation, ask the students to act out the situation, and finally to analyze and discuss the resulting drama tells you a great deal about a child's way of thinking.

Since from such sources you learn about the child, his environment, and his parents, you may have some idea of the cause of his difficulty. You must remember, however, that you are not a psychologist. Most teachers are prone to make psychological statements without enough evidence. You may well record what a mother or a student has said or done, but you must be careful not to make psychological value judgments as a result of these statements. Usually the school psychologist can help you with some of the interpretation of your recordings. When your school has no psychologist and when the problem is a puzzling one, you may be able to get help from your city or state education department psychologist. At other times the school nurse or doctor can be of assistance. Some school administrators hold case conferences with the guidance personnel, the speech teacher, the medical personnel, and the classroom teacher to discuss ways of helping a particular boy or girl.

Recording the Information

You record what you have found out about a particular child on a case history. For school purposes a case history is usually quite simple. It may follow this plan:

CENTRAL HIGH SCHOOL SPEECH DEPARTMENT
CASE HISTORY

Date ....

Name of student ....Address....................

Name of Guardian ....Address.................

Telephone number ....

Date of Birth ....Sex........Homeroom.............

Speech Difficulty ....

....

Father: Age .... Eduction ....

       Occupation ....Speech defect if any............

       Health ....

Mother: Age .... Education ....

       Occupation ....Speech defect if any............

       Health ....

Brothers and Sisters:

Names	Ages	Speech defect if any
....	....	....
....	....	....
....	....	....
....	....	....
....	....	....

Physical Condition: Weight .... Height..............

Abnormality in mouth, throat, nose, or teeth structure.................

....

Motor Impairment ....

Defect in Hearing ....

Defect in Vision ....

Serious Illnesses ....

....

Mental and Educational Development:

   I.Q. .... Test ....

   Scholastic Achievement ....

Scholastic Interests ....

School Attendance: ....

Homeroom Teacher ....

THERAPY

After you have singled out the handicapped students and scheduled them, you are ready to begin therapy. In therapy, your aim
is to replace old habits with new ones. To accomplish this change,
you have both long-range and immediate aims. You hope that Jackie
will learn to say *l* and *r* correctly, to use the new sounds in all
words in all situations, and thereby to communicate more effectively
at the end of the year. The objective of one lesson may be to teach
him to produce the *r* in isolation. Or you hope that Helen, within
a two-year period, will learn to accept her stuttering and to control
it in most situations. The objective of one lesson, however, may be
to help her eliminate certain mannerisms.

Even though you are dealing with a small group or an individual,
you keep your long-term objective firmly in mind and plan a
progression of experiences to reach it. You prepare your procedures
by finding ways of teaching the student to hear his undesirable
speech, by determining means of helping him to make an acceptable
sound, control his stuttering, or change his voice, by hunting for
materials that will fit the needs of the individual, and by making
the practice as varied and as interesting as you can. You constantly
keep in mind ways of reinforcing what he has already learned.

When you are working with a group, you treat them as a group
and not as individuals. For example, you may be teaching a group
of lispers. Early in the term you devise a series of lessons to help
the boys and girls hear their difficulties. The first are general listening exercises; the second are more specific, more closely related to
hearing deviant *s*'s. You may, for instance, first explain the different
kinds of lisps, then demonstrate them, and then say a list of words
containing *s*'s some of which you make acceptably and some not.
Students indicate those that are unacceptable. Frequently at this
point students diagnose each others' lisps. A similar kind of group
activity leading to individual understanding occurs as you teach
students how to produce a particular sound.

After students have learned to hear a sound, to produce it correctly, to incorporate it in words, they must practice it. Finding varying procedures for drill is a challenge. One teacher makes up a story with blanks and provides a list of words from which students may select those that they think appropriate to place in the blanks. Part of one of her stories and a list of her words follow: The sound involved is the initial blend *sn*.

WORDS: snake, snap, snapper, snarl, snatch, sneaky, sneer, sneezing, sniff, snippy, snob, snore, snort, snow, snub, snuggle.

Walking in the jungles of Africa, I met a .... who

.... and .... at me. But I became

friendly with him. I found he was a .... He was

very adept at .... I admired his ability.

There are many ways of making drill-work interesting. You can set up situations or stories to play wherein a particular sound must be used. Such techniques are described in the chapter on voice and articulation. Or you can adapt forms of parlor games like, "I see a ————; it begins with *r*;" but you must keep in mind that the practice and not the game is what is important.

Just as in other work, you and the students evaluate progress. Some teachers ask students to keep their own progress charts. On them the students indicate their eventual goal and a record of their lessons and home assignments. You and they together note their achievement. Comments like "excellent in isolation," "used acceptable *r* in reading," "again reverted to nasal voice" show the attainments of students.

You may make such a chart part of the child's cumulative speech record; or you may keep a log. In the log, you indicate the student's weekly assignments and his progress as a result of each assignment. You summarize his progress at the middle and the end of the semester. At the end of the term, you make a statement which may be included in the child's school cumulative record. Such a statement follows:

6/19/59. Difficulty—*l* and *r*. Can make *l* and *r* and incorporate them in words with the exception of *l* and *r* in the following blends: *pl, bl, pr, br, fl,* and *fr*.

Does not consistently incorporate *l* and *r* in words. Excellent progress. Prognosis good.

You must be aware that this statement is not for your benefit or for the correctionist who may follow you. It is rather a statement which should prove useful to a classroom teacher or a guidance counsellor. You must, therefore, couch it in terms a layman can understand. It should make clear to a teacher the level of achievement in speech which he can expect from a student.

REPORTS

You should prepare two reports for your principal or supervisor: (1) a report indicating the results of your survey and (2) one explaining the nature and purpose of the speech correction program and giving the necessary statistics on the number of students handled during the year. This second report is often needed for statements to a state department of education, because state aid is frequently based on the number of students receiving speech help. You should determine at the beginning of the semester the kind of information required by your state department of education.

Survey Report

The report of the survey for speech-handicapped children includes information on the number of students and the types of difficulties which they have. It gives the total number of students examined, the number of students handicapped by speech difficulties, the percentage of these students, and the breakdown into specific speech difficulties and these percentages. You may well use the categories used by the American Speech and Hearing Association Committee on Legislation:

ESTIMATED NUMBER OF SCHOOL AGE CHILDREN PER 10,000
WITH EACH TYPE OF SPEECH OR HEARING PROBLEM[2]

Type of Problem	Percentage of Children with Serious Problems	Number of Children with Serious Problems
Articulation	3.0	300
Stuttering	1.0	100
Voice	.1	10
Cleft Palate Speech	.1	10
Cerebral Palsy Speech	.1	10
Retarded Speech Development	.2	20
Speech Problem due to Impaired Hearing	.5	50
Total	5.0	500

[2] ASHA Committee on Legislation, "The Need for Adequately Trained Speech Pathologists and Audiologists," *ASHA* I (December, 1959), 138.

You may even wish to include the national figures for purposes of comparison. You also note in this report the number whom you have recommended for help by other school agencies. This figure is again broken down into the specific difficulties.

Term Report

Besides a brief description of the nature of the program and an explanation of its purpose, your term report will include the following statistics:

1. Number of students who have received correction during the term.
2. Number of students receiving correction at the end of the term.
3. Number of students dismissed with reasons for their dismissal during the term.
4. Number of students added during the term.
5. Number of conferences with parents.
6. Number of conferences with students.
7. Number of home calls.
8. Number of referrals—broken down into specifics.
9. Number of meetings with parent groups—broken down into specifics.

ATTITUDES AND ETHICS OF SCHOOL THERAPISTS

Maintaining Professional Status

Since speech correction has now attained a professional status, you should exhibit an awareness of this status. The first part of the awareness is in gaining the necessary training. The American Speech and Hearing Association has listed the requirements for basic certification.[3] In fact, education departments of 32 states now have certification plans which approximate those of the Basic Speech Certificate.[4] If you are doing speech therapy in the schools, you should preferably meet these requirements upon employment. If you do not meet them then, you should take work in summer school to meet them as quickly as possible. A second part of the awareness lies in your relationship to other professions. You must recognize the delimitation of your field from that of the doctor, psychologist, psychiatrist, dentist, and physical therapist. You neither criticize any of these workers nor do you make a diagnosis or even a hint of one in a field other than your own. A third part of the awareness is a knowledge of your own limitations. When you do not understand a voice case, you do not feign knowledge; when you have difficulty with a parent, you do not adopt an I-am-wiser-than-thou attitude. You seek help from those who have been in the field for a longer time than you. Lastly, you keep up with the literature in the field. Since more and more is being learned about the areas of speech correction, you should keep your knowledge up-to-date. Build your own library and recommend that the school library order the important new books in therapy.

Maintaining a Professional Attitude

To maintain a professional attitude toward your students is important. Since you are working in small groups, you feel freer than in the classroom. In addition, you want a permissive atmosphere

[3] Committee on Clinical Standards of Speech of the American Speech and Hearing Association, "Clinical Certification Requirements of the American Speech and Hearing Association," *Journal of Speech and Hearing Disorders,* XXIII (October, 1958), 347-354.

[4] R. B. Irwin, "Speech Therapy in the Public Schools: State Legislation and Certification," *Journal of Speech and Hearing Disorders,* XXIV (May, 1959), 127-142.

in speech correction work. You must, however, be sure that as a result of these two factors, no undue familiarity exists between you and your students. You must in this situation maintain at all times a professional, workmanlike attitude. You can be friendly but at the same time maintain the necessary professional distance.

Even though you are young, you can handle difficult groups effectively. At one time the author saw a college senior, very attractive, very young, not much over five feet tall, handle a group of young, brain-injured, Korean veterans. These men felt the clinician's friendliness and, at the same time, respected her. During the session they worked hard and achieved desirable goals. The author also saw the same young woman handle a group of twenty-five boys in a high school clinic for substandard speech. All of the boys were of low intelligence; and many were behavior problems who, according to the supervisor, caused a large proportion of the disciplinary problems in the school. During one session the teacher and the boys were discussing wrestling. The young teacher knew the names and the weights of all the wrestlers. At another session the topic was baseball. Again the teacher knew the players' names and their batting averages. When questioned, she smilingly admitted that baseball and wrestling were two of her interests. Her knowledge, her desire to learn still more about these two areas, her ladylike demeanor, her gracious good manners, and her attitude of expecting respect may have accounted for her unusual success in handling two quite different but equally difficult groups.

Remaining Unemotional

Part of maintaining a professional attitude is not to respond emotionally to a child's problems. To identify yourself with the child is easy. You must, however, maintain an objective attitude.

Guarding Confidential Information

Closely related to maintaining a professional attitude is the guarding of confidential information. You must feel responsible for all confidential information which you possess. First, you guard your records carefully. You keep your case histories locked in a file when you are out of the room. You make sure that no students are alone in your room with unlocked files. Second, you must not succumb to the temptation to reveal to another teacher information given to you confidentially by a student or his parent even though you may believe that this information will help the teacher handle the child. The information may become common knowledge and, as a result, your relationship with the child or his parents is harmed. When you feel sure that information, not confidential but highly personal, should be shared, you consult the school's psychological counselor or if the school does not have a psychologist, your principal.

A position involving both speech arts and therapy may seem burdensome. Teachers frequently, however, find the area of speech for which they first had least enthusiasm the one which they most enjoy. When one teacher was a college student, she was interested primarily in theater; in fact, she played the lead in several college plays. After doing both drama and therapy in an elementary school, however, she found the most exciting challenge for her was in the field of therapy. On the other hand, one student, primarily interested in therapy, became enthusiastic in her practice teaching about teaching public speaking, discussion, and debate. She said that many of her courses in psychology and in the science of speech helped prepare her for handling of public speaking and debate. She believed that they were a valuable addition to her courses in public address.

SUGGESTED READING

AINSWORTH, S., *Speech Correction Methods* (New York, Prentice-Hall, Inc., 1948). Discusses the policies of school administration on special educational programs. Gives advice on organizing a speech correction program.

———, "Suggestions for a Successful Speech Correction Program in Public Schools," *Quarterly Journal of Speech,* XXXI (December, 1945), 471-477. Makes suggestions about public relations, relationships with classroom teachers and bulletins.

ANDERSON, V. A., *Improving the Child's Speech* (New York, Oxford University Press, Inc., 1953), pp. 299-320. Contains material on integrating speech training with the school curriculum.

BACKUS, O., and BEASLEY, J. E., *Speech Therapy with Children* (Boston, Houghton Mifflin Co., 1951). Explains and describes methods of group therapy.

BARBARA, D. A., "The Classroom Teacher's Role in Stuttering," *The Speech Teacher*, V (March, 1956), 136-141. Explains the emotional difficulties of the stuttering child and the perfectionist parent.

BEASLEY, J., "Group Therapy in the Field of Speech Correction," *Journal of Exceptional Children*, XVII (1950), 102-107. Gives the purposes and methods of group therapy in the field of speech correction.

BERRY, M. F., and EISENSON, J., *Speech Disorders: Principles and Practices of Therapy* (New York, Appleton-Century-Crofts, Inc., 1956). Presents a comprehensive and systematized body of knowledge of disorders of speech.

CHAPMAN, M. E., "The Speech Clinician and the Classroom Teacher," *Journal of Speech Disorders*, VII (March, 1949), 53-61. Describes bulletins used by the correctionist to get co-operation from the teacher. Explains the duties of the correctionist.

CHIPMAN, S., "On Receiving Your First Appointment as a Speech Correction Teacher," *The Speech Teacher*, IV (September, 1955), 173-175. Gives advice about human relationships with teachers and supervisors.

EDNEY, C. W., "The Public School Remedial Program," in W. Johnson, *et al, Speech Handicapped School Children,* rev. ed. (New York, Harper & Brothers, 1956), pp. 406-519. States the problems of the school speech therapist and makes sound suggestions for their solution.

EISENSON, J., ed., *Stuttering: A Symposium* (New York, Harper & Brothers, 1956). Contains discussions of stuttering by O. Bloodstein, J. Eisenson, I. Peter Glauber, J. G. Sheehan, R. West and C. Van Riper. Introduction by Wendell Johnson.

EISENSON, J., and OGILVIE, M., *Speech Correction in the Schools* (New York, The Macmillan Co., 1957), Ch. 14. Contains material on speech correction services.

FOSSUM, E. C., "Cooperating with the Speech Correctionist," *Journal of Education*, CXXXVI (March, 1954), 182-184. Explains the services of the correctionist including surveys and in-service institutes for classroom teachers. Talks about the counselling of parents and the co-operation with physicians.

GARRISON, G., *Speech and Hearing Services . . . A Design for Program Development* (Bulletin 92, State Department of Education, Hartford, Connecticut, June, 1960). Suggests policies and procedures which will help in (1) determining need for such a program, (2) organizing, conducting, and improving services, and (3) clarifying procedures to be followed in securing state funds for speech and hearing services in Connecticut. Contains samples of many forms needed in providing speech and hearing services.

Hirsch, I. J., *The Measurement of Hearing* (New York, McGraw-Hill Book Co., 1952). Describes methods of testing hearing and tells about the significance of hearing losses.

Houchin, T. D., "Notes on Organizing a Speech Correction Program in the Public Schools," *Journal of Speech and Hearing Disorders,* XIV (March, 1949), 53-62. Tells how to organize a new speech correction program in a public school system. Gives procedures on beginning a program. Contains speech correction forms, samples of letters to parents and teachers, and articulatory testing materials.

Irwin, R. B., *Speech and Hearing Therapy* (New York, Prentice-Hall, Inc., 1953). Treats comprehensively speech therapy in the public schools.

————, "Speech Therapy in the Public Schools: State Legislation and Certification," *Journal of Speech and Hearing Disorders,* XXIV (May, 1959), 127-143. Reviews state legislation and certification requirements for speech therapists in each of the states in alphabetical order.

————, "Speech and Hearing Therapy in the Public Schools of Ohio," *Journal of Speech and Hearing Disorders,* XIV (December, 1949), 63-68. Explains the development of the program in Ohio: finding children for service, case load, scheduling of classes, equipment for speech correction rooms, and coordination day.

————, "State Programs in Speech and Hearing Therapy: Organization and Administration, *The Speech Teacher,* V (March, 1956), 125-131. Studies case loads, patterns of organization, and the cost of therapy.

Konigsberg, E., and Windecker, M., "Speech Correction in the High Schools, *The Speech Teacher,* IV (November, 1955), 247-252. Lists types of disorders. Describes the ideal clinic teacher. Tells how to start the class. Gives procedures for teaching remedial work and suggests additional class activities.

Luper, H. L., and Ainsworth, S. H., "Speech Correction Rooms in the Public Schools," *Exceptional Child,* XXII (October, 1955), 24-26. Indicates space, acoustic treatment, and special furnishings needed for the speech correction room.

MacLearie, E. C., "Evaluation and the Effectiveness of the Speech and Hearing Teacher in Public Schools," *The Speech Teacher,* II (September, 1953), 209-211. Discusses briefly personal relationships, physical facilities, rapport with children, lesson planning, follow up, and records and reports.

Newby, H. A., *Audiology: Principles and Practices* (New York, Appleton-Century-Crofts, Inc., 1958). Gives the basic principles and practices in audiology.

Reid, L. *Teaching Speech,* 2nd ed. (Columbia, Mo., Artcraft Press, 1958), Ch. VIII. Contains material on being a clinician in the schools.

Travis, L. E., ed., *Handbook of Speech Pathology* (New York, Appleton-Century-Crofts, Inc., 1957). Contains sound, accurate information on procedures in speech correction.

Van Riper, C., *Speech Correction: Principles and Methods*, 3rd ed. (New York, Prentice-Hall, Inc., 1954). Includes chapters dealing with handicaps, understanding the speech defective, psychotherapy, articulation disorders, voice disorders, stuttering, cleft palate speech, foreign accent, cerebral palsy, and hearing problems. Ch. 13 deals with the speech therapist and discusses his role in the public schools.

West, R., Ansberry, M., and Carr, A., *The Rehabilitation of Speech*, 3rd ed. (New York, Harper & Brothers, 1957). Contains information and remedial procedures for all types of speech defects.

EXERCISES

1. Prepare a paragraph for reading which will detect major articulatory difficulties.
2. Prepare a form for a case history.
3. Prepare a form for recording progress.
4. Work out a schedule for therapy for the following: (Assume that you are free during the fourth, sixth, and seventh periods each day.)

Stutterers:
Freshman A, free 4, 7.
Freshman B, free 6, 7.
Junior C, free 7.
Junior D, free 7.
Senior E, free 4.

Cleft Palate Patients:
Freshman AI, free 4, 6.
Senior AJ, free 6, 7.
Cerebral Palsy Patient:
Senior AK, free 4, 7.
Hard of Hearing Patient:
Freshman AL, free 6.

Patients with Articulatory Difficulties:

Freshman F, free 5, 7; (*l, r.*)
Freshman G, free 6, 7; (*s, l*)
Freshman H, free 4, 7 (*th*)
Freshman I, free 4,7; (*f, v, th, s*)
Freshman J, free 4, 6; (*s*)
Freshman K, free 4, 7; (*s*)
Freshman L, free 6; (*l, r*)
Freshman M, free 6; (*l, r*)
Freshman N, free 6; (*l, s*)
Freshman O, free 7; (*r*)
Sophomore P, free 7; (*th*)

Sophomore Q, free 4; (*s*)
Sophomore R, free 4; (*s*)
Sophomore S, free 4, 7; (*s*)
Sophomore T, free 6; (*s*)
Sophomore U, free 4, 7; (*l, r*)
Sophomore V, free 4, 6; (*r*)
Sophomore W, free 4, 6; (*l*)
Junior X, free 6; (*s*)
Junior Y, free 4; (*s*)
Junior AA, free 4; (*l*)
Junior AB, free 4, 7; (*l, r*)

Junior AC, free 4, 6; (*s, th, f, v*)   Senior AF, free 6, 7; (*s*)
Senior AD, free 4, 7; (*l, r*)   Senior AG, free 4, 7; (*s*)
Senior AE, free 6, 7; (*s*)   Senior AH, free 6, 7; (*s*)

NOTE: All the voice cases and all of the most seriously handicapped are to be taken care of by the school's special speech therapist.

The letters in parentheses indicate the sound or sounds with which the particular individual has difficulty.

VIII

THE CAREER
OF THE SPEECH TEACHER

17

Your Career

as a Speech Teacher

THE BACKGROUND OF SPEECH EDUCATION

ALTHOUGH YOU FREQUENTLY hear, "the discipline of speech has little tradition," today's speech education has its roots in ancient civilization. The faith that Isocrates, Aristotle, Cicero, and Quintilian had in speech education is still held by speech teachers. Even some of the positions that teachers regard as very modern were taken by Quintilian and others of his time. The emphasis on ideas in speechmaking set down by Aristotle closely resembles the emphasis today. The organization of a speech, taught before the birth of Christ, parallels the organization taught today. The importance placed centuries ago on a speaker's having a good character and on a delivery which does not call attention to itself approximates the importance placed on these elements in this current time. Admittedly the acquisition of new knowledge, some of it resulting from scientific inquiry, has had a very considerable effect on the teaching of speech, but the roots of speech education lie in ancient civilization.

Like the ancient rhetoricians, teachers today believe that their students can be taught to improve their speaking and that such teaching is important. Most teachers agree with Isocrates who assumed that a quick and facile mind, good voice and diction, and poise are assets that make for an effective speaker but who also affirmed that students not so generously endowed can improve their speaking and sometimes surpass the gifted speakers. Teachers concur with Aristotle who pointed out that everybody speaks to sift or support theses. They further concur with his insistence on the need for treating the principles of speaking systematically. Speech teachers are in accord with Cicero who refuted the statement that if one knows his subject matter well, he will be eloquent and who emphasized that no speaker is eloquent unless he knows the art of rhetoric.

Modern Trends in Ancient Times

Some of the ideas that teachers think of as peculiarly modern are expressed in the writings of the ancients. Examples follow: Isocrates cited as an advantage of the teaching of speech that the speaker become more gracious in social intercourse. Aristotle recommended a degree of integration of study when he said that rhetoric relies heavily on ethics, politics, and psychology. Quintilian's criterion for a standard of usage was that pronunciation should be based on custom—not what the majority say but the consensus of the educated. He further said that it is ridiculous to prefer the language men have spoken to the language they now speak. Quintilian also believed in providing for individual differences, for he said that some exceed others in natural ability but only to the extent that some will accomplish more and some less.

Character of Speaker

Teachers of the twentieth century approve the idea of Quintilian, that the speaker be a good man to recommend himself to an audience. In their eighteenth century writings so did Ward, Campbell, and Blair. Whately in the nineteenth century, like Aristotle, said the character to be established must be one of good principles, good sense, and good will.

Importance of Ideas

Just as today teachers stress the importance of ideas in speechmaking, Aristotle, Cicero, and Quintilian all emphasized their importance. Nineteenth-century writers also advocated their significance. For example, John Ward said that students of speechmaking should possess "great learning and extensive knowledge." George

Campbell asked that the speaker acquire "everything that seems to improve knowledge, discernment, and good sense." Blair requested that the speaker have "a proper acquaintance with liberal arts.[1] Furthermore, when teachers point out that topics for speechmaking should be related to the speaker, they are agreeing with Whately of the nineteenth century when he suggested that topics come from studies in which the speaker is engaging, from content of conversation to which he listens or in which he participates, and from his everyday activities.

Organization of Ideas

Just as teachers of this generation stress not only the importance of ideas but also of the organization so did the ancients. Corax in 466 B.C. suggested an organization quite similar to the one today's students may follow: a proem to begin the speech, a narrative to tell the story of the case, arguments to show that right is on the side of the client, subsidiary remarks to clarify and influence, and the peroration to conclude. Similarly Aristotle gave this order: proem, statement, argument, and epilogue. Lastly Cicero's *de Oratore* suggested a like organization under *dispositio*. Interestingly enough, the organization of present high school courses in public speaking frequently follow the five divisions noted in Cicero's *de Oratore*: *inventio, dispositio, elocutio, memoria,* and *pronuntatio* (research, adaptation, composition, rehearsal, presentation).

Communication of Ideas

Further, teachers in this age believe that the communication of ideas is the end and that the expression as the means should not call attention to itself. Again Ward, Campbell, Blair, and Whately agreed that in delivering a speech, the speaker should be natural, should concentrate on the material to be delivered, and should earnestly try to communicate his material to his listeners without dependence on artificial rules. These same men based their philosophy of voice and articulation on the idea that the speaker must be understood: to be understood, the speaker uses distinct articulation,

[1] C. W. Edney, "English Sources of Rhetorical Theory in Nineteenth Century America," *History of Speech Education,* Karl Wallace, ed. (New York, Appleton-Century-Crofts, Inc., 1954), p. 85.

speaks at a moderate rate, and avoids monotony. Their advice on gesture was similar to that of teachers today—to guard against awkward motions and to preserve a natural appearance.

Elocutionary Movement

Admittedly remnants still exist in speech education of the elocutionary movement of the seventeenth and eighteenth centuries: Some speech teachers are overly concerned with all signs of bodily action in communication, with the manipulation of the vocal mechanism to achieve response to meaning and feeling, and with a prescriptive approach to articulation and pronunciation. As a result, judges of contests find the student speaker who takes two steps forward, raises his hands palms up, and turns his eyes heavenward while he extols the virtues of providing aid to foreign countries. This contestant is focusing attention on voice, articulation, and movement, instead of on full realization and communication of meaning. The apparent artificiality displeases the audience and fortunately is on the wane. Students of speech today smile when they read seventeenth century's John Bulwer's directions on gestures of the hand from his "Chirologia."[2] Bulwer advises that to wring the hands is a natural expression of excessive grief, used by those who condole, bewail, and lament.

Curiously enough from the elocutionary movement came the foundation for a more scientific study of the physiology of speech, the classification of sounds, and a system for recording these sounds. The writings of Alexander Melville Bell provided the basis of Henry Sweet's *Broad Romic*. Out of this work grew the International Phonetic Alphabet. Thus, began the study of the scientific aspects of speech.

SPEECH EDUCATION IN AMERICA

One of your most fascinating studies is the history of speech education. You will do well to become familiar with the tradition of your subject by studying such areas as classical rhetoric and the Greek theater.

A unique contribution to the literature of the history of speech

---

[2] L. Thonssen, *Selected Readings in Rhetoric and Public Speaking* (New York, H. W. Wilson, 1942), p. 189.

education in United States is the *History of Speech Education in America: Background Studies.*[3]

The purpose of the book is to tell how the field of speech education has unfolded and developed from colonial days to recent times. The editor explains that the authors are writing of "the use of speech in socially significant situations and of the attempts to teach the art of oral communication in a formal educational environment."[4]

The book is divided into three parts. The first section deals with the heritage of speech education and includes the English backgrounds of rhetoric, rhetorical theory and practice in Colonial America, and the English sources of American elocution.

The second part has to do with the American contributions to rhetorical theory, the elocutionary movement, the training in rhetoric and elocution in nineteenth-century colleges, the influence of Steele MacKaye and of Dr. James Rush on speech education. It gives an account of the influences of the literary societies and debating groups on the history of speech education in the elementary and secondary schools and discusses the development of education in speech correction and hearing. It notes the importance of the study of phonetics and pronunciation and of the rise of experimental phonetics. It shows the origin and development of departments of speech in colleges and of national speech organizations. Authors pay tribute to the leaders in the field and the parts they have played in its growth.

The last section deals with the educational theater. It includes material on theater in colleges, high schools, private theater schools of the late nineteenth century, and professional theater schools of the early twentieth century. The role of the national theater organizations in theater education is made clear.

The book, much like a survey course, covers a large amount of ground and gives an over-all picture of the field. As in a survey course, some of the writers have worked from a strict chronological order; others have shown the relationship of the development of the particular area to the social and economic conditions of the times; others have noted the major contributions of individuals;

[3] K. Wallace, ed., *History of Speech Education in America: Background Studies* (New York, Appleton-Century-Crofts, Inc., 1954).

[4] *Ibid.*, p. vi.

and still others have indicated the emerging ideas and theories and have summarized the results of research. As a good survey course gives an over-all view of subject matter, so does this book. The classical tradition of rhetoric and its influence on all speech education is clear. The influence of educators such as Rousseau, Pestalozzi, Froebel, and Herbart is obvious in the sections on speech in the public schools. The picture of the increasing specialization in the field is vivid. You will gain from this book a clear concept of the development of speech education in this country.

BEGINNING YOUR CAREER

Your career, with its considerable and illustrious heritage, begins with your college training. Most high school teachers of speech look back on their training and wish that they had chosen their courses somewhat differently, had spent time on other activities than those which they selected, or had taken advantage of diverse situations in their term of practice teaching. Since you cannot foresee accurately the kind of teaching situation that you will face, you cannot plan your training with complete efficiency. You can, however, follow certain general principles which will make your training more valuable and your first teaching job more comfortable.

Your training should include learning in all the aspects of speech, some knowledge of related areas, and an understanding of today's educational principles and processes. Such training fits you to handle your first year of classes successfully.

Speech Courses

Many college students major in speech because of a feeling of excitement about dramatics, debate, or therapy. As they become acquainted with other aspects, however, they find as much and sometimes even more excitement in them. One student had been interested in theater since childhood. She had gone to a creative drama class, had participated in high school plays, and had been a successful college actress. When she took her first course in speech correction, however, she found a second interest as strong as her first. Now in her teaching she is working in both areas and in her graduate-school career she is following both interests.

The college student who intends to teach speech in a high school should prepare himself in more than one area of speech and should be sure that his training in each area is quite comprehensive, for few new teachers teach just public speaking or radio and none teach just stage makeup or radio script writing. The preparation of the prospective speech teacher should be broad and should include courses in phonetics, speech science and therapy, oral interpretation, theater, public address—embracing public speaking, discussion, and debate—and radio and television. Furthermore, in choosing the courses in the various aspects of speech, the prospective teacher should consider whether or not he is overspecializing. For example, one college girl had elected eighteen hours of acting but had never had any training in other aspects of play production. The production of her first high school play, therefore, posed many problems for her, because she did not know how to prepare a promptbook, to build scenery, to put on makeup, or to costume her cast. One of her courses might well have been in play production; another in stagecraft.

Related Courses

Not only will most beginning teachers teach several different speech courses, but many will teach a second subject, usually English or social studies. These disciplines are intimately related to speech. Surely the relationship between English and speech courses is obvious. A history of drama can provide necessary background for your high school course in theater. A course in Shakespearean comedies and tragedies can help you to connect the work in your theater class to the students' work in English classes. A study of contemporary literature can give you an understanding of the authors of today and their writings which will prove valuable in your teaching of interpretation, creative drama, and even public speaking. The relationship between speech and social studies is also clear. Since the topics of public address often concern themselves with economic, social, and political questions of the day, college courses in the field of social sciences are necessary for the high school teacher of speech. True, you can read contemporary newspapers, magazines, and books but you get sound bases for the analysis of important state and national events in a social science class.

Education Courses

You must not only have a sound background of content in speech courses, but you must also know about human growth and development, about the philosophy and organization of our public schools, and about teaching materials and methods. Education courses are given for these purposes; they should aid you in understanding yourself and others, in knowing the adolescent student intimately, in recognizing the organization of schools and their relationship to our cultures, and lastly in becoming a competent, capable teacher. These courses are not just theory courses. For example, in learning to know adolescents you may work with them through the agencies of the town. Or in learning how to teach, you will plan and present lessons to representative students.

Extracurricular Activities

Your selection of extracurricular activities should be as broad as your selection of speech courses. If you spend all of your time in discussion, in debate, or in the theater, you pursue an avocation that is stimulating, but you neglect your preparation for directing a full program of extracurricular activities in the high school. When you take part in several activities, you realize the problems that exist in them and you are better fitted as a teacher to handle the problems of extracurricular activities. Furthermore, participation in activities outside of the speech department is valuable. One student said that his participation in student government gave him an excellent apprenticeship in handling people and in administration. He remarked, "I often wonder whether I could have successfully completed my first year of teaching if I hadn't had this training."

To summarize: The teacher should be an educated person with training in his specialized area. Secondly, he should have guidance in selecting and putting into practice methods and materials in teaching speech. Lastly, he should know what his students and his school will be like. This last analysis should be a careful one—very like the speaker's analysis of an audience and of an occasion.

Finding the First Job

Placement Bureaus

After you have been trained for teaching you are ready to look for a job. You have the choice of a variety of placement services: the bureaus of placement of your college, the Speech Association of America, your regional and state and city speech associations, and the commercial agencies.

Probably most of you will use your college placement bureau almost exclusively since in all likelihood you will want to teach in the state in which you have been trained. Almost always college bureaus know of a wide variety of openings in their area. For this bureau you prepare statements of your training, experience, and general philosophy of teaching. This material you should prepare with special care. Outline it, write it, read it, correct it, reread it, and recorrect it. A slip in grammar, a misspelling, a carelessly worded sentence, or an extreme statement may cost you the job that you want.

Some of you will use other agencies. When you are interested in a job outside of your state, you may choose to use the teacher placement service of the Speech Association of America. Your first step in doing this is to send for forms to the Executive Secretary of the Speech Association of America whose name and address are listed in both *The Speech Teacher* and the *Quarterly Journal of Speech*. For this service you pay a nominal fee. You also may find a job through the placement bureau of your local, state, or regional speech association. At the time of the convention of such an organization, a placement committee usually provides a service whereby would-be employers and employees are brought together.

Lastly you may join a commercial agency. You must remember that when you accept a job through a commercial agency, you pay a fee which usually consists of about 5 per cent of your first year's salary. You may well depend upon your college bureau to recommend an agency in the area in which you are to be located.

Applying for a Job

Your first contact with your would-be employer is probably through your letter of application and your data sheet. The letter of application should arouse the interest of your employer, should show him that you want to teach in his system, and should provide him with information which will influence his decision. The information usually includes generalized material about your background, your status as to certification, and your special qualifications for the job which you are seeking. For example, if the job is one in which you are to coach theatrical activities, you list your courses in this area and indicate your experience as an actor, a stagehand, and a director in your undergraduate and graduate work and as a high school coach of theater. The letter should be short, expertly typed, and grammatically correct.

A sample letter follows:[5]

206-54 Whitehall Terrace
Queens Village 27, New York.
May 1, 1958

Dr. John Smith
Superintendent of Schools
Central Village, New York

Dear Dr. Smith:

The Queens College Teacher Placement Office has informed me of a speech vacancy in your school system. I am interested in this position and wish to present my qualifications for appointment to your staff. I am enclosing an outline of them on the accompanying data sheet.

I am a senior at Queens College with a major in speech, a minor in education, and twenty-four credits in English and I am currently practice teaching at Jamaica High School. By June, my courses will have qualified me to be certified for teaching speech in New York State.

My extracurricular activities have been for the most part in theater. Since I have begun my practice teaching, however, I have pursued an interest in speech correction by giving individual speech therapy to selected students for twenty minutes before each school day.

As a camp counselor this past summer, I worked with teen-age girls. I guided a counsellor-in-training program in which my responsibilities included directing weekly field trips, sports and crafts activities, and over-

[5] Written by Olympia Parasco while a student of Education 65, Methods of Teaching Speech in the Secondary School, at Queens College.

night hikes. Not only was the experience enjoyable, but I am also certain that it will prove helpful in my teaching.

I hope that you will find my qualifications suited to the position since I would be delighted to be invited to join your staff. I shall be glad to come for a personal interview at your convenience.

Sincerely yours,

Olympia Parasco

With such a letter you send a data sheet which may follow this form:

DATA SHEET OF TRAINING AND EXPERIENCE

Name:
Address: PICTURE
Telephone Number:
Application for:

PERSONAL:

Age .... Sex....... Weight....... Height....... Health.......

Marital Status ....

EDUCATION:
High School:
College:
Graduate Work:

COURSES:
Courses in Speech: (List by title)
Courses in Education: (List by title)
Courses in Related Areas: (List by title)

TEACHING EXPERIENCE:
(Include school, subjects taught, years, and salary. If you are inexperienced, list your experience as a practice teacher.)

EXTRACURRICULAR ACTIVITIES:
(List undergraduate activities or activities which you have supervised in your teaching with years and schools.)

HONORS:
(Give significant honors such as Phi Beta Kappa, or offices held in organizations like the student government.)

OTHER RELEVANT EXPERIENCE:
  (Note other work experiences such as counselling activities, social work, and clinical experience.)

TRAVEL:
  (Include only if significant.)

REFERENCES:
  (Use no more than six. List names of persons who know you well, such as: your supervisor of student teaching, the head of your department, your principal, and college professors who can vouch for your scholarship. Or you may write: Listed in my folder at the X Placement Bureau which will be furnished on the request of the employing officer.)

Whereas the letter of application, the data sheet, and the folder sent by the bureau serve as an introduction to the administrator, the administrator hires you through a personal interview. In the interview you must be careful of your appearance and your manners. You must speak clearly, answer questions readily, and be a good listener. You must not make an immediate issue out of personal matters. For example, undoubtedly finding a place to live and being paid enough to live there are important to you. But the first emphasis should be on the position in all its aspects.

FOLLOWING YOUR CAREER

Once you are hired, you must quickly learn the organization of your school and its hierarchy of authority, so that you can make sure that you consult your immediate superior before consulting anyone above him. It is possible to make an unfortunate consultation quite inadvertently in a more-or-less casual conversation, but even this can prejudice your immediate superior against you.

You must also find out who in the school is responsible for particular requests. Who is responsible for making the calendar of assemblies? Whom do you see when you have a student attendance problem? To whom do you go when you want to use the school auditorium for rehearsal? Who does the mimeographing? Where do you get supplies? Some schools have a handbook which gives you this information. Others follow the trial-and-error system. But you do well to get this information early in your career when you feel free to ask questions.

In acquiring information you meet many school workers. One of the most important is the guidance officer. Becoming acquainted with the guidance officer is essential, for you will need his help frequently. You may quite soon unearth a student who seems perpetually sleepy or is not working up to his capacity. As a result, you may want to know more about this student or to give your information to the guidance officer. You must, however, remember to give only information and not your interpretation of it. In addition, you may learn from the guidance officer whether a system of cumulative records exists and whether the records are available to you.

In making requests and in running your homeroom, you will find that many clerical details are involved. You must, therefore, discover how to take care of them quickly and efficiently; often an older teacher will be glad to give you advice on handling them. Ways of keeping attendance, giving out textbooks, and requesting permission for a class visit to a place outside of the school differ. You should discover the accepted procedures for taking care of these details in your school and follow them carefully and accurately.

Human Relations in the School

Wherever you are living closely with other persons you relate well and easily to some and less well and easily to others. One important factor in relating in a school is your attitude toward your specialty. Although you believe that speech is the most important discipline, other teachers feel that their particular specialties are the most important disciplines. Your school will not revolve around the speech curriculum; it will revolve around the total learning of the students. You must, therefore, see your subject in terms of the total learning and consider its connection with other areas. Often you can help build the connnection between two areas. For example, a drama teacher invited the social studies teacher to her class to answer questions on the social background of *Watch On the Rhine*. Such co-operative endeavor helps link one area with another and promotes appreciation of disciplines other than one's own.

That you understand the philosophy and points of view of those with whom you work is necessary to promote healthy relationships. You and the music teacher can work together on many productions.

You need to know his attitudes about production and even about such practical matters as sharing the use of the auditorium. At the beginning of the year, it is well for you both to plan ahead and decide when each will use the auditorium.

You and the English teacher also have many areas in common. Whereas the English teacher is most concerned with written communication, you are most concerned with oral communication. But you both use much of the same material and methodology and teach many of the same skills. You should supplement each other's instruction. Frequently you can connect the two areas by telling each other your plans and by each utilizing what the other has taught. Since you appreciate that other teachers are also interested in promoting sound learning in their students, you give them what help you can.

Growing Professionally

Reading

Being a good teacher is important but so is growing professionally. Since there is constantly new information in your field, you must keep up in it. For instance, new methods of diagnosis and therapy and new interpretations of principles and practices have resulted from recent research. New plays are being produced. New speeches are being delivered. To keep abreast you should read articles in professional journals and significant texts.

The following are professional journals which contain many meaningful articles in the field of speech:

American Forensic Association Register (American Forensic Association).
American Speech (Columbia University Press).
ASHA (The American Speech and Hearing Association).
Central States Speech Journal (Central States Speech Association) .
The English Journal (National Council of Teachers of English).
Etc: A Review of General Semantics (International Society for General Semantics).
The Journal of Communication (National Society for the Study of Communication).
The Journal of Speech and Hearing Disorders (American Speech and Hearing Association).
The Journal of Speech and Hearing Research (American Speech and Hearing Association) .

The Quarterly Journal of Speech (Speech Association of America).
The Southern Speech Journal (Southern Speech Association) .
Speech Monographs (Speech Association of America).
The Speech Teacher (Speech Association of America).
Today's Speech (Speech Association of the Eastern States).
Western Speech (The Western Speech Association).

The reviews of the recent books in these journals provide suggestions for your reading. You may borrow the books from a convenient library or you may buy them. Most publishers are willing to send a book on approval, giving you time to look it over. Budgeting a certain amount of money to be spent on one's professional library each year is wise.

Speech Associations

Attendance at speech conventions is a second way to grow professionally. Recognizing the values of stimulation and learning inherent in the meetings of such organizations, many administrators encourage their teachers to go by paying either traveling expenses or the total expenses of attendance. Although your school administration may provide some financial help, you should also include in your personal budget, money for this attendance. That you do attend is important, for at conventions you meet other teachers with problems similar to your own, attend sessions devoted to your special areas, and become acquainted with the leaders in your field. Frequently you can begin an active career in associations by working first with your local, then with your state, and then with the regional or the national organization. Ability to organize and to lead well shows up quickly in organizations such as these.

Graduate Study

Going on to graduate study is a third way to grow professionally. Since you usually do graduate study in one of the specialized aspects of speech, you look for the school which can offer you exceptional training in this particular aspect. In this search you take account of several factors. You find out who you want to study with and where they teach. You go through *Speech Monographs* to learn where the research that particularly interests you is done. You investigate the facilities of a particular institution: the speech faculty outside of your own specialized area; the theatrical plant, if you are interested in theater; the speech clinic facilities, if you are interested in therapy. Finally, you may seek help from one of your undergraduate professors who is interested in the same aspect of speech as you are, for he will know the leaders in the field and will be glad to recommend schools to you.

To stay with one school is wise. Attendance at many schools is enticing; you may believe that the wide attendance broadens your background. But you may end up with too little knowledge from too many sources. Moreover, you may find that you have accumulated a large number of credits toward the Master's degree but that no institution will be willing to accept more than six. Most institutions allow six credits to be transferred toward the Master's degree; you should make sure, however, that the institution where you are doing your graduate work will permit a transfer of credit before you take a course in another college or university.

Participation in Community Affairs

Although being a well-trained skillful professionally alert person is important, it is also essential that you participate in community affairs. You have many opportunities to meet representative members of the town where you teach. First of all, Parents' Night is planned for this purpose. In addition, you take part in local organizations like the League of Women Voters, the Little Theater, The American Association of University Women, or the Stamp Collectors' Club. You get to know the inhabitants of the town and they come to know you.

Another kind of community relationship exists in your providing speakers or entertainers for organizations of the town. You try to balance the entertaining aspect with the informative aspect. You indicate what is available as requests come to you. You make a calendar well in advance. When a particular group has performed its alloted number of times, you so advise those requesting a program and suggest other groups. You give many students opportunities to perform in the community.

Rewards of Teaching

Your rewards in teaching are plentiful. Dealing with young and malleable human beings, helping them to solve their problems, and watching them grow are exciting. Your most significant rewards in teaching will not be a raise in salary or a promotion. For example, you will feel proud when one of your students chosen to play the lead in the university play writes you that your training was what made his selection possible, when you see a scholarly article in the *Quarterly Journal of Speech* written by one of your former students, or when one of your best debaters is elected to the United States Senate. Such activity of your students may mean nothing by way of actual prestige or material reward; yet it gives you the feeling of the worth of the job.

Teaching is like a good book. It challenges you and stimulates you. Page after page of the book affects you differently; day after day of teaching affects you differently. Days can be amusing, provocative, tantalizing, stinging, inspiring, and even once in a while tedious, dreary, and insipid—just like the pages of a good book. But reading a good book and teaching children are both infinitely rewarding.

SUGGESTED READING

BALCER, C., "The High School Principal and the Teacher of Speech," *The Speech Teacher*, IV (September, 1955), 183-186. Gives advice about the teacher's relationship with the principal.

BALDWIN, C. S., *Ancient Rhetoric and Poetic* (New York, The Macmillan Co., 1924). Contains material on Aristotle, Cicero, and Quintilian.

BALDWIN, C. S., *Medieval Rhetoric and Poetic* (New York, The Macmillan Co., 1928). Contains a discussion of rhetoric of the middle ages.

BRYANT, D. C., "Aspects of the Rhetorical Tradition; 1. The Intellectual Foundation," *Quarterly Journal of Speech*, XXXVI (April, 1950), 169-176. Shows that the study of rhetoric sticks firmly to "the intellectual—to thought and knowledge—to the sound, the true, the valuable." Stresses the intellectual foundation of the study of rhetoric.

CLARK, D. L., *Rhetoric in Greco-Roman Education* (New York, Columbia University Press, 1957). Tells the story of the literary theories developed by teachers of rhetoric in Greece and Rome. Gives an account of educational methods used by ancient teachers in the schools of rhetoric in training speakers.

GRAY, G. W., "The Development of Graduate Work in Speech in United States," *The Speech Teacher*, II (September, 1953), 173-177. Tells of expansion of graduate work in speech in the last sixty years.

KNIGHT, P. D., "The American Speech and Hearing Association and Your

Professional Growth," *ASHA* I (October, 1959), 50-52. Tells the speech therapist how to evaluate himself on a professional level.

Great Teachers of Speech Series:
1. Emily Kimball Lilly, "The Young Lew Sarett," *The Speech Teacher,* IV (January, 1955), 22-23.
2. Severina Nelson, "Charles Henry Woolbert," *The Speech Teacher,* IV (March, 1955), 113-117.
3. Marie Hochmuth, Richard Murphy, and Herbert A. Wichelns, "Wayland Maxfield Parrish," *The Speech Teacher,* IV (September, 1955), 159-164.
4. M. R. McBride, "Frank M. Rarig," *The Speech Teacher,* IV (November, 1955), 231-232.

HITCHCOCK, O. A. "How to Get a Job as a Teacher of Speech," *The Speech Teacher* IV (November, 1955), 225-230. Gives advice on training necessary for getting a job and on applying for a job, including writing a letter and gaining a personal interview.

REID, L. D. "Graduate Study and Teacher Placement," *Quarterly Journal of Speech,* XXXIV (April, 1948), 177-182. Analyzes the demand for teachers in 1946 and 1947. Suggests trends in growing areas in speech. Still applicable today.

————, *Teaching Speech* (Columbia, Mo., Artcraft Press, 1956), ch. 17. Contains excellent material on the speech teacher's career.

SIMON, C. T., "The Teacher and His Graduate Work, *The Speech Teacher,* I (November, 1952), 231-236. Points out the growth of graduate work. Gives advice on how to select a school and tells the meaning of being a graduate student.

THONSSEN, L. *Selected Readings in Rhetoric and Public Speaking* (New York, H. W. Wilson Co., 1942). Contains selected passages from the more important contributors to the literature of rhetoric and public speaking.

WALLACE, K., ed., *History of Speech Education in America,* (New York, Appleton-Century-Crofts, Inc., 1954). Gives the English background of American speech education. Includes a history of all the facets carefully and interestingly done. Should be part of the library of every teacher of speech.

WEAVER, A. T., BORCHERS, G. L., and SMITH, D. K., *The Teaching of Speech* (Englewood Cliffs, N. J., Prentice-Hall, Inc., 1952), ch. 2. Traces the development of speech education. Relates concepts to present-day teaching concepts.

WEST, R. W., "The Association in Historical Perspective," *ASHA,* II (January, 1960), 8-11. Gives the history of the American Speech and Hearing Association.

EXERCISES

1. Write a letter of application for a position which either:
   a. includes teaching fundamentals and doing speech therapy,
   b. includes teaching fundamentals and theater,
   c. includes teaching fundamentals and coaching debate, or
   d. includes teaching fundamentals and third-year English.
2. Read and outline Aristotle's *Rhetoric*.
3. Read through one volume of Quintilian. Indicate the principles recorded in this volume which you would follow today.
4. Subscribe to at least one professional journal and indicate which two other journals you would prefer to receive. Give reasons for your choice.
5. Read reviews of books in one issue of *The Speech Teacher*. Get one book which was reviewed from your own library. Agree or disagree with the reviewer, giving reasons for your point of view.
6. Conduct a mock interview with another student or with your instructor for a speech position. Working with your classmates, evaluate your performance.

Index